The Fearless
Harry Greb

The Fearless Harry Greb

Biography of a Tragic Hero of Boxing

BILL PAXTON

McFarland & Company, Inc., Publishers
Jefferson, North Carolina, and London

Photographs are from the collection of the author unless credited otherwise.

LIBRARY OF CONGRESS CATALOGUING-IN-PUBLICATION DATA

Paxton, Bill, 1966–
The fearless Harry Greb : biography of a tragic hero of boxing / Bill Paxton.
p.   cm.
Includes bibliographical references and index.

ISBN 978-0-7864-4016-0
softcover: 50# alkaline paper ∞

1. Greb, Harry, 1894–1926.   2. Boxers (Sports)—United States—Biography.
I. Title
GV1132.G67P39   2009   796.83092—dc22   [B]   2008051899

British Library cataloguing data are available

On the cover: Harry Greb in an undated photograph (Bettmann/CORBIS).

Manufactured in the United States of America

*McFarland & Company, Inc., Publishers
Box 611, Jefferson, North Carolina 28640
www.mcfarlandpub.com*

This book is dedicated to my loving wife Kristin Crotty Paxton, who let me take the time necessary to create it and supported me along the way. It is also dedicated to the boxing fans of Pittsburgh. Greb loved the fans who supported him and he loved his city.

I also dedicate it to Harry Greb and how he chose to live life to the fullest. As Dr. Martin Luther King, Jr., once said, "We are confronted with the fierce urgency of now. In this unfolding conundrum of life and history, there is such a thing as being too late. Procrastination is still the thief of time." Greb was very aware of time and chose to savor life and devour it.

And finally to my two sons Jake and Mason. Never give up no matter what the obstacles, follow your dreams, work hard at them and enjoy life.

ACKNOWLEDGMENTS

I would like to thank the following people and organizations that have helped me in my research, and in making this book: Stanley Weston for inspiring me early on in my research, the Carnegie Library in Pittsburgh, Mark Hooper from Angel Editing, Dr. Albert Ackerman, Dr. Scot A. Brower, Dr. Anthony Andrews, Library and Archives of the Historical Society of Western Pennsylvania, Christopher Greb, Tony and Kathleen Triem, Reverend James W. Garvey and the Epiphany Church, Harry Shaffer from Antiquities of the Prize Ring, David Bergin from Collection of Pugilistica.com, Craig Hamilton from josportsinc.com, Veteran Boxer's Association Ring #1 in Philadelphia, Lou Manfra from Heavyweightcollectibles.com, Christopher Tarr from fistianaboxingmemorabilia.com, Stu Saks from Kappa Publishing and *The Ring* magazine, Heather Ryan from the *Pittsburgh Post-Gazette*, Sally Braden, Paul McWhorter from Son of the South, Laura Waayers from the Naval Historical Foundation, the University of South Carolina, Anne Preston, Kevin Smith, and finally Max Kellerman for continuing to spread the word.

CONTENTS

PREFACE

I have been a boxing fan my whole life, and a boxing historian for over a decade. As a casual boxing fan who would watch current fights, I would hear the announcers refer to past boxers, names like Jack Dempsey, Gene Tunney and Mickey Walker. I started researching old-time boxers, and one name kept on popping up on boxers' fight records. Other boxers during the twenty-year period from 1910 to 1930 would have impressive fight records showing they battled the best of their time, names I already knew. However, no matter what weight class a boxer was in, he always seemed to lose to one unknown individual, Harry Greb. This sparked my interest, so I attempted to learn more about this fighter who beat almost everyone he fought. The little I could find out told me he fought more often than any fighter of his time. The heavyweight champion Gene Tunney, who lost only one fight in his entire career, suffered his sole loss at the hands of Greb. I asked myself, "Who is this guy and why have I never heard of him before?"

I searched for a video of him fighting. I had obtained fight videos of almost every important fighter of that era, and those fighters fought less often, so I assumed it would be easy enough to get a fight video of Harry Greb. When I talked to fight film collectors I was met with chuckling; they told me that no fight films exist for Greb. I found this impossible to believe because fight films exist of his opponents, and he was a champion in two weight classes in addition to fighting 299 pro bouts.

When I searched for magazines or books on him, none could be found. The more I dug for information, the more mysterious he became. No one had anything or knew anything about him. Then someone told me an amazing thing. Not only did Greb beat all these Hall of Fame champions, fighting ferociously against all opponents, but he also won these battles while blind in one eye. This story seemed impossible. A boxer needs stereoscopic viewing to see punches coming from the left and the right sides. My interest was sparked further; who was this mysterious man?

At the time I started my research the Internet was in its infancy. It was no help in satisfying my curiosity and only contained two pictures of Greb and one paragraph stating key wins of his career. I heard a rumor of a book that had been written about him in 1946. Unfortunately, all the book collectors I talked to had never heard of it. When I talked to book collectors who focused on boxing, they told me of one collector who may have a copy. That collector told me that he did have one personal copy, and that he would contact me when another one surfaced. He told me to prepare myself because it was a very slim book. He found it disappointing with very little real information, mostly gossip. Most of the information surrounded the stories of Greb never training but always womanizing.

While waiting for the book to surface I was in contact with boxing collectors and discovered that each different collector had one item pertaining to Greb, and it was the rarest and most expensive item in their collection; they would not part with it for any reason. These items would be a photograph, a letter, a fight ticket stub or other similar memorabilia. When interviewed, each collector would seem to have a little nugget of information about Greb. The more I searched, the more it seemed that each collector had a small piece of a puzzle, but no one had put them all together.

After waiting close to two years, I was finally able to obtain a copy of the Greb biography by James Fair, *Give Him to the Angels*. Unfortunately, the book collector I talked with was right. The biography contained very little of his career, was obviously not researched, and contained mostly myths obtained from hearsay. It raised more questions than it gave answers.

I then had an idea to create a Web site that could be a central archive of all these different puzzle pieces. The Web site, www.harrygreb.com, was created in 1996. It was one of the first boxing Web sites on the Internet focused strictly on one boxer, past or present. During the next decade people from around the world contributed copies of what little they had, be it photos, quotes, magazine articles, information or newspaper clippings. Whenever I did find something I could purchase, I paid a large amount of money for it. If it were an item, I would display a photo online; if it were a newspaper or magazine article, I would retype it onto the Web site. Any boxing fan who was curious about this fascinating character could come to the one place where information was free and easily accessible. With each nugget of information I acquired, I slowly discovered the true story of the man *The Ring* magazine says is the greatest middleweight champion who ever lived. I slowly learned why he is put on this pedestal.

His story and accomplishments were remarkable. He reigned as World Middleweight Champion from 1923 until 1926. He won the American Light Heavyweight Championship in 1922. He is the only man to have ever beaten heavyweight champion Gene Tunney. In a time when boxers fought frequently, he fought the most. He was in over 300 fights with 299 of them being official bouts. He fought thirty-seven times in 1917 and forty-five fights in 1919, without losing a single time in either year. He was one of the only Caucasian fighters to cross the color line. Weighing only 160 pounds, he boxed heavyweights weighing over 200 pounds; Greb beat every single heavyweight he ever boxed. He fought eleven future Hall of Fame champions and beat each one of them. He was nicknamed "The Pittsburgh Windmill" because of his unique fighting style that had never been seen before, and has never been duplicated since. After his untimely death, it was discovered he accomplished most of these things while secretly blind in one eye. In 1990 he became part of the inaugural class of inductees into the International Boxing Hall of Fame.

The contents and research from the Web site provide an extensive foundation for this book. However, this book includes a wealth of information not available on the site. I have researched newspapers and magazines for over a decade. I have focused mostly on newspaper articles to construct this book for accuracy and legitimacy. Studying the newspapers is very important because most of Greb's fights were "newspaper decisions," which meant the sportswriters in the local newspapers determined who they thought won the fight. The sportswriters acted as the judges so their opinions were of the greatest importance. The newspaper accounts of Greb's fights also help describe his unique fighting style and how he beat his opponents.

While living in Chicago, I acquired most of my research when I traveled to Pittsburgh. At Pittsburgh's Carnegie Library I studied microfilm from many different local newspapers, including the *Pittsburgh Press*, the *Pittsburgh Post* and the *Gazette Times*. I have examined microfilm covering every day of Greb's amateur and professional career spanning from 1913 to 1926. I have cross-referenced many facts with major newspapers of the day from outside Pennsylvania, including the *New York Times*, the *Washington Post* and the *Chicago Tribune*. The only things I have used from magazines are rare quotes from his opponents and friends. Magazine articles tend to focus on the mythical stories of Greb while rehashing the same unsubstantiated stories. I have interviewed people throughout the years, including Greb's relatives, his opponents' relatives and collectors. My intent is to present his true story so the real man is presented instead of the myth. Accurate descriptions of all key fights throughout his entire career are also told for the very first time. His one-of-a-kind "windmill" fighting style is also described in detail, fight by fight.

On mysteries surrounding Greb, I have consulted specialists in that field who were able to shed some light on the subject. Before researching this book I was unsure exactly when Greb became blind, and how it progressed through the years. For the book I have interviewed three specialists in the field of retinal detachment. They apply their professional knowledge to construct the most probable diagnosis of his blindness. After examining the facts, newspaper accounts and the timetable of events, all three specialists have agreed on what truly happened to Greb's eyesight, and when.

Other myths or mysteries have also been investigated, including the rumors of his fighting with a glass eye, never training, being a heavy drinker, being the dirtiest fighter who ever lived, and constantly womanizing, and that his name wasn't even Greb.

The book is generally presented chronologically, with many chapters covering a single year. To make some subjects more easily accessible I have some chapters that are based on a specific subject matter, which may span across numerous years. For example, chapters 3, 4, 5, 7 and 9 each cover one year of Greb's life. The remaining chapters cover a subject or one specific event. An example is chapter 12, "The Tunney Rematches." This chapter covers all four rematches Greb had against Gene Tunney over the years. Chapter 14, "The Bulldog Meets the Windmill," covers the one fight Greb had against Mickey Walker. These subject chapters are placed in the book chronologically, so if they generally occurred near the beginning of his career, they are placed near the beginning of the book. If they occurred later in his life, they are placed later in the book.

The final chapter, "The Myths Grow While the Legend Fades," focuses on the myths that surround Greb and answers whether they are true or not. The chapter also tells why the general boxing fan has never heard of Greb compared to the other champions he defeated.

The book includes Greb's complete fight record, which I believe is the most comprehensive and accurate one that exists. Each fight record before mine either is missing his amateur and exhibition bouts, or has incorrect dates, locations or results. This fight record includes all amateur bouts and exhibitions. Each fight has been cross-referenced with various sources to ensure accuracy of date, year, opponent, location, and result. This biography is the only book which pulls together pieces of knowledge from countless sources to present the complete picture of Greb's incredible life.

1.

FROM A STREET CORNER
TO A RING CORNER

They loved him because it was as though each fight fan had taken a ball of clay and formed it to his own idea of what a prize fighter should be, and it came out Harry Greb.

— Stanley Weston

Like any legendary fighter should, Harry Greb was born coming out of a corner. This corner, however, wasn't in a boxing ring; it was a street corner. On June 6, 1894, Harry Greb was born at the corner of Dauphin and Fitch Street (also known as Millvale Avenue).[1] Greb's father, Pius, was driving his pregnant wife Annie to the Western Pennsylvania Hospital, which was located less than a mile away from where they lived. Annie started delivering the baby in the car before they could get to the hospital. It wouldn't be the last time a car would affect Greb's plans.

Pius Greb was born on October 15, 1860, in Rossdorf (Amoeneburg), Germany. At the age of twenty Pius left Germany to come to America. He had nine brothers and sisters, and three accompanied him to America. Pius chose a great city at a great time. When Pius came in 1880 he was joined by a major influx of German immigrants. One of these immigrants was the father of Henry J. Heinz, who founded the H.J. Heinz Company in 1872. In addition, during this important time in Pittsburgh, industrialists like Andrew Carnegie and George Westinghouse built their fortunes. By the turn of the century Pittsburgh had grown to become an industrial and commercial giant; this is probably what attracted Pius to the city. Many other immigrants came looking for employment in Pittsburgh, mostly in the factories and mills of the "Steel City."

After Pius had immigrated to the U.S. for work, he met his future wife, Anna Wilbert. Anna M. Wilbert was born in April 1863 in Pennsylvania. It is believed that Pius called her "Annie." Pius and Annie had several things in common, including their German heritage. Both of Annie's parents were born in Germany. It has been said that Harry Greb was half Irish on his mother's side, but that is untrue. Both of Harry Greb's parents came from German families, with no Irish background whatsoever. It is believed this rumor was spread to help make Harry more marketable because Irish boxers drew better crowds.

Pius and Annie got married around 1892, when Pius was thirty-one and Annie was twenty-eight. They bought a rental property at 4902 Alhambra Way, in the Allegheny District of Pittsburgh. Pius and Annie lived in the property while also renting sections of it out to two other couples. Pius worked as a stonemason at that time and Annie stayed at home to raise the children.

It has been said that Harry Greb, born Edward Henry Greb, took the first name of an older brother who died at a young age. The story goes that Greb looked up to his older brother, so when Greb started fighting he took his name, Harry. This hasn't been verified, but what is documented is that Annie gave birth to a total of six children, and only four survived. Pius and Annie had a daughter named Lillian, who was born in 1892, the year they got married. Lillian lived at least until the age of seven but passed away sometime within the following ten years. Greb was only two years younger than Lillian. The name of Greb's other older sibling who passed away is unknown, but the child died before Edward Henry was five years old.[2]

After 1900 Greb's parents then moved the family one block away when they bought their own house. His childhood home was at 138 N. Millvale Avenue in the Garfield neighborhood on the east side of the city.[3] It was three miles away from the juncture of the Allegheny, Monongahela, and Ohio Rivers, and near the heart of the city. Garfield was a community with a solid, working-class population.

After his older siblings passed away, Greb became the older brother to three younger sisters. In June 1896 his younger sister Ida was born. Ida and Greb were two years apart, were friends growing up, and stayed very close throughout Harry's life. When he was six years old his second little sister was born, and christened Catherine. Then at the age of ten his little sister Clara was born.

It was around this time that his sister Ida remembers his first aspirations to be a champion. In an interview Ida recalled, "He would scurry down into Father's basement, stand on a box, strike a fighting stance and proclaim himself the world's champion."[4]

Pius once told a story about when his son was growing up. There were neighborhood bullies that would try to pick on Greb. There were four particular bullies who would come around trying to stir up trouble, making Greb run away. Then one day Pius saw these four older and bigger bullies come around again, but this time Greb didn't have a chance to run away. These troublemakers grabbed him and tied him up to a wagon wheel. If Pius was telling the truth, then he was witnessing all this and never lent a hand to help his son. Greb had to fend for himself. Greb was able to break loose, but this time he didn't run away. Something clicked inside him and he decided not to be a victim anymore, he chose instead to be a fighter and face these bullies head

Pius Greb in 1923 or 1928 when he visited relatives in his home village of Rossdorf, Germany (collection of Christopher Greb).

on. After Greb broke loose, Pius said, "He ran them down and whipped them so bad they never came around the neighborhood again."[5] Greb would be known for fearlessly fighting bigger and stronger men throughout his career and it all began right there and then.

Every boy needs a hobby, and Greb was no exception. As a boy he spent time on the roof of his house playing with pigeons. He kept a pigeon coop up there and tended to his pigeons to help pass the time. By all accounts he was very fond of them.[6]

Greb fancied the girls even when he was going to school. A former grade school student colleague of his was interviewed years later. She said, "With the girls, he was the berries. I used to see him strutting down the street with them, carrying their books. When he came to a mud puddle he would pick them up and carry them over it with gusto. If other boys approached, Greb butted them off the sidewalk like a billy goat."[7]

Pius was a firm father and expected his family to follow his rules in his house. Even as an adult Ida wouldn't refer to their childhood home as "their" house; she would refer to "father's house" or "father's basement."

Harry seemed to be a pretty rambunctious child so it was inevitable that a father with "old school" ethics and rules would eventually not see eye to eye with his exuberant son. One subject of disagreement concerned

Harry Greb's mother, Anna Greb (*Pittsburgh Post-Gazette*).

Greb's focus on boxing. Pius agreed with his fight with the bullies, but it seemed that would be the first and *last* fight that Pius would agree with. Pius was known to have said that Greb was great at baseball and Pius believed he should have pursued that sport instead of boxing. Happy Albacker, a future friend of Greb's, said he saw him play baseball later in life and that Greb wasn't any good. Pius wanted Harry to pursue baseball because he had no respect for the sport of boxing. During Pius's life, the sport of boxing went from bare–knuckle brawls to a sport with gloves and rules. However, in Pius's mind it wasn't as respectable as baseball, and it seems he wished his son were known for playing a more respectable sport than boxing. Pius never went to see his son box. While his mother and sisters traveled to and attended his boxing matches, his father refused to even go to one. Luckily for the sport of boxing, this never stopped Greb from pursuing what he wanted to do.[8]

Sometime after June 1908, when Greb was fourteen years old, he ran away from home. Some believe that Pius kicked him out of the house because he caught Greb involved in a boxing match. Greb's sister Ida was there and she refutes that. Ida said in an interview that Greb chose to leave home, and that he wasn't kicked out. Greb was out of the house for around a year before he came back. It is believed he stayed with his friend Walter Gemmel, who was the same age. Walter had a younger brother William whom Greb was also friends with. The Gemmels lived on the other side of the same block at 4930 Dearborn Street.[9] Greb eventually returned home because Ida sent word to him that Pius was going to sell the pigeons. Greb didn't like the thought of his beloved pigeons' being sold so he hurried home to persuade his father not to sell them. Although what Pius said was usually final, Greb successfully persuaded his father to keep the birds. He then stayed at home for around eight months.

As of April 22, 1910, Greb was still living at home and became an electrician's apprentice at the age of 16. He was working in the east Pittsburgh plant of the Westinghouse Electric and Manufacturing Corporation.[10] An electrician's apprentice with the company would earn twelve dollars a week at that time. The Westinghouse plant was a little over two miles from his home and was located near the corner of North Dallas and Hamilton Avenue. This is a few blocks northwest of Westinghouse Park near the Pennsylvania Train System. It has been said that Greb ran the two and a half miles to and from work every day. Streetcars were in use between Garfield and the plant on Penn Avenue, but Greb chose to run, despite working ten-hour days.

Sometime in the second half of 1910, Greb would leave home for the second and last time. Greb lived with friends for some years while continuing to work as an apprentice.[11] It is unknown if he stayed at the Gemmels' house again. Greb was seen around town by the locals and got the nickname "Icky," often spelled "Ickie." The nickname followed Greb in local newspapers throughout most of his life.

In early 1913, when Greb was eighteen and still working at the Westinghouse Plant, he started hanging out around the local boxing gyms. He learned how to box whenever he had a chance. George Engel, who would years later manage Greb, said that Greb worked as a runner for his brother August Engel at the Westinghouse plant. While George Engel was managing Frank Klaus, the middleweight champion of the world, he was contacted by his brother August. George Engel was based in New York at the time, so his brother wrote him a letter telling him about this young kid named Greb. August wrote that he "watched him a couple of times and was greatly impressed." George Engel would later say,

> My brother took a liking to Harry and finally lent him enough money to go see me in New York. It was tough getting fights then, but I worked Greb into some good spots and he stood up beautifully. I managed him through thirty fights and never had a contract. Eventually no one wanted to fight him and the inactivity, together with his longing for Pittsburgh, split us up.[12]

The Westinghouse Interests, East Pittsburg, Pa.   No. 1068

A postcard of the Westinghouse Manufacturing Plant in East Pittsburgh, where Greb worked for years.

Whether Engel actually managed Greb in New York for thirty amateur fights is unconfirmed. It may be that Engel's claim is false.

In March of 1913 a big amateur boxing and wrestling tournament was being held at Waldemier Hall. Waldemier Hall, often also spelled Waldemeir or Waldemeer, was located at 44th Street and Butler in Lawrenceville. Waldemier Hall was just a mile away from Greb's boyhood home. These amateur boxing tournaments took place there periodically so Greb and his pals, Emanuel Kelly, Walter Gemmel, and some other boys had probably been to see these tournaments on previous occasions. Greb would spend time seeing the regulars fight, and he looked upon their ability with high regard. At this time Greb decided to answer the call of adventure by entering the tournament.

Skipper Manning was a local who groomed amateurs to take part in the tournaments, and he worked with Harry to get him ready. The first night of the tournament was on March 10, 1913. The first opponent Greb met was W.J. Miller. William J. Miller had already been fighting as an amateur for at least a year, and was at that time boxing out of the famous O'Toole club. He was a pretty tough boxer for Greb's first opponent. Two months earlier Miller had entered and won a different amateur boxing tournament in Waldemier Hall. Miller had entered the 158-pound division and won the final in three rounds. Miller had also knocked somebody out the previous year. So here was an experienced amateur boxer facing someone who had never officially fought before.[13]

The first round of this three-night tournament started around eight o'clock. Greb and Miller fought in the 145-pound weight class. The fight went the scheduled three rounds and, incredibly, Greb won on points. There wasn't much time to celebrate the victory because the next round of the tournament would take place the following night.

The Waldemier Hall building as it looked in 2007 (Library and Archives Division, Historical Society of Western Pennsylvania, Pittsburgh).

James "Red" Mason is shown smiling beside Greb in 1925. Mason would manage Greb for most of his career (Antiquities of the Prize Ring).

On March 11 Greb's opponent was Al Storey. Storey was another amateur boxer who had confidence and experience in abundance. Storey fought out of the local East Liberty area and had won the previous night against M. Donovitch. The Greb-Storey bout again went the full three rounds and Greb looked great. A local paper would write: "Greb's fighting last night was a revelation."[14]

The third and final night was on March 12. Greb's final opponent in the tournament was his toughest one yet. William A. Cumpsten went by the name "Red" Cumpsten. He had been fighting for at least a year and knew what he was doing in the ring. Cumpsten had easily beaten his previous opponents the last two nights, and one of them he knocked out. Cumpsten would eventually turn professional and have a local pro career. The referee for all the bouts during this tournament was Leo "Yock" Henninger. Henninger would eventually end up refereeing sixteen of Greb's professional fights. Including these three bouts, then, Greb and Henninger were in the ring a total of nineteen times, spanning over a decade.

A good-size crowd was present for the night's bouts. Greb handled himself well and eked out a win to get the gold medal. It was announced that night that all the winners in the boxing events had qualified themselves for a trip to another tournament. The next tournament would be held in Cleveland around a month later, and they would be battling against boxers of the Cleveland A.A. Club.[15]

A few weeks went by and April 4 arrived. Greb traveled with seven other Pittsburghers to Cleveland, Ohio, for the intercity boxing tournament, which was to be held at the Cleveland Athletic Club. Billy Evans was the referee for all the four-round bouts. Greb's opponent was George Koch from Ohio. Greb ended up winning the 145-pound weight class. The fight went the whole four rounds and Greb won by decision.[16]

Greb didn't stay an amateur for too long. While other boys boxed in the amateur ranks for years, anxious Greb only had five fights in less than a three-month period. Greb always lived in the moment at a very quick pace. Life in the working-class Garfield area didn't have many options for the youth of the day. When they finished the school years then there were the working years. They woke up and went to work in a plant, mill or business every day for the rest of their lives. If boxing didn't work out, there would always be the factory jobs to fall back on. Greb chose to enter the adventurous world of pro boxing.

Mike Gibbons, the St. Paul "Phantom," was arriving in town from New York to fight a local Northside welterweight, Jimmy Perry. The fight was to take place at Exposition Park, but preliminary bouts had to be arranged. Word got out that there was money to be had, so Greb thought this might be a good time to turn pro. However, he couldn't do it without a manager. Greb found James "Red" Mason, who was a manager of a few local boxers at the time, and approached him. Mason asked Greb, "Are you game?" Greb's response was, "Well I guess yes. I fell off a three-story house and lit on my head without being hurt."[17] Mason decided to take Greb under his management and set him up for a fight. Mason had probably seen Greb fight in one of his amateur bouts; if so, that had certainly helped in the decision-making process.

Mason had been managing fighters around Pittsburgh for decades. He was also connected to the history and development of Pittsburgh boxing during the turn of the century. Boxing wasn't far removed from bare–knuckle fighting back then. In 1892 the first world heavyweight champion under the Queensberry rules gained the title. As late as the last decade of the 19th century boxing was restricted legally and socially in Pittsburgh. In the 1890s boxing matches took place in outlying mill towns like Allegheny, Millvale, Homestead, and Aliquippa. Boxing matches were even held on barges in the Ohio River because technically that would make them outside the jurisdiction of local authorities. Boxing gloves started being worn during these fights because the Queensberry rules were gaining popularity in the 1890s.[18]

The Pittsburgh newspapers became a very important part of this scene. Sportswriters like "Jimmy Jab" would inform readers about the local boxing news, comment on the fights, and state their personal opinions about the quality and quantity of the bouts that took place. No actual commission existed for fight promotion or boxing regulations, so all the responsibility fell on the shoulders of the newspapers. The prizefighter, or his manager, would issue a challenge to some other fighter in the city by placing the challenge in the newspapers. Back in April 1899 Mason used this technique and deposited money with a local newspaper for Jack Bennett to fight Ed Kennedy. Kennedy would end up refereeing many of Greb's fights.[19]

In the early 1900s athletic clubs started sponsoring ring activity, so this aspect of the newspapers' role declined. Athletic and social clubs began supplying the boxing ring, and this brought about more standardization and regulations for promoting boxing matches. Reforms that were introduced by the local Pittsburgh athletic clubs made it possible for Pittsburgh citizens to support boxing, even though it was technically still illegal. At this point, Mason, as well as other managers of the time, would arrange for a fighter from one club to fight a boxer from a different club. They would also get a boxer from one area of town to fight a boxer from another part. This was the situation of local Pittsburgh boxing when Mason started managing Greb. Greb was from 138 N. Millvale Avenue, so he was touted as "Harry Greb of Millvale" or "Harry Greb of the East End."[20]

The fight results weren't official, so each newspaper would have its own reporter covering the fight, and they would describe in their columns who they thought won the bout and why. Nat Fleischer, the creator of *The Ring* magazine, described these "newspaper decision" bouts this way: "Newspaper decisions are rendered when the state does not allow an official decision and the sporting writers give their opinion as to who won the fight in the newspapers." "No Decision" fights, as they were also called, were still the norm in Pittsburgh when Greb started fighting. For example, fighting was legal in New York, so there could be judges with an official decision. Most of Greb's fights were No Decision bouts. Therefore, in the record books you will see "ND 6," which means a newspaper decision fight scheduled for six rounds.[21]

Mason took Greb under his wing in May of 1913. Mason would turn out to be a great mentor to help guide Greb through learning the sport in and out of the ring. His first bout was on the undercard of the Mike Gibbons vs. Jimmy Perry bout. This fight took place on May 29, and Greb's first professional fight was against Frank Kirkwood. The *Pittsburgh Press* advertised "Knockout Kirkwood of Coraopolis" against "Harry Greb of Millvale."[22] The bout wasn't the smoothest for Greb, but he won the newspaper decision. The *Pittsburgh Post* printed the next day that Greb and Kirkwood "opened the show with a somewhat clumsy but earnest bout. Greb had a bit the best of it."[23] Therefore, he had successfully found a manager and now his first pro fight was under his belt.

Greb had his second scheduled fight on July 19 against Battling Murphy at Old City Hall. The *Pittsburgh Press* the next day described the fight this way:

> The lads were excited at the bell and swung wildly. In one clinch Greb had a close call to a fall through the ropes. Greb had the weight and punch and Murphy was joyous when the round ended. Less than a minute after the second round was under way Murphy looked like a passenger and the referee stopped the carnage. Murphy had a leaky nose, but was otherwise uninjured.[24]

Greb won the fight in the second round by a TKO. He also won his next fight by knockout. On August 13, 1913 Greb fought Lloyd Crutcher in Punxsutawney and knocked Crutcher out in the first round.

His next fight would be Greb's toughest battle yet. He was scheduled to fight Harvey "Hooks" Evans on October 11. Evans had an amateur background and had been fighting regularly as a pro for a couple of years. Greb's lack of experience was about to catch up with him. The six-round fight took place at Old City Hall in Pittsburgh and it went the full distance. The next day the *Pittsburgh Post* gave the fight to Evans. The *Post* wrote that it was "a good bout and Greb was going strong, although outpointed."[25] This was Greb's first official loss on record.

There wasn't much time for Greb to be disappointed about his first loss because his next scheduled bout was less than two weeks later on October 22, 1913. The fight was against Mike Milko, who had been fighting for a total of at least six years and was of Slavic-American heritage. Milko was a well-known Western Pennsylvanian amateur lightweight champion who had fought in the amateurs for at least five years (1908–1912) while living in the Homestead and Munhall areas of Pennsylvania. He was also a workout partner for Owen Moran in 1910. For a while in 1912 Milko officially changed his name to "Mickey Jerome," thinking that a more Irish-sounding name might open up better opportunities for him. He eventually went back to using his real name.

Milko fought Greb twice in 1913. The referee for both fights would again be Yock Henninger. Their first meeting was October 22 at the Young Men's Republican Tariff Club in Pittsburgh. Before the fight it was written that Greb

> is taking the coming battle very seriously and training faithfully in order to put his husky opponent out of his path. If he can dispose of Milko by the knockout route he feels that his future in the pugilistic firmament is assured. But Milko also is confident, and the fact that he carries a heavy punch in either fist and can assimilate enough punishment to put an ordinary man out makes Greb's task a tough one.

This was only Greb's fifth professional bout and Milko certainly gave Greb a fight to remember. It was a very tough battle and the next day the newspapers said it was a draw.

The two boxers fought again one month later on November 17 at the Southside Market House. It was written: "It was fight, fight, fight all the way."[26] Greb's footwork and cleverness in the ring made the difference in the fight, so the newspapers gave him the decision, but it was close. The *Pittsburgh Post* wrote: "The fans want to keep an eye on Young Grebbs [sic]." It was observed that "in their second meeting Mike Milko hit the Pittsburgh Windmill so hard he cracked a couple of Greb's ribs, thus softening him up for Joe Chip."

Greb's next fight would be one he would never forget. He was set to fight on the undercard of the November 29, 1913, match between Bob Moha and Tom "Bearcat" McMahon. Greb was originally supposed to go up against Hugh Madole, but George Chip's manager, Jimmy Dime, supposedly put some pressure on the promoter to put George's younger brother, Joe Chip, on the card. George Chip was middleweight champion at the time, so he had enough pull to make it happen.[27] It was therefore set for Joe Chip to fight Greb in the preliminaries that night. Joe Chip was known as a puncher, but with an awkward style. Before the fight the newspapers were saying the bout "should prove good, as it will give Grebbs [sic] the test needed to bring him around to where the public will notice him."[28]

The fight took place at Old City Hall in Pittsburgh, and Tom Bodkin, who also promoted the fight, refereed it. Greb weighed 142 pounds and gave away fourteen pounds to the 156-pound Joe Chip. When the first round began, Chip started like "a wild man, missing some leads by four feet."[29] Sometime during the first half of the first round, Chip made Greb's lip bleed. This didn't stop Greb, however, who ended up leading the fight at the end of the first. Supposedly, during the fight Greb's second was negatively commenting about Chip. This got under Chip's skin, so it was an angry Chip who came out for the second round.

At the opening of the round no one was worried for Greb, least of all Mason. The second round was going Chip's way when Greb made a major error. He didn't keep his guard up for a second and Chip caught up with his speed, landing a major

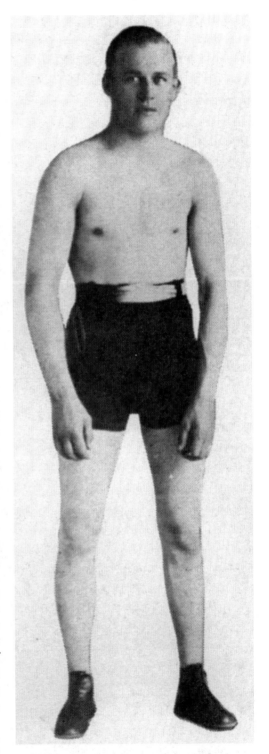

Joe Chip, the younger brother of champion George Chip. Joe was the only man to have knocked out Greb with a punch (Veteran Boxers Association, Ring One).

Old City Hall, from an issue of *Palmer's Pittsburgh*, 1905. Many local boxing matches took place here (Library and Archives Division, Historical Society of Western Pennsylvania, Pittsburgh).

right hand directly onto Greb's unprotected jaw. Greb fell back and bumped his head against the ring floor. The punch against his jaw was one hit, and his head hitting the floor was another. Greb was dazed but tried to get up in time for the count. However, he was unable to rise up off the canvas in time. One story states that Buck Crouse, a stablemate of Greb's, made an effort to reach the bell before the count could finish to save Greb from a knockout. Crouse was going to sound the bell to make it seem like the round had finished, although there was plenty of time left to go. Unfortunately, Greb was counted out and lost the fight, but the activity in the ring wasn't finished. The crowd at Old City Hall was watching a thriller.

After Greb was counted out and walked back to his corner, he was greeted by his manager, Mason. Mason took a bucket of water and splashed it all over Greb to help wake him up. While this was going on, Chip went over to Greb's corner and supposedly kicked Mason. Chip was still upset about the bad things he had heard coming from Greb's corner during the fight. Mason was obviously none too happy at this turn of events. Before he could think of what to do next, someone in the crowd handed him a cane, and he started swinging the cane at Chip. Before contact could be made between Mason and Chip, people from the crowd entered the ring, intervened and cooled things down. It was written the next day: "Bystanders prevented a flare up. The 'kayo' was a thriller."[30]

In the record books for Greb is a KO loss in the second round to Joe Chip, the first year he turned pro. This was to be the first and only time Greb was truly knocked out by a punch. In the future he was to have one technical knockout where the referee stopped the bout, but the fight with Chip was something completely different. The next day Greb was seen around town without a scratch on him; it was like he had never been in a fight. When asked about the fight, Greb had no excuses to offer. He simply said he met a better man that night. He also said that from then on, "I will not go out of my class and meet a man who weighs 156 pounds in the afternoon, while I only scale 142."[31] Greb didn't think that for long. During the rest of his career he was famous for fighting men that were bigger and heavier than he was.

The last month of the year, Greb had two more fights. On December 6, just a week after he was knocked out, he went to Old City Hall to fight again. Greb fought at Old City Hall (pictured) many times in his early career. It was a well-known venue for boxing and was located on Market Street between 4th and 5th. Greb had a scheduled six-rounder against Harvey "Battling" Sherbine. Sherbine was from McKeesport, Pennsylvania, and had previously fought Greb's old opponent Mike Milko. "Battling" Sherbine was tall and thin, around 150 pounds or lighter. He was known for good footwork and some clever defensive maneuvers in the ring. Greb won the bout in six rounds.

Six days later, on December 12, Greb fought his last fight of 1913. It was against Terry Nelson at the Mishler Theatre in Altoona, Pennsylvania. Greb made sure to finish the year right by knocking Nelson out in the third round. This third-round KO capped off his first year as a professional prizefighter.

Greb experienced a lot in this year. He boxed for the first time, fought as an amateur in tournaments, traveled, found a manager and turned pro. As a pro he experienced his first win, first loss, first loss by KO, and his first pro wins by KO. Harry Greb certainly didn't get this much excitement clocking in and out at the Westinghouse factory.

2.

THE EARLY ROAD OF TRIALS

The following year, 1914, began with Greb fighting Whitey Wenzel twice in the month of January. Wenzel was a Pittsburgh lad who would eventually battle Greb ten times in all. This is the most any fighter would ever fight Greb. Their battles became local favorites that everyone wanted to see. When these two fighters met, the fans knew they were going to see a good tough fight. Wenzel wasn't to become a famous boxer, but during the first few years of Greb's pro career he provided the tough "schooling" Greb needed in the ring.

Otto "Whitey" Wenzel was a middleweight who originally fought out of the north side of Pittsburgh. Wenzel had been fighting professionally for four years, learning a lot in the ring and accumulating a big local following, before he fought Greb in the first of their many contests. Newspapers would write about his upcoming fights, have interviews with him, and publish pictures of him all the time. He was one of the local boys a fighter would have to go through if he wanted to move up the ranks. Wenzel would fight many of Greb's opponents, including "Irish" Gorgas, Al Grayber, George Lewis, John Foley, "Battling" Sherbine, Fay Keiser, Al Rogers, Jerry Cole, Kid Manuel, Buck Crouse, and many others. Some fights Wenzel would win, some he'd lose, and some would end in a draw, but all were exciting because he would always give a hundred percent of himself. The crowds loved him because he was a scrapper. There was no easy fight with him because every time he entered the ring, he intended to do whatever it took to win.

Greb's first two meetings with Wenzel, who was a little taller and heavier than Greb, took place at Old City Hall, and both fights were scheduled to go six rounds. The contests were rough, tough and bloody. Each fighter would alternate winning a round or two. The early rounds saw them throwing a lot of punches back and forth in which Greb would come out slightly ahead. At this point, however, it would start getting ugly.

During their second fight, on January 10, 1914, Greb split Wenzel's lip and then puffed his cheek in an early round. Wenzel came back and punched Greb so hard his face started to bleed. This upset Greb so much he started fighting wildly until the round ended. The middle rounds were full of hard fighting, but with Wenzel getting a little tired and slowing down slightly. Greb would pick it up a little in the last couple of rounds to eke out a very close win in the newspapers the next day.[1]

They fought two more times in 1914 and both fights ended in draws, according to the newspapers. The bouts were tough and close, but Greb would finish stronger, winning the last round with Wenzel a little leg-weary. The fights had a box office draw total of about $600 a fight, with general admission costing fifty cents, and a dollar for closer seats. The audience consisted of mostly local followers of Greb and Wenzel.

The next year saw Greb and Wenzel fighting in March, April, and May, with Greb winning two out of the three matches. The crowds started getting bigger as people heard what great fights they were and would consist of around 1,200 fans. Greb would start a round against Wenzel

A young Harry Greb, around 1915. Many boxers during this time would wear decorative sashes around their waists as Greb is doing here. Starting at a young age and continuing throughout his career, Greb would slick back his hair for photographs and before entering the ring (Craig Hamilton collection, www.josportsinc.com).

with a right hand or an uppercut and would be able to land it without too much of a problem. Wenzel would usually try to throw a lot of uppercuts hoping one would land. It was around this time that Greb started figuring out Wenzel's style and beating him easily at his own game.

Harry Keck of the *Pittsburgh Post* would write the following about the March 5 fight:

> Wenzel did quite a little scoring himself, but most of his punching lay in jabs, occasional straight lefts to the head and face and uppercuts, only a few of which landed. He also did a little

work inside, but in no department did he measure up to Greb's standard. There is no doubting the fact that Greb's terrific swings to the stomach as he rushed in, sapped a goodly part of Wenzel's speed and stamina. Greb counted best with this style. Strange, to say the least. Wenzel was beaten by an opponent who employed exactly the same methods used by Whitey in all his previous bouts. The right swing and hook to the body, accompanied by the additional momentum of a speedy rush, always has been one of Wenzel's best assets. Forced to combat the same style, he was unable to utilize it himself.[2]

In 1916 they fought their final two bouts, but by then Greb had become much better. Greb easily won the May 6 bout by winning every round. He confused Wenzel with "clever footwork."[3] Their last fight took place on June 17, 1916, and was a ten-round bout; all their previous fights had not been over six rounds. Wenzel hadn't fought many ten-rounders so it ended up being too much for him. Greb won six of the rounds, with Wenzel only winning one and three rounds even. This fight took a lot out of Wenzel, who stopped boxing entirely for over a year afterwards, taking up management instead. Greb had grown as a fighter, learned everything he needed to win against Wenzel and completely dominated while finishing with energy to spare. Wenzel would eventually return to boxing as a fighter later the following year. He would then go on later in his career to fight Hall of Fame members George Chip in 1921 and Gene Tunney in 1922.

Greb started fighting another opponent in 1914 whom he would clash with often. His name was Fay Keiser, and he fought out of Cumberland, Maryland. Keiser was a middleweight who

stood 5'10½" tall. Greb and Keiser battled a total of nine times throughout their careers, and their feud would span a total of ten years from 1914 to 1924. Most of their fights were newspaper-decision bouts with two official decisions that Greb won. Keiser was only able to muster two draws against Greb during their early battles.

Greb and Keiser fought twice in 1914 with both fights being six-rounders. The first bout took place on April 14 at Duquesne Gardens in Pittsburgh. The contest was on the undercard of the Buck Crouse vs. Gus Christie match-up. Greb would eventually meet and beat both these two headliners in years to come, but as he was just starting out and trying to get a name for himself, many of his fights were on undercards of bigger fights. Yock Henninger was the referee for the first meeting between Keiser and Greb. According to the newspapers, Greb won the bout. Their next fight was on May 13, this time at the Southside Market House, and the six-round bout was said to be a draw.

Fay Keiser battled Greb a total of nine times. The last time they fought was for the world middleweight title (collection of Pugilistica.com).

Greb and Keiser fought three more times the following year; the first of these was on May 31, 1915, in Connellsville, Pennsylvania. Greb was fighting with an injured right hand, which he had hurt in his fight a week earlier against Wenzel. The hand hadn't had time to fully heal, but Greb still fought with it. The bout was a very fast-paced six-rounder which was pretty even until the final two rounds, when Greb picked up the pace and won. The newspapers said the next day that Greb won the fight while fighting most of the time with only his left hand.

Greb and Keiser fought again a month later on June 25 in Cumberland, Maryland. This tough fight ended in a draw, according to the newspapers. Then on July 22 they fought at Old Moose Hall in Cumberland, and went a full ten rounds. Greb was so dominant that the *Pittsburgh Press* said he won every round except for the first and fifth. Near the end of the bout Keiser was losing strength and was getting close to being knocked out, but he held on. When the bout was finished, Greb left without a mark on him while Keiser looked bruised and battered all over his face and body. Although the previous fights were close, including two draws, Greb had learned what he could from Keiser and was now completely overwhelming him.[4]

The next year Greb and Keiser met again in Cumberland on September 4, 1916, in a ten-round fight that Greb won. Then on January 29, 1917, Keiser and Greb were matched to fight a grueling twenty-round bout in Lonaconing, Maryland. This fight would be an official bout with an official decision. It was such a long bout it eventually ended at 11:45 P.M. and was witnessed by two thousand spectators. Greb was said to have won seventeen of the rounds with two rounds even; Keiser won only the fifth. The fifth round was also the time when Greb opened up a cut over Keiser's mouth which continued to bleed throughout the fight. When the extremely long bout finally ended, Referee Matt Hinkle raised Greb's hand in victory.

Years later Greb and Keiser met each other twice more. On December 6, 1921, the two fought in Philadelphia. The *Pittsburgh Post* wrote the next day that Greb "battered [Keiser] in the 6th round with lefts and rights until it seemed impossible for a human being to withstand the blows, but Keiser consumed the beating and was actually trying to fight back at the bell." Greb ended up winning the eight-round fight, according to the newspapers.[5]

The feud finally ended when they fought their final bout on March 24, 1924. Greb was middleweight champion and the fight took place in Baltimore. Keiser was bleeding and beaten up when he was dropped to the floor in the twelfth round by a right to the chin. Keiser had barely made it to his feet when the referee decided he had seen enough and awarded Greb the win. The bout was so one-sided that Greb's slicked-back hair wasn't even mussed up until a clinch in the fourth round. It ended as a TKO in the twelfth round and they would never fight again. It says something about Greb that he at least gave his old nemesis a shot at the middleweight title once he had won it.

Keiser had a successful career fighting such Hall of Famers as Gene Tunney, Young Stribling and Tommy Loughran, and ended up retiring from the ring soon after his last bout with Greb in 1924. Keiser and Wenzel are responsible for battling Greb a total of nineteen times between them. The two fought each other on September 28, 1915, in Cumberland in an official ten-round fight where Keiser was awarded the victory.

One of the things Greb is known for in his career is fighting men much heavier and larger than himself. Greb fought most of his pro career weighing between 158 and 168 pounds, but he often fought against men in the heavyweight division. Greb enjoyed fighting heavyweights because they were so much slower than he was. He learned early that he could take their punches so he was never afraid of them.

The first heavyweight that Greb tested his chin against was John Foley. When Greb traveled to Cleveland for the amateur tournament, one of his teammates was the heavyweight John Foley. On July 20, 1914, Greb stepped into the ring against Foley, a match he didn't even know would take place until minutes before the bout.

John "Honey" Foley was a local Pittsburgh boy who outweighed Greb by a full thirty pounds. The fight took place at Greb's frequent venue of Waldemier Hall. On the night of July 20, 1914, Greb was originally scheduled to fight Fay Keiser or Ray Parks, but they canceled. John Foley came in at the very last minute and offered to fight Greb to keep the ticket holders happy and save the show. Greb had been boxing men around his own weight up to this point and was surprised to have to step into the ring at the last minute against a heavyweight.

Greb used his speed to fight rings around Foley. He would circle his opponent and quickly go inside and punch, then distance himself before Foley could respond. Once in a while slow-footed Foley would throw a punch that landed, but they were so phoned-in that Greb had a lot of time to prepare for them. Most of the time Greb just evaded Foley's slow punches and "executed tangos" around him. When the six-round bout ended Greb was awarded the victory.[6]

The following month Greb met Foley again for another six-round bout at Waldemier Hall. The fight was on August 31, 1914, and each man had plenty of time to prepare for his opponent this time, no surprises and no excuses. The outcome was exactly the same, with Greb using his speed to dash around his opponent. Greb was "raining in blow after blow while avoiding and blocking heavy returns." Greb was awarded another victory with a headline reading "Foley Victim Of Worst Ever Ring Beating."[7] Greb would go on to fight many heavyweights, and he always enjoyed it. Foley gave him the first taste of what it would be like, and Greb continued to feast on these big men for the rest of his career.

Greb fought a future Hall of Famer early in his career by the name of Jack Blackburn. Blackburn is famous for training Joe Louis, but before this he had a very impressive career as a boxer himself. His career spanned over twenty years, from 1901 to 1923, in which he fought the likes of Joe Gans, Sam Langford, Philadelphia Jack O'Brien, Kid Norfolk and many others. In 1915, when Greb and Blackburn were scheduled to battle, Blackburn had been released

Jack Blackburn (right) with George Chip. This photograph was taken in 1914 upon Blackburn's release from prison (Antiquities of the Prize Ring).

from prison the year before, and Greb knew not to take this fight lightly. Greb was shorter than Blackburn but was carrying a little more weight. Blackburn had acquired a reputation of fighting men bigger and stronger than himself and being a great fighter against any man who would step in the ring with him. Years earlier the great middleweight champion Stanley Ketchel had refused to fight Blackburn because he was so tough.[8] Even though Blackburn hadn't fought between 1909 and 1913, Greb knew he had to train really hard if he was to have any chance when he stepped in the ring against him.

This fight would also be the first fight Greb had against an African-American prizefighter. During this time in boxing history, white fighters, managers and promoters would not give African-American fighters a chance to fight against Caucasians. Since Jack Johnson had become the first African-American Heavyweight Champion and had dominated the division since 1908, the white boxing establishment had done everything in their power to dethrone Johnson and make sure it never happened again. Johnson was to eventually lose his title on April 5, 1915, to Jess Willard, but Greb and Blackburn fought a few months before this happened. During Johnson's reign and even after he lost the title, the white boxing establishment didn't want white boxers fighting African-Americans because the African-American fighter might win, forcing whites to deal with another champion like Johnson.

Unlike many of his fellow white boxers during his time, Greb didn't subscribe to this prejudice; Greb just wanted to get better as a boxer and constantly fight the best. That meant fighting some African-American boxers, no matter what some people may have thought about it. Greb eventually fought African-Americans "Allentown" Joe Gans, Willie Langford and Kid Lewis. Greb also had famous scraps against Hall of Famers Kid Norfolk and Tiger Flowers.

Greb was scheduled to face Jack Blackburn on January 25, 1915, at Duquesne Gardens in Pittsburgh. His usual training regimen included going six rounds with relays of different boxing partners, which included men from many different weight classes. Greb would also run ten miles, do extensive exercises in the gym and finish with a rubdown. According to the January 22, 1915, issue of the *Pittsburgh Post*, Greb was sparring with a heavyweight so hard that Greb knocked him "down for the count."[9]

Local Boy to Oppose Clever Ring Veteran

Greb shown in an early newspaper ad promoting a fight between him and Jack Blackburn (*Pittsburgh Post-Gazette*).

When the six-round fight began Greb started throwing a lot of punches; some were hitting, but most missed. Greb was the aggressor, constantly going after Blackburn. Early in the first round Blackburn slipped and used Greb's extended arm from a punch to help get back up to one knee.

Greb's arms never stopped throwing punches. While he was punching, Blackburn blocked, moving to the side, ducked punches and tried to get out of the way of this constant assault. From the first round to the last, Greb kept Blackburn on the defensive. Blackburn only managed to throw a tenth the punches Greb did, but he tried to make them connect and count. When Blackburn's punches connected, they hit Greb's middle but didn't do too much damage.

In the third round Greb started understanding Blackburn's defense and was able to land more frequently and make the punches land harder, making Blackburn's nose start to bleed at the end of the third. The first three rounds went to Greb.

By the fourth round Blackburn was getting better at fighting back Greb's rushes, but Greb was landing more consistent punches. Greb was aiming his punches at Blackburn's jaw and a lot landed. Blackburn fought back while aiming his blows at Greb's body and head; the fourth round was said to be even.

Greb held back in the fifth round and didn't use up too much energy; he was saving some for the next and final round. This was a nice tactic that proved Greb was becoming an experienced boxer that used strategy. However, this meant Blackburn was able to land more punches compared to all the previous rounds. The fifth round was awarded to Blackburn.

When the sixth round began it was like watching the first. Greb came out swarming his opponent with constant punches. The "Pittsburgh Windmill" was earning his name. Blackburn couldn't do anything but cover up and play defense. Once in a while he would tie up Greb when he would rush in, but to no effect other than an occasional counterpunch. Greb finished strongly and was the busier man. The final round was awarded to Greb, as was the fight in the newspapers the following day.

Greb successfully kept the pressure on Blackburn from the first to the sixth, forcing Blackburn off his game so he had to play defense. Greb didn't tire because he had trained properly for the fight, which gave Blackburn no window of opportunity. The newspapers would write that Greb was using his arms like "piston rods" and that Greb threw "a million punches." This was a major win and showed people Greb was starting to be a boxer who needed to be taken seriously.[10]

The next month Greb was scheduled to fight Harry "KO" Baker. This fight was to become the benchmark fight that started Greb on his course to the middleweight championship. A title bout was many years away, but this fight was against a Philadelphia star middleweight that everyone in the state of Pennsylvania saw as the strong young contender who was on the rise to stardom.

Local rising star Harry "KO" Baker from Philadelphia. Baker would get heavy coverage in the local newspapers and was expected to become the next local contender (*Pittsburgh Post-Gazette*).

Baker weighed around 160–165 during this time of his career and fought middleweights and light heavyweights. "KO" Baker had just beaten Blackburn twice in the previous month and was now ready to face Greb.

Their fight came on February 10, 1915, in a six-round bout at the famous Duquesne Gardens. Up to this point Greb had fought at the Duquesne Gardens for his big bouts with Keiser and Blackburn, and he would go on to have many more fights here. The Duquesne Gardens was located on Craig Street in the East Liberty area of Pittsburgh. It hosted lavish events, concerts and many sporting events, including hockey and boxing. Greb knew he was in a major fight if it was being held in the Duquesne Gardens.

If Greb were going to climb a notch higher toward being considered as a real middleweight contender, it would have to be done against the rising star of Baker.

The bell sounded for the first round and it seemed as if Baker was feeling Greb out, trying to gauge him. Greb noticed this and immediately took the offensive, landing several left jabs and right crosses onto Baker's head. Baker tried to retaliate with a timed left uppercut, but Greb moved out of the way and rushed Baker with a bunch of short punches to the head. Greb was always moving, so when an opponent missed it gave him an opening to take advantage of. Before this fight Greb would often lead with his right arm extended. Greb knew Baker was aware of this, so Greb mixed things up. He led with his left hand during some of the first round and always kept in Baker's face. This helped Greb time a one-two punch that he used quite often in this round. When the round was coming to an end, Greb threw a hard left to Baker's jaw that sent Baker retreating back to his corner. Greb followed Baker and started showering him with punches while Baker could do nothing but cover up. Right before the bell rang Baker found an opening and hit Greb with a stinging left to the head which forced Greb to back up. This was the end of round one. Greb won it and the crowd knew they were in for a good fight.[11]

In round two Greb continued to lead with his left hand and then mixed things up every four or five leads by using his right hand instead. Baker continued to try to time his punches and use them economically. Baker mostly used his left hand but timed them wrong so Greb was able to duck underneath them. This wasn't working for Baker so he tried to change his tactic by focusing more on Greb's body instead of his head. Baker was then able to land some body shots successfully when he threw several rights and lefts. The end of the second round came and it looked like Greb had won this round by a larger margin than the first.

It was clear Baker needed to step up his attack if he was to win this bout. He started the third round by rushing out of his corner and going straight for Greb. Greb saw this rushing attack and sidestepped out of the way. Greb's quick sidestep made Baker lose his balance and he stumbled onto the floor of the ring. When Baker rose to his feet again both men started punching wildly to each other's heads. However, Baker couldn't keep up the pace and started to tire. With Baker tiring from Greb's continuous onslaught, Greb was starting to land punches more easily. Baker was used to fighting with his right leg and arm extended. Greb noticed this and continued to alternate from left lead to right lead. Baker was mentally caught off balance by this, and Greb had won this round by the biggest margin yet. When the bell rang and Greb turned to his corner his followers in the crowd started yelling in excitement.

Baker began the fourth better than any of the other rounds. He hit Greb on the head with a left, and then in a clinch he landed a hard right onto the back of Greb's skull. Both men in this round generally stood in the center, swinging aggressively with both hands. Baker was able to land a few lefts and rights to Greb's stomach. Greb then retaliated with a bunch of sharp jabs to Baker's mouth. Baker returned with a left swing and a left uppercut, slowing Greb down a little. Greb returned fighting hard and the round was given to Greb by a very slim margin.

Early in the fifth round Baker gained the advantage with his left swings. Baker then threw a powerful left uppercut but because Greb was quickly moving, the punch landed under Greb's

Above and opposite: Inside and outside views of the Duquesne Gardens. Greb had many fights here early in his career. It was a multipurpose arena that held lavish events, concerts, boxing and hockey games. Shown here is the inside with a skating rink (Library and Archives Division, Historical Society of Western Pennsylvania, Pittsburgh).

arm instead of his jaw. If it had landed on the jaw, it could have changed the fight considerably. Greb started fighting behind his jab from a distance. He was probably slowing things down a little to save some energy for the final round. Baker continued throwing his left uppercuts, trying to hit a vital area, but Greb wouldn't let that happen. Baker threw these uppercuts with so much power that they would lift his own body a few inches off the canvas. He was obviously trying to change the course of the fight with just one blow. That may have worked for him in the past, but not tonight against someone so quick and crafty. At the end of the round Greb landed two left hooks and a solid right to Baker's head. This was the closest round yet and was said to be even.

The final round began and Baker again rushed out of his corner but was immediately met with a left to the face. Greb then connected to Baker's face again before hitting him with a left and right to the head. This made Baker lose his balance a little. Greb's stamina was on full throttle and Baker just couldn't stop it. Baker would land sometimes onto Greb's stomach, but Greb continued to rush and he completely dominated the final two minutes. Greb was dancing around Baker now, landing lefts and rights to the face and occasionally the body. As in Greb's last fight, his opponent had no alternative from here on out than to cover up and defend himself from the onslaught.

After the fight Greb was called "a human dynamo" and "an enraged tiger." Baker threw his left mostly and Greb was able to respond to it easily. Greb finished so well it was said to be the fastest finish the experts had seen in the entire season.

Following his win against Baker, Greb decided to have a little party to celebrate. One of the people who attended the party was Mildred Reilly, his future wife. Greb and Mildred were said to have started dating around this time. After the party, a local newspaper wrote about the gathering and referred to "the young lady" as "the belle of Little Washington, her hometown." A friend gave the newspaper article to Greb and he read it over very carefully. When they referred to Mildred as "the belle of Little Washington," Greb asked his friend what "belle" meant. Greb's friend didn't know what the word meant either. Greb tried to figure out if the word was derogatory or not. Some time passed and Greb was found looking through a dictionary to find the word. He finally lifted his head from the book and said, "It's all right, that guy didn't call her any names."[12]

Greb and Baker had a rematch the following month so as to make sure there was no confusion about who truly was the best. The rematch took place at the Duquesne Gardens again and the outcome would also be the same. Yock Henninger was the referee and everyone saw Greb duplicate his victory. The fight was said not to be as fast as their first meeting. Greb was forcing the action throughout and was referred to as a "human jumping jack in motion."

When Greb fought the rematch he had brought a girl to witness it. At the fight, the papers said, was "Greb's best girl." Although the papers didn't print her name, it was believed to be Mildred. This could have been the very first fight of Greb's she saw in person.[13]

After Greb beat Baker a second time, all the attention Baker had been getting as a real contender was now transferred to Greb. Greb was now seen as the rising star that people had to fight, and his newspaper coverage skyrocketed. The newspapers started covering Greb when he signed to fight someone, then wrote about him training, then wrote some more in days leading up to a fight. Now Greb's fights went from preliminary bouts on the undercard to being the headliners. Beating Baker made everyone realize Greb was now a Pittsburgh contender on his way to the championship one day.

Now that Greb was considered a contender, he was about to challenge other real middleweight contenders. Greb was matched to fight Joe Borrell, who had just fought for the middleweight title against champion George Chip on January 26, 1914. Borrell lost the fight against Chip but put on a good show.

Greb had revenge on his mind against Borrell because they had fought four months earlier and the newspapers said Borrell had won the fight. Greb had taken that fight at a moment's notice and was not given the time to properly train and prepare. Now he wanted to show how he had progressed as a fighter.

Leading up to the Borrell fight Greb was training as usual at the Garfield Athletic Club. He was secretary of the club and a few days before the Borrell fight the club had a vote and decided on blue and white as the colors to represent the club. Then they passed a motion for the whole club to go to the Greb-Borrell fight en masse and make a big showing wearing a lot of blue and white. The members asked Greb to call the *Pittsburgh Post* and tell them all about it. Greb contacted sportswriter Harry Keck, who would eventually become one of Greb's closest friends.

Greb talked on the phone to Keck, who wrote their conversation in the newspaper the next day. Greb said,

> Well, to make a long story short, they asked me to wear blue and white tights when I fight Borrell and they'll all wear blue and white ribbons or badges or blue and white somethings. I always wear green tights, but I had to promise to wear blue and white ones this time. If I get licked I'm going back to the green ones, but if I win, I'm going to stick to the new boys. What do you think of the idea?

"It listens all right," said Keck. "And it sounds like a pretty good story."

"You bet your life it does," said Greb. "Guess I'll say goodbye," concluded Greb. "Don't forget to put a piece in the paper about it tomorrow. All the boys will be looking for it."

"Goodbye," Keck replied and hung up the receiver. A few minutes later Jimmy Mason, Greb's manager, blew into the office and was told about it. He came back with:

"Blue and white's not such a bad combination at that; all he'll need is to spill a little blood and he'll look like the American flag."[14]

This rematch fight against Borrell, who outweighed Greb by fifteen pounds, took place on April 22, 1915, at the Duquesne Gardens. During the first two rounds Greb was driving Borrell around the ring with his rushes of lefts and rights. Borrell was unable to do any actual fighting during this time because of the force of Greb's assault. Greb would throw long-distance lefts to the face and when the fighters were close Greb would throw lefts to the body. Greb dominated the first two rounds. Borrell put in more of an effort in the third round, but Greb still forced the fight and won that round as well.

In the fourth and fifth rounds Greb tried to keep Borrell at a distance using his jab, but Borrell would get close and throw punches to the body. Both worked hard and fast while Greb used very quick footwork. Although it was close, these rounds went to Borrell because of his more aggressive fighting and better effectiveness during the clinches.

The sixth and final round began and Borrell had a lot to make up for. It started with a lot of clinches, during which Borrell was able to pry his arms free and hit Greb's head using both of his hands. Greb tried keeping him at a distance using his jab, but Borrell would go for a clinch, where he was much more effective. Borrell's body blows in this round worked and Borrell won the final round.

With Greb winning the first three rounds and Borrell winning the last three, the bout was declared a draw. Considering the disadvantage in weight and Borrell's many years of experience, Greb made a great showing. Greb was constantly improving and the way he handled himself in the first half of the bout showed it. Greb would continue to fine-tune his technique, and he was able to demonstrate this when these two fighters met for a third and fourth time, which will be covered in the next chapter.[15]

Later in 1915 Greb was to have one of his most memorable fights, one which made him change the way he fought forever after. On December 16, 1915, Greb fought Perry "Kid" Graves at the Power Auditorium in Pittsburgh. It was a scheduled six-round newspaper decision bout refereed by Joe Donnelly, who would referee fourteen of Greb's fights. Kid Graves was a welterweight who was fighting out of

Joe Borrell in a fight pose (Craig Hamilton collection, www.josportsinc.com).

Brooklyn at the time. His real name was Perry Ivan Graves and he was an inch and a half shorter than Greb. Before he met Greb in the ring he had fought the likes of Young Ahearn, Jack Britton, Mike Gibbons, Soldier Bartfield, Mike Glover and Ted "Kid" Lewis.

For many days leading up to this bout there was a lot of buzz. These two boxers were said to have a rivalry because each considered the other one an obstacle in his path. Greb needed to beat Graves so he could fight Mike O'Dowd in his next bout. Both fighters were expected to fight fast and furious and each trained to the greatest extent. The *Pittsburgh Press* would write on December 14, a day before the fight, that each was working out in training gyms in preparation for the fight. The article was titled "Graves And Greb Finish Training." The *Press* would also write: "Both are crowding in as much labor as possible into the final conditioning sessions, with a view to being in their very best form when they step to the center of the ring."[16]

On December 15 the *Pittsburgh Press* wrote: "Trained to a degree of perfection that will enable them to go the entire six rounds, if necessary, at their utmost speed, Harry Greb and Kid Graves are impatiently awaiting the sound of the bell."[17]

Fight night finally arrived, and when the first round began, Graves boxed smart and comfortably. He was throwing a nice left hook along with his left jab. Greb was throwing punches, but Graves either blocked them or moved away before they had a chance to land. Graves was using his welterweight speed to his advantage during this round, and the round went to him.[18]

Then the bell rang for the second round and both boxers began to fight. There was a mix-up early on and Greb hurt his arm when he punched Graves on the head the wrong way. Then they were both in a clinch, but when Greb stepped back he dropped his left arm. Greb was now more determined to fight so he started to make a desperate attempt to win this round. The two had some exchanges in the ring and Greb won them; he was outfighting Graves in this round by a slight margin. When the bell sounded to end the round, something very surprising happened. Greb's left arm fell limp to his side. The *Post* would write: "His face, screwed up, bore testimony to the pain he was suffering."

When Greb was in his corner after round two a physician examined his arm and found that the radial bone was fractured. He had broken the bone in his left arm when he punched Graves's head early in the second round. Greb didn't stop then, but instead continued to fight and win the second round while his arm was broken. The referee had to call the bout because he couldn't allow Greb to continue; therefore, it was a TKO for Graves.

The following day Greb's arm was in a splint. He presented his X-ray to people and it clearly showed that the radius was completely fractured, "and the jagged ends were overlapping."

Greb was originally scheduled to fight Mike O'Dowd five days later on December 21 in St. Paul, Minnesota. He couldn't be in that fight because of his broken arm, so the promoters started looking for a replacement. Kid Graves fought O'Dowd in place of Greb, and he ended up winning the ten-round newspaper decision.

Greb had to take a couple of months off to let the arm heal. He should have taken longer, but he was anxious to get back in the ring. His manager, Red Mason, was interviewed on February 22, 1916, about the accident and how the recovery was going. Mason said he thought the accident was a good thing because it would "make a two-handed fighter of Icky." The *Pittsburgh Press* on February 22 wrote that before the accident Greb was "notoriously a left-handed boxer. With the southpaw he could hit at all angles, but with the right he has been awkward and slow." Mason had a theory that Graves may be the "unwitting cause of the development of Greb's right hand."[19]

The broken arm didn't stop Greb from continuing his aggressive daily training schedule, which now included running longer distances. The *Pittsburgh Press* wrote that "a fine distance runner was lost to the world when Greb decided to enter the ring." This was stated by professional long-distance runner Hughie Bruce, who at this time would accompany Greb every single morning at the crack of dawn for long-distance runs. It was also said that Greb had now "developed a pair of lungs and a wind that ought to carry him through any ordinary bout at top speed."[20]

A couple of key changes occurred after his arm was broken. When Greb trained he was now working on his right arm, so it got stronger. Instead of being less powerful than his left, it had now become equal or better. His distance running increased his stamina in the ring. This would allow him to stay swarming throughout the fight instead of slowing down to take a breather before the final round.

Mason's theory was put to the test with Greb's first bout after the accident on February 26, 1916, against Walter Monoghan. Greb was able to use his left only during the first two rounds, then it was all right hand for the remainder of the bout. After the second round his left was injured again so it took the new strength of his right hand and his improved stamina and leg quickness to carry him through the rest of the contest. It was a very close and exciting fight so a rematch was asked for. However, Greb's re-injured arm still needed more time to heal, so the rematch, originally scheduled for March 11, was called off.[21]

Greb had a bout scheduled against Herman Miller, a Baltimore middleweight, on March 18. It had to be canceled because a physician took a look at Greb's arm the day before the bout and reported that he wasn't yet fit to box. Greb had been concealing how bad his arm truly was because he was so anxious to return to boxing. The boxing physician reported that if Greb fought Herman Miller that night, he would be running the risk of permanently losing the use of his left arm.[22]

On March 27 Greb had another medical examination of the arm. He proved he was physically fit enough to schedule a fight against Kid Manuel on April 1, 1916. Greb was confident in his return to the ring because his left was working as it used to and his right was vastly improved. The *Pittsburgh Press* wrote that Greb "doesn't intend to fight with one arm, as he had to do against Walter Monoghan a month ago."[23]

The Greb-Manuel fight was very close, and Greb finished with a lot of energy and at a terrific pace, probably due to his extensive training. Because it was such a close fight they were set for a rematch on June 3. The fight again took place at the Power Auditorium (the Power House) on Penn Avenue and 34th Street. If there

Perry "Kid" Graves is the only boxer to have beaten Greb by a technical knockout (courtesy of Tracy Callis).

was any doubt, Greb showed just how much stronger his right hand had become when he knocked out Manuel in the first round with "a vicious right hook." The right punch was so strong that Manuel was unconscious for several minutes afterwards.[24]

Mason's theory was proven correct. Graves was the unwitting cause of Greb's new development as a better and stronger boxer. This would be confirmed the following year — 1917 — when Greb would do what he had never been able to do before. He would have the busiest fight year of his life and go on a powerful knockout streak.

Near the end of 1916 Greb set his sights on fighting a stablemate of his, middleweight Al Grayber. Grayber, as well as future Greb opponents Buck Crouse and Walter Monoghan, were all fighters under the management and promotion of James "Red" Mason. All three boxers, as well as others, shared the same training facility. Grayber was a good fighter and was getting a lot of attention. Grayber's real name was Andrew Albert Valentine, but he was always known at this time as Al Grayber. Once Greb hurt his arm, Grayber got more attention from Mason, and this just aggravated the intense rivalry between the two boxers. In late March Greb notified everyone that he wanted to fight Grayber in the ring. "Icky" Greb wanted to settle, once and for all, the matter of who was the best fighter in the stable and who deserved the premium treatment for being groomed to be a champion.[25]

Mason agreed to the grudge match and it was scheduled for August 7, 1916. It would be another fight to take place at the Power Auditorium. Greb was looking forward to this fight and said, "A good stiff poke on the jaw will tumble Al Grayber just as quickly as it'll make any other man flop. I never heard that he was an iron man, and if I reach his chin as cleanly as I reached Kid Manuel's, he'll go."[26]

Grayber was a little taller, heavier and stronger than Greb, but it didn't change Greb's belief that he'd beat Grayber in the ring. Greb's intention was to use his own speed against Grayber's strength. They both increased their training schedules so as to be in top physical shape for this intense grudge match. It was well understood that the loser of this fight would go down one rung in the stable, while the winner would be "the cock o' the walk." Mason agreed to stay neutral and not be in either boxer's corner. He liked both boxers equally and was "praying for a good hard draw."[27]

The day of the fight arrived and the two boxers finished their intense training. Greb and Grayber even added to the importance of the fight by betting money on the result. The two combatants wagered almost their entire gate on themselves. Whoever won would get the other person's purse for the fight, winner take all. Each also promised a knockout and now the loser would be "a loser financially as well as pugilistically."[28]

That night the announcer stepped into the ring and introduced them as "Al Grayber and Ickie Greb, feudists for years."[29] The fight was scheduled for six rounds. For the first three rounds the two boxers let their aggression get the best of them. They threw wild punches that missed a lot, when they weren't grabbing and clinching each other. They didn't pay any attention to their timing or their distance when throwing punches.

During the fourth round Grayber got out of control and "jackknifed" Greb over the ropes. While Greb had his back to the ropes, Grayber pushed and leaned on Greb so he was leaning halfway over. After being on the receiving end of this tactic, Greb would apply it to opponents later in his career. The referee called a time out to let Greb, and his back, recover. Once the fighting started up again Grayber put Greb's head in an arm lock and held him there until the crowd started yelling. Grayber's dirty tactics were getting this fight out of control fast.

The crowd was yelling and going wild during the fourth round but they were calming down in the fifth. There were a lot of policemen in attendance that night because everyone had expected a wild bout. Grayber was said to have won the fourth round through his hitting ability, while Greb was throwing some bombs that were missing. The fifth round was as ugly as the previous rounds, with a lot of stunts but little boxing.

At the start of the sixth and final round, Greb leapt into the center of the ring ready for Grayber. Greb threw some great punches to the face that landed easily. Grayber was unable to return any blows and Greb was making a good show this round. When the round ended some of Greb's fans were saying he won the fight, but everyone else agreed it was a draw. The next day the papers announced, "Grayber and Greb in Draw."

The match-up ended just the way Mason had wanted it. Now that it was a draw the side bet was off because there was no winner, so each was able to keep his end of the purse. Greb and Grayber never fought again and never had to. This fight got all their frustrations out and they were now able to deal with each other in the same gym while training. Greb would become

Mason's main breadwinner in the stable when he started on a massive fight schedule the following year.

Starting in 1917, Greb's arm got even stronger while he was still fighting for the top spot in his stable. This would cause Greb to fight constantly and have more fights in one year than any other time in his life. He would also have a string of KOs and finally get Mason's full attention as the top boxer in Pittsburgh.

3.

ICKY'S BUSY YEAR

Harry "Icky" Greb had a massive fan base who always came out to root for him. "The Garfield fans were the making of me in the boxing game," said Greb. "They were out rooting for me every time I boxed as an amateur, and they have kept it up in every bout I have had around here since I entered the professional ranks. Their encouragement has helped me to win many a fight."[1] They witnessed Greb fight more frequently in 1917 than in any previous year.

Greb had his first fight of 1917 on January 1 against Joe Borrell at the Power Auditorium in Pittsburgh. Greb had already fought Borrell to a draw in 1915. Greb now had two more years of experience under his belt and was a much better boxer.

Greb started the fight furious with activity. The papers called him a "wildcat." This time Greb didn't try to keep Borrell on the outside using his jab. Greb rushed in and started fighting with ferocity. It looked like Greb was trying for a knockout every second and Borrell was trying to avoid it. Borrell had been able to throw effective punches in the previous bout, but this time Greb didn't give him the opportunity. Greb swarmed, constantly threw punches and kept Borrell on the defensive with no opportunity to throw anything. The second and fourth rounds were the best for Greb when he landed some nice punches that really shook Borrell. The first round was declared even, but the second through the fifth were all Greb.

The sixth round began and Greb continued to demonstrate that he had become far superior compared to his previous bouts. Previously Greb had been just a year or two into the pros and Borrell had been able to capitalize on Greb's inexperience, but not any more. Greb swarmed his prey and battered him to the head and body during the sixth round. Borrell was barely holding on in the sixth, "dazed and rather groggy," and was thankful for the bell. Borrell stopped trying to win the fight and focused more on trying to survive it. Greb would go in and out so quickly that his victim didn't have time to set himself up defensively or to counter the attack. Greb dominated the final round, as he did the whole fight, and was duly awarded the victory.[2]

By the end of March, Greb had accumulated four knockouts already for the year. Then on April 2 Greb was matched up against a top contender, Young Ahearn. Ahearn was a New York middleweight who had fought Jack Britton, Al McCoy, Mike Gibbons, Soldier Bartfield, Leo Houck, George Chip and Jack Blackburn. Ahearn had fought the middleweight champion, Al McCoy, the previous year. Ahearn beat McCoy but didn't receive the title because it was a newspaper-decision bout. He would only have won the title from the champion in an official decision fight, or if he had knocked McCoy out. Ahearn staked a claim to the middleweight championship for a while, although unofficially. It was written: "With the exception of Mike Gibbons, Ahearn owns the biggest 'rep' of any chap Harry has ever faced."[3]

The fight took place at the Power House with 1,200 people in attendance. At the bell for the first round both fighters rushed to the center. While Greb went forward, Ahearn threw a left into Greb's eye. Greb then rushed Ahearn to the ropes, but Ahearn slipped away and was able to switch positions to get Greb on the ropes. Then Ahearn started throwing his left. Greb immediately did an incredible move by leaning far to his right to avoid a punch. He leaned so far to his right that his head was level with his waist. This maneuver made Ahearn miss by a mile.

The third rush resulted in Greb's sending Ahearn back into his corner. Greb threw a big right hand that made Ahearn lose his footing while trying to avoid the punch. While Ahearn regained his footing, Greb threw a vicious left hook to Ahearn's stomach. Ahearn started to get weak in the knees and wobble. While Ahearn was trying to recover, Greb threw a short right hand that landed right on Ahearn's chin. Greb's opponent dropped on the ropes and hung there, half in and half out of the ring. While Ahearn lay drooping over the ropes, Referee Ed Kennedy counted him out.

The timekeeper guessed that the knockout occurred at one minute and thirty-five seconds into the first round, but many observers thought it was less than a minute.

Harry Greb, rising Pittsburgh star, around 1917 (Getty Images).

When Ahearn was interviewed after the fight he said, "I was hit on the jaw. That's all." When asked about Greb's knocking him out he replied, "Of course it was an accident." He then said, "Just to show that it was luck, pure and simple, I'll come back and meet this fellow for nothing. I won't even ask for cab fare."[4] Greb replied a day later, "The knockout was no fluke. I hit Ahearn with one of the cleanest and most solid punches I ever landed on an opponent. It was the last right-hander that turned the trick."[5]

Ahearn never attempted to fight Greb again. This was Greb's third KO in three successive fights, all within two weeks. The other two had come against Tommy Gavigan and Young Herman Miller.

Later in April it seemed like Greb would finally get his chance to fight for the middleweight title for the first time. Al McCoy was the current champion and Greb was scheduled to fight him on April 30. Unfortunately, there was a catch. The fight wasn't going to be an official decision, but a newspaper-decision bout. For a championship fight this meant that the only way the champion could lose his title was by a knockout. An opponent could win every round of the fight, but if he didn't knock the champion out by the end of the final round, the champion would still keep the title. Greb was in no position to state demands so he took the offer to fight McCoy under these conditions. McCoy had had a claim as the middleweight champion of the world, on and off, since Greb's second year of boxing in 1914. He originally claimed it in June of 1914 when he knocked out previous titleholder George Chip in the first round.

When Greb stepped into the ring to fight for the title, he was mentally ready. Some young athletes get stage fright when they step into the big game for the first time. An article in the *Pittsburgh Post* a few days before the big fight talked about this specific subject. The story was titled "Greb Won't Be Affected By Fright In Big Bout."[6]

The story, written on April 27, consisted of explaining how some fighters think they are confident, but leading up to the big fight they may worry, lose some sleep and train differently. Then when they finally step into the ring and have to deal with the situation as a reality, they lose their confidence and end up fighting well below what they are capable of. This scenario was not going to affect Greb. The article stated that Greb "looks upon all opponents in the same light — as chaps to be beaten and gotten out of the way as soon as possible — and never for an instant is he bothered by the slightest thought of what the other fellow is going to do to him."[7] Greb was going into the fight "in just the right mental attitude to carry the battling right to the champion, take him along at top speed, hit him as often as possible, allow him no rest, wear him down and stop him."[8]

The championship bout took place on April 30, 1917, at Exposition Hall, also called Exposition Music Hall or simply Expo Hall. It was located in an area called "the point" because it was a juncture point for the Allegheny and Monongahela Rivers. Greb had his professional debut there against Frank Kirkwood and would have more fights there in the future.

There were 5,000 people in attendance for the start of the bout. Greb entered the ring first with his manager, Red Mason, and some cornermen, and he was met by great applause when he entered the ring. Then McCoy entered the ring with the referee, Jimmy McAvoy. McCoy had personally hand-picked McAvoy to referee this bout. Greb's tights were black, not his usual color, with an American flag belt. Al McCoy's trunks were deep green, also with an American flag belt around the waist.[9]

The bell rang to start the fight. Round one was relatively uneventful and fairly slow with Greb doing most of the work. At one point Greb held with his right hand and landed eight quick punches to McCoy's jaw.

Round two began and McCoy was doing a lot of clinching. Greb started throwing every punch imaginable, and they were landing. Greb was always the aggressor while McCoy wasn't being active. Greb was able to back McCoy into the ropes and continue his punching there. At one point the crowd got so fed up with McCoy that they started yelling at him to fight. Greb was easily awarded that round by a large margin.

Greb started round three by quickly leaving his corner and going after McCoy. Greb began his famous dancing around the opponent while peppering him with punches. McCoy didn't know what to do; Greb was so fast that he couldn't catch him. McCoy was unable to ready himself to throw a punch because Greb was never in one place long enough for him to take aim. Then Greb was able to get McCoy to the ropes, where he landed a lot of punches to his body. That was working so easily Greb started landing punches to the jaw. This became so effective that the champion turned his back to Greb and started hanging onto the ropes as a way to stop getting beaten up. McCoy's nose was bleeding when the bell rang to end the round. Not only did Greb win that round, but it was said that Greb may never have had an easier opponent because the fight was so one-sided.

In round four Greb was in control and completely dominating the champion. McCoy's face was getting pounded constantly, and then Greb threw a right into McCoy's chest which made him go straight in for a clinch. It was another easy one-sided round for Greb.

When the fifth round started McCoy still had a lot of water left on his back that his corner men had applied to him in between rounds. The dripping water started getting the floor very wet. There was so much that the crowd started yelling to the referee to wipe it off. Greb started throwing a right-hand punch and then lost his footing, slipping on the wet floor. When he was rising back to his feet McCoy rushed in and landed a left uppercut. This should have

Exposition Hall, a boxing venue located at "the point." It was at the confluence of the Allegheny River and Monongahela Rivers where they form the Ohio River in Pittsburgh. Greb fought many of his opponents here including Al McCoy, George Chip, Buck Crouse, Captain Bob Roper, Jack Renault, Larry Williams and Mickey Shannon (Library and Archives Division, Historical Society of Western Pennsylvania, Pittsburgh).

been a foul but nothing was called. Greb eventually jabbed three times in a row with his left and brought over his right just as the bell rang.

By the sixth round McCoy was just trying to survive the fight without getting knocked out. Greb was winning every round dominantly, but he needed that knockout. Greb got McCoy backed up to the ropes again and forced him "to lean back over them by raining a fusillade of punches." The crowd was going crazy, yelling and screaming. Greb was able to really rock McCoy right before the bell by landing a powerful left to the jaw which hurt and weakened McCoy considerably.

The seventh round was all Greb with McCoy trying to cover up or land a left-hand punch. Greb was overwhelming him. By the eighth McCoy's mouth was starting to bleed. McCoy was still trying to land a left hand but had no chance of timing it with Greb moving so quickly. The champion then realized he was getting pummeled and had to at least try to be more aggressive to stop this slaughter. Now that McCoy had made an attempt to fight a little harder, Greb increased his punching by hitting McCoy constantly with both his hands with highly effective, full, straight-on punches. When the bell rang to end the eighth round, McCoy was a bloody mess. The titleholder was described at this point as "gory."

When round nine started Greb rushed after McCoy and got him against the ropes, where Greb bombarded him with constant punches until McCoy "staggered." He regained his legs and got to the center of the ring. McCoy threw his left once in a while but with no effect. Greb then started catching him on the jaw again and again. A normal fighter would have gone down under this barrage, but McCoy was trying to stay on his feet to save his title. This was a massacre in which Greb was said to have thrown "500 punches to 1." McCoy was barely on his feet when the round ended.

The tenth and final round began and both fighters shook hands before fighting. The crowd was screaming and yelling for a knockout. To start the round Greb "followed McCoy like a cat

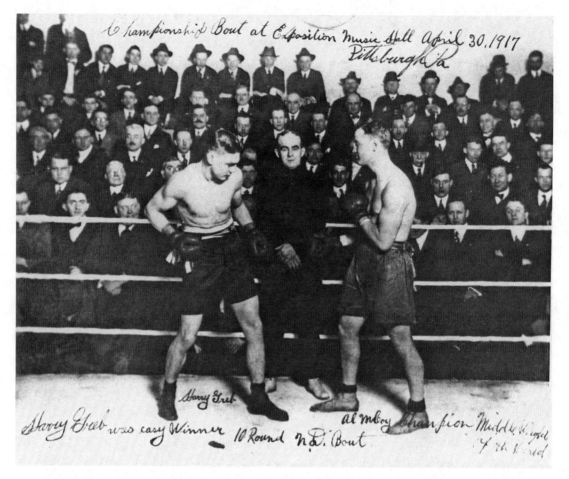

Championship Bout at Exposition Music Hall April 30, 1917 Pittsburgh Pa

Harry Greb was easy Winner 10 Round N.D. Bout

al mCoy champion Middle Weight of the World

Harry Greb (left) with middleweight champion Al McCoy and referee Jimmy McAvoy (center). This would be Greb's first chance to fight for the title. Greb could only obtain the title if he won by a knockout because it was a newspaper-decision bout (Antiquities of the Prize Ring).

and drove him into the corner, then upon the ropes." McCoy made a last-ditch effort by throwing a big left hand, but it missed. Then Greb countered with a barrage of rights and lefts to the jaw and face. Greb was throwing everything at McCoy, but he was still staying on his feet, albeit barely. The champion was taking an immense amount of punishment when the final bell rang to end the fight. Greb didn't get the knockout he needed. He won every single round against the "champion," Al McCoy, but he didn't get the title.

When Greb started walking to his corner the crowd started cheering and screaming for him. As soon as Greb left the ring to go to his dressing room he was swarmed by admirers congratulating him on his victory. The newspapers the next day all said the same thing, how Greb won each round and was the complete master over the "champion," who was backing up and defensive the whole fight. McCoy always had his arms raised outward trying to stop Greb's onslaught.

McCoy admitted after the fight and before he left Pittsburgh that it was the worst ring beating he had ever received as a fighter. This was saying something, since Al McCoy had faced a lot of great fighters, including Mike Gibbons, George Chip, Jimmy Clabby, Zulu Kid, KO Brennan, Joe Borrell, Soldier Bartfield, Young Ahearn and Jack Dillon. After this fight McCoy was referred to as the "cheese champion" because it was obvious to everyone that he lost the fight overwhelmingly. This fight was so easy for Greb that he fought again three days later.[10]

MIDDLE WEIGHT
CHAMPION
OF THE WORLD

LIGHT HEAVY WEIGHT
CHAMPION
OF AMERICA

HARRY GREB
GARFIELD, PGH., PA.
PROPERTY OF "Bo" KELLY

A rare photograph showing a young Greb early in his career (Antiquities of the Prize Ring).

As for the money the fighters received for the fight, McCoy was guaranteed 35 percent of the receipts, meaning he got $2,800. Greb's share was 17½ percent so he received $1,400 for the fight. If Greb had knocked McCoy out he may have reigned as middleweight champion for nine uninterrupted years.

A couple of weeks later, on May 19, Greb was matched up against one of the all-time greats, Jeff "Globetrotter" Smith. Smith's career résumé is filled with the top boxers of his time, including Hall of Famers Gene Tunney, Tommy Loughran, Georges Carpentier, Les Darcy and Mike Gibbons. He also fought such great champions as Mike McTigue, George Chip, Eddie McGoorty and Jimmy Clabby.

Before Smith met Greb in the ring for the first time, Smith had previously won the World Middleweight Title. Smith won the title in 1914 by beating Eddie McGoorty in a twenty-round fight in Australia. He then successfully defended his title against Jimmy Clabby. Smith eventually lost the title and regained it by fighting against Mick King later in the year in two great fights. In 1915 Smith actually fought the legendary Les Darcy. Darcy only lost to three men in his entire career and Smith was one of them. When Smith regained the Australian World Middleweight Title, he had to defend it against Darcy on January 23, 1915. Smith won the fight by a fifth-round disqualification.

Greb and Smith met in the ring on May 19, 1917, at the Broadway Auditorium in Buffalo, New York, in what was to be a scheduled ten-round newspaper decision. It was a hard-fought battle and Greb was able to knock Smith down twice. The ten-round bout ended with Greb being awarded the victory in the newspapers.[11]

One boxer people wanted to see Greb step in the ring against was Les Darcy. Part of this interest was because Darcy had recently come to America to fight. Darcy had beaten everyone in Australia so big fights that would bring in big money were starting to get scarce for him there. Unfortunately, it was tough for him to get fights in the U.S. for several reasons. Some would say it was because he hadn't created a big fan base yet, and others would say it was because he was so good people were hesitant to step into the ring with him. Another reason given for Darcy's not getting fights was that he wasn't in a union, so doors were automatically closed for him. In contrast, other Australians coming over to fight who were union men, like Mick King, were able to get fights easily.[12]

Darcy was soon hospitalized with a tooth infection. It was really touch-and-go for Darcy in the hospital around the time Greb beat Jeff Smith. At times Darcy wasn't expected to make it through the night, but he would find the strength to recover. If Darcy could survive this infection, there was still hope for Greb to someday meet him in the ring. This was Darcy's condition when Greb met his next opponent, the ex-middleweight champion George Chip.[13]

George Chip was scheduled to fight Darcy on May 22. Since Darcy was ill and couldn't fight, the search was on for a replacement for the contest. Mason started wheeling and dealing until he was able to get Greb to take Darcy's place.[14]

Chip became the middleweight champion of the world when he won the title from Frank Klaus in 1913. Chip successfully defended the crown many times until he lost it to McCoy in 1914. He unsuccessfully fought to regain the title from McCoy in 1915, and again in 1916. Chip was trying to battle his way back for another shot at the title when he fought Greb.

The fight took place at Exposition Hall and was a ten-round newspaper-decision bout refereed by Eddie Kennedy. Over 4,000 people were in attendance for an extremely tough fight. In the first round Greb was the most effective and was able to land lefts and rights to Chip's face. Greb threw some uppercuts and landed a vicious left while Chip was coming in. It was clearly Greb's round.[15]

At the start of the second, Greb landed a right to Chip's jaw, then constantly moved around him, circling him while throwing punch after punch from different positions. This confused

Chip and he didn't know how to respond so he just took it. Both fighters started landing many blows, but the round was given to Greb by a small margin.

Greb had a shade in the third round, but again it was close. Then in the fourth round Greb almost knocked Chip out. It was at the beginning of the round and Greb lunged at Chip, throwing a right hand that caught him behind his left ear. This staggered the former champion, but he was able to save himself by leaning one arm on the nearby ropes to keep himself up. Chip was able to recover and get back to fighting by the end of the round. That was the closest thing to a knockout either fighter would get.

In the fifth both fighters were landing powerful punches. Chip was able to land some, but they were not effective against Greb's great chin. Chip saw the fight slowly slipping away from him so he continued to load up his punches in an attempt to land a great knockout, but it never came. Then in the fifth, with Chip getting more frustrated, he started head-butting Greb, and Referee Kennedy had to warn Chip to stop. The crowd started hissing at Chip while he was being reprimanded by the referee. By the end of the round Chip's left ear was starting to bleed.

At the start of the seventh, Chip started head-butting Greb again and was warned again by the referee. This may have led some boxers to retaliate with dirty tactics, but Greb just continued to throw punches at Chip and land them easily. Greb then landed a right to Chip's jaw which made the ex-champion clinch. Chip was slowly moving around with his right hand cocked back, hoping to throw a desperate knockout punch. It was another round for Greb. Half of Chip's face was completely covered with blood and his ear was bleeding freely.

Greb was also awarded the eight and ninth rounds. When the tenth and final round started it was clear Greb was winning the fight by a wide margin. The two fighters started the round by shaking hands. Then Greb turned his aggression up a notch and gave it his all. Each boxer landed lefts and rights to the head and body. Both fighters were trying their best when the final bell sounded. It was said to be one of the best fights seen in Pittsburgh for many years.

The next day, May 23, the headlines read, "Greb Defeats Chip in Sensational Battle." Greb was to fight George Chip again later in the year. He won that battle also by an even more comfortable margin.

A day after the fight, when the newspapers were informing people of Greb's victory over Chip, there came terrible news for boxing. On May 24, any hopes for a fight between Harry Greb and Les Darcy were lost forever. In Memphis, Tennessee, Darcy, the great Australian middleweight champion, lost his final fight in the hospital and died that afternoon. What started as an infected tooth developed into streptococcus poisoning. The poisoning reached his heart and Darcy passed away. Many historians wonder what the result would have been in a fight between these two boxers.[16]

Greb's next opponent was scheduled to be Frank Mantell on May 29, 1917. By this time in the year the papers were already printing that Greb had "been the busiest fighter in the United States." Only five years into the pros, he was recognized as "the leader in the middleweight division."[17] However, he still hadn't been given an official decision bout for the title. Greb knew his shot at the title would come soon enough so he not only kept this unprecedented fight schedule, but he maintained his training regimen.

Greb sometimes trained at the Pittsburgh Lyceum Gym, located at 110 Washington Place (the site of the Chatham Center today). It was a building devoted to organized sport and was across the street from the Epiphany Church that Greb belonged to. The Lyceum was constructed by Father O'Connell, who also constructed the Epiphany Catholic Church.

When training, Greb would sometimes spar with heavyweights, which could be dangerous for a middleweight. While training for the Frank Mantell bout, Greb sparred with heavyweight George Hook. Hook was a local policeman and a regular sparring partner of Greb's. When big George Hook threw a punch on May 27 his elbow bone collided with Greb's scalp and caused a three-inch gash. The cut went deep to the skull above Greb's left ear and took four stitches to close. Mason immediately called the promoters and postponed the Mantell fight.[18]

The cut healed and the fight finally took place a couple of weeks later on June 15. It was a ten-round fight at the West End Theatre in Uniontown, Pittsburgh. Mantell had previously claimed the middleweight championship back in 1912 when he beat Billy Papke. Although Mantell was a veteran middleweight, Greb had an easy time with him.

As soon as the bell rang Greb started his attack fast and strong, as he usually did. Within a minute Mantell's nose and mouth were bleeding. Then Greb threw an uppercut which sent Mantell to the floor. He was able to get to his feet but Greb immediately met him with a left to the gut and then a right to the jaw. The right was so powerful Mantell was knocked clean out. The referee, Yock Henninger,

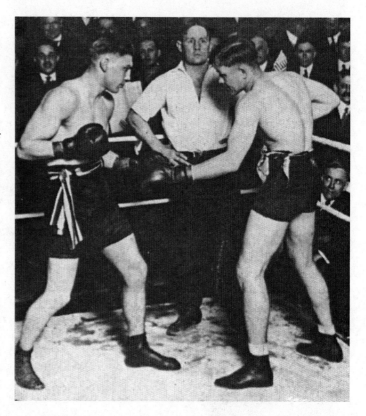

Greb, before his battle with ex-champion George Chip (right). Referee Ed Kennedy is in the middle. Chip had won the middleweight title in 1913 when he knocked out Frank Klaus. Chip held the title until 1914, when he was knocked out by Al McCoy (collection of Pugilistica.com).

called the bout a KO for Greb with a time of only seventy seconds into the first round. Greb was unstoppable. Mantell was so destroyed by the bout that he took four months off. He then came back to have one final fight against Mike Gibbons before retiring from the ring for good.[19]

Greb's next fight took place at Exposition Hall, where he had fought Al McCoy. The fight was to be the long-awaited match-up between two Pittsburgh middleweights, Harry Greb and Albert "Buck" Crouse.

Buck Crouse was a local Pittsburgh middleweight who had been the shining star rising through the ranks a few years earlier. When Greb was getting started as a pro it was Crouse that everyone was talking about as the next middleweight to fight for the championship. Crouse had beaten George Chip and also fought Leo Houck, Jack Dillon, Tommy Gibbons, Eddie McGoorty, Les Darcy and many other great fighters. This fight was what fans were waiting to see.

The bout took place on July 2, 1917, and was scheduled for ten rounds. Greb tried to fight on the inside because Crouse had a very long reach. They were both evenly exchanging punches when Crouse landed a left onto Greb's face. This got Greb's attention and he started battering Crouse across the ring and into a neutral corner. He kept on pummeling Crouse in the corner against the ropes while Crouse couldn't do anything but cover up. This show of aggression gave Greb the first round.[20]

Greb started the second round by launching himself across the ring and into Crouse's corner. Greb was definitely getting the better of the exchange. He realized that he was much faster

Greb, before his fight with Albert "Buck" Crouse (right). Referee Ed Kennedy is in the middle. The Pittsburgh fans had waited years to see these two local boxers finally fight (collection of Pugilistica.com).

than Crouse so he kept up this speed and aggression. Greb then "leaped in his jumping jack fashion and hurled himself upon Crouse." Greb started hitting Crouse with lefts and rights and never let up the pressure, eventually winning this second round by a bigger margin than the first.

The third round was Greb's with Crouse just fighting defensively. In the fourth round

Crouse's nose started to bleed. Then Greb threw a hard punch to the stomach that made Crouse grunt. Greb saw this weakness and focused more punches on the stomach, making Crouse try to cover up. Again, it was Greb's round all the way.

In the fifth round Greb was able to land punches to the head without any trouble. Then Greb caught Crouse around the neck with his left while landing his right into the face repeatedly. It was a tactic Greb had used against George Chip recently. The fighters started exchanging punches again, but Greb was moving around too fast for Crouse to land anything. Greb was landing ten punches to Crouse's one. When the bell rang it was said that Crouse was very tired and was taking a great beating.

When the sixth round started Greb immediately ran to Crouse and started pummeling him again. This fight was looking like "a typical Greb fight, with his opponent always on the receiving end and unable to figure out a defense." Sometime in the round Crouse went to the referee to speak to him, but his face was so inflamed and puffy that he couldn't even form understandable words. He was trying to stop the fight but couldn't talk through the inflammation and blood. By this point the crowd was yelling for a knockout and Crouse was praying for the bell to ring. It finally did, and the fighters went to their corners.

When Crouse was sitting on his stool in the corner in between rounds, one of his seconds grabbed a sponge and threw it into the ring to symbolize that Crouse had quit. Supposedly it was Buck Crouse's suggestion to end the fight there; he had taken too much and there was no reason to continue the fight any longer. When they looked at Crouse's injuries they found a cut lower lip and a mouth filled with blood and cut-off flesh. Greb was just too fast, elusive, aggressive and smart for Crouse. One big power punch didn't give Greb the seventh-round TKO; it was the constant and relentless punishment from both hands coming from different angles with no defense to stop the onslaught.

The day after the fight it was written: "Greb is just about as close to the middleweight championship of the world right now as any of the contenders, and he will be a hard man for anybody to beat." Already the *Pittsburgh Post* was writing: "Pittsburgh stands a good chance of having the future middleweight champion in Harry Greb. In his own way, he is a veritable Stanley Ketchel."[21]

On July 16 Greb had claimed the title of middleweight champion because of his mastery over champion Al McCoy and his beating of all the other contenders. After his win over Buck Crouse he was ready to call out that he was the legitimate champion and that he deserved a decision bout against champion McCoy. The boxing fans and newspapers supported Greb with a headline stating, "Greb's Title Claim Popular With Fans."[22]

In the middle of August Greb took a short but well-deserved one-week vacation. He vacationed approximately from August 19 to 26 at Conneaut Lake, where he took it easy from boxing. Greb had spent the last eleven months fighting practically nonstop. Conneaut Lake is located in Pennsylvania about two hours north of Pittsburgh. It was founded in the 1880s for hunters and fishermen. In the 1890s there was an amusement park added. So by the time Greb vacationed at the lake there was plenty to do, including fishing, hunting, dining, golfing, a roller coaster, and everything an amusement park and a lake with a beach front have to offer. It is believed he vacationed there with a bunch of friends, including his steady girlfriend, Mildred Reilly. They had been dating for years now and it was starting to be a serious relationship.[23]

The lake area was in rural northwestern Pennsylvania, and Pittsburgh newspapers were hard to come by there. Therefore, Greb even had a hard time keeping up with the state of boxing during this week. For example, Georges Carpentier had arrived in the States from France during this time on "war business." Carpentier was setting up a few boxing exhibitions, but Greb didn't know any of this until he arrived back in Pittsburgh. By that time it was too late to set up an exhibition for him to fight Carpentier. Greb was very unhappy about not being able to meet the French boxer in the ring.[24]

Years later Greb would build a permanent training facility on Lake Conneaut. He built a house with an outdoor boxing ring where he trained in 1923 for his first fight against Johnny Wilson for the middleweight championship.

When Greb returned from Lake Conneaut he was ready to resume training for his upcoming ten-round bout against Battling Levinsky at Forbes Field. Greb was training so hard that he damaged a ligament in his leg, so the fight was postponed for four days. The leg healed and Greb gave an open training exhibition at the Lyceum Gym a couple of days before the fight. The *Pittsburgh Post* stated that "most of the work consisted of hard bouts with his numerous sparring partners." One of the sparring partners was George Hook, the big policeman. People were interested in seeing how Greb would handle this big man because Battling Levinsky, the light heavyweight champion, outweighed Greb by twenty to twenty-five pounds. After the exhibition the *Post* wrote: "Levinsky's weight, reach and height advantage is not going to save him from defeat unless he can show a great deal in addition to that. Greb's speed and aggressiveness discount that advantage."[25]

Levinsky claimed the light heavyweight title when he beat Jack Dillon on points on October 24, 1916. Levinsky weighed a little over 180 pounds to Greb's 160 pounds. Levinsky was also three inches taller than Greb, with Greb 5'8" and Levinsky 5'11" tall. Levinsky also had a longer reach that Greb had to go against. With all this against him, Greb was still extremely confident of a win. He even urged friends to place bets on him to win. Since Greb first saw Levinsky fight he had asserted that he could whip him.

The fight took place at Forbes Field, the baseball stadium. An estimated eight to nine thousand people were in attendance. The ring was placed between home plate and the backstop. Greb easily won the fight and was called "a perpetual-motion fighting machine." Levinsky responded to his poor showing when interviewed in his dressing room after the fight. "Wasn't I rotten. Gee wasn't I rotten. I couldn't get my left working, I couldn't plant my right. Gee! Wasn't I rotten!"[26]

Less than a week after the Levinsky fight, Greb fought Jeff Smith for the second time. Greb had beaten Smith in May and they fought this rematch on September 11, 1917. This bout was a ten-round affair at the Auditorium in Milwaukee, Wisconsin.

Greb won the fight while keeping Smith on the defensive. Greb's clever and awkward style confused Smith, and he simply didn't know how to combat it. After the fight Harry Keck, Greb's friend who wrote a sports column in the *Pittsburgh Post*, reprinted a very insightful story that was originally written by Chicago writer Ed W. Smith. Smith used to be a boxing referee and was now a sportswriter. He traveled from Chicago to the Greb-Smith fight in Milwaukee. Harry Keck reprinted the article because the story "shows a keen insight into Greb's manner of fighting for a first impression; it picks out the local man's peculiarities and pictures him as just what he is; a man with no particular style, who fights according to a code all his own that is so mystifying as to make it almost impossible for his opponents to successfully combat him."

Here is some of the story written by Ed Smith describing Greb's victory over Jeff Smith. The title of Harry Keck's article was "Interesting View Of Greb Is Taken By Western Critic."

> Harry, who is a clean, decent young man with all the appearance of good habits and excellent morals, is one of the weird freaks of the ring.
>
> From the opening bell he tears in with an assortment of punches that are freakish and quaint. He regards nothing that was ever written in any authoritative book on the art of self-defense. He constantly leads with his right, which is strictly in discord with all the proper teachings of the ring, and does other things so foolishly that he proves a wonderful fellow.
>
> Against Smith last night he tore in for the full thirty minutes, never gave Jeff a chance to set himself for a telling punch and when the end was reached he had the Jerseyite gasping for breath and glancing around for a rocking chair.

Harry scores every second of the time with something or other, no matter how foolish it may look. He hooks and swings, he jabs and uppercuts, he ducks and sidesteps and the man in front of him, clever as he may be, is made to look foolish.

Jeff, being a great defensive fighter, was able to block and throw off many of Greb's punches, but in doing so he was made to appear slow and unskillful. Greb is so awkward and comes at an opponent in such a variety of ways that there is absolutely no way of figuring him.[27]

Previous champion Jeff Smith had won the world middleweight title in 1914 (Antiquities of the Prize Ring).

Ed Smith would continue to write and to referee boxing matches. He would even go on to referee three Greb fights in the future, against Eddie McGoorty, Mike Gibbons and Ed Gunboat Smith.

In the last month of the year Greb fought a rematch against a fine welterweight boxer who had moved up to middleweight, Terry Martin. They had first boxed in 1914 with Greb winning that six-round fight. Now it was time for a rematch. Martin had fought middleweight champion Billy Papke and was a veteran boxer who knew his way around the ring. Martin had fought for the welterweight title in 1907 against Billy "Honey" Mellody but had lost the decision.

On December 8, 1917, Greb and Martin fought a ten-round newspaper-decision fight at Charleroi, Pennsylvania. Martin started the fight well and kept up during the first and second rounds. Then during the last minute of the third round Greb knocked him down twice. Each time Martin stayed down until he rose to his feet on the count of nine. This was a veteran boxer who knew how to use the count until he regained his senses. However, Greb then threw a short right which knocked Martin out for a long time. Five whole minutes passed before they were able to revive him.[28]

The knockout of Martin was Greb's 13th and final KO of the year. The *Pittsburgh Post* had a headline: "Harry Greb Was Busiest Boxer In Country Last Year; Earned $28,753." He had completed a record thirty-seven fights in fifty-two weeks. Boxers fought very frequently during this time, but not to this degree. To put this in context, Benny Leonard was the lightweight champion during 1917 and was known for being an exceptionally busy fighter. However, his busiest year only totaled twenty-six bouts, which averages out to be one fight every two weeks. Greb fought eleven more times than Leonard, which averages out to be one fight every ten days. It was written that "Greb's record stands out as one of the most remarkable chapters that have been written into Queensberry history."[29]

It was a good thing Greb put so much effort into getting the whole country to know his name in 1917 because the following year he would not be so busy in the fight game. Greb would spend his time in a different fight, one which affected the whole country: World War I.

4.

In the Navy

While Greb was having battles inside the ring, America had recently entered a bigger battle, World War I. In 1917 the United States had entered "the War to End All Wars." The war had been going on since 1914, but the United States only began its active involvement by the president's declaration in April 1917. A cease-fire, which led to the end of the war, eventually took place in November 1918. This was roughly the time span of America's involvement in the "Great War." During this time the United States drafted four million men to serve. As early as January 7, 1918, the newspapers were already writing about Greb's inevitable call to duty. One of the local papers wrote in January that Greb was "figuring on keeping as busy as possible, for he is likely to be called to army service before long, and he wants just as many scraps as possible before joining the olive drab."[1]

The first major fight of the year for Greb was against the then middleweight champion Mike O'Dowd. It was another newspaper-decision bout, so Greb would again have to win by a knockout to get the title. Greb had proven himself to be more than qualified for a legitimate shot at the title in a judged decision bout, but O'Dowd didn't allow that. Greb decided to take the fight anyway. The ten-round bout took place in St. Paul, Minnesota, on February 25, 1918.

This fight was extremely close with different newspapers not agreeing as to who won. There was no knockout, so O'Dowd kept his title by default, but many papers said Greb outpointed O'Dowd. Many papers also reprinted the same article stating that O'Dowd had won. One of the factors that contributed to the difference of opinions was that nothing very decisive took place in the bout, "nor was either fighter badly punished."[2]

Many Minnesota newspapers voiced their local opinions about the outcome of the fight. The *Minneapolis News* gave the fight to Greb. George Barton wrote: "Easterner's Jumping Jack Tactics Puzzle St. Paul Harp." Barton would go on to referee the last Greb-Tunney fight, but that would be many years later. As a referee, Barton knew how to judge a fight, as he had been the third man in the ring many times before. Barton explained that Greb's unique style of quickness and moving confused O'Dowd and he was "unable to fathom" Greb until Greb outpointed him.[3] The title of the article was: "Greb Outpoints O'Dowd in Ten-Round Struggle."

Barton scored the fight with Greb winning five rounds: 2, 3, 4, 6 and 7. He gave two rounds, 8 and 9, to O'Dowd, with rounds 1, 5 and 10 as even.

Another Minnesota sportswriter who was at the fight was Fred Coburn, working for the *Minneapolis Tribune*. Coburn saw Greb's aggressiveness as the difference. He went on to write: "Greb's dancing, in-and-out style was a puzzle to O'Dowd for the major portion of the encounter and at no time was Michael able to solve it with any stupendous effect."[4]

Sportswriter John R. Ritchie, working for the *Minnesota Journal*, also awarded the fight to Greb.[5] Even though all these newspapers declared Greb the winner, there were just as many papers that didn't. The *Pittsburgh Post* would even write: "It was that close of a fight."[6] Often times in newspaper decisions, when many newspapers have the different boxers winning, the bout goes down as a draw. However, O'Dowd is usually credited for the win in this case.

The *Chicago Tribune*, the *Washington Post* and the *New York Times* all reprinted the exact same article. Its verdict had O'Dowd winning "by a shade." It also described Greb as doing "most of the leading" while O'Dowd fought "a strong defensive battle."[7]

What was confusing for O'Dowd was Greb's unique style. Greb was "hopping in and out and flashing a left hook to the face and body, Greb prevented O'Dowd from getting set for his right-hand haymaker."[8] O'Dowd did land a solid punch in the ninth round, but because Greb had a great chin he just took the time to shake it off, cover up then continue with the fight. It was also said that Greb had the advantage on the infighting.

Harry Keck, from the *Pittsburgh Post*, scored the fight with Greb winning five rounds: 3, 4, 6, 7 and 10. O'Dowd won three rounds: 5, 8 and 9. Keck wrote that two rounds, 1 and 2, were even.

Greb had been weighing 165 pounds for his recent fights and had lost a full ten pounds before this bout. He surprised people at the weigh-in when the scales read 155¾. People were expecting him to weigh 165. Greb was said to have trained extensively and had maybe over-trained. This may have made a slight difference in the fight, but people wrote that it wasn't noticeable because Greb was full of aggressive energy from the first to the last round. If it had been an official decision title fight, there would have definitely been a rematch to clarify any doubts to this extremely close fight. Unfortunately, these two great champions were never to meet in the ring again.

After the fight Greb spent three days entertaining people in a "vaudeville stunt."[9] He used his boxing skills on stage at a burlesque house. Many popular boxers were known to entertain crowds in vaudeville during this time. It was a practice made popular by champion James J. Corbett, who often headlined vaudeville theaters throughout Greb's lifetime.

In March Greb fought African-American Willie Langford. Langford was a middleweight fighting out of Buffalo, New York. The *Pittsburgh Post* wrote that Greb, "waiving the color line, obtained a decision in the six-round bout with Willie Langford."[10] Langford was the second African-American Greb had chosen to fight, the first being Hall of Famer Jack Blackburn.

Then in April something happened to Greb while he was in Muncie, Indiana. He got a boil on his forehead and was forced to get it lanced off. By the time he returned to Pittsburgh he had become seriously ill from the lancing procedure and had to enter Pittsburgh's Mercy Hospital. The complications that Greb got were blood poisoning as well as the threat of pneumonia.[11]

Greb had to take the entire month of April off from boxing and try to recover from this situation. He finally got healthy again and was ready to re-enter the ring.

By the beginning of May, Greb said that he was feeling "fit and strong again," and was wholly recovered from his illness the previous month.[12] Now he was set to do some exhibition bouts on a "Land Battleship" in Union Square, New York. A stablemate of his by the name of Johnny Ray was

Sailor Greb in his 1918 navy uniform (*Pittsburgh Post-Gazette*).

Middleweight champion Mike O'Dowd (**Antiquities of the Prize Ring**).

also going to fight in this exhibition. Johnny Ray was a lightweight boxer who also was under the management of James "Red" Mason. Greb and Ray used to train together at the Lyceum Gym in Pittsburgh. Both fighters started boxing professionally in the same year, 1913. Both boxers also had the same manager and training facility, so they became friends. Ray was around 130 pounds while Greb was around thirty pounds heavier.

The New York open-air boxing exhibition was to be part of a big navy recruitment and liberty loan event. The man in charge of the event was Commander Newton Mansfield, who at one time was in charge of the navy recruiting office in Pittsburgh. A replica of a big navy battleship was hand-built on location in Union Square. The ship was called the USS *Recruit* and the boxing exhibitions were held aboard the ship, attracting around 40,000 people.

This navy recruitment event was important to get people to enlist. During this time of World War I there was a selective service act that required local, district, state and civilian boards to register men for service who were between the ages of twenty-one and thirty. Once the men enlisted, the government would then know who they were and where they lived so they could send them their draft cards.

The feature for the event was Greb fighting two heavyweights, Jim Coffey and Joe Bonds, with the preliminary being Johnny Ray boxing Walter McCaffrey.[13] The event took place on May 4, 1918.[14] In the preliminary bout, Ray had a fun time beating his opponent, who he almost knocked out during the three rounds. Coffey was a 200-pound heavyweight from New York. It was written that Greb "almost stopped Coffey by the way he tore after him every minute of the three rounds they fought."[15] Greb's second fight that day was against heavyweight Joe Bonds from Tacoma, Washington. Greb kept Bonds busy for the full three rounds.

Four days after the event, while still in New York, Greb heard the call to duty and officially enrolled in the Naval Reserve Force.[16] Greb had originally registered for the draft in June of the previous year, 1917. However, before he was drafted he now chose to enlist, which gave him the choice of which branch to serve in. Greb and Ray were both now enlisted in the navy. Greb was officially sworn in and awaited further orders for his training. While waiting for his navy training orders to arrive, Greb traveled back to Pittsburgh. He started his training for a big upcoming fight against Soldier Bartfield.

The date for the Bartfield match-up was May 20, which was less than two weeks away. The

The USS *Recruit* being built inside Union Square, New York. It was made in the park for recruiting purposes during World War I and had a navy crew demonstrating life aboard a battleship. Harry Greb had
his boxing exhibition on the quarterdeck of the ship where thousands of people could see (Paul
McWhorter from Son of the South).

fight was scheduled for Forbes Field, the baseball stadium, as it was expected to attract a very large crowd. Greb scheduled two fights before the big Bartfield bout. This was an example of how Greb would use smaller fights to help train for bigger fights. He planned to battle Al McCoy and then Clay Turner. Greb would also train every day to add to his preparation.

The Al McCoy fight took place in Cincinnati on May 13, and was a ten-round newspaper-decision bout. They had met in the ring before, on April 30 of the previous year. Greb had won that first bout.

Greb started the contest, as he always did, like a "whirlwind." He went straight after McCoy and hit him square on the nose, which immediately started bleeding. By the fourth round Greb was hitting McCoy easily and was clearly winning the fight. Greb never let his opponent get set to throw a clean punch. He was using both his hands to land plenty of punches and won most of the rounds; some were even, but McCoy had no rounds at all to his credit. It was written that Greb "showed the local fans what sort of stuff Uncle Sam's sailors are made of. He went after his opponent at the very start, never leaving the issue in doubt, and he leaves Cincinnati to return to his country's service a more popular man than ever."[17]

After beating McCoy, Greb left

Johnny Ray, who would eventually become famous for managing Billy Conn. Ray would tell all his Greb stories to Conn, so Conn grew up in Pittsburgh idolizing Greb (courtesy of Tim Conn, Billy Conn's son).

Cincinnati and traveled to Bridgeport, Connecticut, for his fight against light heavyweight Clay Turner. Johnny Ray also traveled with Greb. Ray was in Greb's corner for the fight and acted as his second. Turner was referred to as "Chief Turner" or "Joe Turner, the Indian boxer." This was the first of seven bouts that Greb and Turner would have in their careers. The *Pittsburgh Post* would write that this fight was a "training bout for Greb to condition himself for his meeting with Bartfield at Forbes Field Monday night."[18] It was to be very good training because it was a full fifteen rounds.

Turner outweighed Greb, was four inches taller and had a much longer reach. During the fight Greb did a "jumping jack" punch. This consisted of Greb's swinging and landing a punch while leaping into the air. This allowed Greb to get through defenses and punch from any angle. The punch couldn't have been too powerful because his feet weren't planted, but it still must have unnerved his opponent. Turner couldn't have known what was coming next from Greb. All of Greb's aggressiveness kept his opponent on the defensive for most of the bout, and

Form 1 2866 **REGISTRATION CARD** No. 105

1	Name in full	*Harry E. Greb* — Age in yrs 23
2	Home address	*114 N. Millvale Pittsburg Pa*
3	Date of birth	*June 7th 1894*
4	Are you (1) a natural-born citizen, (2) a naturalized citizen, (3) an alien, (4) or have you declared your intention (specify which)?	*Natural Born Citizen*
5	Where were you born?	*Pittsburg, Penna*
6	If not a citizen, of what country are you a citizen or subject?	
7	What is your present trade, occupation, or office?	*Boxer*
8	By whom employed?	*Self*
	Where employed?	
9	Have you a father, mother, wife, child under 12, or a sister or brother under 12, solely dependent on you for support (specify which)?	*Mother None*
10	Married or single (which)?	*Single* — Race (specify which) *Caucasian White*
11	What military service have you had? Rank	*none* ; branch
	Years ; Nation or State	
12	Do you claim exemption from draft (specify grounds)?	

I affirm that I have verified above answers and that they are true.

Harry Edward Greb
(Signature or mark)

Above and opposite: The two sides of Greb's Draft Registration Card. He registered for the draft on June 5, 1917, around a year before he started serving in the Navy (collection of Tony Triem).

as a consequence Greb won the fight easily. He used his "torpedo style" to win eleven of the rounds, with two rounds going to Turner and two rounds even.[19]

With these two bouts behind him, Greb was now ready for the long-awaited fight against Soldier Bartfield. Greb arrived in Pittsburgh a few days before the fight and immediately started training in the gym. He trained each day leading up to the fight and even sparred with lightweight

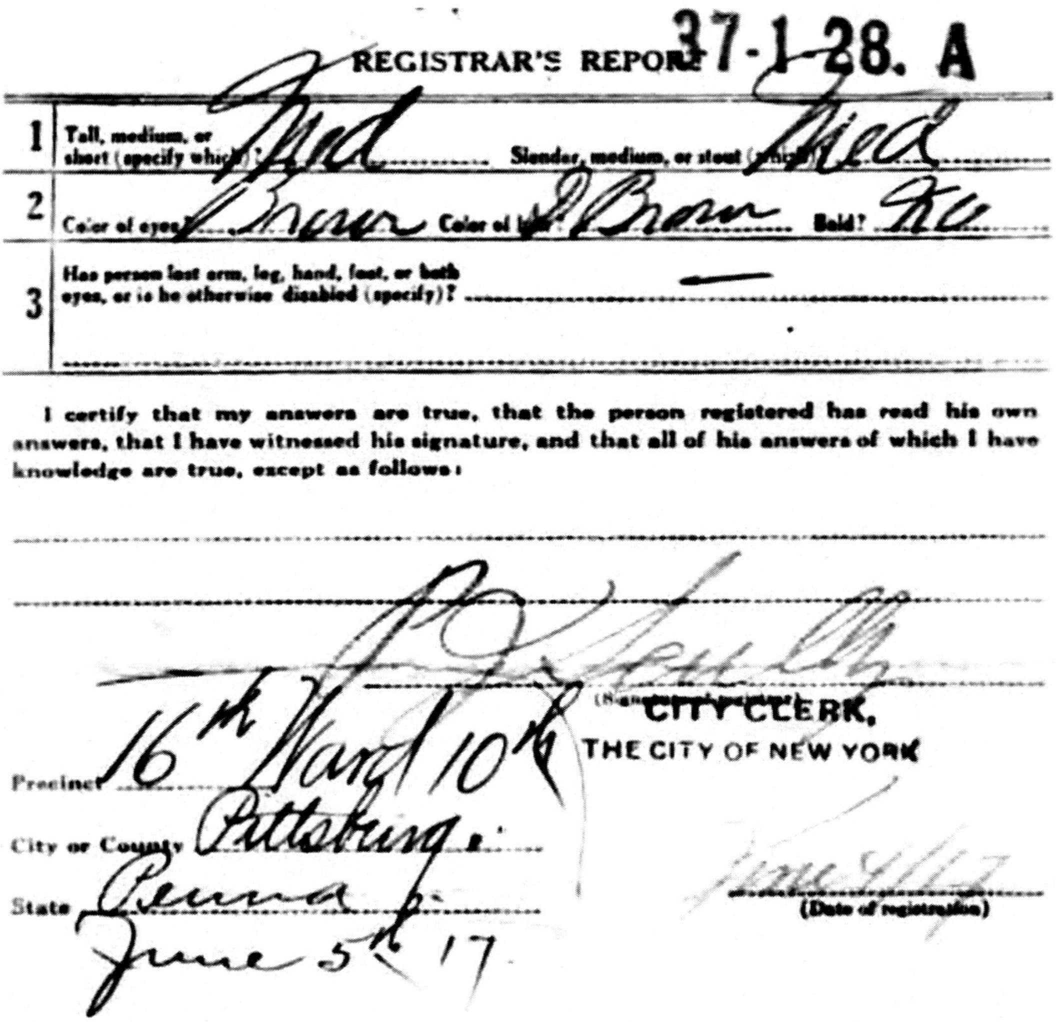

REGISTRAR'S REPORT 37-1-28. A

1 | Tall, medium, or short (specify which)? *Med*   Slender, medium, or stout (which)? *Med*

2 | Color of eyes *Brown*   Color of *Brown*   Bald? *No*

3 | Has person lost arm, leg, hand, foot, or both eyes, or is he otherwise disabled (specify)?

I certify that my answers are true, that the person registered has read his own answers, that I have witnessed his signature, and that all of his answers of which I have knowledge are true, except as follows:

CITY CLERK,
THE CITY OF NEW YORK

Precinct *16th Ward 10th*

City or County *Pittsburg*

State *Penna*

June 5th 17

(Date of registration)

Johnny Ray for a while. Training went so well that "Greb worked off five pounds in a fast but not too strenuous gym session."[20]

Greb and Bartfield had fought a close newspaper-decision fight before, so this was a rematch. Sportswriters asked the two combatants what they expected would happen this time. Greb was going into this fight very confident and said, "I know his style now, I'll win."

Bartfield was also confident and stated, "I know just what he's got. I can beat him easy this time."[21]

The night of May 20 came and 4,000 people attended Forbes Field for this ten-round clash. Bartfield entered the ring first and took the corner facing left field. Greb then entered the ring with Mason and Ray. Greb was wearing his customary bright green trunks and also was wearing a small American flag sash that dangled over his left leg.[22]

The first five rounds were easily Greb's. He started off strong, fast and aggressively. Greb was landing five punches to one. In the fourth round Greb landed a right-hand punch that got Bartfield totally off balance. The only thing that saved Bartfield from going down were the ropes. That was Greb's biggest round up to that point. Then in the fifth the two combatants stood toe to toe and swung constantly for half a minute until Bartfield was the first to back away. It was said to be a thrilling round with Greb eventually winning it.

The sixth round was a very close one that came out even. Greb usually fought full steam ahead with plenty of energy every round. If it was a ten-round fight or fifteen-round fight he would finish the bout ready for more. However, in this bout he started slowing his energy down a little in the second half of the fight. It was believed to have been caused by the illness that made him take the entire previous month off. Therefore, although Greb won the seventh round, it was obvious that he was tiring just a little.

The eighth round was the first to be awarded to Bartfield. Greb was able to throw some effective lefts, but Bartfield was landing a lot of punches to the body, and Bartfield's harder body punches won him the eighth round. He was able to take the ninth round also, when Greb was throwing a little wild, while Bartfield threw more effectively.

Greb must have known he hadn't been giving his best the last few rounds. When the tenth and final round started he tapped into his reserve and made a great showing. He was throwing a lot of accurate lefts that landed with power. In this round Bartfield fought dirty by head-butting straight into Greb's chest, just over his heart. It was described as "the foulest pieces of work ever seen in the ring here." Greb didn't return in kind, though. He wasn't put off his game, nor lowered to that level; he instead "fought back with all his might and literally pounded Bartfield all over the ring." The last minute was full of punches and some went low. "They were fighting like tigers at the finish. It was Greb's round and fight."[23]

The next day a headline read "Sailor Beats Soldier In Torrid Battle." Greb won the fight six rounds to three, with one round even. Some people said it was the most punishment Greb had received in years, but that was on account of Greb's just recovering from his illness and Bartfield's size advantage. Nevertheless, Greb won the fight and would say the next day that Bartfield gave him the toughest fight he could remember. It was also written that Greb had "nothing but praise on his lips for Soldier. He thinks him a first-class fighting man."[24]

Greb and Bartfield met again just nine days later on May 29 in Toledo, Ohio. This third fight ended up being a much easier one for Greb now that he was healthier; he won thirteen of the fifteen rounds. Bartfield was throwing illegal punches in the bout and twice had to be cautioned by the referee. Nevertheless, nothing stopped Greb and he was awarded the victory. Greb's "continual jabbing proved too much for Bartfield." He opened Bartfield's right eye in the eleventh round, "and kept jabbing it until it was closed." Greb continued at a terrific pace and was able to win with a lot more energy left than in the previous bout.[25]

On May 30 one of Greb's stablemates was leaving to go to boot camp. George Hook, the heavyweight sparring partner and former policeman, was leaving to go to Camp Dick, Texas, for six weeks of training. People around Greb were being sent off to training and to war, and Greb knew it would soon be his time to go also.[26]

Now that Greb was in the Naval Reserves he represented the navy in boxing tournaments. A Red Cross tournament took place on June 20 at Madison Square Garden. The event was hosted by the War Hospital Entertainment Association and it raised over $18,000 to help benefit wounded soldiers. Greb was matched up against Zulu Kid of Brooklyn. According to the *Pittsburgh Post*: "The Pittsburgh fury played with the rugged but clumsy Italian for six rounds, going at speed and throwing gloves so fast that his opponent could do little but cover."[27]

This was the third time Greb had beaten Zulu Kid. The first time was in 1917 in Pittsburgh. The second time was in January of 1918 when Greb "cleaned the floor with Zulu."[28] They would meet in the ring a fourth and final time one year later in November 1919. In that final bout Zulu Kid suffered a severe beating.

By July of 1918 Greb was attached to the land battleship in New York. The USS *Recruit* was the same ship Greb had boxed his heavyweight exhibitions on back in May. On July 24 he wrote a letter from the battleship to all his fans in Pittsburgh. The *Pittsburgh Post* printed the letter with a picture of Greb in uniform, the same picture shown earlier. Here is the letter:

Just writing you a few lines to let you know that I am still alive and attached to the land battle-ship here in New York. I expect to see some active service before long, though, and so does Johnny Ray, who is here with me.

I have several bouts booked ahead, for most of which I will require only short furloughs. These bouts all help in the recruiting work I am listed for, as we never fail to get some recruits everywhere I box.

Ray is doing the same work as yours truly and also expects soon to be put on active service. So one of these days the pair of us will be placed on deck of a real ship on the ocean and sent to "points unknown."

Just let my friends back in Pittsburgh know that our recruiting work is not the cinch it is generally thought to be. We work and work hard, and besides, Johnny and I act as boxing instructors to a big bunch of fellows.

Here's sending my best to all my friends in Pittsburgh and hoping to have a hand in deciding the biggest battle I was ever in.[29]

In July there was an idea in the military to hold a boxing contest between the army and navy to see who could win the title of the Middleweight Championship of the United States Armed Forces. The current champion of the army was famous middleweight Eddie McGoorty, who was now a corporal at Camp Grant. While McGoorty was representing the army, Greb was representing the navy. The fight between them took place at Fort Sheridan, Illinois, with the victor winning the service title. The contest was to have an official decision, judged by the referee.

Greb left his station in New York and traveled to Chicago with Mason for the bout. McGoorty arrived in Chicago early and was training at Kid Howard's Arcade Gymnasium. The winner would receive a diamond-encrusted championship belt, while all proceeds went to army recreational funds. The promoters received no money at all for this event; they were just doing their duty for Uncle Sam.[30]

Around 5,000 people packed the big drill hall at the fort to witness who would win the service title in this ten-round bout. Sailor Greb was immediately the aggressor. He moved to the left and to the right then threw punches with both hands. One of the ringsiders yelled, "That fellow is a fighting fool." The first round was said to be even, with Greb the aggressor and Corporal McGoorty cleverly holding his own.[31]

During the second round Greb's aggressiveness was starting to take hold. Inflammation began to appear over McGoorty's left eye, which made him slow his fighting down a little bit. It was Greb's round. In the third round Greb was able to almost close McGoorty's left eye completely. He kept taking the fight to his opponent while McGoorty could do nothing but block and try to defend himself. It was said that McGoorty "stuck out the round and wearily walked to his corner."[32]

Greb was in control for the remainder of the fight, winning every round except the fifth and seventh. The headlines the next day read, "Greb Wins Service Title By Handing McGoorty Licking." The referee gave Greb the decision and crowned him the Middleweight Champion of the U.S. Armed Forces.[33]

Greb had just three more fights in August and September, and then he was sent on active duty. Those final three fights finished his involvement with the recruiting branch of the navy. Starting at the end of September, Greb was strictly focusing on being a sailor in the navy aboard the land ship in New York.

On October 5 Greb arrived home in Pittsburgh for a three-day leave. He is believed to have met up with his girlfriend, Mildred Reilly, while he was home. They were still dating and it was obviously a serious relationship. She was anxiously waiting for Greb to finish his time in the service. While Greb was at home most of the sailors on board his ship were in quarantine due to illness.

The USS *Recruit* land battleship was a full-size, hand-built wooden battleship. This was where Greb was stationed. It was used for recruiting purposes to help demonstrate life on board a battleship. Actual navy sailors worked on board the ship doing everyday chores while people watched (Paul McWhorter from Son of the South).

Greb had just received his orders informing him that when he reported back to the USS *Recruit* he would then be transferred to go to sea at once. Greb was told, "When he reports back next Thursday he will get his belongings ready to leave in about two weeks."[34]

On October 11, after Greb had returned to the USS *Recruit*, his manager, Mason, went to see Harry Keck at the *Pittsburgh Post* to tell him about a scare he received from driving with

Col. Guthrie waves his hat on the quarterdeck of the USS *Recruit*. That section is where Greb originally staged his exhibition bouts back in May 1918. Notice how many people are on the quarterdeck.
This helps show how large the battleship was (Paul McWhorter from Son of the South).

Greb. The article was titled "Greb Drives New Car Like He Fights; Help!" Greb had bought a
new and expensive car a while before, and he had stored it in his garage for his family to use
while he was away. When Greb was in town for a furlough he drove it around.

Mason described to Keck how relieved he was that Greb was back on the ship because he
was safer there. Mason went on to explain, "He's safe when he's there. You know that car? The
one he bought a while back? Well, that's the ruination of the young man, or will be. Yes, siree.
The ruination of him. Came darn near being the ruination of me. Never again — never on my
word of honor — will I take another ride with that young fella. Never."[35]

Mason continued his rant, "Say, you know how that guy Greb fights, doncha? Just fights
and fights and fights, huh? Allatime going, huh? WELL, THAT'S JUST THE WAY HE DRIVES
THAT CAR![36]

"Yes, sir," Mason continued.

> Just like that. Misses things narrower than anybody I've ever seen. Added ten years on to my
> life to ride with him. Don't exactly bust any speed laws, or anything like that, you know, but —
> well, all I gotta say is, EXCUSE ME from riding with him in the future. He can ride to suit
> himself and he gets a lot of pleasure out of it. But he drives too gosh-hanged much like he
> fights to suit me![37]

Mason was right to be concerned. He unknowingly foresaw the many auto incidents that
Greb would be involved in, including the accident that would contribute to his death.

An unidentified sailor points a gun on the deck of the USS *Recruit*. Notice the large crowd on the ground. There are also civilians on board in the upper left-hand corner. They are touring the ship so they have a better understanding of what is in store for the navy sailors (Paul McWhorter from Son of the South).

Around the end of October, Sailor Greb was placed as part of the crew on the battleship USS *Sierra*. This was a real battleship, not a fake one like the USS *Recruit*. Also part of the crew with Greb was his old boxing stablemate Johnny Ray. This must have made the experience a little more comfortable with a friend on board.[38]

The USS *Sierra* would take many soldiers from America to the European theater during World War I. Usually the *Sierra* would transport fresh navy soldiers from the U.S. to France. The ship would drop them off, pick up soldiers going home, then start the trip all over again. When stationed on the USS *Sierra*, Greb was part of the gun crew.

Around November 10 Greb would write to his sportswriter friend Harry Keck, at the *Pittsburgh Post*. Greb wrote, according to Keck, "that he finds life on board ship better training for fighting than his former task with the recruiting branch of the navy. Wrestling 108 pound shells for the biggest gun on the ship is much to his liking."[39]

While Greb was on board the battleship and heading to France, there were plans for a major boxing event to be held in England called the "King's Tournament." The captain of the *Sierra* showed Greb a telegram "in which it was stated that as the navy champion Greb was to be transferred to London for the bout as soon as the *Sierra* reaches its French destination."[40] It was believed at the time that many members of the American Navy Boxing Team were onboard the ship with Greb. On his way to France, Greb was expecting to fight against the French and European Heavyweight Champion, Georges Carpentier.

Top: The USS *Sierra* docked in a European port in 1918, the approximate time Greb was a crewman on board. A camouflage is painted on the outside of the ship (Naval Historical Foundation). *Bottom:* A six-inch gun at a gunning station aboard the USS *Sierra*. Greb was part of the gun crew on board the ship (Naval Historical Foundation).

As of November 15 Greb was still on the USS *Sierra* on his way to France.[41] However, while Greb was on board the ship a very exciting thing occurred: the Allied forces won the war. The final ceasefire stopping all combat with Germany had occurred on November 11. The war was over and troops were celebrating victory. By the time Greb stepped off the ship, the Germans had signed the Armistice.

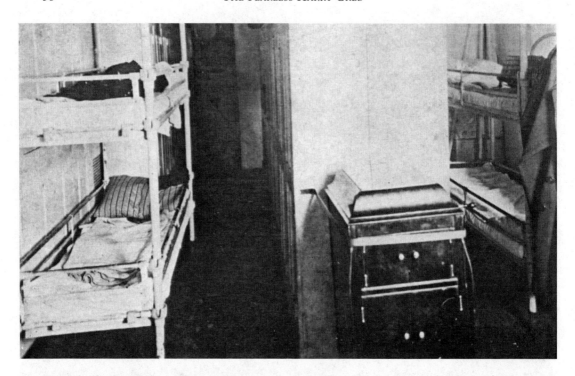

Top: The Chief Petty Officers' sleeping quarters on board the USS *Sierra* (Naval Historical Foundation). *Bottom:* The troops' and crews' mess hall on board the USS *Sierra*. Notice there are no chairs because all the sailors ate while standing up (Naval Historical Foundation).

The soldiers of the Allied forces were looking forward to having a fun boxing tournament to help celebrate the victory. Sometime after November 15, Greb and Ray finally arrived in France and then traveled to London for the "King's Tournament." The tournament took place at Royal Albert Hall on December 11.

When the tournament began Greb was matched against Corporal Baker of South Africa, not Georges Carpentier as originally expected. There was initial confusion about who exactly Greb fought on the first day. The United Press, the *Wisconsin Daily Northwestern*, Ohio's *Sandusky Star Journal*, Nebraska's *Evening State Journal,* and the *Pittsburgh Post* all stated that on December 11, 1918, Greb had knocked out a "Corporal Green of South Africa" in the first round.[42] However, starting the next day all newspapers started referring to Greb's opponent as "Corporal Baker" of South Africa.[43] Whoever it was, either Corporal Green or Corporal Baker, he was definitely from South Africa and was knocked out by Greb in the first round on December 11 in London.

The next day, December 12, was the final day of the tournament. Greb entered the light heavyweight division, not the middleweight division, so his next opponent was a Private George Ring. His opponent's name was sometimes spelled "Private Wring" and he was in the British Army. This final day would determine who would receive the most trophies from the twelve that were up for grabs. It would either be the British forces or the American forces. The American Army and Navy men eventually won ten out of the twelve battles against the British. Greb, however, didn't win his match against the light heavyweight Ring. It was a four-round bout judged by a referee and the decision went to Private Ring.[44]

Greb soon got on board a ship and returned to the States. His exact return date is unknown, but he was definitely back in Pittsburgh by December 30 according to Harry Keck.[45] Once Greb arrived back home he was met by his long-time girlfriend, Mildred Reilly. They were both anxious to have the war over so they could get on with their plans for the future.

5.

First Year of
Marriage and the #45

As soon as Greb arrived home from his service in the war, he announced his plan to marry his girlfriend of three years, Miss Mildred Kathleen Reilly. Mildred lived at 3421 Ward Street in the Oakland area of Pittsburgh, around three miles away from where Greb grew up. She was eighteen years old and Greb was twenty-two. They were rumored to have been engaged for the past year, but no wedding date was announced until January 7, 1919. On that date they made a formal announcement that their wedding would take place on January 27.

It was also announced that the two lovebirds had originally planned to get married the previous year, but the war had delayed their plans. So several days before Greb entered the service they were betrothed with wedding plans to be delayed until the war was over. Greb arrived back from the war around the last week of December and he wasted no time, presenting Mildred with an engagement ring on New Year's Day. The engagement ring was set in platinum with a karat and a half diamond.[1]

Mildred had been working "as a long-distance operator for the Bell Telephone Company."[2] It has been written that Mildred was once a chorus girl at George Jaffe's old Academy Theatre on Liberty Avenue, but this has never been confirmed. In an interview I had with Harry Greb's grandson, Harry Greb Wohlfarth, he said, "It's not well-known but Mildred was a beauty contestant. Before they were married she won a beauty contest that years later developed into the Miss America contest."[3]

Mildred had been to a bunch of Greb's bouts, including several over the previous year. Mildred was expecting that Greb would soon become the middleweight champion of the world. She stated, "I know he can win the championship if he ever gets another match with the champion." Greb agreed with his fiancée: "I am confident I can clean up the whole world now."[4]

The wedding ceremony was to take place at the Epiphany Catholic Church, "to which Greb belongs." It was located at 1018 Center Ave, at the corner of Center Ave and Washington Place. The church was situated right across the street from the Lyceum Gym, where Greb trained. After the morning ceremony the couple was planning a wedding breakfast for friends and family. They were then planning to take a short honeymoon trip to the east before returning to their new home. The new house was in the East End, "where preparations already are under way to have the domicile beautifully furnished and all ready to welcome them upon their arrival."[5]

Greb's plans for the future didn't include fighting in the ring forever. Sportswriter Harry Keck, who interviewed Greb, wrote: "He plans a great campaign for the next two years and, if he cleans up all the money he wants in that time, intends to retire and enter business. He is one of the most thrifty, clean-living and popular boxers Pittsburgh has turned out."[6] It is surprising to hear Greb referred to as "clean-living," but during this time of his life he was. Up to this point in Greb's career he hadn't received any of the false images that would be applied to him later in his career.

Greb planned on keeping really busy before his wedding day. On January 12 he had already planned on fighting four times before his wedding a couple of weeks later. Another big fight was presented to him against Soldier Bartfield, but it could only take place on January 27 in Columbus, Ohio, which was the original date of the wedding. Greb didn't want to pass up a big payday against Bartfield again so he changed the date of the ceremony to three days later.[7] Now that the date was changed to January 30 it gave him time to fight Leo Houck, Earl "Young" Fisher, Paul Sampson-Koerner, and Soldier Bartfield before his wedding.

Greb easily beat Leo Houck in Boston on January 15, then beat Young Fisher in New York five days later on January 20. Greb fought again three days after that. His next opponent was Paul Sampson-Koerner, who was also known as Paul Sampson. Harry Keck referred to the fight as a "typical Greb fight, with 'Icky' bobbing up and down on Mr. Sailor Sampson's ocean all the way."[8] After the fight Sampson was looking for a rematch. "I took the bout on short notice when Len Rowlands had to cancel it and really had no special training for it. Greb did not hurt me and I think I can give him the fight of his life if I am properly primed for a bout with him."[9] Sampson never had the chance because they never fought again.

Greb's next bout was another one against Bartfield on January 27. The fourth Greb-Bartfield fight took place in Columbus, Ohio, and Greb won the twelve-round bout. At the beginning of the fourth round Greb landed a great punch to the chin that sent Bartfield straight to the canvas. Bartfield eventually got up and continued to fight, but it was a losing battle. Greb was said to have won the fight, which was "a very tame affair."[10]

With Greb taking care of these four distractions in the past two weeks, it was now time to focus on his wedding day. The papers were full of stories and pictures leading up to this big Pittsburgh event. A Pittsburgh newspaper would declare: "The biggest social event in Pittsburgh's fistic history will be the wedding of Harry Edward Greb and Miss Mildred Kathleen Reilly at the Epiphany Church next Thursday."[11]

A few days before the ceremony, it was time for Greb and Mildred to get their wedding license. Mildred's mother, Mrs. Irene Reilly, joined them. Like always, Greb was in a hurry so the three of them rushed into the marriage license office. They met with the clerk, Charles Hendrickson, who was about to close up for the day. Greb had waited until the last minute, just before they were about to close. Luckily for them Clerk Hendrickson recognized who Greb was so he stayed open and gave the happy couple their marriage license with no problem.[12]

The wedding day finally arrived and over 1,000 people were in attendance. Keck would write: "Of course, Greb arrived at the church LATE. He has a habit of doing things snappily and in a hurry."[13] Although the

Greb Weds Tomorrow
Boxer and Bride-to-Be

Harry Edward Greb.   Miss Mildred Kathleen Reilly.

This announcement appeared in the *Pittsburgh Post* on January 29, 1919 (*Pittsburgh Post-Gazette*).

Outside and inside views of the Epiphany Church, where Harry and Mildred were married in 1919. The Lyceum Gym, where Greb often trained, was located directly across the street from the church entrance (courtesy of the Reverend James W. Garvey).

ceremony was to start at 9:00 A.M., the wedding participants arrived at the church in taxis at 9:30, a half-hour late. The wedding party then entered the church along with the 1,000 people who were waiting outside for them.

The reason for the delay was that Greb was caught up in training for a future bout. "Bright and early he arose," Keck would write,

> and at 7:15, less than two hours before the time set for Mass to begin, he set out for a run on the road. He covered some miles on the sprint, and it was fully thirty minutes before he returned, covered with perspiration. In a jiffy he bathed and changed clothes, and a short time later was on his way to engage in the most important match of his life.[14]

Greb's best man was Emanuel Kelly, "his lifelong pal."[15] Emanuel Leo Paul Kelly was born on March 25, 1892, in Pennsylvania. He was from an Irish family with immigrant parents. Greb and Kelly lived near each other when they were growing up and are believed to have met at school or when playing outside. The Kellys' house was at 407 Winebiddle Avenue, which was only four blocks away from the Greb household.[16] It is unknown if they worked at the Westinghouse plant together when they became teenagers, but Kelly was a machinist's apprentice the same time Greb was an electrician's apprentice. Kelly went on to serve in both World Wars and as a civilian worked as a laundry driver, then a laundry salesman.

The maid of honor was Greb's sister, Miss Katherine E. Greb. Others that were present were Greb's two other sisters, Ida and Clara, both his parents and Mildred's mother, Irene. Red Mason was also there with his wife and three-year-old daughter, Dorothy. Harry Keck was there and wrote: "The bride wore a dark blue traveling suit and in the parlance of the ring, was a virtual knockout."[17]

After the ceremony there was a wedding breakfast at the Ford Pitt Hotel for a hundred guests. People arrived a little after ten o'clock. The wedding breakfast with entertainment went on until after two o'clock in the afternoon. It was written: "A great time was had by all."[18] One thing that happened there was a surprise announcement from Mason. The wedding date had been rescheduled to January 30 for a reason. It could have taken place a day or two later than originally planned, but Mason himself had suggested January 30 because that was the eighth wedding anniversary for him and his wife. Greb and his manager now had the same wedding anniversary dates.

After the breakfast the newlyweds went to Union Station to take a train to Cleveland, where Greb had a boxing match to take care of the next day. Many guests accompanied them to see them off. Mason was also traveling to the fight with Greb and Mildred, and he brought along his wife and daughter.

They arrived in Cleveland the next day. Greb fought Tommy Robson and easily won. During the fight Greb's "kangarooish tactics, in which he leaped about the mat like a jumping jack and swung, uppercut or jabbed from every angle, all but completely bewildered the rugged Robson." It was a ten-round fight and Greb was said to have won seven of those rounds with two rounds even. Robson never had a chance against Greb, who "possessed a freak style that better boys than Robson have tried in vain to solve."[19]

The newlyweds soon arrived back in Pittsburgh and started living in their new house, located at 6444 Jackson Street in the East End. Greb had people working on it for weeks in preparation for them to move in; he would own this house for the rest of his life.

Now that they owned a home together, Mildred was a housewife, greeting Greb when he arrived home every day. The frequency of out-of-state matches was increasing, though, because Greb was becoming very much the in-demand boxer. Mildred is believed to have traveled with him by train to some of his out-of-state fights as well as watching the local bouts.

Greb kept very busy with a lot of bouts in 1919. He may have been making up for lost time

Harry with his wife Mildred. This photograph was taken a couple of years after they were married (Antiquities of the Prize Ring).

Greb's home at 6444 Jackson Street as it looked in 2007. The only difference in how it looked when Greb and his wife lived there would be the second-story addition coming out of the middle of the roof. That three-window addition was built decades later by another owner, but the roof itself is still original. The house still even has the original details from when Harry and Mildred lived there, including the front door's original stained glass.

after being in the navy the previous year. If he kept this pace up he would beat his own record for the most fights in a year. In 1917 he accumulated thirty-seven battles and was setting a pace in 1919 to match or exceed that mark.

On March 17, 1919, Greb was scheduled for a rematch against heavyweight Bill Brennan. Brennan had fought his first fight against Jack Dempsey the year before. Brennan's famous championship fight against Dempsey was to come in 1920.

Brennan and Greb had fought their first battle a month earlier in New York, and Greb won almost every single round in that fight. Brennan was now saying he hadn't been in the best of shape then, but he was now, so this fight should be different. Dempsey was actually planning on coming to Pittsburgh to see this match-up, but unfortunately had to be in New York on business.[20]

The Brennan-Greb rematch took place at the Duquesne Gardens. Heavyweight Brennan and middleweight Greb met in front of a packed house. The fight was very similar to their first one; Keck would write: "It was Greb's fight by a mile; he won every round and in the last round he had the vanquisher of Levinsky, Coffey and a host of other crack heavyweights arm-weary, leg weary and groggy." The headline the next day was "Bill Brennan Beaten In Every Round Of Bout." It was said to be Greb's fight from start to finish. Brennan outweighed Greb by thirty to

Harry and Mildred are playfully sparring inside their home (collection of Don Scott).

forty pounds, was taller and had a longer reach, but none of that mattered to Greb. He took the fight to Brennan, was always the aggressor, and Brennan had to be on the defensive for the whole bout. The *Post* would write: "He beat a heavyweight, who next to Dempsey, probably is the best man in his class in the country today, and he beat him decisively."[21] Greb would battle Brennan a total of four times in 1919 and completely dominate his opponent every time.

Heavyweight "KO" Bill Brennan (Wilhelm Schenck) is well known for his two tough fights against Jack Dempsey (Heavyweightcollectibles.com).

Red Mason suffered a tremendous loss just two days later. On March 19, 1919, Mason's wife, Mrs. Caroline M. Mason, died at her home at 3529 Claybourne Street. The Masons lived on the East Side just two miles away from the Grebs' new home. Mrs. Mason had gotten sick with a slight cold a week earlier, but it had then progressed quickly to double pneumonia and influenza.[22] Mason was at her bedside for days and left it only to be at the Greb-Brennan fight for a few hours.[23]

Mason had had a rough couple of years, with his wife being the fourth relative of his that had died during that time. Mason's father died, then his sister passed away after that. Then just after the previous year's Christmas, a tragedy struck his only son. James Jr. was searching for toys he thought were in a cupboard and was somehow burned to death. The exact details of the situation are unknown, but there may have been some hazardous chemicals in the cupboard which were flammable. Now, just a few months later, while he and his wife were still mourning their son, Mason lost his wife.[24] Now all Mason had other than boxing was his three-year-old daughter, Dorothy.

Less than two weeks later, on March 31, Greb was scheduled to fight heavyweight Billy Miske. They had fought a year earlier with Greb winning five rounds, Miske winning three, with two rounds even. People were excitedly awaiting the rematch because Miske was four inches taller and thirty pounds heavier. Keck would write of Miske: "He possesses every physical advantage, with the possible exception of endurance, over Greb." This rematch was originally

Greb and Miske---They Clash Again Tomorrow Night

A Greb and Miske newspaper picture a day before their fight on March 31, 1919. The caption underneath originally read, "Left-Billy Miske. Center-Miske doing road work at St. Paul a week ago in preparation for his bout with Greb. Right-Harry Greb, claimant of World's light-heavyweight title and still a contender for the middleweight crown" (*Pittsburgh Post-Gazette*).

planned for later at Forbes Field, but Greb was too anxious. Greb said, "I'm ripe now; bring him on. I'll show 'em if he can lick me."[25]

The fight started at 10:30 at night inside a packed Duquesne Gardens. When Miske was entering the ring he was handed a telegram bearing great news, which he read in his corner. The telegram was from his dad and it was to inform him that his wife had just given birth to a healthy baby boy. "Baby boy arrived at 6:30; Everything going well. Father."[26] With that good news out of the way Miske was now ready to start the fight.

Miske was throwing a lot of body punches in the early rounds. Near the end of the third round, one of his punches landed below Greb's belt. Greb "writhed in agony, though he did not go to the floor, and Miske hastened over to apologize, while the crowd rose up in a threatening attitude toward Miske."[27] Miske went to Greb's corner and apologized for the low blow, then went all around the ring apologizing. It was clear that it hadn't been intentional, and Miske didn't want the fight to end this way. While Miske was apologizing the bell rang to end the round. When the next round started Greb was his old self again, dominating the fight.

During their first fight at Forbes Field Miske had been able to open a cut over Greb's eye late in the bout which made the fight look closer than it actually was. Miske wasn't so lucky this time and it was obvious to the packed crowd that Greb was the winner. To accentuate this point: "Miske's face was badly puffed when he left the ring, while Greb did not bear a mark." This was yet another dominating win for Greb over a heavyweight contender; he won eight of the ten rounds.

On June 16, 1919, Greb battled Joe Borrell for the fourth and final time. By this time Greb had developed as a fighter and was well on his way to being the legend he was to become. Borrell was about to experience a completely different caliber of fighter than he had previously stepped into the ring against.

Borrell rushed Greb on the inside just like he had in their previous bouts, but Greb was clever enough to avoid it this time and include a left to the face. Then Greb didn't try to stay on the outside like before. By this time in his career Greb had no respect for the likes of Borrell, so he held Borrell's left while constantly landing right-hand punches into his opponent's face. Greb continued to land lefts and rights while Borrell could do nothing but hold onto Greb and try to clinch. This continued for the whole first round with Greb landing at will and Borrell not being able to do anything about it.[28]

When the second round began Greb started focusing his lefts and rights to the body. Then Greb landed a left which made Borrell drop to his knees. When Borrell was finally able to take some more punishment, Greb landed a short right to his jaw that sent Borrell rolling on the floor. He took the nine count and the bell rang as soon as he was able to make it to his feet. Borrell was starting to feel the awesome power that Greb had developed.

The third round had Greb starting off with one left to the body and then another to the face. Greb then landed a right to the jaw which made Borrell go in for a clinch. Greb landed another right to the face, a couple of lefts to the body and then added a left and right to the face. Borrell could do nothing but desperately try to cover up.

In the middle of the fourth round Greb landed a left to Borrell's jaw which made him drop to one knee again. Borrell tried to clear his head and finally made it to his feet on the count of eight, but he was still very groggy. Borrell backed up into his corner and tried to cover up his face and body with his arms and gloves. While he was covering up the crowd was yelling, "Stop the fight!" They had seen enough of this massacre; Borrell was being outclassed to the point where people were feeling sorry for him.

The referee let the fifth round begin and Greb was able to land any and all punches at will. Borrell continued to cover up so Greb danced around him looking for an opening. He was able to find plenty of these and landed lefts and rights with ease. Borrell ran to his corner and turned his back to the ring; he went so fast he almost went through the ropes. Referee Lew Grimson finally stopped the fight as Borrell was so beaten he couldn't even lift his hands. Greb finally got the TKO he was looking for at two minutes and five seconds into round five.

By the middle of June, Mason was trying to set up a rematch between Greb and Mike Gibbons. They had fought a close fight in 1917, and Greb had been trying to get him back in the ring ever since. Mike Gibbons and his manager, Eddie Kane, were asking for a lot of money and making other demands that continued to delay a rematch. To put their own spin on the situation, Kane was saying how the rematch hadn't happened because Greb's camp was trying to avoid the fight. Greb responded to this claim by saying, "I never sidestepped Gibbons in my life. I have been trying to get him to agree to reasonable terms for a bout for years. I'll make him eat his words when I get him in the ring."[29]

Terms were finally agreed upon and the fight was scheduled for June 23, 1919, at Forbes Field. Mason responded to Gibbons and his manager by saying,

> Harry will settle the hash of this paper champion at Forbes Field Monday evening. Greb is not, and never was, afraid of Gibbons. I made effort after effort to bring them together, but Kane, knowing that the outcome would be unfavorable to his man, dodged the issue by making demands that it was impossible for any club to meet. At last, he was cornered and compelled to come to terms.[30]

Over 7,000 people were in attendance at Forbes Field on June 23 to witness this ten-round newspaper-decision fight. Round one was very fast but even, with both fighters landing plenty of left hooks and body punches.[31]

The entrance to Forbes Field, major league baseball's second steel and concrete stadium. It opened in 1909 and included elevators, electric lights and trolley lines. It was home to the Pittsburgh Pirates baseball team and the Pittsburgh Steelers football team.

During the second round Greb landed a lot of punches and was the more aggressive of the two, forcing Gibbons to the ropes and landing a left hook. Greb was throwing a lot of punches, and some were missing, but the overall effect was keeping Gibbons off balance. When Gibbons returned to his corner after the round he was spitting blood; it was Greb's round.

In the third round Greb landed his best blow of the fight so far, a very hard right to Gibbon's face. Greb followed it up with some additional lefts and rights to the face. Gibbons was having difficulty locating Greb at close range, but he did land some good body shots. This close round was awarded to Greb.

The fourth round was awarded to Gibbons because he was able to block some swings while landing good punches to Greb's body and head. The fifth round was constant action. Greb started out throwing a lot of body punches while Gibbons was throwing to the head. Greb was able to get Gibbons in the corner and land "a back hand to the face," followed by lefts and rights to the stomach. By the end of the fifth round it was clear that Greb won the round and that his opponent was starting to look "weary."

In the sixth Greb was the aggressor once more, taking the fight to his opponent. Greb backed him to the ropes again and landed a left to the body. After a few more exchanges Gibbons's nose was starting to bleed from a cut. He tried to rally at the very end of the round, but it was too late by then; this was another round for Greb.

Forbes Field. Greb had some of his biggest fights there, including battles against Jack Dillon, Battling Levinsky, Soldier Bartfield, Billy Miske, Mike Gibbons, Bill Brennan, Tommy Gibbons, Kid Norfolk, and Jimmy Darcy. The field was also home to the Homestead Grays of the Negro league from 1939 to 1948. The stadium was eventually demolished in 1971.

The previous round took a lot out of both fighters, so the seventh round started slow. Greb was showing a cut under his right eye, but it wasn't affecting him. He was throwing a lot of punches that were missing the target; therefore, the seventh round was awarded to Gibbons.

The eighth round started with Gibbons trying to be the aggressor. The punches from both fighters were seen to "lack steam." Then things got interesting when "Mike taps Greb on the head and smiles. Harry musses Mike up with three right-handers to the face." It was a close round but observers gave it to Gibbons by a shade. It was to be the last round Gibbons was awarded.

In the ninth round Greb backed Gibbons up to the ropes with a left swing to his face. He followed it up with some quick lefts and a right to the face. Later in the round, "Harry hooks a hard left to the stomach. Mike keeps his gloves close in front of his face."

When the tenth and final round began both participants shook hands. Then when the fighting started, "Greb's left is first to land." This was followed up when "Harry lands a backhand right to the face." Gibbons replied with a right to the face. After a clinch Gibbons blocked a left hook before saying something to the referee, but no one heard what it was. Gibbons threw a left jab to the face which made Greb throw more punches to Gibbons's body. Gibbons threw a right to the face, and at this point it was noted that Gibbons wasn't using his left hand. Both the fighters got into a clinch where Gibbons focused on Greb's stomach while Greb landed lefts and rights to the chin. After the clinch Greb slipped on the canvas, and while he was getting up Gibbons hit him. It was no use, however, because Greb won that round and was awarded the fight.

The next day the headlines read, "Barrage Of Gloves Launched By Harry Confuses Phantom." Six rounds were awarded to Greb with Gibbons winning just three. Gibbons was said to have fought a "cautious battle," while Greb was "always on top of Mike." Greb was seen throughout the fight keeping "his left glove to the face, moving it around like a range finder, while figuring for a place to put his right." Gibbons not only allowed this throughout the fight, but it was clear by the end that "Gibbons was plainly puzzled by Harry's windmill style."

After the battle against Mike Gibbons, Greb continued to fight at a terrific pace. He was taking every fight he could get and was on course to beat his incredible record of thirty-seven fights in a single year. He eventually was not only going to beat the record, he was going to demolish it. Greb had already exceeded his previous mark of thirty-seven by September and had a whole three months left. This was unheard-of. He was on pace to reach fifty-two fights in fifty-two weeks, and these weren't easy fights, either; they were against heavyweight contenders, light heavyweights, and middleweights. What makes this even more amazing is that more than half the fights were out of state. Greb had to travel by train to and from all these matches, which were located in Massachusetts, Ohio, New York, Michigan, West Virginia, Oklahoma, and Missouri.

On September 7 a *Pittsburgh Post* headline read, "Greb Will Set New Boxing Mark For Year." Here is the beginning of the article:

> That Harry Greb this year will break all records ever made for the number of fights fought is a sure thing, as right now, counting the two fights he had during the past week with Jeff Smith and Battling Levinsky the total is thirty-six. This number, with almost four more months to go of this year, will likely run it up to fifty fights, something unheard of in the ring up to the present time. In the thirty-six fights already fought only four of them have taken place here in Greb's own hometown, and this more than anything proves what a great attraction Greb is wherever he fights.
>
> In all these fights not one of them has been even called a draw by any of the newspapers where the battles have been fought.[32]

It seemed like nothing could get in the way of Greb's reaching fifty fights, but by the end of September the first stumbling block came along. On September 21 it was announced that Greb had to cancel three fights due to illness. He was starting to suffer from boils which had weakened him to the point where he couldn't fight. It was reported: "Greb is physically at low ebb, and suffering from boils so much that he has been forbidden to fight, and consequently has cancelled three moneymaking battles."[33]

The exact development of this condition was described by Mason. He said that in Greb's last triumph against Silent Martin, he had had a difficult time accomplishing this task because of his boils. Mason said, "A boil on the back of his head was broken open by a blow from Martin's fist, and that night he got deathly sick."[34]

Greb was supposed to fight Mike McTigue in Cumberland, Maryland, the next month, but Mason had to cancel the bout. When Mason called the fight venue, the Cumberland Club, he informed them that Greb was suffering from "boils and a broken little finger, received in his last fight at Canton last week." Mason went on to say that the boils had become so severe that he decided to "not only call off his match here but two others during the next two weeks."[35]

Greb didn't fight for a whole month and stayed at his home under Mildred's care. Greb eventually had his first fight back from his illness on October 13. The fight was against "Sailor" Ed Petroskey in Philadelphia, and Greb won the fight easily in what was said to be the most one-sided fight people had ever seen.[36] Speculation existed that Greb may not have fully recovered from his broken finger a month earlier because he injured both his hands in the Petroskey fight.

After the bout Greb had plaster casts put on both hands. By October 27 Greb had "removed his right hand from the plaster cast," but "his left hand, which was also broken, is still encased." It was written that Greb "hopes to have it free in a few days and then will resume active training for whatever bouts are arranged for him."[37] During his month off many bouts had to be canceled, including ones against Tommy Robson and Clay Turner.[38]

With Greb forced to slow down, he spent his time at home with his wife and newborn child. On October 16, Mildred had given birth to a baby girl. They named their daughter Dorothy Mildred Greb, and she would be their only child.

Then on November 17 Greb started fighting again, beating George "KO" Brown in Ohio. It was reported: "Harry didn't spare his hands. He let his punches go hard, and lots of them landed on Brown's cast-iron brow, seemingly without damage to Harry's hands."[39] Greb won every round but the fifth.

He then continued on his fighting streak, fighting every few days. By December 22 Greb had accumulated forty-five fights and forty-five victories. He needed to squeeze in five more fights by the end of the month to reach fifty, but it wasn't meant to be. Just days after his victory over Clay Turner on December 22, Greb became ill again and was forced to cancel all fights for the rest of the month. He suffered an "attack of ptomaine poisoning."[40] Greb was supposed to fight Augie Ratner, but the fight was canceled when news of his illness was revealed.

Greb's fight schedule was slowed down late in 1919, but it didn't stop him from accumulating the highest number of fights in one year any champion in fistic history has ever accomplished. This was a benchmark that Greb was never to get close to again; neither did anyone else, for that matter. That is almost a fight a week, and the fact that he was forced to take a couple of months off due to illness makes it even more remarkable.

The "Pittsburgh Windmill" arrived back from World War I and made sure no one had forgotten about him. As a boxer, he was back to where he was before joining the navy, or maybe even further. When Greb announced his engagement earlier in the year he said, "I am confident I can clean up the whole world now."[41] And that is exactly what he did. His record by a champion of forty-five fights with forty-five wins in a single year still stands today, and will probably never be broken. The year 1919 marked the time Greb entered the prime of his boxing career. Add to this his marriage and the birth of his daughter, and these were certainly happy times indeed.

6.

JACK DEMPSEY AND THE HEAVYWEIGHTS

Harry Greb spent his entire career at a fighting weight of around 158–168 pounds. Back in Greb's time, there were only the eight original weight divisions, before the many "super," "junior" and "light" classes that we have today were added. Greb fought men in the top three weight classes: heavyweight (unlimited weight), light heavyweight (175-pound limit) and middleweight (160-pound limit).

Greb naturally met the middleweight limit when he needed to for fights. He would not have to worry about his weight for the light heavyweight division because he would normally be well below the limit. He was constantly fighting and training so his weight didn't fluctuate compared to fighters today who don't fight as frequently, and when not in fighting shape often weigh up to twenty pounds more than they do the day of a weigh-in. Fighting and training on a regular basis gave Greb the ability to easily meet the weight for middleweight and light heavyweight bouts.

Greb also had extraordinary ability to fight and beat heavyweights despite only weighing around 160 pounds. He would fight men who sometimes outweighed him in the ring by over thirty pounds.

Weight classes are currently separated by six- to eight-pound increments. This is done to make fights more competitive. When a fighter is outweighed by his opponent by over eight pounds, it is extremely difficult for the lighter man to win. It means the heavier man has more muscle mass and can hit harder. They can also use their weight advantage to try to tire their opponents in clinches or against the ropes. If they outweigh their opponent by eight pounds, they are put in a different weight class so a fight is a more even contest.

Greb didn't just fight people who outweighed him eight pounds; he also fought light heavyweights who outweighed him by an incredible 10 to 15 pounds. There is currently a "super middleweight" division that has a weight range of 161 to 168 pounds. This division didn't exist in Greb's day so he would skip this range entirely when fighting light heavyweights. Greb would not only fight these light heavyweights and win, but eventually he would become the champion, dominating all others in this division.

Greb also took on heavyweights who outweighed him by an amazing twenty, thirty or over forty pounds, and he would beat them decisively on a regular basis. To put this in modern terms, Greb was weighing in as a middleweight (currently between 155 and 160 pounds) and skipping as much as three weight classes to fight men who today would fit in the cruiserweight and heavyweight classes.

His ability to defeat all comers, regardless of size, is one of the incredible accomplishments in fistic history and establishes Greb as one of the greatest boxers who has ever lived. He didn't slowly move up in weight over the years and gradually fight heavier men as he got older and

Jack Dempsey (left) and Harry Greb at Dempsey's training camp in 1920 (courtesy of Scott Yaniga).

heavier. Greb would weigh around 160 pounds and fight a middleweight one day, beat a heavy-weight the next week, then a middleweight a week later, then a light heavyweight after that.

He was able to accomplish this incredible feat by using his natural speed, his great conditioning, and what was probably one of the best chins in boxing history. Greb used his speed to get inside and punch when he wanted to and move away from the big slow punches of his larger opponents. He would use his great conditioning to maintain this high level of energy and speed throughout the entire fight. Then if Greb did get hit by these big fellows—and hit with punches that would knock out other heavyweights—he would be able to weather the storm and take the punch in his stride. This great combination of traits gave Greb the ability to win round after round until his heavyweight opponents found themselves helpless and unable to knock him out. By the end of the fight they would be confused, bewildered and exhausted. Greb once said, "I like to fight as often as I can, for that keeps me in shape. I also like to tackle the big fellows around 200 pounds, for they are slower and easier to hit than the little fellows. The bigger they come, the easier they generally are when they have to face speed."[1]

Another factor which made all this possible was that Greb didn't possess the emotion of fear. He knew without doubt there was no man on earth that he couldn't beat in a boxing match. It didn't matter if the man was heavier, taller, had a longer reach, was more experienced or was holding a championship belt. Harry Greb would fight any man alive, and that included the heavyweights. He beat every one of the top heavyweights of his time that were willing to fight him.

Greb barreled through life, in and out of the ring, and never stopped to look back. Any boxer in the path of the "Pittsburgh Windmill" had to prepare himself to be beaten, or else refuse to fight. Jack Dempsey would eventually do both of these things.

When Jack Dempsey started getting a lot of attention in the boxing world, Greb immediately wanted to fight him. Even before Dempsey became heavyweight champion in 1919, Greb was calling him out for a fight. On August 6, 1918, soon after Greb had disposed of Battling Levinsky, Greb challenged Dempsey to a fight for the first time. A newspaper headline read, "Greb Beats Levinsky; Challenges Dempsey." The article stated that Greb "announced that he was anxious to take on Jack Dempsey."[2]

Dempsey, however, would not accept Greb's offer. Instead, Dempsey chose to fight Battling Levinsky himself in November of that year. Levinsky, a man Greb had just beaten for the second time, got to fight Dempsey but Greb didn't. Greb would eventually fight Levinsky a total of six times and win every single one of them.

Greb fought and beat many of the same men Dempsey fought: Willie Meehan, Ed "Gunboat" Smith, Terry Kellar, Battling Levinsky, Tommy Gibbons, Billy Miske, Joe Bonds, Bill Brennan, Homer Smith, Jimmy Darcey and Gene Tunney, to name a few. By beating these heavyweights Greb demonstrated that he was more than qualified to step into the ring with Dempsey himself.

In July of 1919, about a year after Greb began calling out Dempsey, promoters began putting together a boxing match between the two. Dempsey had won the heavyweight championship on July 4 by beating Jess Willard. A few weeks later, on July 21, 1919, a headline read, "Greb-Dempsey Fight Probable; Two Promoters Offer Purses."[3]

The proposed fight was to take place on Labor Day, and there were two promoters willing to set the fight up. One promoter, Matt Hinkle of Cleveland, was willing to put up $65,000 "for the men to fight for Labor Day night in Cleveland's American League Park."[4] This fight was to be a ten-round bout. Matt Hinkle was also a referee and worked many of Harry Greb's fights. Hinkle would eventually referee one of Greb's matches with Gene Tunney.

The second promoter willing to set up a bout between Greb and Dempsey was Jimmy Shelvin, who was willing to pay for the fight to happen at the Cincinnati Reds' ballpark, also on Labor Day. This fight was planned to be a fifteen-round affair. There were two possible venues and two proposed fight lengths for a Dempsey-Greb showdown.

Greb wanted the fight badly, firmly believing he could beat Dempsey. It didn't matter if it was a ten-round fight or a fifteen-round fight; there wasn't a heavyweight he had fought that he hadn't beaten. When Greb and his manager were asked about the fight they both quickly said yes. "Greb is more than willing. He is asking for the bout. Both Greb and Jimmy Mason say so. It's up to Dempsey."[5] Harry Greb wanted the fight so badly that Jimmy Mason was in talks with both the promoters to make it happen; all that was needed was Dempsey's acceptance.

The *Pittsburgh Post* wrote: "So it's up to Dempsey. And it's going to be difficult for Dempsey to say 'Go get a reputation,' for Greb's fought four fights to Dempsey's one, and licked as many, if not more, heavies than Dempsey."[6]

Jack Dempsey was in negotiations at the same time to fight heavyweight Bill Brennan. Greb had already fought Bill Brennan in 1919 and had won practically every round of all three fights. Greb had beaten Brennan easily in February, in March and a few weeks earlier in July. Instead of wanting to fight the conqueror in these fights, Dempsey chose to fight the loser. After fighting with Greb and Dempsey, Brennan would later say, "If Dempsey was fightin' that little buzzsaw instead of me, I would bet on Greb."[7]

The fight between Greb and Dempsey in 1919 never took place because Dempsey didn't want to fight. Dempsey knew it was going to be a tough battle for him to win, and that Greb could win on points. Dempsey may have also been afraid of looking bad against a smaller and faster man, even if he did manage a win. Dempsey was given the nickname "The Giant Killer" after he beat a very large Jess Willard for the heavyweight championship. No one knew more than Dempsey about what a smaller man could do to a much larger man. Dempsey had everything to lose and absolutely nothing to gain. Therefore, he would continue to fight men that Greb had already beaten rather than fight Greb himself.

This was to be a recurring theme throughout Greb's career. In the October 1953 issue of *Male* magazine there was an article dedicated to the subject of Dempsey's refusing to fight Greb. It was written by author Bill Stern and was titled "The Man Dempsey Wouldn't Fight." The article tells of Dempsey's manager, Jack Kearns, not wanting his fighter in the ring with Greb. "Kearns refused to entertain any notions about a Dempsey-Greb bout. But many of Greb's backers and well-wishers did entertain the notion, and were convinced Greb would have made a bigger fool out of Jack in a regular bout. Greb, himself, was so certain about the outcome of such a fight that he needled Dempsey whenever he saw him. 'Hey, ya bum, when ya gonna fight me?'"[8]

After Dempsey refused to fight Greb in 1919, he only fought one exhibition bout for the rest of that year, while Greb fought fifteen more times in 1919. Dempsey's first ring encounter in 1920 was in March. On March 5, 1920, Dempsey fought heavyweight Terry Kellar in a three-round exhibition bout. The two had fought four times already with Dempsey winning every time.

Kellar was another heavyweight that Greb had already beaten. Greb had fought Kellar back in 1918 and beaten him in a ten-round fight. A headline read, "Harry Greb Laces Kellar." Greb threw a punch in the first round that "staggered Kellar," and he dominated the fight from start to finish. A newspaper wrote that he won every single round except maybe the fourth and sixth, which may have been even. People were wondering how Kellar could be "absorbing such a royal and gratuitous beating as the one Harry Greb ladled out."[9]

On March 23, 1920, Greb fought Larry Williams. Williams became a sparring partner of Dempsey's in the following year, but there was time for Greb to beat him first at Exposition Hall in Pittsburgh. A newspaper wrote that Greb took eight of the ten rounds in the fight. The *Post* wrote: "The sheer bewildering speed of Harry's attack was simply too much for Larry, who, willing, game and aggressive at all times, was unable to avoid or block the flocks of gloves Harry launched himward [*sic*], or to land more than occasional punches of his own."[10]

Greb fought Williams again a few months later in Buffalo, New York, and was the point winner in that bout also. After the fight a paper wrote: "And tonight locally there is much respect for Harry's challenge of Jack Dempsey, which it is hoped will lead to a Buffalo engagement of the pair."[11] There were rumors spread by Greb's manager that Dempsey and Greb were going to fight a ten-round battle in Buffalo on May 31, 1920.[12] People in different cities were all wondering what would happen if Greb and Dempsey fought in an official fight.

Dempsey refused to fight Greb in that official bout in May, but he was willing to spar with him. Three days in a row, July 27 to 29, 1920 Greb sparred with Dempsey. It is believed that Greb approached Dempsey and asked to spar with him. Greb did this to meet Dempsey and forge a relationship that could someday lead to an official fight. The sparring sessions took place at Dempsey's training quarters at Broadway and 57th Street in New York. Around 2,000 people paid fifty-five cents to see the two meet in the ring. On July 27 they met in the afternoon and "boxed four hard rounds."[13]

It was written the day after they first sparred that Greb "will work with Dempsey again today and Thursday, leaving for home that evening."[14] It would be a good workout for Greb because in a few days he was heading back to Pittsburgh to fight another future heavyweight opponent of Dempsey's, Tommy Gibbons.

July 29, 1920, was the third and final day that Dempsey and Greb sparred. People came in droves again to see these two combatants in the ring. So many people turned out that the doors had to be closed early. The famous actor Douglas Fairbanks traveled to New York just to be the honorary referee. Greb couldn't contain himself and had to capitalize on this opportunity because it was possibly the last time he could get Dempsey in the ring.

The *Pittsburgh Post* would write later that same day: "A big surprise was sprung on those present by the way Greb tore into the champion and in the middle of the second round time had to be called when the Pittsburgher landed a hard right on Dempsey's left eye and split it open." After the eye was damaged, Dempsey didn't want to lose face so he agreed to continue boxing, but after a couple more exchanges, "he told them he would have to call it off for the day."[15]

It was also written that "Greb looked as strong as a young bull." The crowd loved Greb and he was "surrounded on all sides."[16] Dempsey had been apprehensive about battling Greb before these sparring sessions, and he sure wasn't in a hurry to fight him afterwards.

After Greb split Dempsey's eye on July 29, 1920, "everyone expressed themselves that he would be a sure winner against Gibbons Saturday afternoon."[17] He left Dempsey's training quarters later that day and headed straight to Pittsburgh for his fight against heavyweight Tommy Gibbons. Gibbons would become famous in the future for fighting Dempsey in Shelby, Montana, but Greb was going to fight him first.

Greb arrived in Pittsburgh ready for the July 31 fight. The ten-round, newspaper-decision bout took place at Forbes Field in front of nearly 12,000 eager spectators. These two fighters had met earlier in the year so people were anxious to see what would happen this time around.

The first round was awarded to Greb because he had landed some punches from

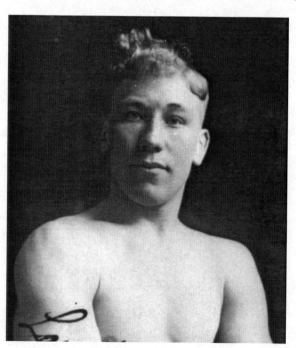

Larry Williams (Antiquities of the Prize Ring).

a distance. He wouldn't allow Gibbons to be effective on the inside either at the start. Gibbons was awarded the second round because of his effective body punching and short hands to the head when he got on the inside.[18]

Greb became wise to Gibbons's effectiveness at close range, so in the third round Greb stayed on the outside. Harry would "land from a distance" in the third and would try to tie Gibbons up when they were close. Although it was a better showing for Greb, Gibbons was still awarded the third round.

In the fourth round Greb raised the heat by fighting a little more aggressively. He would go inside, score and then return to the outside before Gibbons had time to throw a return punch. Greb was "swinging and hooking punches from all angles." He made Gibbons miss so often in the fourth round that "for the first time, Gibbons seemed doubtful of the direction of his punches, he was failing to find the tantalizing Greb." The fourth round was subsequently awarded to Greb.

Harry Greb and heavyweight Tommy Gibbons (right) in the ring during their fight on July 31, 1920, at Forbes Field. Referee Jack Dillon stands behind them. Greb weighed 160 pounds the night of the fight while Tommy Gibbons is believed to have been around twenty pounds heavier. Gibbons refused to weigh in the night of the fight (*Pittsburgh Post-Gazette*).

In the fifth round Greb was even more in control. He landed his first big punch of the fight when he threw "a right swing to the chin and stood Tom straight up on his heels for a few seconds. Then he put a right to the chin and dug a left to the stomach without the semblance of a return." The fifth was another round for Greb.

The sixth round was pretty uneventful while both fighters were searching for openings. Between the sixth and seventh rounds, rain started to fall. By the time the bell rang to start the seventh round, "it was pelting down merrily while the exposed spectators broke to the stands." The rain must have woken Greb up because he started the seventh with a rush of energy. He threw a flurry of unanswered punches that all landed on his opponent. "He put a right to the face, a left to the stomach and right to the ear, a left to the face and a right to the neck." Then Gibbons landed one big punch that slowed Harry down a little. It was a knockout punch that had floored many opponents before, but Greb took it and just shook it off. Before Gibbons could land another punch Greb had recovered from it completely. It was Gibbons's best punch of the night, and it wasn't good enough.

The last three rounds were said to be very wet from the rain while Greb became ever more dominating.

Harry handled Gibbons with the most absolute disregard for big punches. He pulled and hauled and punched, hooked and swung, and, finding that his blows were landing easier and scoring

Shown here is middleweight Harry Greb shaking hands with heavyweight Tommy Gibbons (right). Note the height and size advantage that Tommy Gibbons had over Greb (courtesy of Heavyweight collectibles.com).

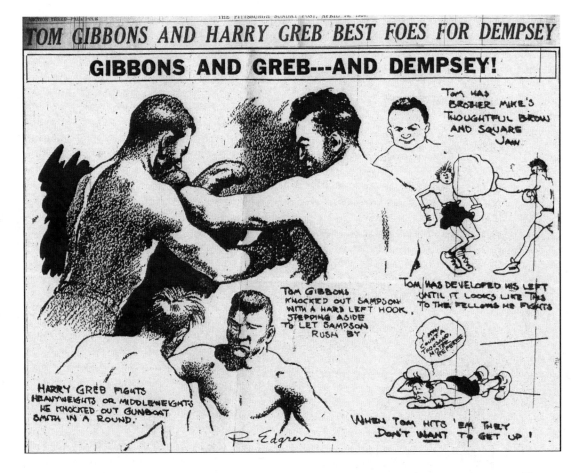

This illustration depicting the powerful fighting ability of Tom Gibbons and Harry Greb appeared in the *Pittsburgh Post* on April 10, 1921 (*Pittsburgh Post-Gazette*).

more effectively than ever before, he got more confident than ever and battered merrily away. And he was hurting with his hitting too.

Greb was in usual form, bringing the fight to his opponent and being the aggressor. He wouldn't give his opponent time to set up a punch and Tommy was always "off balance." At the end Greb "just manhandled him gleefully and seemed to get a deal of satisfaction out of it."

When the bell rang in the rain-drenched ballpark it was clear Greb had won. Harry had beaten heavyweight Tommy Gibbons, and had enjoyed doing it. Greb was awarded seven of the ten rounds. The headline the next day in the *Pittsburgh Post* read, "Greb Gives Gibbons Good Thumping In Furious Fight." Tommy Gibbons had just become another heavyweight victim of Harry Greb.

One of the major accomplishments Greb is known for in his career is that he was the only man to have ever beaten Gene Tunney—the same Gene Tunney that would go on to beat Dempsey twice.

Another fighter that, like Tunney, beat Dempsey more than once was Willie Meehan. Dempsey fought Meehan five times and lost to him twice with two other bouts judged draws. For a fighter that gave Dempsey so much trouble, Meehan was no problem for Greb.

When Greb fought Meehan for the first time it was on December 4, 1917. This was the same year that Meehan had already beaten Dempsey and also fought two bouts against him to a draw.

Nevertheless, when Greb stepped into the ring against him it was a whole different story. Greb easily punched Meehan hard "about his fat stomach." Most of the time Greb was throwing punches to Meehan's face using lefts and rights. These one-two punches "bothered, annoyed and also hurt the fat fellow."[19]

Greb was outweighed by over 25 pounds that night. He weighed 161 pounds for the fight while Meehan weighed 187. Even with all that extra weight Meehan was "outmauled and out-roughed" by Greb. Greb was landing so many punches to Meehan's face that his eyes were "damaged" near the end of the fight. Dempsey seemed to have trouble against Meehan, but against Greb, Meehan "was hurt repeatedly by his opponent's savage punches." It was a six-round bout that Greb easily won. A headline the next day read, "Greb Proves Easy Victor Over Meehan." [20]

The next time these two boxers fought was on May 8, 1919, in a ten-round bout. Greb weighed 166 pounds for the fight while Meehan outweighed him by over thirty pounds. Greb, however, won again, this time taking nine out of the ten rounds. It was said that Greb entered the ring with a black eye and two boils, but this certainly didn't stop him from beating such an easy opponent. Greb was said to have disregarded Meehan's punches while he continued with his constant attack.[21]

Ed "Gunboat" Smith was a 6'2" heavyweight considered a "white hope." He fought all the top boxers, including Jack Dempsey, Georges Carpentier, Kid Norfolk, Fred Fulton, Billy Miske and Harry Wills. Some of the fighters he defeated were Sam Langford, Jess Willard, Carl Morris, "Fireman" Jim Flynn, "Bombardier" Billy Wells, Battling Levinsky and Frank Moran. He even had exhibitions with Jack Johnson and Stanley Ketchel. He won the white heavyweight title in 1914 against Arthur Pelky. He was a great heavyweight boxer whose weight ranged from 170 to 186 pounds.

Dempsey and Ed "Gunboat" Smith fought twice in their careers, in 1917 and 1918, with Dempsey winning both times. Greb also met "Gunboat" Smith in the ring twice. Their first fight took place on May 24, 1918, at Madison Square Garden. It was a six-round fight refereed by Kid McPartland. Greb was outweighed by fifteen pounds and gave up almost half a foot in height, but these disadvantages didn't slow him down at all. When the first round started Greb began lunging at "Gunboat." Smith didn't seem to understand Greb's style and had great difficulty landing punches. It was written that "Harry was the personification of perpetual motion, boring in continuously

Ed "Gunboat" Smith in 1915 (Antiquities of the Prize Ring).

on the lanky Gunner with both arms going like flails." Greb's most effective punches came from using an "overhand right chop to the jaw." By the last two rounds "Gunboat" started tiring a bit. The headline the next day was "Greb Defeats Gunboat Smith."[22]

The next time Greb and "Gunboat" Smith fought was on October 21, 1920, in Indiana. This fight didn't last as long because after a few clinches Greb "landed a hard left on Smith's right eye, injuring the optic nerve and blinding him. A second later he landed a right on Smith's jaw, knocking him out."[23] The fight ended with Greb getting a first-round knockout.

Homer Smith was another heavyweight who fought both Dempsey and Greb. Smith fought many great heavyweights of his time including Bill Brennan, Billy Miske, Fred Fulton, Luis Angel Firpo, Jack Johnson, Jack Sharkey and Harry Wills. Homer Smith lost to Dempsey by KO in 1918, but it was a few years later when Greb would have a crack at him.

Greb finished off Smith with a fifth-round TKO on November 25, 1921. Greb weighed around 165 pounds while Smith weighed around 190. The fight took place

Homer Smith circa 1928 (Fistianaboxingmemorabilia.com).

in Brooklyn and was over quickly. During the first five rounds Greb gave Smith "a fine pasting." During the whole fight "Smith did not land an effective punch."[24] Then at the end of the fifth round Smith quit. He claimed that middleweight Greb had broken his ribs. Greb wasn't just surviving in fights against heavyweights, he was punishing them severely.

Greb even fought and beat a few of Dempsey's heavyweight sparring partners such as Jack Renault, Jock Malone and Walter Monoghan.

Greb would battle Jack Renault twice in 1921. The first fight was on March 16, 1921, at Exposition Hall in Pittsburgh. It was a ten-round fight and Greb was said to have won nine of the rounds. Greb weighed 165 pounds for the fight and Renault fought at 187 pounds, over twenty pounds more than his opponent. Greb was mostly using left hooks and right swings during the bout. Although it was a pretty tame fight, Greb won the fight without a problem.[25]

The second time these two fought was around a month later on April 6, this time in Canada. Although the fight took place in a different country, the result was nearly the same. Greb defeated Renault for a second time with Renault outweighing Greb again by about twenty pounds.[26]

Greb tallied up a win against any and all of Dempsey's opponents that he fought. Not too bad at all for a middleweight. Greb would also fight many heavyweights who didn't battle Dempsey, such as Bartley Madden, Paul Sampson-Korner, Whitey Allen, John Foley, Zulu Kid, Joe Cox, Charley Weinert, Al Roberts, Mickey Shannon, Al Benedict, Capt. Bob Roper, George Hauser and more. Greb didn't just use speed against these heavyweights; he also had a very good punch on

Jack Renault (collection of Pugilistica.com).

occasion. For example, when Greb fought heavyweight Whitey Allen in 1921, he broke Whitey Allen's jawbone with a strong left jab. The scheduled six-round fight had to be stopped immediately. Several other heavyweights worth mentioning here are Bartley Madden, Al Benedict and Joe Cox.

Bartley Madden was a heavyweight who fought Hall of Famers Tommy Gibbons, Joe Jeannette, Battling Levinsky, Harry Wills and Gene Tunney. His most impressive wins came against

Clay Turner, Larry Williams, Homer Smith, Tom Cowler, Martin Burke, Leo Gates and Jack McAuliffe. Other significant boxers he fought were Fred Fulton, Joe Cox, Bill Brennan, Jim Coffey, Billy Miske, Tom Heeney and Jack Renault.

Greb and Madden fought twice, once in 1919 and a year later in 1920. The first fight was ten rounds and took place in Buffalo. Greb's speed was just too much for Madden to handle. In the very first round Greb was able to land a great punch that made Madden fall to the canvas and receive an eight-count. He was able to get up and finish the fight, but not much changed. Greb cut Madden around both eyes and when the bout was finished it was obvious that Greb had "greatly outpointed" Madden.[27]

Their second fight took place in Kalamazoo, Michigan, and was another ten-round newspaper decision. Although Greb was unable to knock Madden down in this fight, his speed was still too much for Madden to handle. Greb was able to hit him whenever and however he wanted while being totally unaffected by Madden's punches. Greb won eight of the rounds while the other two were judged as being even. Even with Bartley Madden's extensive heavyweight experience against great competition, against Greb he couldn't even win one round.[28]

Al Benedict was a heavyweight boxer that always weighed more than 200 pounds. He was a big man who fought many great heavyweights of his time including Arthur Pelky, Jim Coffey, Joe Jeannette, Carl Morris, Bill Brennan, Battling Levinsky, Charley Weinert, Capt. Bob Roper, Jack Renault and many others. Harry Greb fought Al Benedict on September 26, 1922, in Toronto, Canada.

In the first round Benedict threw a big punch that rocked Greb. After staggering for a second Harry recovered

Bartley Madden (Antiquities of the Prize Ring).

and went on to control the fight. This was another example of Greb's having a great chin that could take a heavyweight punch and recover from it. Greb very quickly took control and knocked down Benedict in the second round. Benedict got up, only for Greb to drop him a second time in the same round. Greb then floored his heavyweight opponent a third time before the round came to an end. By that time the referee didn't even bother to count. Harry Greb was awarded a second-round TKO against a man that weighed 200 pounds.[29]

The final heavyweight opponent of Greb's worth noting was Joe Cox. Cox was a big heavy-weight who weighed 200 pounds or more and was 6'5" tall. This was an extremely big man who had a lot of experience against heavyweights, including "Fireman" Jim Flynn, Jess Willard, "Sailor" Jack Carroll, Luther McCarty, George "Boer" Modell, Arthur Pelky, "Gunboat" Smith, Bill Brennan, Jim Coffey, Bartley Madden and others.

Cox fought Greb on September 20, 1921, in Brooklyn. Greb weighed 161 pounds while Cox was a pound shy of 200. Greb was fighting a man thirty-eight pounds heavier and nine inches taller in a twelve-round fight.

In a fight against a much bigger and taller man Greb didn't back down at all. In the fifth and sixth rounds it was reported that Greb and Cox "stood toe to toe and pasted each other with a steady stream of lefts and rights."[30] When the fight was over Greb was officially awarded the fight by the judges.

To put this weight and height disparity in perspective, Dempsey was four inches shorter than Cox and Dempsey usually weighed in ten or more pounds lighter than Cox. Greb was fight-ing bigger and taller men than Dempsey and was having no problem beating them. Greb eas-ily beat every single heavyweight opponent that he ever fought.

In late 1920, Greb was about to have his second set of sparring sessions with Dempsey.

The *New York Times* announced on August 27, 1920, that Greb was to be a sparring part-ner for Jack Dempsey, in Jack's preparation for his fight against Billy Miske. Greb had already fought and beaten Billy Miske.

On September 1, 1920, in Benton Harbor, Michigan, Greb was back in the ring against the heavyweight champion. There was to be three days of sparring sessions between Dempsey and Greb. The first day's sparring match was three rounds, and Greb wasted no time. Greb "went into him like a hurricane, piling up points with his rapid, erratic style, and eluding the cham-pion's retaliatory efforts with ease." This sounded like a typical Greb fight. Greb was the aggres-sor, throwing a lot of punches and keeping the opponent on defense while the opponent was unable to land any effective punches. Greb was throwing many "assorted" punches and was landing these "into the champion from all angles."[31]

The *New York Times* stated that Greb gave "the champion a real honest-to-goodness bat-tle." The article went on to say, "Greb was all over him and kept forcing him around the ring throughout the session. Dempsey could do little with the speedy light heavyweight, while Greb seemed to be able to hit Dempsey almost at will. Time and again Greb made the champion miss with his famous right and left hooks."[32]

Greb was said to have been "a veritable whirlwind" against Dempsey. He even did his jumping-jack style of leaping into the air while throwing a punch. The *New York Times* stated that Greb jumped "off the floor to hit Dempsey in the head when the latter was standing straight, but managed to do it and landed without leaving himself open to Jack's snappy hooks and short swings."[33]

People were experiencing a glimpse of what a real fight may have been like between these two fighters. Greb was taking the fight to his opponent, and while Dempsey was trying to solve the riddle of Harry Greb, he was unable to land effective punches. When Dempsey did try to land punches, Greb was "eluding the champion's retaliatory efforts with ease."[34] The first day of sparring was over with two more remaining.

The second day of sparring took place the following day, on September 2. The *Washington Post*'s headline would read, "Greb Splits Dempsey's Tongue." Between 1,500 and 2,000 people paid to see this second day of sparring between these great combatants.[35]

In the first round Dempsey "held his own with one of the most shiftiest [*sic*] youths." The *New York Times* would describe the beginning of the first round like this: "Greb rushed Dempsey. The onslaught was so sudden that Jack was caught off guard and it took a solid left hook into the body, plied with all the forces at Greb's command, which is considerable, to jolt Dempsey into action. Then the fur began to fly."[36]

In the second round, "Greb reached Dempsey with a crushing right-hander flush on the chin." Harry then "broke loose and popped away at Dempsey as the bell rang." The *New York Times* would go on to

Joe Cox early in his career (**Antiquities of the Prize Ring**).

say that the bout "caused the crowd to burst into cheers and prolonged applause. In fact, during the intermission between the second and third rounds, Ted Hayes, who acted as announcer at the Dempsey camp, was compelled to request the spectators to refrain from urging either of the men to greater efforts."[37]

When the third round began Dempsey landed some body punches, two of which "lifted Greb clear off his feet." Greb continued to take the fight to Dempsey and make Jack "block" and "duck" from Harry's punches. Early in the third round they were in a clinch when Greb's head butted Dempsey's jaw. The contact was so severe that Dempsey "spat blood for the remainder of the round."[38] It was obvious by Dempsey's performance that he knew he had to fight against Greb. When the three rounds ended Dempsey was out of breath. He was experiencing what it was like trying to keep up with Greb, who fought at this fast pace for every round and even picked it up in later rounds. It was written that Dempsey "was puffing very hard after boxing Greb. Of course, it was an unusually fast workout, but it seemed to take him longer than it should to recover his wind even after so strenuous a session."[39]

The third and final day of sparring took place on September 3. The previous day of sparring had taken so much out of Dempsey that he only allowed two rounds with Greb on this final day. The *New York Times* would write: "Harry Greb, looking as chipper as ever in his U.S. Navy jersey and his black tights, climbed into the ring to take Dempsey over the jumps for two rounds of three minutes each."[40]

The fighting the day before had been so intense it seemed there was a specific intention to take it easy on the last day. It is unknown if Jack asked Harry to lighten up a little on this last day. It consisted of "the lightest kind of boxing, consisting chiefly of feinting and footwork." The *New York Times* would go on to write:

Just as soon as they squared off it was apparent that there was to be none of the continuous slam-bang stuff which had accompanied their previous engagements. Greb did not rush the champion and they feinted and pranced about for a full minute before either made a real lead. Toward the close of the round they met mid-ring and there was a sharp exchange of body punches. The second round was a little livelier, but it wasn't a cyclone, and the crowd was somewhat disappointed. The fans had expected to see more of a real battling than had featured the jousts between these two.[41]

After this second set of sparring exhibitions with Dempsey, Greb was more convinced than ever that he could win a decision over the heavyweight champion if he were given the chance. Later in 1920 another attempt for an official fight took place. The *New York Times* on November 30, 1920, had a headline, "Greb May Meet Dempsey." Promoter Floyd Fitzsimmons of Benton Harbor, Michigan, traveled to South Bend, Indiana, "en route to New York, where he expects to sign Jack Dempsey for a ten-round fight with Harry Greb."[42]

The article would go on to state, "Greb has been trying to get into the ring with Dempsey for several months, and he has been especially eager to meet the champion since beating Gunboat Smith in one round of a ten-round battle." Greb was all for the fight while "Fitzsimmons is reported to have promised Greb to do his best to sign the Dempsey match."[43] Unfortunately, this attempt wasn't successful either. Dempsey simply did not want an official fight against Greb.

A month later, in December of 1920, Greb beat heavyweight "Captain" Bob Roper. A headline the next day read, "Greb Defeats Roper; Gives Fans Surprise — Touted As Logical Contender For Dempsey." The article talked about the fight between Greb and Roper and went on to talk about how Greb would fare against Dempsey, if they ever fought. The article stated that Greb was the next logical contender to fight Dempsey and that the result of the fight would probably be the same as all the other fights Greb had had against heavyweights.

Those at the ringside marveled at Greb's speed, hitting power and ring generalship, and freely predicted that it boded ill for Champion Dempsey should Greb ever succeed in getting the former in the ring. It was the general belief that Dempsey would find considerable trouble in landing any decisive blow on the elusive Greb.[44]

This general belief that it would be a very difficult fight for Dempsey was not just held by the public and sportswriters, it may have even been held by Dempsey himself.

7.

A Time for Change

James "Red" Mason had been Harry Greb's manager ever since he turned pro in 1913. Mason used his vast experience in Pittsburgh boxing to help groom Greb into a great fighter. However, Mason's greatest contribution to Greb's development was the ability to constantly feed him so many fights. Mason kept Greb busy by scheduling fights almost every week, which kept Greb in great condition, gave him the opportunity to experience the styles of many different fighters, and allowed Greb to gain a large following of fans.

All of this was about to end. On December 31, 1920, the *Chicago Daily Tribune* printed the headline "Greb Breaks with Manager; Goes to Engel."[1] Greb's new manager, George Engel, was based out of New York City. The article described why Greb had dropped Mason as his manager: "It is said the trouble between Greb and Mason began last summer, when Greb was beaten by Tom Gibbons at Forbes Field. The local battler also told friends he was not getting a large enough percentage of his purses to suit him."[2]

A week later, on January 6, 1921, Greb wrote a letter to his new manager, who was still based in New York. Greb was now training out of the Motor Square Boxing Club in Pittsburgh and wrote the letter on their stationery. He used to train out of the Lyceum Gym but now that he was no longer managed by Mason, he had started training elsewhere. The location of the Motor Square Garden in Pittsburgh was listed as "Baum Blvd, Beatty, Centre and Trade Sts." Below is a transcript of the first letter that Greb wrote to his new manager. (Any missing punctuation is how it was written in the letter.)

Jan 6.

My Dear Pal George,

Your letter received today and was very glad to hear from you. George I sure am glad I made the change I did in making you my manager. Now since it is done I am really very happy and would not take twenty thousand dollars cash to go back to him.

He has his hammer out knocking already but everybody knows Red Mason. Well George I have been training for the last four days and now I am in pretty good shape and from now on with about four days notice will be able to take on any fight you arrange.

If I were you I would get in touch with Tartorick in New Orleans as Mason had me matched there with Happy Littleton for 15 rounds to a decision and he was to receive twenty five hundred with the privilege of twenty five per cent of the house with all expenses, but I am sure you can get more than that.

I was talking to John McGarvey, matchmaker of the Motor Club here and I gave him your address he is going to get in touch with you for a bout with Tommy Gibbons he said he would give 33⅓ per cent of the house but I think you can get a guarantee of five thousand with the privilege that would be ten rounds no decision and I am sure I can beat him but try to get him to make one sixty three at three o'clock the last time we were to do that weight but he lost his forfeit and I weighed in at one sixty one and he weighed 168, but still I beat him easy. I think it would be a good match for me here.

89

Well George how about the Flat we are anxious to go to New York City and you and I can work together better see what you can do for me to go there the first of next month.

That certainly was a nice write up Walter St. Denis(sp) had about you. Am enclosing a clipping out of the days paper what Mason said try to send a story in the papers here that I am a big booster for Pitts and that I will travel all over the world to box but it will always be Harry Greb of Pittsburgh and that will show that Red headed bastard up.

Will come to an end hoping to get a long letter like this from you soon.

Regards From Mrs Greb and Myself to you and your Family
Harry Greb

Get my clipping books from Boston, Hugh McGan(sp) has them.
The bills you got out are fine. We will have some pictures taken later.

So began the two-year relationship between Greb and his new manager. During this time Red Mason began being the matchmaker for the Keystone Club. This was a boxing club that fought at the Southside Market House and Exposition Hall. Mason was now responsible for setting up all the fights, and he was thought to be the right man for the job because he was on speaking terms with almost everybody in the Pittsburgh boxing community.

For the next two years Greb was going to find out, the hard way, that Mason had in fact been doing a pretty good job for him after all. Mason wasn't only a friend, he also kept Greb very busy and set up a lot of big fights in his career. Engel talked pretty smoothly to Greb and promised him a lot of things, a bigger percentage of the purses among them. Greb believed these promises and gave Engel a try, but their relationship was rather short-lived. Greb was about to spend two years learning that George Engel certainly wasn't everything he was cracked up to be. The moment Engel's contract was up for renewal Greb would seize the opportunity to go back to Mason.

During 1921 the extremely busy fight schedule Greb was maintaining started to taper off. He only fought twenty-one times in 1921, much less often than in previous years. Engel was based out of New York so Greb would end up only having five fights in Pittsburgh. Instead, Greb would travel to many different cities across the nation, and even fight in Canada.

One of Greb's first fights under Engel was against Pal Reed. Reed had boxed while serving in the navy during World War I, just like Greb. Reed was now a southpaw middleweight fighting out of Massachusetts. The fight took place on January 29, 1921, in Boston. Boston sportswriter Jack Conway wrote that 6,000 people came to see the fight between Greb and Reed. Greb won the ten-round contest easily, but the fight wasn't without its moments. It was written: "Reed didn't have a chance of winning the decision, but he proved willing at times, and risked an exchange of wallops with his rugged rival whenever he got to close quarters."[3] The *Boston Post* wrote the

George Engel, a famous New York boxing manager (Antiquities of the Prize Ring).

Pittsburgh,Pa,   December,30th, 1920,

Harry Greb of Pittsburgh Pa, now employs George Engel of
New York City as his business manager under the
following terms,

FIRST. the said Greb is to devote all of
his ability as a boxer or otherwise to the carrying out of
this contract and is to assume no emplyment of any kind,
that shall not be considered as undertaken under and
controlled by this agreement,

SECOND. This agreement shall continue in
force for a term of Two Years from date, unless sooner
dissolved by mutual consent,

THIRD. The said Engel shall have all the
rights and all the powers and perform all the duties that
are usually had by a boxing manager,

FOURTH.The said Greb shall receive SEVENTY
(70) percent of the net profits of this agreement and the
said Engel shall receive THIRTY.(30) percent thereof,

FIFTH. From the Gross receipts of this
engagement shall be deducted the training expenses of said
sum, and any expense incurred by the said Engel in carrying
out this agreement, and the balance shall constitute the
net profits above referred to,

SIXTH.In all matters of business policy
to be pursued hereunder the said Engel shall have the
controlling voice,

The intention of this agreement is
that said Greb shall devote all his personal time and
efforts to the carrying out of the same, and the said Engel
shall act as his business manager, and in the construction
of this agreement where itsterms are in dispute or do not
cover the custom that usually prevails in such agreements
shall govern,

Signed in duplicate,

A copy of the management contract between Harry Greb and George Engel. Notice that it was only for two years, starting on December 30, 1920 (Antiquities of the Prize Ring).

following day: "Pal brought the fans to their feet when he sent Greb reeling to the ropes twice in the fourth, and in the sixth a right to the chin almost upset the champion."[4]

These two fighters met twice more, once in 1923 and the final time in 1924, with Greb winning each time. In his career, Pal Reed would go on to fight Mickey Walker, Tiger Flowers, Jack Delaney, Tommy Loughran, and Johnny Wilson.

Pal Reed was interviewed later in life and looked back at his fights against Greb:

> A unique style is very important in becoming a champion. I think Harry Greb's boxing will best illustrate this. Harry was known as the "fighting windmill." There never was a man who typified Harry's style of boxing. He threw blows from every angle. He rained uppercuts and blows that were used by no other boxer. He had a great faculty for starting a blow and stopping it in midair, but countering with another blow.... I should say that the greatest I ever fought was Greb.[5]

Once when interviewed Reed pointed to several scars on his face and said, "Greb did this and this and this. You couldn't hit him. He would stand in the corner with his hands down and you still couldn't hit him."[6]

Engel matched Greb to fight another tough boxer, this one by the name of Chuck Wiggins. Wiggins was a strong, rough boxer who fought the likes of Battling Levinsky, Gene Tunney, Tommy Gibbons, Tommy Loughran, Les Darcey, Mike Gibbons and Tiger Flowers. This wasn't to be the first time Greb and Wiggins met in the ring; they had met on four previous occasions with Greb receiving the win each time.

Greb and Wiggins would fight a total of three times in 1921. The first fight of this year took place on May 28 in Wiggins's home state of Indiana and was said to be a ten-round draw in the local papers. An immediate rematch took place on June 23 with the same result, a ten-round newspaper-decision draw. Then on September 5, 1921, in West Virginia they fought for a third time, this time on neutral ground. The fight was also a ten-round no-decision bout, but the outcome was not to be as close as the last two fights. This time Greb clearly won by taking five rounds, with Wiggins winning just one round and the others being judged as even. The bout was said to be "a rough house affair from start to finish. Wiggins hit Greb low at least ten times during the melee and was frequently warned by the referee. As early as the third round Referee Seales stopped the fight and told Wiggins if he didn't cease hitting the belt he would be disqualified."[7]

This rough fight was said to have contained "elbowing and butting with the head." Wiggins and Greb would go on to fight a total of nine times between 1919 and 1923. Greb was later quoted as saying about Wiggins, "He was the best butter I ever butted with."[8]

Greb was to fight another Dempsey opponent more than once in 1921. This time he was to battle middleweight Jimmy Darcy, who was known to have a very powerful right-hand punch, once in May and then again in October. Darcy was fighting mostly out of New York during this time in his career. Their first fight was a ten-rounder and took place on May 13, 1921, in Boston. Greb easily won this fight and was even able to knock Darcy to the canvas in the fourth round. Although Darcy was still fighting strong until the final bell, it was later discovered that he had broken his left hand sometime during the contest.[9]

The rematch took place months later on October 24. This was also a ten-round fight, but this time it was staged in Buffalo, New York. Greb dominated the fight and won by decision. His best rounds were the 7th, 9th, and 10th when he really gave Darcy a beating. He was most effective on the inside, while Darcy was doing a lot of clinching.[10]

The following year Darcy fought for the heavyweight title against Jack Dempsey. Once again, a fighter Greb had beaten got a chance to fight Dempsey for the title, instead of Greb getting the chance himself. Darcy lost the title bid and went on to fight Greb again in 1923. The

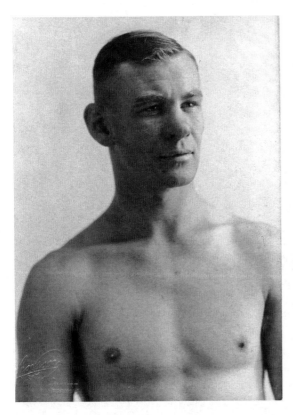

Chuck Wiggins was a much rougher fighter than Greb ever was. Wiggins was disqualified for dirty tactics eight times in his career, while Greb was only disqualified once (collection of Pugilistica.com).

1923 fight between the two was for the middleweight championship, and once again Greb came out the winner.[11]

A major fight Greb had in 1921 was in Madison Square Garden against Charley Weinert. Weinert, born in Budapest, Hungary, had fought such Hall of Famers as Gene Tunney, Jack Dillon, Harry Wills and Jack Sharkey. This bout took place on November 4, 1921, and was the first of a series of elimination bouts to help choose a light heavyweight challenger for Tommy Gibbons's American title. Greb was said to have been giving up around twenty-five pounds to his heavyweight opponent.

In the first round of the fifteen-round fight, Greb threw a left and right that floored Weinert. He rose on the count of four, but the bell rang to save him from any further damage.

Greb was said to have fought "one of his typical battles, letting punches fly from every angle, every second. His favorite trick was to crush in with both maulers flying and then pinion Weinert's arms in a clinch and keep on hitting with one hand."

As early as the fifth round Weinert's face started to be "puffed and bleeding." The fight was said to be "one glorious fifteen-round lambasting, at the end of which event the judges agreed on Greb as the winner." The headline the next day read, "Weinert Takes Great Lacing from Icky."

In November Greb was set to fight a light heavyweight champion from Australia. Although originally from California, Billy Shade traveled to the land down under and captured their versions of the welterweight, middleweight, light heavyweight and heavyweight titles. Shade arrived back in America and started fighting in October of 1921. He came from a family of fighters that included his two brothers Dave and George.

The Greb-Shade contest was a ten-round no-decision bout and took place at Motor Square Garden in Pittsburgh. This was the same place from where Greb wrote his letter to George Engel.

Unlike previous fights, Greb started off fighting "flat-footed." He was fighting a more conventional style and "boxed according to the book." This was a completely new description of his fighting style. This "conventional" style gave Billy Shade the ability to land "a couple of stiff right-handers to the head." Once he experienced the best Shade had to offer, it was all Greb from there on out, and he was able to do whatever he wanted, whenever he wanted. "If he wanted to box, he did and jabbed Shade repeatedly. If he wanted to fight, they stood toe to toe and slugged until one broke ground. If Greb wanted to be Greb, he did so and cut loose with his old-fashioned aerial attack that unleashes punches from everywhere."[12]

By the tenth round Shade's lip was split and his face was puffed, while Greb appeared "as fresh as when he started." The newspaper headline the next day read, "Greb Carries Shade Along,

Charlie Weinert on the cover of *The Ring* magazine. The issue, from 1925, also shows Harry Greb, Mickey Walker and Harry Wills (*The Ring*, Kappa Publishing).

Winning in Motor Square Bout."[13] After winning this bout Greb was only to fight three more times in 1921.

Greb was said to have changed his style now that he was fighting more often in New York. Regis M. Welsh from the *Pittsburgh Post* wrote near the end of the year that Greb learned "many tricks in New York." Welsh would go on to write:

> Greb has finally hit into the style which is going to get him a lot of money around Madison Square Garden and other Gotham Emporiums. Because Harry, the wild, ferocious, sometimes comical fighter has finally adopted a style which makes any fighter look good with him no matter how far he outclasses him.

Welsh's point was that Harry would now carry a fighter a little during the fight instead of embarrassing him badly. This made for what looked like a more competitive fight so people thought they were getting their money's worth, instead of watching a fighter get totally beaten from start to finish, which is what Greb used to do.[14]

This sudden change of fighting style was being attributed to his recent fights in New York under his new manager. Some new trainers may also have taught Greb a new thing or two. Nevertheless, there was another significant occurrence that happened later in 1921 which could shed more light on why Greb was starting to have closer fights than usual. It could answer why Greb was fighting slightly differently later in the year, and why he had even started fighting a little rougher, thumbing opponents in the eyes for the first time in his career.

During Greb's recent fight with Charley Weinert back in November the papers wrote that Greb had "rammed his thumbs so deep into Weinert's eyes that you looked for them to come poking out of Charley's ears most any time."[15]

Greb's fight descriptions up to this point had always been relatively clean. Even when Greb was fighting someone who fouled him, he didn't respond in kind. Greb would always fight his fight and not resort to rough tactics. Now, however, he was doing a little more than the usual holding or elbowing that was normal practice in the boxing ring. He started upping the ante. In the November bout against Weinert the newspapers noted that Greb "for some reason cut loose with every shady practice known to the ring except kicking. He butted, held on, held with his gloves and rammed his thumbs ... deep into Weinert's eyes...."[16] What could have made Greb change his style and start fighting so rough?

Even before he got to New York the first string of "rough-house" fights started on September 6 in the Chuck Wiggins fight in West Virginia. After the fight it was said that "the fight was a rough house affair from start to finish," with "a good deal of elbowing and butting with the head, both men being the offenders."[17] What else might have happened before September that could have made Greb alter his style of fighting? Maybe the answer can be found back in Greb's recent fight against Kid Norfolk.

On August 29, 1921, Greb was scheduled to fight future Hall of Famer Kid Norfolk for the first time. Kid Norfolk was born William Ward in Belmont, Virginia. When he started boxing professionally in 1914 he started using the name "Kid Norfolk" after the street he was born on. He was a light heavyweight but fought many heavyweights of his time. The list of boxers he fought before boxing Greb included Sam Langford, Jeff Clark, Bill Tate, Sam McVea, Arthur Pelky, Tom Cowler, Gunboat Smith, John Lester Johnson, Billy Miske, Joe Jeannette, Clay Turner, Jack Blackburn, Jamaica Kid, and Lee Anderson. After fighting Greb he would go on to battle Tiger Flowers, Harry Wills, George Godfrey, Tut Jackson, Battling Siki, and Tommy Gibbons.

Norfolk outweighed Greb by at least 17½ pounds when they first met. Many white heavyweights refused to fight Norfolk and give him a chance at a title because of his color, and his talent. These white boxers all drew the "color line," but Greb thought differently. Greb knew

Norfolk was one of the best light heavyweights out there so he chose to take him on in the ring. This fight would end up being one of the most memorable bouts of Greb's career.

The ten-round fight was scheduled for Forbes Field in Pittsburgh, where Greb had fought many times before. Days before the fight was to take place there were rumors floating around Pittsburgh that a fix was in. This was totally untrue, but the rumor was affecting ticket sales and both camps knew they had to put up a great fight. And they did just that.[18]

Norfolk, who was fighting out of New York, was seen around town training hard for the fight. Greb was also training hard and was seen at a police benefit a couple of days before the bout, where it was reported that he looked good. So both fighters were prepared and in condition when the fight started.

When the bell rang to start the bout there were 5,500 people in the baseball park. Most of the first half of the fight was all Norfolk. According to the *Pittsburgh Post* the first round was awarded to Norfolk while Greb was "crowded every inch of the way" and was "forced to abandon his jumping jack attack." The second round, "which Greb carried by sheer aggressiveness, was awarded to Harry."[19]

Then in the third round Norfolk landed a great right-hand punch to Greb's jaw which made him "hit the floor like a sack of oats. He was up in an instant, though." He wasn't seriously hurt, but Greb immediately went after Norfolk to prove that the punch hadn't affected him too much. After Greb rose from the canvas he "tore loose" into Norfolk. Although Harry had recovered quickly, the round was still awarded to Norfolk because of the knockdown.

The next couple of rounds were also awarded to Kid Norfolk. During these rounds, however, Greb was being very physical with his opponent when they were in clinches. When the sixth round started, "the purpose of his tussling and tugging around in the repeated clinches soon showed. It sapped the steam from the ebony giant and made him look just like any ordinary Greb opponent."

Harry Greb (IPC Media).

With Norfolk starting to tire in the sixth, the crowd started cheering for Greb. This encouraged Greb, who then "unleashed both hands in the opening of the sixth round and never ceased for a minute thereafter, completely bewildering Norfolk, who looked wearily to his corner for some sort of advice." When the sixth round ended it was clear that Greb had won that one.

From the seventh round until the end of the fight in the tenth, it was all Greb. He was fighting aggressively with both hands while "the usual jumping and throwing his hands carelessly at his target were missing." The final rounds were tough, but Greb was able to capitalize on Norfolk's tiring and "lacking steam" in his punches.

Greb was even able to re-open an old cut over Norfolk's eye. This was an injury that Norfolk had originally suffered at the hands of Lee Anderson months earlier during a colored heavyweight title

Kid Norfolk, known as "The Black Thunderbolt," was one of the top light heavyweight boxers of his era but was never given a title shot. He turned pro in 1913, the same year as Greb. In his career he fought around 100 bouts and only lost fifteen times. He retired from boxing in 1926 at the age of thirty-three. He was inducted into the International Boxing Hall of Fame in 2007 (Antiquities of the Prize Ring).

bout. Lee Anderson had permanently damaged Norfolk's eye so the fight had to be stopped and he took a couple of months off to recover before stepping back in the ring to fight Greb. This gave Greb "a target to shoot at, and this Harry did in the closing rounds to such an extent that the Negro's lamp was torn open and the blood flowed freely."

With Greb dominating the second half of the fight and also being awarded the second round, he won the bout. He was awarded six rounds while Kid Norfolk was only awarded four. He had won a close battle by coming on strong at the finish. The headline the next day was "Harry Greb Is Winner Over Kid Norfolk in Forbes Field Bout." At the very end of the fight Norfolk's eye was cut and he was also bleeding from the mouth, while "Greb's only mark was a puffed left eye."

So Greb had won a very close and rough fight. He had received his first flash knockdown in many years but may have also received something else, something far more debilitating and long-lasting. The puffiness over his left eye was not the only damage Greb had suffered in the fight. Something had happened to his other eye also, something that was never mentioned in the newspapers during his lifetime.

Years later, after Greb had passed away, his doctor dropped a bombshell from Atlantic City. In the *New York Times* on October 27, 1926, Greb's personal physician, Dr. Carl S. McGivern, made the following formal statement: "Harry Greb was made blind by a blow on his right eye during a fight with Kid Norfolk, Negro heavyweight, in New York City in 1921."[20] His blindness was said to be caused by a retinal detachment.

Ophthalmic surgeons have been consulted on this subject to get a clearer picture of what Greb went through. Most important is the question of whether the detachment actually happened in the Norfolk fight at all or occurred later in another bout. Dr. Albert L. Ackerman is one specialist that was consulted for this book. His credentials include decades of personal experiences concerning retinal detachments suffered by boxers. Dr. Ackerman has been a retina surgeon for almost half a century, beginning in the early 1960s. In 1969 he treated the actor George C. Scott for a retinal detachment around the time the movie *Patton* was being made. George C. Scott was a boxer in his early years, but his detachment wasn't caused by boxing.

One of Dr. Ackerman's first experiences with retinal detachment in fighters came when a boxer arrived to see him one day escorted by prison guards. This boxer was Rubin "Hurricane" Carter. "Hurricane" was in jail and was complaining of loss of sight and asking to see a doctor. No one working in the jail believed him at first so a lot of time passed and his symptoms worsened. Finally "Hurricane" Carter was allowed to leave the hospital to see an eye specialist and he knocked on Dr Ackerman's door. Dr. Ackerman then examined and diagnosed "Hurricane" as having a retinal detachment that unfortunately had progressed because it hadn't been treated earlier.

This was one of Dr. Ackerman's first cases with a boxer and it began his research into how common eye injuries were with boxers. Dr. Ackerman sent a letter to the New York Boxing Commission in 1965 informing them that they should be routinely examining boxers for eye injuries; at that time it was not done. Years later in the 1970s this examination was finally installed as a normal practice. A friend of Dr. Ackerman's was the retinal surgeon who treated Sugar Ray Leonard for his retinal detachment. Throughout the decades Dr. Ackerman has treated retinal detachment in many boxers, including young boxers in the Golden Gloves.

Dr. Scot A. Brower, another ophthalmologist, was also interviewed for this book. Dr. Brower has performed special procedures dealing with retinal tears and detachments. The

Greb wearing boxing gloves of his era. Notice the free-moving thumbs that gloves had back then. They contained very little padding and were very flexible (Carnegie Library of Pittsburgh).

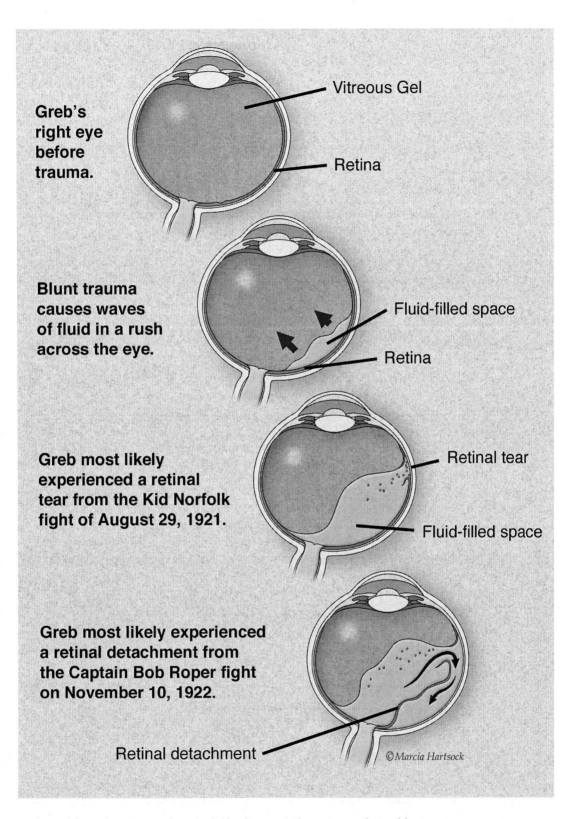

Greb's right eye before trauma.

Vitreous Gel

Retina

Blunt trauma causes waves of fluid in a rush across the eye.

Fluid-filled space

Retina

Greb most likely experienced a retinal tear from the Kid Norfolk fight of August 29, 1921.

Retinal tear

Fluid-filled space

Greb most likely experienced a retinal detachment from the Captain Bob Roper fight on November 10, 1922.

Retinal detachment

©Marcia Hartsock

Shown here is the process of a retinal detachment. It demonstrates how a blunt trauma progresses to a tear and then finally to a retinal detachment. Many boxers are currently treated for this and are cured using modern surgery that was unavailable during Greb's lifetime (Illustration © Marcia Hartsock).

third surgeon interviewed was Dr. Anthony Andrews, who is a retina/vitreous surgeon. Dr. Andrews has also treated a boxer suffering from a detached retina.

These three specialists described exactly what a retinal detachment is. The eye has a lining inside it called the retina that converts light to a message sent to the brain; this message allows you to see. When there is a blunt trauma to the eye it can sometimes affect this lining. Trauma can be caused by car accidents or other injuries, but boxers receive it by direct punches to the eye. Dr. Ackerman believes Harry Greb probably suffered from the most common type of tear in boxers, known as retinal dialysis.[21] When someone lands a punch to the eye it causes the eye to compress. Dr. Brower described it as "sending waves of fluid in a rush across the eye." When the glove is taken off the eye "it causes a decompression when the eye re-expands. This compression then decompression causes retinal tears."[22] Retinal tears are like cracks in the lining that seldom heal on their own. Often these cracks don't heal at all and slowly get bigger until the lining starts to peel away from the back of the eye and fluid seeps from the center of the eye through the crack. When fluid starts seeping through it causes a retinal detachment. Dr. Brower describes it to his patients in this way: "Imagine if you were applying wallpaper in your home with weak adhesive then peeled a little wallpaper back near the top. If you then poured water in between the wall and the wallpaper the wallpaper would easily peel away. This is similar to what happens in a retinal detachment." First there is a tear, also called a break, and if that doesn't heal it progresses to a detachment.

Surgery can now be done to reattach the lining and fix the detachment. Sugar Ray Leonard took advantage of these new procedures and was able to fix his eye, enabling him to box again. Retinal breaks which cause a retinal detachment were first understood and successfully treated by surgery in 1929 by a research surgeon name Dr. Gonin.[23] However, in 1921, when it happened to Greb, there was nothing any doctor could do. Dr. Ackerman described the situation as "helpless." When someone like Greb went to a hospital he was told to take some quiet time and rest his eyes. This didn't actually help prevent the detachment from progressing, but the doctors at the time thought it might; they didn't know any better. The patient was often given patches over both eyes to limit their use. This rest was supposed to help the eyes, giving them a chance to heal and repair themselves. If the rest didn't work, and it seldom did, then the patient was stuck with whatever sight he had. Nothing whatsoever could be done about it.

Dr. Ackerman, Dr. Brower, and Dr. Andrews were supplied with all the key dates and information about Harry Greb's case. All of these retinal detachment specialists made it very clear that although Greb could have suffered immediate and complete loss of sight in his right eye, he probably just suffered from a retinal tear during the Norfolk fight.

After Greb's death his condition was described as a retinal detachment. Back then a retinal tear and retinal detachment were said to be one and the same. Retinal tears are cracks and often occur in the periphery of the eye. In the 1920s a doctor was only able to see directly to the back of the eye so many retinal tears would go unnoticed until they progressed to a full detachment. When Greb's condition was described as a retinal detachment, which could easily have been a retinal tear that progressed later to a full detachment. This is what probably happened in Greb's case.

The blunt trauma of Kid Norfolk's punch to Greb's right eye in August 1921 probably caused a retinal tear (break) that would eventually progress to become a full retinal detachment. Dr. Andrews even explains, "A boxer can develop retinal tears due to blows to the head and not necessarily to the eye itself." Immediately after the Norfolk fight Greb "complained of seeing lights of many colors."[24] This is a symptom of a retinal tear (break), or of a concussion. Other than the immediate flashes of light, Greb probably experienced no other visual side effects for many days. Dr. Brower stated, "Retinal detachments often start occurring four or five days after the tear occurs. When a detachment does occur it starts in the peripheral vision." This means Greb may not have needed to go to a doctor immediately, and a doctor wouldn't have been able to see anything anyway. Dr. Andrews also agreed, stating, "He would not have gone blind immediately. Sometimes blindness can happen within several days but usually takes several weeks."[25]

So when Greb fought on September 5 against Chuck Wiggins, less than a week after the Norfolk fight, his vision may not have been impaired at all yet. A retinal tear may have been present, but no retinal detachment. Once a retinal tear is present it may take up to two weeks before the person starts to have the visual impairment associated with a retinal detachment.

Greb's next fight after Chuck Wiggins was against heavyweight Joe Cox on September 20. This would have been almost exactly two weeks after a retinal tear may have started. This bout would start Greb's string of New York fights that would last until November. If he was beginning to see symptoms of a retinal detachment around September 20, that would have given him an entire month to seek treatment.

Greb took an entire month off from fighting between the September Joe Cox fight and his next fight on October 24. His eye physician, Dr. McGivern, was based in Atlantic City, which is just a couple of hours from New York. It is very feasible that Greb started experiencing vision impairment and went to see Dr. McGivern after the September 20 Joe Cox fight. This would have given him an entire month to receive treatment, which at this time would only consist of resting the eyes by having patches over them.

In my interview with Dr. Ackerman he described what Greb might have been seeing at this point. Although he could have received sudden and complete loss of sight, he may also have been experiencing "sections of blindness, fading sight, cloudy or blurred vision." Greb could have also been experiencing "floaters," which are small floating objects you see that are really the parts of the tear and are floating inside your eye. Dr. Andrews suggests he "would have lost side vision." Any of these symptoms could have occurred in Greb and nothing would have been done about it. Over time they could have healed, stayed the same, or progressed.

Therefore, what may have happened is that Greb received the trauma to his eye from a punch in the Kid Norfolk fight. A retinal tear occurred five days later with visual impairment starting up around two weeks after that. Once he started experiencing the visual problems, it was possibly partial blindness in different quadrants of the eye. He went to see a doctor at the end of September, then took an entire month off for treatment, in spite of which his condition gradually worsened until he was blind in his right eye.

Greb would keep this a secret from the general public for the rest of his life; he would tell only a few close friends and his family. He was sensitive about the condition and didn't want other boxers to know about it. If anyone who was boxing him knew he was blind in his right eye, they would use this to their advantage and throw more punches from that side as Greb wouldn't be able to see them coming. If the boxing commission knew he was blind they may not let him continue to box. Fortunately, Greb's unconventional style helped him to continue boxing with only one eye. If he had always used a conventional stance of standing flat-footed in front of his opponent, it would have left his right side open for punches he wouldn't have been able to avoid; luckily Greb didn't fight that way. Greb's windmill style was based on constantly moving in and out and around his opponent, which gave him the ability of not relying on stereoscopic vision as much as other fighters. He was constantly moving, which made it easy for his left eye to constantly see his opponent from different angles. This lessened the number of "blind spots" due to the loss of the right eye.

It was only after his retinal trauma in the Norfolk fight of 1921 that Greb started thumbing people in his fights and being extra rough. This was the dangerous tactic some boxers were using back then: to make an opponent back off, just thumb him in the eye. It happened to a number of boxers, then it happened to Greb, and now it seemed that he was using the tech-

Harry Greb

nique himself. Those were dangerous times for boxers. They didn't receive a lot of money by today's standards, but they were putting their lives on the line in every bout. Greb didn't let his blindness stop him or even slow him down. He continued fighting and winning by any means necessary, even if it meant using some rough tactics he had learned along the way to help compensate for his handicap.

It is believed that Greb never held any animosity toward Kid Norfolk for what happened to him in the ring. He supposedly figured that it was just one of the many risks he took when he stepped onto the field of battle. Back at the turn of the 20th century when Greb was fighting, boxing wasn't that far removed from bare-knuckle fighting, and there were deaths in the ring periodically.

Greb knew how dangerous, or even fatal, the sport of boxing could be. Just eight months before he fought Norfolk, one of Greb's previous opponents had died in the ring. The fight was between Al Roberts and Mickey Shannon. Greb had beaten heavyweight Mickey Shannon back in 1920 and would beat heavyweight Al Roberts in 1922.

Al Roberts (right) before a fight with Willie Meehan (left) in 1920. The man standing between them is unidentified. This photograph was taken a few months before Roberts' deadly bout with Mickey Shannon (Antiquities of the Prize Ring).

These two boxers met in the ring on December 7, 1920, and the fight resulted in the death of Mickey Shannon. Shannon's real name was Raymond McMullen, and he boxed out of Frostburg, Maryland, and Newark, New Jersey. Al Roberts fought out of Staten Island, New Jersey. Their bout took place in the Fourth Regiment Armory in New Jersey. Roberts knocked Shannon out in the sixth round with a solid blow to the jaw, but Shannon never regained consciousness and died in hospital the next day. Roberts was immediately arrested, taken to jail and charged with Shannon's manslaughter.[26]

Opposite: Harry Greb (Antiquities of the Prize Ring).

According to the *Chicago Daily Tribune*, "Shannon fell toward the corner of the ring and his head hit on the floor with a resounding thud. It was said by several witnesses that his head had struck an iron ring to which was fastened a support for the corner post. Others present stated that his head struck the post."[27] These were the dangers Greb was facing every time he stepped into the ring.

The charges against Al Roberts were eventually dropped when the cause of death was declared to be an intracranial hemorrhage caused by the impact to Shannon's head during the fall, not from the punch. Both the boxers' purses for the fight were given to Mickey Shannon's mother.

These were serious times and boxing was seen as a very dangerous sport. That was one of the reasons why many states didn't even allow boxing to take place, while other states didn't allow official decisions. This was the environment Greb was a part of when he was blinded. He had boxed his whole life, it was how he made a living, and it had become his identity. Everything he had received in life and achieved had come through boxing. It wasn't something he was easily going to give up doing, even with the loss of an eye.

DEATH IN KNOCKOUT ENDS RING CAREER OF POPULAR BOXER

MICKEY SHANNON.

Mickey Shannon picture from the *Pittsburgh Sun* after the fatal bout (*Pittsburgh Post-Gazette*).

8.

A CITY CELEBRATES

The year of 1922 started off with some promising events for Greb to look forward to. He was scheduled to fight Tommy Gibbons again, and this time in an officially judged bout, not just a newspaper decision. Early in January there was even discussion about his finally being able to fight for the middleweight title against Johnny Wilson. Wilson had won the middleweight title with the help of his connections with people from both sides of the law. Now that he had the title, the last thing he wanted to do was defend it against men who could beat him. Wilson knew he couldn't keep the title very long by fighting the best there was.

New York promoter Tex Rickard had set up a title fight between Wilson and Greb, to take place in February in Madison Square Garden. Both boxers signed the contracts, but when the time was getting close to actually fight, Wilson started acting like he wanted to back out. On January 2, Johnny Wilson's manager stated that Wilson was backing out of the fight.[1] The following day the New York Boxing Commission immediately suspended Wilson and his manager for repudiation of contract.[2] The ban became nationwide a couple of weeks later when sixteen more states banned the champion from boxing.[3] The whole country was witnessing the middleweight champion refusing to fight the top contender. Wilson was just a paper champion because everyone knew he wasn't the best middleweight out there; it was just a matter of time until Wilson would be forced to fight Greb. Greb was used to being ducked by now so he continued on his normal schedule. He was looking forward to his big rematch with Tommy Gibbons in March.

The fight against Gibbons was to take place on March 13 in Madison Square Garden. It was to be a fifteen-round fight with an official decision. At that time an "official" decision meant there were two judges at ringside that gave the referee the verdict to announce after the fight. If the judges disagreed, then the referee would cast a vote and be the deciding factor. However, if the judges agreed about the outcome, the referee's opinion didn't matter.

The previous fights between these two men had been newspaper decisions so this official ruling was eagerly anticipated. The winner was to be considered the top contender for the light heavyweight title. A couple of years had passed since they had last fought each other and both boxers had been on great winning streaks since then. Gibbons had knocked out a lot of men in the past two years and had also been fighting heavyweights. Many people believed that Gibbons was the favorite in this fight, but this didn't matter at all to Greb. He was very confident when he was interviewed in New York the day before the bout. He stated, "I'm not afraid. No fighter living has ever scared me. I've fought tougher men than Gibbons and they couldn't stop me, and I've fought him three times and he couldn't do it." Greb would go on to say, "This is the one chance I will have to prove to many that I really am in his class. If condition, confidence and eagerness to do my part has any bearing on the result, then I will win."[4]

As for Tommy Gibbons, he was also very confident that he would win the fight. Gibbons was scheduled to fight Dempsey if he won, so he was certainly going to give it his all. When

Gibbons was interviewed he said, "Greb's speed will not worry me. He is no better now than before when I hit him often. If I hit him as often tomorrow as I did in the rain the last time we met, he'll go out in the first round. That is my intention, to end it as soon as possible." Gibbons thought he would be able to knock Greb out, and do it early in the fifteen-round fight. Gibbons would go on to say, "And once my right connects Mr. Greb will be removed from my path. Still I look for a hard fight, a fast fight, and one where the punch will have more concern than the speed. This, weighing heavily in my favor, almost makes me believe that the fight will not go more than six rounds."[5]

On March 13 Greb was a 2½ to 1 underdog, while 13,400 boxing fans filled Madison Square Garden for the fight. What these fans didn't know was that Greb was not only the underdog, was not only outweighed 171 to 163, but was also going to fight with a damaged right eye. By this time Greb's eyesight problems would have progressed to such an extent that he would only have partial vision in his right eye. His vision would have been cloudy, blurry or completely gone in quadrants of the eye. Greb was probably better at hiding it now and dealing with this handicap in the ring, but the fact that his sight was diminishing would only add to the huge task he had in front of him. He was going into the ring against a man who outweighed him, had a knockout punch, was taller and was able to see perfectly out of both eyes. Even with all this stacked up against him, Greb stepped into the ring fearless and confident.

The fight was a highly anticipated event with many notables in attendance, including opera stars and movie stars. It was even sponsored by Mrs. William Randolph Hearst. Boxers Jack Dempsey, Benny Leonard, and Johnny Dundee were also in attendance, rubbing shoulders with taxicab drivers, bootleggers, and ordinary fight fans in what has been worked up as the greatest fistic argument since the "Battle of the Century."[6] Everyone was waiting to see if Harry Greb had what it took to accomplish his greatest career achievement up to this point.

Greb's wife Mildred was also in attendance, seated in the tenth row. Their three-year-old daughter, Dorothy, was probably being watched by Greb's mother, Annie, and two of his sisters, Ida and Catherine, who had all traveled to New York for the fight. His immediate family members were among just a handful of people who knew of Greb's blindness so they must have been on the edge of their seats to find out if Greb could accomplish this unprecedented feat while handicapped.

Before Greb left the dressing room that night he had a visitor who thought he could use a little luck. The visitor was Brooklyn Fire Department Captain Frank Sample. Captain Sample had just returned from Ireland a few weeks before and presented Greb with a fresh shamrock. Captain Sample told Greb, "These are the luckiest things in the world and my wife says that in view of the fact that I couldn't be stopped from taking a slice of that two-to-one-stuff, I had better ask you to wear this in your right mitt."[7] Greb figured he shouldn't turn down a lucky shamrock; after all, he had grown up in Garfield, which was an Irish neighborhood, so he knew the shamrock's symbolic significance. Greb placed it carefully in his glove, and now he was ready to enter the ring.

The first round started fast with Greb forcing the fight. Throughout the round there were exchanges while Greb was taking the fight to Gibbons. Greb was jabbing and landing power punches with his left.[8]

In the second round Gibbons was much more effective and landed some good right-hand punches to Greb's body. By the third round Greb started to be more elusive. He landed a left and right punch, but when Gibbons attempted to retaliate he only found air with two right-hand swings. Then Greb landed another one-two punch with a left then a right. Gibbons tried to respond with a left and right of his own, but they missed their target again; Greb had quickly slipped away. Then Greb landed two lefts to Gibbons's body and finished the round with a final left at the bell. Greb's speed was starting to be effective and Gibbons was only finding air with a lot of empty swings.

In the fourth round Greb started to be a little more aggressive on the inside. It was written that Greb had Gibbons "off balance" for the majority of the round. Greb was moving around frequently and would measure the distance to his opponent by using his left. When the fifth round began Greb landed a big right punch to Gibbons's jaw. When they clinched afterwards Greb landed two more rights, this time to his opponent's ear. Greb later hooked a couple of punches to Gibbons's ear before landing another left to the jaw. Gibbons landed a right uppercut to Greb's chest, and Greb returned with a right to the ear. Greb continued to land some good lefts all over Gibbons's head while Gibbons landed some lefts of his own, but not as frequently.

Greb started the sixth round with a hard right to his opponent's jaw. There were some exchanges and clinching in the middle of the round, but by the end of the sixth Gibbons was missing with lefts and rights while Greb was able to land his punches with ease. Greb was

Harry Greb and Tommy Gibbons (right) before their bout in 1922. Referee Kid McPartland is in the middle (collection of Pugilistica. com).

stepping in and landing punches, then quickly stepping out of the way and making Gibbons miss.

By the seventh round it was clear that Greb was landing his punches effectively, but they didn't contain a knockout punch. Greb then "feinted Gibbons into an opening" which allowed Greb to land a few lefts to Gibbons's mouth. Then Gibbons hooked a powerful left to Greb's head. There was a lot of infighting in this round that Greb was said to have gotten the better of. Greb was able to throw a great right punch to the chin which made Gibbons "wince." Gibbons returned with a left to the stomach and a right to the jaw to end the round.

In the eighth round Greb was able to "stagger Gibbons with two lefts to the chin." This made Gibbons throw wild punches again, missing with most of them. Then Greb landed a straight right onto Gibbons's mouth "which sent Tom back on his heels." He was hurt and had to clinch to survive. Greb was "fighting fiercely" and continued to force the fight on his opponent. Greb was throwing right-hand punches and left-hand punches while "Gibbons is bewildered and can't get over an effective blow." This continued through the tenth round while Gibbons was trying to land a "haymaker," but Greb was just too elusive. By this time in the fight it was noticed that Gibbons was "bleeding from the mouth and eyes."

In the eleventh round Gibbons landed some powerful punches. During this round Gibbons was "the stronger of the two." Greb was seen to have slowed down due to the pace he had set in the fight up to this point. In the twelfth round Greb had recovered his wind while the two exchanged a lot of punches. By round thirteen the "Pittsburgh Windmill" was swinging in full force while he "made Tom look slow at the bell."

The *New York Times* described the last half of the fourteenth round:

> Greb danced away from a hard left and drove home a left to the stomach. Greb landed a left to the jaw. They rushed into a clinch in a corner and Greb was short with a right swing for Gibbons' jaw. Just before the end of the round Greb landed lefts and rights lightly on Gibbons' body and jaw. The Pittsburgh boy appeared to get stronger, while Gibbons slowed up considerably as the battle neared the close.[9]

There was some clinching, but both were throwing punches when the final bell rang to end the bout.

The *New York Times* wrote: "Greb opened the final round with two rights that caused red blotches on Gibbons' body." The two fighters exchanged blows the entire round while standing "toe to toe." "They were going at it hard in Greb's corner when the bout ended."[10]

When the bell rang the fighters went to their corners to wait for the judges' verdict. It was a unanimous decision by the judges that Greb had won the fight and overwhelmed Gibbons. The *Pittsburgh Post*'s front page headlines the next day read, "Greb is victor over Gibbons," "Garfield Boxer Carries Battle To Larger Opponent," "Although Outweighed, Local Boy Dazzles Crowd With Speedy Attack; Makes St. Paul Man Look Foolish."[11]

Tommy Gibbons was only awarded two of the fifteen rounds, the second and seventh, "when Greb let Gibbons lead." At the end of the fight people rushed into the ring to congratulate Greb. The crowd "fondled Greb like a baby" while his manager, George Engel, "planted a big kiss on his brow." Gibbons knew he had lost the fight and walked over to Greb's corner and congratulated him.

Greb had set an incredible pace for the entire fight and just never let up. His speed and timing were so great that he played a nice trick on Gibbons during the fight. Greb was said to have let his hands down while he was fiddling with the belt around his waist. Greb "was plucking at his belt with both hands as if to pull up his tights." This made Gibbons think that Greb had left himself open with his hands down and occupied. Therefore, Gibbons started to throw a right-hand punch while Greb had apparently lowered his guard. This was what Greb wanted his opponent to think. "Greb had waited cunningly for just that move. Before the other fellow's blow has even started on its journey Greb is under and up with a right cross of his own."[12] Greb used this trick on Gibbons so he could land a punch of his own first; Greb's speed was just that good. Greb's hands could be down to his sides when an opponent started a punch and he could still land his punch before his opponent could hit him. After the fight Greb would say, "There are few things a fighter must have besides size, among them being aggressiveness, footwork, cleverness and courage."[13] Greb had all of these in spades.

The *Chicago Daily Tribune* would write: "For nearly the entire distance Gibbons was on the receiving end of the greatest shower of blows he had ever seen in his life." The *Tribune's* article would go on to say, "The defeat was a severe one for Gibbons who had entertained the hope of one day meeting Jack Dempsey for the championship. He blew his last chance tonight when the Pittsburgher literally picked him to pieces nearly every step of the way."[14]

After the fight Greb wrote an article for the *Pittsburgh Press* newspaper titled "Gibbons Struck Only Three Hard Blows." He described in the article how Gibbons had landed only three blows that affected him, two in the second round and one in the eleventh. He also went on to describe how and why he used his unique style:

In my bout with Tommy Gibbons I entered the ring with two definite ideas, one was to throw as many gloves as I could in the general direction of Gibbons, the other was to keep out of the way of his right hand. Gibbons is a hard puncher, I will concede that he hits harder than I do. However, he must be set to be effective. On the other hand I never set when starting a punch, often I am going away when it lands. That, of course, is the real reason why Gibbons has greater punching power. If I adopted flat-footed tactics I probably could put twice as much steam back of my blows. However, such a system would immediately rob me of one of my best assets, a nimble pair of legs. If good footwork can neutralize punching power by keeping a fighter off his balance then I am for good footwork. I believe I made it apparent that such a thing was possible by my showing against Gibbons.[15]

Gibbons was never allowed to land a big punch and clearly lost the fight. He later said he thought Greb was a "contortionist." Gibbons not only lost this fight, but also lost his chance at an upcoming bout against Jack Dempsey. When Dempsey was interviewed after the fight he said, "Greb was a busy bee and fought a most admirable contest."[16]

The newspapers were saying this victory for Greb was "the greatest pugilistic upset in recent years."

Greb and his wife were staying at the Hotel Theresa at 125th Street in New York. After the big fight he was "being swarmed with theatrical companies and newspaper syndicates asking for interviews with Greb."[17] Two theatrical companies offered Greb a contract to stage some performances. While Greb was thinking this over he had plans on returning to Pittsburgh in a few days, then taking a couple of weeks off.

While still in New York, Greb had finally chosen which theater company he would entertain with. He signed a contract with the Gayety Theater in Pittsburgh and would appear in every performance of *The Bowery Burlesquerers*. Greb's vaudeville tour would be performed at the theater every day for a week, then go on the road for ten to twelve weeks to "make the circuit of the biggest towns in the country, showing the style of attack which has made him the most talked of fighter in the country today." The highlight of his performance would consist of a "boxing stunt, just to give those who know and those who don't know a glimpse of the style which has mystified the fistic world."[18] After a boxing and gymnasium act he would also speak to the audience.

Harry, his wife Mildred, and their daughter Dorothy were all arriving back home in Pittsburgh on Monday, March 20. Not only did Greb have his vaudeville tour to look forward to, which started the day he arrived home, but a special homecoming had been scheduled for him by the city earlier in the morning. This was going to be a very busy day for Harry.

The day started as soon as Greb and his family stepped off the train at Union Station around 9:30 A.M. A welcoming party greeted him which consisted of thousands of Pittsburghers who wanted to see the underdog who had upset the famous light heavyweight Tommy Gibbons.[19]

A brass band helped welcome the Greb party off the train. Then Greb was escorted into a car to be part of a parade through the streets of Pittsburgh. A fleet of hundreds of cars took part in this victory parade which traveled from Liberty Avenue to Fifth, up Fifth to the final destination at the City Council Building, where a big reception was waiting. Thousands of Pittsburghers were cheering wildly in the streets along the route in celebration of their hero. The swarming fans then hoisted Greb onto their shoulders and carried him to the next scheduled event.

Once Greb arrived at the City Council Building he was greeted by the mayor of Pittsburgh and other dignitaries. To satisfy the cheering crowd, Greb was escorted to the 5th floor of the building, where he made a speech. He told the crowd how his fans "helped him wonderfully to perform the biggest feat of his life." He went on to promise to beat the light heavyweight champion, Gene Tunney, then the middleweight champion, Johnny Wilson, next. There was even a

Top: The happy Greb family of Harry, Dorothy and Mildred. The photograph was taken in New York right after Greb beat Tommy Gibbons. Greb and his family were staying together at the Hotel Theresa. This photograph was originally supplied by Dorothy's son, Harry Greb Wohlfarth (Greb's grandson), and by Maria Boscia (Greb's great-granddaughter) (collection of Pugilistica.com). *Bottom:* Greb's family arriving at the train station with him. From left to right are Harry's sisters Catherine and Ida, his mother Annie, his wife Mildred, Harry, and his manager George Engel (*Pittsburgh Post-Gazette*).

quartet with him who sang a few songs until the celebration ended. It took a while for the crowd to disperse while they collected in the lobbies and exits waiting to see glimpses of Greb. It was declared that this day's victory parade "was the greatest turnout ever in the history of the city."[20]

The homecoming parade ended around noon; then it was time for Greb to be swept off to his next scheduled event. He was escorted to the Gayety Theater to take part in the start of his

A crowd in the city of Pittsburgh welcoming Greb home (Antiquities of the Prize Ring).

vaudeville tour. Greb was to have two performances every day for a week, starting with this one. He began with a short speech to the crowd in the packed theater before starting the stunts of his act. The first stunt was shadow boxing, and the crowd was in awe of his speed. He followed that up with skipping rope for a while. Then came a three-round sparring exhibition. His sparring partner for this first day was Young Gotch.

After his two performances at the theater Greb's day was still not over yet. He went to the *Pittsburgh Post* building to make an international radio address. He was at the Pittsburgh Post-Westinghouse Electric radiophone to tell the story of his great victory over Tommy Gibbons. Greb also described his plans for the future to everyone listening. His speech was broadcast all over the United States and "Canada, Mexico, South America and far out to sea."[21]

Greb's big homecoming day finally ended after the radio broadcast. He would continue his theater performances twice daily in Pittsburgh for a week, and the celebrations would continue with banquets held in his honor after every night's performance. He would end the last show at around eleven P.M., then go to a banquet hall at a main dining room in a major hotel. The parties would last for hours. Each night at the Gayety Theater, Greb would spar against a different opponent. Johnny Goodwin would referee and some of Greb's lucky opponents on stage were Young Frank Gotch, Jack McFarland, Patsy Scanlon and Jack Barry.[22]

After one of the performances that week Greb was presented with a large silver cup. Inscribed on the award was the following: "Presented to Harry Greb by his Pittsburgh friends, March 24, 1922, as a tribute to his victory over Tommy Gibbons at Madison Square Garden, New York, March 13, 1922." This was an incredible week full of honors constantly bestowed upon him.

At the end of the week Greb left and traveled to Toronto to continue his theatrical tour. He was there for the tour's second week of performances, then continued traveling all over the United States for around eight more weeks. All the shows were sold out because everyone wanted to see the amazing boxer everyone was talking about.

While Greb was on his tour a picture of him was placed on the cover of a brand-new boxing magazine. Shown here is the cover of the new magazine, titled *The Ring*. It was created by president and editor Nat S. Fleischer. Greb made the cover of the April 1922 issue. The magazine that we now know as "the bible of boxing" had just started publication a couple of months earlier, and Greb made the cover of only the third issue that was ever published.

Now that Greb had soundly defeated Tommy Gibbons, who some believed was the main light heavyweight contender, this made Greb the number one contender. Light heavyweight was the next weight class below the heavyweights, and it was common practice for light heavyweights to fight against the heavyweight champion. This bout was supposed to determine who Dempsey's next opponent would be. Gibbons was expected to win, so Dempsey was making plans to fight him. Now with Greb winning the bout it should have been his opportunity to fight the heavyweight champion.

While Greb was still on his ten-week vaudeville tour people were talking again of a Dempsey-Greb boxing match. The *Oklahoman* newspaper had a headline: "Dempsey Will Give Greb Chance To Win Heavyweight Crown." Dempsey was traveling and had stopped over in Chicago on March 20, a week after Greb had beaten Gibbons. Dempsey had just stopped off for a few minutes while waiting to pick up another train when he was asked about when he would finally fight Greb. Everybody wanted a fight between the two and Dempsey simply couldn't avoid addressing the issue. Dempsey's response was:

> It is possible that I might get a match with Harry Greb, and if I do and there is a call or demand for it, I surely will take it. There is just a chance that Greb might have an idea that he can beat me. I like to have a lot of persons with good drawing power think they can beat me. It would make business for me. Just now I can't see much in sight, unless it is a European trip.[23]

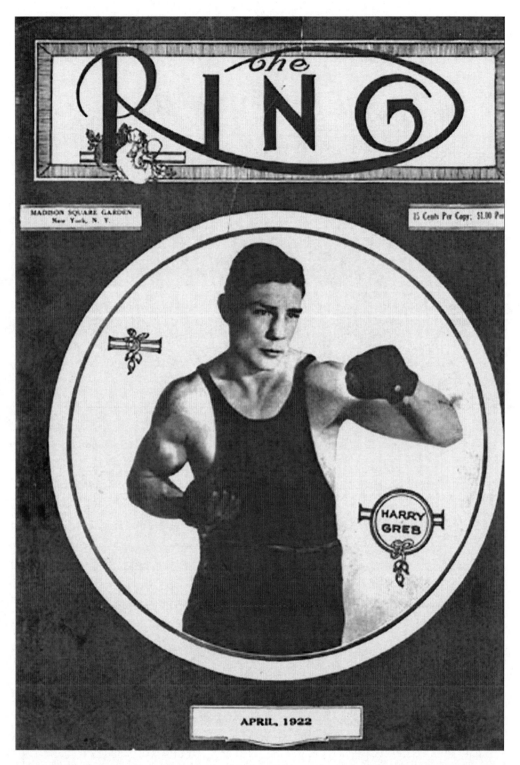

Greb on the cover of the third issue of *The Ring* magazine, April 1922. From the birth of the magazine until the year he died, Greb would always be honored with *The Ring* magazine yearly awards. In the magazine's first year of publication Greb would win "1922 Fighter of the Year" and be in the "Fight of the Year." In 1923 Greb would be in the "Upset of the Year" and win "Best Middleweight of the Year." In 1924 he would win *The Ring*'s "Fighter of the Year" again. In 1925 he was awarded another "Fight of the Year" and also won "Best Middleweight of the Year" (*The Ring*, Kappa Publishing).

A *Pittsburgh Post* cartoon, from July 23, 1922, showing the top five contenders to fight Jack Dempsey. Harry Greb is in the upper right-hand corner hanging from a missile. Also shown are Harry Wills, Georges Carpentier, Jess Willard and Bill Brennan. The *New York Daily* ran a poll asking readers to vote for who they think Dempsey should fight next for the heavyweight title. The top five candidates in the May 1 issue were Harry Wills leading the poll with 4,835 votes. Next was Bill Brennan (1,320 votes), Harry Greb in third (725 votes), Jess Willard (700 votes) and Georges Carpentier (360 votes). Other notables lower on the list were Jack Johnson (305), Gene Tunney (298), Luis Firpo (112), Tommy Gibbons (98) and Billy Miske (88) (*Pittsburgh Post-Gazette*).

A month later, on April 12, 1922, there was a *New York Times* headline: "Dempsey Will Box Greb After Tour." Dempsey's manager was stating:

> Dempsey will probably return home in time to take on Harry Greb in an eight-round, no-decision affair outdoors in Philadelphia. I am reliably told the public really wants the affair to be brought off, and we would like to see Harry make some money, even if he gets mussed up a bit in doing it, to convince him that the best middleweight isn't heavy enough for the big fellow in the game.[24]

Greb and his manager, George Engel, agreed to the eight-round fight in Philadelphia between the "Pittsburgh Windmill" and the "Manassa Mauler." Engel didn't think Greb was going to knock out Dempsey, but he was very confident that Dempsey couldn't do any damage to Greb. In a newspaper article titled "Greb Is Willing To Meet Dempsey" it was written that the eight-round bout in Philadelphia was expected to "lead up to an official decision bout of longer duration if Greb could make the champion extend himself." This was a time when Dempsey's next opponents were expected to be either Greb, Tommy Gibbons (whom Greb had just beaten), or Gene Tunney (whom Greb was about to fight). People thought Greb's speed would be too much for Dempsey. Greb wasn't expected to knock out the champion, but Greb was capable of winning more rounds with speed, activity and endurance.

In a newspaper article titled "One-Punch Fighter Cannot Beat Greb, Belief Of Expert," the way Greb would beat Dempsey was described. "Greb could slip in, out, around and under Dempsey's whistling fists in a short bout."[25]

Greb would write an article for the *Pittsburgh Press* titled "Size Not Only Asset For Champion." In the article Greb describes why Dempsey's size advantage wouldn't be a deciding factor when the two of them stepped into the ring. "A fighter doesn't need to be a giant to be a champion. Because I am shy of the six-foot mark by several inches, and don't weigh in the neighborhood of 200 pounds, I suppose a lot of people are not taking me seriously as a heavyweight contender." Greb would go on to describe various smaller men who had beaten heavyweight champions:

> When Jack Dempsey was matched to meet Jess Willard the bout was ridiculed by a lot of fight critics. Most of the fight fans thought Willard was too big for Dempsey. In the Toledo bout Dempsey, who was a little man compared to Willard, proved that size wasn't the only thing needed to be a fighter. Willard probably still remembers the lacing he took that evening. When I was matched to fight Gibbons the public viewed the bout in much the same manner as it did the Willard-Dempsey go. Gibbons, with an advantage of ten pounds in weight and four inches in height, was regarded as far too husky for me to have a chance with him. I feel that I demonstrated the folly of size being a fighter's most important asset.[26]

Greb was in his prime so this would have been a great time for him to fight Dempsey. Unfortunately, Dempsey didn't want to sign for the fight, he decided to fight the man Greb had just beaten, Tommy Gibbons. We can only speculate what the outcome would have been in a Greb-Dempsey bout. Greb had wanted this fight for so many years that he would have been in top physical and mental condition. The bout probably would have been filmed and we would have all seen the "Pittsburgh Windmill" in his prime. After being denied the match-up, Greb finished his lengthy ten-week vaudeville tour. It was then time to return to the ring and battle Gene Tunney for the American Light Heavyweight Championship.

9.

ALL GOOD THINGS

Now that Greb had soundly defeated light heavyweight Tommy Gibbons, the country wanted to see him fight for the American Light Heavyweight Title against Gene Tunney. The fight was set for May 23, 1922, in New York. Tunney was known as the "Fighting Marine" because of his service during the war. Tunney was undefeated and had claimed the American Light Heavyweight Title by beating Battling Levinsky in January of the previous year. Greb had beaten Levinsky six times. Even after Greb was signed to fight Tunney he was looking past him and trying to sign a fight against World Light Heavyweight Champion Georges Carpentier. Everyone expected Greb to beat Tunney because of Tunney's lack of experience. The betting odds for the fight made Greb the 3–1 favorite. The bookies had learned their lesson, and weren't going to make the mistake of underestimating Greb, as they had with the Gibbons fight.

A few days before the fight Harry's wife Mildred wasn't feeling well so she went to see a doctor. The doctor said she shouldn't travel to New York for the fight and suggested she confine herself to her home until the illness passed. Now that Greb was in the spotlight it meant she was in the spotlight too. This in turn meant everyone wanted to know what she was doing for the fight and what her reactions would be. Mildred had traveled to many of Greb's biggest fights in the past and had watched them from the audience, so they were concerned when she wasn't going to see her husband box.[1]

Someone had the idea that this would make a good publicity opportunity so a Post-Westinghouse radiophone was brought to her. A radiophone receiver was installed in the Greb home a few days before the bout so she could hear the fight blow for blow.

Mildred listened on the radio as her husband was about to enter the ring. If Greb won this bout, it would be the first time he had become a championship titleholder. As a light heavyweight champion he would have the power to choose most any fight he wanted against any fighter in any weight class. He couldn't get the middleweight champion to fight him for the title, but if he became light heavyweight champion, things would have to change.

The momentum was building in his career and his years of hard work were finally starting to pay off. However, to keep this momentum going he would have to win. The partial blindness in his right eye didn't seem to have affected his performance in the Gibbons fight so he must have gone into this fight against Tunney very confident that his secret handicap wouldn't stop him this time either. Greb would just have to keep on moving so he wouldn't get hit with punches he didn't see coming, keep on moving so he could see his opponent better and fight a little rougher on the inside to compensate for his partial blindness.

Greb was fighting a boxer with only fifty-three fights under his belt over an eight-year period. Greb had fought almost that many bouts in a single year (1919). People were expecting Greb's experience to be one of the deciding factors in the fight; the odds, with Greb as the 3–1 favorite, made that clear. Tunney wasn't affected by the odds, though; after all, he was almost thirteen pounds heavier than Greb, had a height advantage and even had a longer reach. Tunney

MRS. GREB "HEARS" FIGHT

Mildred Greb listens to the first Greb-Tunney fight. The radio was specially installed in their home because of her illness (*Pittsburgh Post-Gazette*).

was the titleholder with youth and all the physical advantages on his side. People were betting that Greb's experience, speed, endurance and aggressiveness would overcome all of Tunney's physical advantages.

Tunney had been preparing for this fight at a dairy farm in Red Bank, New Jersey, which had been made into his training camp. The idea was that he would find sparring partners who had styles similar to Greb's. This way he could learn how to properly combat Greb in the ring. Tunney's camp soon realized there was no boxer on earth that possessed Greb's unique talents. If they had, they wouldn't be sparring partners, they would be champions. The heavyweight

Pictured here is the second Madison Square Garden, located at Madison and Fifth Avenues, from 23rd to 26th Streets. It contained seating for 8,000 people with standing room for thousands more. It was said there were 13,000 packed in for the Greb-Tunney fight. It was eventually torn down in 1925, after Greb fought many of his greatest fights there (*Pittsburgh Post-Gazette*).

champion, Jack Dempsey, gave some tips to Tunney on how to deal with Greb in the ring. Dempsey was interviewed by sportswriter Hype Igoe before this big title match and referred back to his exhausting and bloody sparring matches against Greb a couple of years earlier. Dempsey said, "Funniest hitter in the world. He makes you think you're in a glove factory and shelves of them are tumbling down on you. He can slap you to death, I tell you. I found that the best way to get him was at close quarters. Getting close to him, however, isn't the easiest thing in the world."[2]

The fifteen-round American Light Heavyweight Title bout took place on May 23, 1922, with Kid McPartland as the third man in the ring. McPartland was a former boxer and had refereed many championship bouts, but he was about to witness a clash that he would never forget. When the bell rang to start round one Greb immediately pounced. He treated this fight the same as any other, rushing his opponent while swinging and never letting up. Greb started by lunging at Tunney while landing a right to his jaw. Then Greb landed a powerful left hook directly onto Tunney's nose, instantly drawing blood. It was only seconds into the fight and Greb already had Tunney bleeding. The punch was said to have broken Tunney's nose in two places, and the blood would continue to pour for the rest of the contest. Greb kept on easily going in and out of his opponent's defense. Tunney threw uppercuts and punches to Greb's body while Greb was swarming in. Tunney's defense was no match for Greb's offense as Greb easily traveled in and out of Tunney's longer reach. Nothing was stopping Greb, who continued to aim for Tunney's face with rights and lefts while circling his wounded prey. When the round ended the combatants were in a clinch on the ropes with "splattered" blood from Tunney's broken nose on both of them.[3]

In between rounds Tunney's corner was "inserting a heavy dose of adrenalin chloride into Tunney's broken and bleeding nose" to help stop the pain and the blood.[4] Gene Tunney later described the situation in his autobiography *A Man Must Fight*. Tunney wrote, "Doc Bagley, who was my chief second, made futile attempts to congeal the nose-bleeding by pouring adrenalin into his hand and having me snuff it up my nose. This I did round after round."[5]

The bell rang to start the second round and Greb landed two quick left jabs to Tunney's face, which just made his nose continue to flow. Greb landed another left to the face and when they clinched Tunney was able to land a left and right to Greb's body. Greb returned these blows with a barrage of punches to the face and body. Tunney could do nothing against Greb's onslaught but hold on in a clinch so as to weather the storm. Tunney was finally able to respond with some lefts to the stomach. When the bell rang both fighters were again against the ropes.

At the start of the third round Tunney was able to duck under Greb's lead punch and counter with a left to the stomach. Greb replied with a left jab to Tunney's face. They exchanged punches on the ropes and Tunney was almost "forced out of the ring" while Greb continued to throw rights and lefts to his face. Tunney then ducked under one of Greb's right swings and threw a right hook of his own which landed again in Greb's stomach. It was clear that Tunney was taking Dempsey's advice and trying to aim for the body. When Tunney tried to throw punches to Greb's face, the swings ended up short because Greb was able to quickly maneuver away from them.

When the fourth round began Greb landed a solid left to the face. When they clinched afterwards, referee Kid McPartland tried to break it up; McPartland was also now covered with Tunney's blood.[6] Greb couldn't stop throwing punches and was warned by the referee for hitting on the break. Tunney was able to land a nice left jab which "sent Greb's head back" and then threw a right to Greb's stomach. Greb returned this with a right and left to the face. Tunney landed another body punch and the two warriors were exchanging some good punches when the bell rang to end the round.

The fifth round began with Tunney beating Greb to the punch and landing a right to his chest. Greb threw a left jab and swung a right punch to the face, but they missed their intended

HarryGreb vs Gene Tunney
Old Madison Sq Garden ~ Referee Kid McPartland

Greb and Tunney (right) in the ring before their first fight. Referee Kid McPartland is shown in the center (Antiquities of the Prize Ring).

target. Then Greb successfully landed a left and right to Tunney's face. This was followed by Greb's accidentally slipping on the canvas and losing his footing. He shot up in an instant, and everyone saw that the fall hadn't been caused by any action of his opponent. Tunney then landed a right to the stomach and face. Greb returned this with "three lefts to the face in quick succession." Tunney then drove Greb to the ropes and landed some good body punches. Nat Fleischer would write: "Tunney began to show improvement in the fifth, which was the first even round."[7]

The sixth round began and it was to be another important round for Greb. He started so quickly that he met Tunney near his corner. Tunney didn't even have time to get to the center of the ring. Greb quickly began the round by landing a solid left to Tunney's face. Then Greb's "wild attack" continued with both fighters almost landing outside the ropes. After this exchange "their heads came together and an old cut was opened near Tunney's left eye." Blood started gushing from the wound. Tunney had received a cut over his left eyebrow two weeks earlier. Tunney's camp were hoping it wouldn't be a problem and had injected adrenalin chloride into the left eyebrow before the fight in the dressing room. It was even said that Tunney received injections of Novocain into both of his knuckles to help him in the fight. Nevertheless, nothing could prepare Tunney for what the "King of the Alley Fighters" had in store for him.[8]

Greb's constant assault from all angles landed on every inch of Tunney and revealed all the weaknesses that Tunney had. Tunney's broken nose and the gash over his left eyebrow were both spewing blood everywhere, covering both fighters and the referee. Greb then "tore in furiously, leading with lefts and rights to the stomach." Tunney returned with the same body attack while they both again ended the round against the ropes. When the bell sounded, McPartland's once lily-white shirt and pants were soaked and red with Tunney's blood. It truly was a bloodbath and was starting to become difficult to watch for even the most hardened of fight fans. Nat Fleischer wrote, "Greb took the sixth by five punches to one."[9]

The carnage continued in the seventh and eighth rounds with Greb opening Tunney's cut over his left eye even more. Greb was also warned again for hitting on the break. Sometime in the eighth round Greb threw a left and right to Tunney's face which created an additional wound over Tunney's right eye. This new gash was so deep that it actually severed a vein. By this time in the fight the flesh over his left eye "was sliced to the bone" and his right eyebrow was now a geyser. Tunney was still bleeding from his nose as well. Nat Fleischer recalls, "All of Tunney's attempts to reach Greb's jaw were futile. The challenger always had flitted out of range by the time Tunney got a jab or hook started to the face. In the eighth, Greb was a marvel of speed."

At the start of the ninth round Greb drove his opponent to the ropes with a hard left hook. Greb then landed another left hook to the face. Tunney was able to land a left hook to the body, but Greb answered it with a left jab to Tunney's crimson mug. By the end of the round the canvas was covered with the blood flowing from Tunney's eyes, nose and even his mouth. Referee McPartland had never witnessed such a slaughter in any fight he had participated in as a fighter or referee. McPartland was constantly separating the two fighters to wipe the blood off their gloves. It was said he went through half a dozen towels to wipe the blood off Greb's gloves during the carnage. The bell finally rang to end the ninth round, and some fans in the crowd were beginning to yell for the fight to stop. However, this was a title bout and that simply was not going to happen. Greb's wife Mildred, who was at home listening to this battle, must have had no idea how gruesome it was getting in the ring. It was probably a good thing she wasn't at ringside for this fight because Greb was relentlessly butchering Tunney like he was a slab of raw meat.

The fight continued at a terrific pace while the "Fighting Marine" was barely able to stay on his feet. Throughout the fight, "Greb's speed seemed to increase and his bombardment became more furious."[10] When the twelfth round started Tunney swung a left hook that missed, then he threw another which landed on Greb's stomach. Greb responded with a left hook to the jaw and two unanswered left jabs to Tunney's face. As in a usual Greb fight, Harry was getting faster in the later rounds while his opponent was gradually being worn down. With a surge of energy Greb unleashed a torrent of punches. This "spirited rally" continued with Greb outpunching Tunney. As the round ended Tunney was able to land some blows to the body when he was at close range.

When Tunney made it to his corner in between rounds he was met by his manager and second, Doc Bagley. The adrenalin that Tunney had been receiving to help stop the bleeding had run out a few rounds before so Tunney's corner was searching for other things to use just to help him make it through the fight. In the corner after the twelfth Doc Bagley gave Tunney a special concoction of his own making. It was a mixture of brandy and orange juice. Tunney took a big swig of this to help him finish the fight.[11] The drink was meant to help strengthen Tunney, who had become weak from blood loss.[12]

With three more rounds to go, the bell rang to start the thirteenth. The fighters continued to battle with Tunney focusing on the stomach and Greb throwing punches everywhere with his ruby-soaked leather. Just as the crowd was wondering when Tunney's corner was going to throw in the towel, a straw hat "came sailing into the ring" from somewhere in the audience. It wasn't from Tunney's corner so Greb answered this distraction by driving a right to Tunney's face, which ended the round.

Throughout the fourteenth round Greb continued his relentless attack. He slipped once on the now slippery canvas, but it wasn't from a punch so he sprung right back up. When the fifteenth and final round began, both fighters met in the middle of the ring and shook hands. This was the common practice back then when starting the final round of a boxing match. Afterwards Greb landed a left and right to the face. Tunney responded with a right to Greb's face. Greb was still full of energy, as he usually was, and landed another quick one-two punch to the head. Both fighters landed blows "at long range."

With the final seconds of the fight approaching, Greb didn't want to leave anything to chance. Tunney was the titleholder and it was Greb's job to convince the judges that he had successfully taken the title from him. So Greb dug deep and capitalized on his conditioning and training to end the fight with complete domination. Greb started showering his victim with lefts and rights while driving Tunney to the ropes. Tunney could do nothing but back up and take it. As the bell rang the last blow of the fight was Greb landing a jab to Tunney's blood-soaked face. It was later discovered that Tunney had lost almost two quarts of blood during the fight.[13]

Greb and Tunney met in the center of the ring before Greb was announced the new champion. Minutes before the announcement was made Tunney went to Greb and said to him, "Harry, you're the winner tonight, Congratulations."[14] Greb responded, "Won the championship."[15] Tunney had entered the ring an unbeaten champion and was now realizing what it was like doing battle with the "Pittsburgh Wildcat."

Joe Humphries pointed to Greb in his corner and announced him the new American Light Heavyweight Champion.[16] When the verdict was announced Greb's corner hoisted him onto their shoulders in wild celebration. Greb won almost every single round, only three rounds going to Tunney. Not only did Greb become a champion, he had to do it by bypassing the middleweight division. Johnny Wilson, the middleweight titleholder, still refused to fight him, so Greb had traveled up to the heavier division to win a title that way. Tex Rickard had said of Greb, "If there ever was a champion there is one, and as I have helped him to this chance, I stand willing to give him a crack at the middleweight championship if I can get Wilson in the ring with him."

Greb had done what no other man could do: he had beaten Gene Tunney and done it decisively. Proven yet again was the fact that Greb could beat anyone, even if his opponent possessed every physical advantage over him, including two good eyes.

It took a very long time for Tunney to properly recover from the brutal beating he was forced to endure. After his recovery Tunney said of that night, "He was never in one spot for more than half a second." He went on to say, "All my punches were aimed and timed properly but they always wound up hitting empty air. He'd jump in and out, slamming me with a left and whirling me around with his right or the other way around." Tunney finally summed up his exercise in futility this way: "My arms were plastered with leather and although I jabbed, hooked and crossed, it was like fighting an octopus."[17]

After nine long years, hundreds of fights and only one good eye, Greb had finally won a title. His speed and endurance mixed with almost a decade of experience and a will to win had finally paid off. He had taken the title away from a man younger, taller, heavier and with a longer reach. It was a time to celebrate and that was just what he did. While Tunney was bedridden from the beating he had received, Greb went out on the town to celebrate his championship victory.

Greb had cleaned up in the dressing room and was met by many Pittsburgh fans who had traveled by train to cheer him on. These Pittsburgh fans filled the trains to travel to Greb's out-of-town fights. A train filled with Pittsburgh fans on their way to his fights was nicknamed a "Greb Special" or "The Iron City Express." A good friend of Greb's, Happy Albacker, would many years later tell a story of what happened after Greb won the championship.

The story goes that someone was congratulating Greb on his impressive victory by yelling, "He gave the big ape twelve pounds, and murdered him! He spotted him half a foot of height!" Then Albacker chimed in, "Weight, height, hell! He spotted him one eye!" Greb was said to have turned and told Happy Albacker to "Shut Up. What the hell are you talking about?" Albacker quickly recovered by replying, "I was just kidding." Albacker had almost let the cat out of the bag by divulging the secret of Greb's one good eye. Luckily nobody knew what he was talking about and immediately overlooked the comment. It saved his friendship with Greb and kept the secret hidden for many more years. Whether this little anecdote is true or not is unknown, but we will have to take Albacker's word for it; he told this story when he was interviewed over twenty years later.[18]

Once Greb left the dressing room he was escorted by a bunch of friends to different speakeasies to drink and dance into the wee hours. Greb loved dancing outside of the ring as much as he did in it. His leg strength and endurance never ceased. Although he usually danced with Mildred, she wasn't there that night so he celebrated his victory without her. While his friends were drinking beer and mixed drinks, Greb usually ordered ginger ale. However, this was a special night, so it is assumed he had a drink or two to celebrate his life's ambition: first title win.

He had finally won a championship, and it was the weight class between the middleweights and the heavyweights. No one would have excuses not to fight him now. Good things continued to unfold for Greb, and he had earned them. After the night's celebration he took the train back to Pittsburgh to go home to his wife.

Mildred's illness wasn't going away, and shortly after Greb arrived home she went to her doctor again. Mildred was diagnosed with tuberculosis. TB was also known as consumption because it attacked the lungs and seemed to "consume" people from within. The symptoms were fever, a bloody cough, constant fatigue and "a long relentless wasting." Mildred was probably suffering from chest pains, a prolonged cough, fever, chills and weight loss. This can be seen in photos of Mildred that were taken during her illness. Mildred's doctor was probably who suggested she go to New York's Saranac Lake to help her condition and that was just what she did.

Back in 1922 there wasn't much treatment for someone with tuberculosis. The vaccine was first tested on a human patient in France in 1921, but didn't start seeing widespread use until decades later in the 1940s, after World War II. The people who were infected with TB in 1922 were encouraged to go to spas or "sanatoriums." These were available to the middle and upper classes and were said to have "excellent and constant medical attention." The only benefits were fresh air and rest. A person entering a spa, as Mildred did, had just a 50 percent chance of surviving. The other 50 percent would die within five years.[19]

Saranac Lake was one of the premiere places to treat tuberculosis at the turn of the century because of its fresh air and serenity. Back in 1884 Dr. Trudeau founded the first sanitarium in Saranac Lake, where people stayed and were treated in "cure cottages." By the time Mildred arrived in 1922 the facility was as big as a town and had its own post office. Unfortunately, the time for TB to be cured by antibiotics was decades away. Mildred's chance of survival was a flip of a coin and Greb knew it.

This was the news that greeted him soon after arriving home after his victory. The year had started off great, but had suddenly taken a drastic turn for the worse. Not only was he losing sight in his right eye, but now he may be losing his beloved wife and mother to his child.

Later in the year, while Mildred was still at Saranac Lake trying to battle her illness, Greb fought Captain Bob Roper in New York. The official decision bout was scheduled for twelve rounds and took place on November 10, 1922. The two men had fought four times before with Greb dominating in each one; this fight was no exception. When Bob Roper entered the ring and shook Greb's hand before the fight, Roper was wearing a live snake around his neck, which kept Greb at a slight distance when shaking hands. It was written that Roper "should have worn it all during the fight as it would have helped him a lot."[20]

This was a tough fight with a lot of clinching, holding, and "mugging." At the end of the second round the two fighters even continued to fight after the bell rang until the referee had to break them apart. In the third round Greb opened "a cut over Bob's eye." In the fifth round Roper continued to clinch and fight on the inside until Greb knocked him outside the ropes. Roper was such a dirty fighter that when Greb leaned over with a hand to help Roper back into the ring, Roper "let fly two punches at Greb."[21] Neither came close to landing, but Greb now knew Roper would do anything during the brawl. Roper was probably upset about the cut eye and wanted some revenge.

The next few rounds continued to be all Greb with his opponent noticeably tiring. By the tenth round Roper got some of his strength back and made a last-ditch effort to inflict some pain on Greb. The *Pittsburgh Post* would write: "In the tenth Roper came to life and

Harry and Mildred in their home. This picture shows how drained of energy she had become from her illness (Antiquities of the Prize Ring).

Sarnac Lake Village in 1899

A Saranac Lake postcard showing the tuberculosis treatment facility. This sanitarium grew to be the size of a town and had its own postal code (from the Jon Kopp collection "My Adirondacks" at http://www.tupperlake.net).

rushed Greb to the ropes, where he mugged him until the referee parted them and warned Roper."[22] Mugging is a dirty technique whereby a fighter opens his glove and rubs its palm all over the opponent's face. The glove's laces scrape the face while the fighter also applies pressure with his thumb.

By the time the twelfth round ended it was clear Greb had won the fight easily. Roper was clinching and mugging Greb on the inside the whole fight. Roper's mugging of Greb through the entire fight was not described in the newspapers, though they noted that Roper "was booed from the start to finish by the packed house."[23]

Greb had won the fight, but may have lost something much more important during the bout. Many believe it was during this fight that Greb completely lost the sight in his right eye. Unlike after the Kid Norfolk fight, when Greb didn't immediately go to a doctor, he was immediately seen with patches over both his eyes days after this fight. When Roper was mugging Greb at close range it is believed he may have thumbed Greb's eye, which may have worsened Greb's retinal tear and caused a full retinal detachment. This would still agree with the statement after Greb's death by his eye physician, who stated his retinal detachment occurred from a punch in the Norfolk fight. Back in the 1920s retinal tears and retinal detachments were viewed as one and the same. His physician would have viewed it as simply the progression of the same ailment.

Greb usually fought every week, but he had to take an unprecedented two months off after this fight against Roper. On November 25 the *Washington Post* wrote, "Harry Greb, the Pittsburgh flash, came to town with patches over two sore eyes, but full of fight."[24]

As stated previously, I interviewed three retinal detachment specialists, Dr. Ackerman, Dr. Brower and Dr. Andrews, about Greb's situation. During my interview with Dr. Ackerman he describes the treatment: "Bi-lateral patches were placed over the eyes to help them rest. Some bed rest may have been given also because they didn't know how to treat detachment back then." I asked Dr. Brower why they would cover both eyes if only one was injured and he replied, "The doctors would want to keep the eyes immobile. Because both eyes move together you need to patch both." Dr. Andrews explained, "Bed rest with bilateral patching would also be used and would stop a retinal detachment in about 10 percent of cases."[25]

The *Washington Post* made it very clear on December 2 that Greb's eyes were "injured in a recent bout with Bob Roper." The papers were also being given a cover story so they wouldn't know how serious the injury was. The newspapers were being told that Greb had patches over both eyes because they were "infected with a cold."[26]

On December 2 there was an article entitled "Greb Enters West Penn Hospital For Treatment." It states how Greb's eyes were injured in the Roper fight and that Greb checked into the West Penn Hospital on December 1. He was being looked at in Pittsburgh by a Dr. D.J. Lerch.[27] Greb stayed in the hospital, where he received bed rest, for a full week. Greb finally checked out of the hospital, where he was "having his eyes treated and enjoyed a general rest, on December 7."[28]

When the doctors finally took the patches off Greb's eyes it didn't matter how bad the right eye was, the doctors couldn't do anything else about it. Whatever his condition was at this point was what Greb was stuck with. Dr Ackerman mentions, "Because no treatment was available they could have determined there was nothing to do and sent him on." Dr. Andrews states, "It

appears that the patching failed. I highly suspect that he had a detachment in November 1922." Greb was probably fully blind in the right eye at this point or it progressed to full blindness soon after.

Greb took it easy for a few weeks and continued to take time off from fighting. On December 19 a newspaper continued to talk about Greb's cancellation of fights. The papers also mentioned that he went in to the hospital again for further treatment. "This afternoon the doctors treating his ailing lamp will render a verdict as to whether the light heavyweight champion can take to the ring again and on their decision rests the battle. His eye was cut in a recent fight with Bob Roper."[29]

Greb was in the hospital bedridden for a week with patches over both eyes, not knowing if he would be permanently

"Captain" Bob Roper, whose real name was William E. Hammond, had a knockout punch. He fought great heavyweights including Jack Johnson in 1919. Roper, known as a rough fighter, was disqualified in at least six fights during his career and some ended in riots (Antiquities of the Prize Ring).

sightless or not. Then he was told there was nothing the doctors could do for him, so he was released. His wife was away with tuberculosis and he now found out that he was completely sightless in his right eye. Greb was still champion, but he hadn't been able to celebrate for long.

While Greb was trying to deal with his blindness, there were rumors spreading about a possible split between him and his manager, George Engel. On November 14, when Greb was in New York, there was a newspaper headline that read, "Greb-Engel Split, Rumor In Gotham." Engel had been Greb's manager for less than two years so this was a surprise to everybody. No one knew where this rumor started or whether there was any truth to it. When Engel was interviewed about it he said, "I would like to lay hands on the scoundrel who is responsible for such a senseless tale." Engel would go on to say, "There is not a word of truth to it."[30]

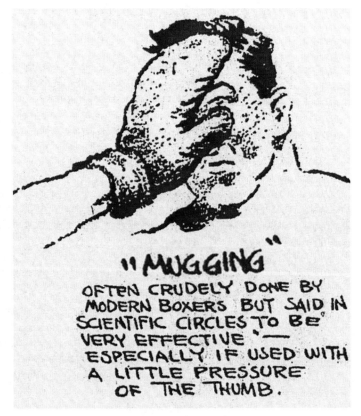

This is an illustration of what boxing circles referred to as "mugging." Bob Roper often inflicted this illegal technique upon his opponents. The crowd usually responded with boos and yells (*Pittsburgh Post-Gazette*).

The following day, on November 15, the basis of the rumor was discovered. It was found out that Greb's contract with George Engel was about to expire very shortly. Because a new contract had not been signed, it was believed Greb might have wanted to break with his manager.[31]

The rumor was soon to be well founded when Greb confirmed that he didn't wish to renew his contract with Engel. The exact reason was never exactly stated; Greb simply said, "I'd like to do my own business for a while, but in time will take on another handler."[32]

Now completely blind in one eye and without a manager, Greb set his sights on revenge against Bob Roper. After a two-month absence from the boxing ring, Greb's next bout was on January 1 of 1923 against the man who had blinded him. Greb fought Roper the first day of 1923 at Motor Square Garden in Pittsburgh.

"Captain" Bob Roper entered the ring weighing 188 pounds, well over twenty pounds heavier than light heavyweight champion Harry Greb. It was a "rough and tumble go from start to finish." Roper wasted no time continuing the dirty tactics he had inflicted on Greb in their last fight:

> Certainly there was anything but good feeling between the two, with Roper rubbing Greb's injured eye — the one Roper cut in Buffalo recently — with his glove at every opportunity, bending Greb over the ropes at times until it seemed Harry's spine would snap, and sticking his thumb in the champion's eyes every now and again.[33]

In the second round, Roper "started his roughhouse stuff by using the heel of his glove to massage Greb's face and injured eye. Henninger [the referee] fought hard to separate them and the crowd 'booed' as the round ended."[34]

Greb was winning the fight, but that wasn't stopping Roper from continuing his dirty tactics. At times Roper would not only roughhouse Greb, but would manhandle the referee, Yock Henninger. Roper would then punch Greb after the bell in both the ninth and tenth rounds. In the final round Roper cut Greb's eyebrow and it bled down his face. After the fight Roper had to be accompanied by police to his dressing room because the crowd was about to attack him for such a terrible display of dirty tactics. Greb was finally declared the winner once the brawl had finished, but not without some consequences.[35]

As soon as the day after the fight, both Roper and Greb were suspended by the boxing commission until they "could explain why the rules of the organization were disregarded in the bout."[36] When Greb finally met with the commission he "insisted that his actions, generally, were governed only by the conduct of his opponent, who undoubtedly called into play more foul tactics than local fight fans have witnessed in any bout hereabouts in a long time." Greb's meeting with commission chairman G.M. Sixsmith was well received and he was reinstated on January 8.[37]

Around this time *Ring* magazine, in its first year of publication, announced its year-end results. The magazine's "Fighter of the Year" award was bestowed upon Greb. They also awarded Greb the "Fight of the Year" for his win over Tunney.

A week later Greb's old manager, James "Red" Mason, was seen in Greb's corner during other fights. Although no contract was officially signed yet, it was clear the two were finally getting back together. By the end of the month it was official: Red Mason was Greb's manager again.[38]

Back with his old manager, Greb was able to look to the future after a lot of recent hardship. However, the bad news would continue to pile up on Greb's plate. By the end of February, Mildred had left her spa at Saranac Lake and started living at home again. This wasn't because she was getting better, but because she was getting worse. The tuberculosis had progressed to the point where she wasn't expected to live much longer. So Greb stayed home and took care of her.[39]

Greb had previously made plans to have another bout with Tommy Gibbons, but it had to be called off on March 7 because Greb's wife "is ill and is not expected to live many days."[40] She had pneumonia as well now. Greb stayed by his wife's side for a month while her condition worsened. While taking care of Mildred and looking after his daughter, "Greb had become a good family man and remained deeply religious and attached to the Roman Catholic Church. While home that March, Greb would pray daily at St. Joseph's Church that

Harry and Mildred (Antiquities of the Prize Ring).

Harry reading a book to his three-year-old daughter Dorothy (Craig Hamilton collection, www. josportsinc.com).

Mildred would pull through."[41] It was the last bit of time they would be able to spend together. She died in her home on March 18, 1923.[42] He was left to take care of their three-year-old daughter Dorothy now, but fortunately his sister Ida and her husband would help raise her. Mildred was also survived by her mother, Mrs. Anna Reilly, and her brother, George Reilly. Harry Keck, who was a sportswriter for the *Pittsburgh Post* and a friend of Greb's, once mentioned how Greb handled the death of his wife after her long battle with tuberculosis. According to Keck, "Greb accepted the inevitable with much the same courage he always displayed in the ring."[43]

Until recently Greb's life had been going well, starting when he beat Tommy Gibbons, then won the American Light Heavyweight Championship against Gene Tunney. But then events took a turn for the worse when he lost all sight in his right eye, separated from his manager, and had now lost his beloved wife Mildred. All the good things had seemingly come to an end, but Greb would weather the storm. Some people would just stay on the canvas and stop fighting, but that wasn't in Greb's nature. He picked himself up and got ready for another round. He was a fighter in and out of the ring. Greb would persevere and continue living life to its fullest.

10.

ACHIEVING THE GOAL— THE MIDDLEWEIGHT CHAMPIONSHIP

Greb had been dreaming of becoming a world boxing champion ever since he was a kid who stood on a box in his father's basement, struck a fighting stance and proclaimed himself "world champion" to all within earshot. Being a natural middleweight made this division the one he cherished most of all. Greb had become the American Light Heavyweight Champion, but what he wanted most was the title that had eluded him, the World Middleweight title.

Everyone in the country considered him the better man compared to current champion Johnny Wilson. Greb had been the number-one challenger for the title for some time, but he had never been given an official chance. Wilson was even barred from fighting in most states because of his refusal to fight Greb for the title. Greb had had to bypass the 160-pound middleweight division and jump all the way up to the 175-pound light heavyweight division to capture that championship title.

Wilson's refusal to defend his title against Greb made the boxing board's decision that much easier. After not allowing Wilson to fight in most states, the boxing board stripped him of his title, then awarded Greb the honors of "middleweight defender." This meant Wilson was no longer recognized as the middleweight titleholder; Greb was, although the title hadn't been exchanged inside the ring. Greb was a man who knew titles were won and lost inside the ring, and he didn't much care for this honorary middleweight title. It was flattering to be recognized but Greb wanted to earn it in the ring.

This title had been held and defended by great middleweight champions such as the original Jack Dempsey, Bob Fitzsimmons, Al McCoy, Stanley Ketchel and Billy Papke. These men respected the title and defended it against the best challengers of the day. However, Wilson was a champion in name only. Once he had gained the title against Mike O'Dowd in May of 1920, Wilson had only fought four more times for the rest of that year. In the following year Wilson fought no more than seven bouts in total, defending the title three times against men Greb had already beaten. In the entire year of 1922 Wilson fought only two times, against a couple of relatively unknown boxers, while never defending the title at all. During this time period that Wilson was middleweight champion, Greb had fought over fifty times, gained the light heavyweight championship, defended that title against future Hall-of-Famers, fought the top middleweight and light heavyweight contenders and fought some heavyweights as well. If Greb had been allowed an official title match against Wilson earlier, he would have been middleweight champion for years already.

Shown here is a cartoon from a newspaper in October of 1922 making fun of middleweight "champion" Johnny Wilson. Wilson was the laughingstock of boxing and had been for a long

Johnny Wilson was often ridiculed in newspapers for not fighting the top contenders (*Pittsburgh Post-Gazette*).

time now. It was expected that Wilson would lose his title immediately if he ever defended it against the best contenders. However, the last time he signed a contract to defend the title was with Greb, and Wilson backed out of the contract when the time got close to actually stepping into the ring and fighting.

The rumor was that Wilson had the help of gangsters. They had helped get some easy opponents for Wilson, and may have rigged some questionable fights, while they were able to collect some money on the side. The last thing these "associates" of Wilson's wanted to do was lose their gravy train. Having Wilson remain champion meant easy money for them so they pressured Wilson into making some of the decisions he did. Wilson was also known for not being the most intelligent person and he didn't have any integrity, so the end result was that the middleweight championship title was being disgraced.

By May of 1923, just a couple of months after Mildred died, the famous promoter Tex Rickard was trying to set up a fight between Greb and Wilson. The title bout would possibly be scheduled for sometime in June at Madison Square Garden, if Tex Rickard could get Wilson to sign a contract. Greb was hopeful it would eventually happen, but he wasn't holding his breath. Greb continued to keep busy by training and fighting as often as he could.

In early May, Greb continued training to make sure if a fight did take place in June, he would be ready to easily make weight for it. He had been fighting a lot of light heavyweights lately and wanted to make sure he would easily make the middleweight limit and be in great condition. Around May 3 Greb was preparing for an upcoming bout against Jimmy Darcy. He made sure to train hard, not because Darcy was extremely tough, but because he was using this fight to help condition himself for a possible fight with Wilson. Greb was weighing 163 pounds while fully clothed so making weight shouldn't be a problem.

While in training for the Darcy fight Greb received a bad scratch on his right arm. He was training with sparring partners Harry Fay and Ditty Woods at the time. The scratch was on the upper part of his right arm, near the elbow; it was just a scratch, so Greb continued his strenuous and aggressive training for the bout, which was to take place in a few days.

A day or two later the scratch started progressing into something else until training had to be stopped. A physician was called into the training camp to take a look at the arm. The doctor thought the arm might have gotten infected so he insisted Greb immediately go to Mercy Hospital for a proper examination. At the hospital it was discovered that the right arm had not only got infected but Greb had got blood poisoning from it. The scratch had been aggravated by excessive use. Greb was soon losing all use of his right arm and the physicians at the hospital were afraid that if they didn't do something about it soon, he might lose the use of his right arm permanently. This meant Greb would have to quit his career as a boxer. He was able to hide his blindness from people, but he wouldn't be able to hide the fact that he had no right arm.[1]

Blood poisoning was a very serious condition back then that could even lead to death. A future opponent of Greb's, Jimmy Delaney, died at the age of twenty-six due to blood poisoning. Just two years after Greb fought him, Delaney got a cut on his arm, and resin that used to be put on boxing gloves got into his blood; Delaney died just a few weeks later.

The physicians immediately lanced a large growth that had developed on Greb's arm. The day after the boil was lanced, and against physician's orders, Greb went back to Motor Square Garden, where he had been training. When he arrived the boxing commission examiner looked at his arm and officially called off the Darcy fight, which was to take place the following day, May 9. Darcy and his camp were questioning if this cancellation was all on the up and up. They wanted to look under the bandages to see for themselves if Greb wasn't trying to pull a fast one by lying about an injury. Greb duly unwrapped the arm bandages and showed everyone the infected and lanced arm.

Once Darcy took a look at the damaged arm he immediately replied, "Gee, that's more than I could do to you in a week, I guess it's all off." Greb was asked why he had waited until the last minute to tell Darcy about the infection instead of canceling the fight days ago. It was then discovered that Greb still expected to go through with the fight, but his doctor had finally refused to permit it. Greb said, "If you think I can fight, then I will, even though I'm knocked out."[2] But there was no way doctors were going to permit it. The infection had spread from his arm and reached into his chest now. There was considerable pain and the doctors at Mercy Hospital wanted Greb to stay in bed, not go running around at training camp.

He was then rushed back to the hospital and after a consultation with four physicians, it was decided Greb might be on the verge of having to permanently lose his arm. With the painful infection now reaching his chest, an immediate operation was scheduled for the next day. They kept Greb at the hospital so they could keep an eye on him and make sure he didn't scurry off again. The operation was very serious and the outcome was to determine if Greb was to stay in the fight game or be forced to stop boxing forever.

The surgery the next day was a complete success. His arm was expected to make a full recovery. A day after the operation Greb was asked how he felt, and he answered that he was "feeling pretty good."[3] He stayed in the hospital bed for a few more days, then was well enough to go back to his home and finish recovering there. It was a close call, but he got to keep his arm.

After recovering well at home during the remainder of May, the impatient Greb was itching to get back in the ring. By June he was physically ready to go back to the gym, and Mason had scheduled Greb's first fight back to be against Len Rowlands on June 16. Greb had plenty of training to do to get back into shape. Greb and Mason had decided it would be best for Greb to continue his training up at the new training camp that had recently been built for him.

The specially constructed camp was located up at Conneaut Lake. This was the same lake where Greb had vacationed with Mildred before they were married back in 1917. It was located around ninety miles north of Pittsburgh and was two hours away from any Pittsburgh distractions. Many years later boxing champion Max Schmeling would also train at Conneaut Lake. Greb's training facility was permanent and consisted of a big cottage that served as the headquarters. There was also an outdoor boxing ring and other training necessities, as well as cottages for living in.

Greb was making more money since becoming light heavyweight champion, and Mason had just recently been reunited with Greb, so they both thought it was a good idea to splurge a little and have their own place to train. They were away from the hustle and bustle of the city with all the usual distractions that came with it. Greb could get the personal attention he needed for training without other boxers around. Now Greb could do whatever he needed to do without delay. To Mason and Greb, getting back together with a fresh start at a new training camp seemed like a good idea. They would work at Conneaut Lake Camp only for the big fights, but those big fights were becoming much more frequent.

The remoteness of the camp gave Greb the privacy he needed while practicing different techniques. Mason had Greb working on some different footwork and punching power that would come in handy if he were to ever fight for the title. If the fight between Greb and Wilson were actually to happen, Greb would have to fight a very clean and traditional bout. He didn't want any point deductions or warnings to take place from the championship judges. Therefore, what he was working on at that time was a little less of his jumping style of milling. His camp believed that the judges may not appreciate his windmill style for the title fight so Greb was practicing without it; Greb was boxing flatfooted in a more traditional technique. This gave him more power in his punches, but lessoned his maneuverability and elusiveness.

After getting in great shape and fully recovering from his illness, Greb was ready to get back into the ring for the first time in four months. This was his longest layoff from the ring ever, including when he was in the navy. People were wondering what kind of shape he was in and if he had a chance at the middleweight title. This comeback fight against Len Rowlands was going to answer a lot of the questions people had. The fight was originally scheduled for June 15 but had to be canceled because of rain.[4] The bout finally took place the next night at Uniontown, Pennsylvania. The bout was scheduled for ten rounds, but Greb didn't need all that time; he was in such great shape he knocked out Rowlands in just three rounds. Greb made sure to practice his flatfooted technique, which he was hoping to use against Wilson. The extra power that is created when a boxer plants his foot to throw a punch was all that was needed to get rid of Rowlands quickly. Although this was not the style Greb preferred, it was one he could implement when needed.

Around this time it was confirmed that a fight between Greb and Wilson would finally take place, but Greb had to fool Wilson into agreeing to it. Greb was said to be so upset at Wilson for ducking him for so many years he said, "The sonovabitch stayed champion three years by keeping away from me. I'll fix him!" The great sportswriter and *Ring* magazine editor Stanley Weston decades later wrote that Greb supposedly traveled to New York just to trick Wilson into thinking he was out of shape. Weston tells the story this way:

> Enlisting the aid of some New York bartenders, all of whom liked him, Harry spent hours drinking colored water and acting like a drunk. The news got around that he was "training" as

usual, and finally reached the ears of Wilson. Johnny said to his manager, "Now's the time for me to fight that bum. The only time."[5]

Wilson signed the contract to fight Greb because he thought Greb was so out of shape, "He'll be carted out of the ring in a stretcher."[6] It is unknown if Weston's story is true or not, but Greb did have a lot of time to travel to New York and pull this stunt off. With Greb canceling so many fights and being away from boxing for so long, it is believable that Wilson thought this was the best time to fight Greb. A scheduled championship title bout was to take place at the end of August. Wilson was a competent boxer, who had a strong enough right hand to win the title and beat Mike O'Dowd twice. However, it was generally believed that Greb, when at the top of his game, would beat Wilson without a problem.

The only concern Greb's camp had for the fight was if the fix was in. Wilson and his gangster associates had been said to have fixed some fights in the past. It was the general belief that Greb not only had to win but had to win dominantly just to have a chance to squeak out a judges' decision. The rumors were that a famous "New York Decision"[7] would take place. This meant that one or more of the judges were given money to lean the scorecards more favorably to Wilson during close rounds. So Greb continued to change his style for this one fight so these possibly dirty judges wouldn't have the opportunity to disqualify him or deduct points. Another rumor was that Greb would be another opponent of Wilson's that would be paid off to take a dive. Anyone close to Greb knew this notion was absolutely absurd.

On July 6 Greb was driving in the town of Connellsville, Pennsylvania, and had a run-in with the local cops. The *Washington Post* wrote an article about the altercation that described how Greb ended up in jail:

> Harry with his three-year-old daughter and sister, Mrs. Edwards, her husband and Miss Helen Austin, in his car, was stopped by Connellsville's giant policeman, Andy Thomas, for violating a traffic rule. He was taken to jail, and according to Harry's story, was beaten by Thomas and another copper when they forced him into a cell. Their blows, according to Greb, opened the wound left by an operation performed for an infected arm several weeks ago.

Greb was then put in a cell until the mayor of the town could give him a hearing. The article went on to describe how, when Greb was finally released, the fighting continued. "When Harry was released, he made a rush at Thomas and with a smash on the jaw dazed the officer."[8] Greb and the giant policeman were then separated.

By early August, Greb was staying at the Conneaut Lake Camp full time and more people were brought in to help him prepare. A couple of his sisters and their families also stayed there for a while. Greb's sister Ida was taking care of his daughter, so Dorothy was brought there too. Many newspapers sent cameramen up to the camp to take pictures and get stories because this was expected to be the middleweight fight that transferred the title. Everyone wanted to find out what the possible future World Middleweight Champion was doing to get ready.

The title fight was to take place on August 31 in New York. A couple of weeks before the fight Greb and his training group changed locations. On August 19 everyone left Pennsylvania and traveled to a new temporary training camp at Manhasset, Long Island. Greb's sisters and daughter also traveled to the new camp.

Greb stepped up his training a notch and really gave it his all. Some of the techniques he used were sparring, using the medicine ball, jumping rope, running and punching a sandbag. After a long day of training in the hot sun, Greb needed to stay hydrated. Mason had been around the boxing game for many decades and had picked up a lot of old tricks. One of Mason's unique methods of cooling off a boxer after a hard training session was to use his famous "Chinese Spray." It consisted of filling his mouth with water and then spitting a spray of it onto the boxer's face. The boxing commissioners had told him not to do it in the ring corner any more because it was unsanitary. Even during a fight Mason would spray his fighters returning to the corner after a hard round. The fighters welcomed it and found it refreshing. It was said that friends would frequently yell in the ring, "Give him Niagara Falls, Red!"[9] and it would be part of the show.

After an extensive and successful training camp it was finally time for the fight. The bout was scheduled for fifteen rounds at New York's Polo Grounds. Greb's outdoor training made a lot of sense because this bout was to take place in the open air. The Polo Grounds was the home of the New York Giants baseball team, and was an incredibly large stadium now ready to host the middleweight championship fight.

The bout took place the night of August 31, 1923. First, however, there was an official weigh-in that afternoon. Both fighters weighed 158 pounds and Greb was expected to drink enough liquids to bring his weight up to 162 pounds when he stepped into the ring. Wilson was said to have looked "fresh, strong and confident."[10] Greb, on the other hand, was described as slightly thin. Greb looked in "perfect shape," but because he had been fighting light heavyweights lately, he had been seen carrying a little more weight than he was at the weigh-in, and this made him look a little thinner than people were accustomed to.

The boxers entered the ring that night a few minutes before ten P.M. Mason entered the ring with Greb and was dressed up, wearing a necktie, which he would normally not do. Then Greb's two seconds entered, Tom Dolan and Tommy Holleran. Tom Dolan was said to have been a friend of Greb's and would eventually be one of his pallbearers. Dolan had been sitting with Happy Albacker in the crowd watching the preliminaries earlier in the evening.

Finally, Wilson entered with his manager, Frank Harlow. The announcer, Joe Humphries, announced Wilson as the current champion. The crowd gave him a "great ovation." Humphries described Greb as "his worthy opponent and leading contender." The crowd then went wild and applauded Greb's name heartily. The referee was announced as Jack O'Sullivan. Both fighters posed for photographs in the center of the ring.

After the photographs were taken, referee O'Sullivan gave the two combatants the instructions for the evening. Immediately afterwards the bell rang to begin what Greb had dreamed for all these years: an officially judged title bout for the middleweight championship. This wasn't a newspaper-decision bout where Greb had to knock Wilson out to win; all Greb had to do was win the judges' decision.

Greb's manager, Red Mason, applies the "Chinese Spray" to help cool Greb off. This picture was taken at the Manhasset training camp (Antiquities of the Prize Ring).

As soon as the bell rang to start the first round it was Greb who rushed out of his corner to meet Wilson. The champ

Greb at the Manhasset Camp before the Wilson bout. Greb is playing a ukulele for his daughter Dorothy and sister Ida. Ida was spending a lot of time with Dorothy since Harry's wife Mildred had passed away (© Bettmann/CORBIS).

threw a left to the head and then a right to Greb's body. After a clinch Greb landed a right to the jaw and then forced the champion to the ropes. The round was full of clinches and finally ended as Greb held Wilson's head with his left arm and then "hammered away with his right." This was Greb's typical inside technique of holding with one hand and pummeling his opponent with the other.

Wilson began the second round anxiously and was immediately greeted by a right hook. Greb tried to get in close, but Wilson successfully kept him away. Then Greb drove Wilson's head back when he landed a powerful right uppercut. After some exchanges Greb drove him to the ropes again and "jolted Wilson considerably" with a hard left hook. Wilson tried to reply with a big swing, but he caught nothing but air. Greb just grinned at the big miss, then landed a good left hook to Wilson's jaw. It was clear that Greb had won the second round.

By the start of the third round Greb was starting to feel pretty comfortable; he knew he was going to handle Wilson easily. Greb came out of his corner for the third round smiling as he drove his opponent to a corner. It was written that "Greb seemed all confidence, while Wilson looked harassed and worried." When Greb landed a hard right punch to Wilson's body the

Shown from left to right are Johnny Wilson, referee Jack O'Sullivan, announcer Joe Humphries and Harry Greb before the fight. Greb and Wilson are shown to be almost exactly the same size. Not only were they physically very similar, their ages were very close. Wilson was thirty years old and Greb was twenty-nine (Heavyweightcollectibles.com).

champ started to clinch. Wilson tried to land a right to Greb's jaw, but Greb just grinned back at him. After Greb landed a left punch a little low, the referee gave him a warning. Then Wilson punched Greb with a low left. Neither was intentional; it was just that they were both trying to aim for the body and were landing punches "dangerously close to the foul line."

Greb opened the fourth focusing on Wilson's head and chest. Then somewhere in the left-field bleachers a fight broke out in the crowd. Patrons seated around the ring had their attention sidetracked by the ruckus in the crowd. The distraction didn't affect the boxers, as Greb continued to force the fight. Wilson was already starting to show the effects of Greb's powerful punches. It was noticed that "Wilson's very prominent nose became bulbous and swollen." Wilson landed a punch to the body, but Greb just looked at him and grinned again; Greb was in control and Wilson knew it. The flat-footed training seemed to have helped add some power behind Greb's punches, as proven by Wilson's swollen nose. Everything was going as planned.

Continuing to enjoy his own handiwork, Greb came out of his corner with a big smile on his face to start the fifth round. First there were some clinches, then a rush to the ropes. Greb began to walk around the champ like an animal circling its prey, looking for an opening. It was written that "Wilson seemed utterly bewildered" with Greb's prowling. Greb finally found the opening he was looking for and went straight to Wilson's head with a shower of lefts and rights until Wilson was up against the ropes. Wilson was starting to weaken considerably in this round.

The sixth round started with both fighters throwing from the outside, exchanging lefts and rights. There was more clinching until Greb broke it up when he measured the distance to Wilson's face before landing a big right hand to the jaw. At this point Wilson's seconds started shouting at their boy to "step in," but when he did, it was into yet another clinch.

Stanley Weston later wrote about something that happened in the sixth round. Weston wrote that during the clinches a conversation took place between Greb and the referee, "who shoved Harry aside and bawled him out for thumbing Wilson's inflamed eye for the tenth time." The referee asked Greb, "What do you think yer doing?" Greb just stared at the official and simply replied, "Sticking my thumb in Johnny's eye. What does it look like?"[11] Greb then continued his attack.

By this point in the fight it was clear that Greb had Wilson completely where he wanted him. All it took was for Greb to just shift his feet and the paper champion immediately "cowered in bewilderness." During the bout so far Wilson was trying to focus on a body attack, but Greb was far too much of a "shifty and elusive target."

The seventh round began with each fighter staring at his opponent from long range, trying to gauge the situation. Wilson eventually landed a couple of left swings to the body, but Greb ducked under the third swing and quickly landed a hard right to Wilson's body. Then Greb landed a hard right directly onto Wilson's jaw that made "a loud smack." By the time Wilson replied with two left punches, the bell had rung to end the round.

Greb "quickened the pace" in round eight by starting with a hard left punch to his opponent's ribs. Then he landed a big right shot onto Wilson's eye, which immediately started to swell. This made a great target for Greb, who "shot a volley of rights and lefts to Wilson's head." By the end of the round Greb threw more punches "that had Wilson bewildered at the bell."

The ninth round opened with a right to Wilson's jaw. Afterwards "the champion seemed very depressed." Greb drove Wilson to the ropes and threw leather to his opponent's body and head. During the round Greb slipped to his knee when he lunged with his right. "He was up in an instant." Greb quickly landed another right to the ribs that "sounded like the beat of a bass drum." Near the end of the round Wilson landed "two light lefts," but Greb answered them with a big right to his head as the bell rang.

The crowd let out "a loud howl" when Greb started the next round with a hard right "to Wilson's overhanging nose." Wilson tried to clinch, but Greb instead pummeled him with rights and lefts to "the champion's beak." Wilson was obviously hurt and tried to weather the storm by covering up. When he finally came to, the champion "landed two straight lefts to Greb's jaw."

By the eleventh the crowd was yelling "taunts" at Wilson to get him to be more active. Greb became more "deliberate in his punching" by circling his prey and looking for an opening to land a big punch. Greb found that opening and shot a big right directly onto Wilson's jaw.

When the twelfth round began, Wilson's seconds shouted, "Let's go!" The champion didn't have a chance because Greb immediately landed a right onto Wilson's sore eye. Wilson was tiring and was seen "fighting very sluggishly." There was a lot of clinching while "Greb had all the better of the in-fighting." During the fight, while Greb was on the inside he "held and hit, hit on the breakaway and was interrupted several times in the act of using the thumb of his left hand much after the manner of a man gouging an adversary."[12] It was becoming clear that Wilson was losing the fight, but if Wilson "realized that his title was slipping he did not appear to care very much."

The thirteenth round was much the same as the previous round. By the fourteenth round Wilson's left eye was "practically closed." Now that it was near the end of the fight and his opponent was tiring, Greb used his great conditioning and endurance to speed things up in the ring. "Greb ran in, shooting rights to the body and whipping more up to the sore eye, with a hard right to the jaw." All the punches that landed in this round were from Greb. "They seemed to realize in Wilson's corner that the title was passing and were shouting hysterically to their man."

The fifteenth and final round began and "Greb was fresh and alert, while Wilson still seemed bewildered. There was a smile of confidence on Greb's face." Greb had been in enough fights to realize he was going to be judged the winner. Greb landed a hard right to the body that made Wilson hold on to Greb "convulsively." Wilson threw a right to Greb's head at the end, but it was too little too late. "Greb threw his arms around Wilson's shoulders at the end. He seemed to know that he had won."

While the judges were getting their verdict ready, the soon-to-be ex-champion looked on "with his left eye virtually closed and with blood dripping from cuts about his mouth." With the crowd having witnessed Greb winning almost every round, they soon heard him being announced the new World Middleweight Champion. Greb's dream had been achieved. He could now bring the title back to his home state of Pennsylvania, which had been home to two other middleweight champions of the past, Frank Klaus and George Chip.

The headline in the *Pittsburgh Post* the next day read, "Harry Greb Is New Middleweight Champion Of The World." Another headline stated, "Johnny Is Puzzled By Harry's Tactics, With Closed Optic Fights Desperately." Days after the fight the *Chicago Tribune* would write this about the championship reign of Johnny Wilson: "Wilson probably was the most unpopular fighter that ever held the title." The article would also state that Greb "won the world's championship by fighting rings around Johnny Wilson."[13]

During the fight, Greb (left) is seen ready to throw a punch at Wilson, with referee Jack O'Sullivan looking on (Craig Hamilton collection, www.josportsinc.com).

Greb was staying at the Hotel Pennsylvania while still in New York. At the hotel he was being swarmed by friends and

The announcer Joe Humphries, on the far left, declares a new middleweight champion. Next to Humphries is one of Greb's seconds, Tom Dolan, with manager Mason entering the ring. Another second, Tommy Holleran, is hoisting a smiling Greb up in celebration. Referee Jack O'Sullivan is on the far right leaning against the ropes (Antiquities of the Prize Ring).

admirers. The *New York Times* wrote: "The Pittsburgher was elated with the new prominence he has won, but, as is characteristic of him, carried himself modestly." The *Times* interviewed Greb about the fight and he said, "But I knew my speed would be too much for Wilson." He went on to state:

> I think I showed everybody who saw the bout that I am Wilson's master. Now, any middleweight in the world can have a crack at the title. I don't intend to remain idle. If Wilson wants a return bout and a promoter will arrange the match I am agreeable. I am sorry that there were reports that I had agreed to any arrangement, but the bout proved them to be false. My record speaks for itself.[14]

While he was still in New York there were banquet celebrations for Greb. His last manager, George Engel, was based in New York, and after the bout Engel followed Greb around just to be in the spotlight. There were rumors floating around, spread by Engel himself, that they might get back together. Seated at the head of a table at a large banquet in his honor, Greb stood up and announced to everyone that this was not to be. Greb said, "Mason and I are friends, have been and will be, probably until I have fought my last fight and longer."[15] Greb and Mason signed a managerial contract while training in Conneaut Lake for this fight and Greb was intending to honor that contract for years to come.

Just like when Greb had beaten Tommy Gibbons, theater companies were now bombarding him with contracts for him to appear on stage. Greb's first appearance was planned to be one week after the fight in Wilson's hometown of Boston. Then he was to appear for a week's worth of performances at the Gayety Theatre, the same burlesque venue where he had done his vaudeville performances before. The plan was for Greb to have four full weeks of theater performances around the country.[16]

On September 2, while deciding if he was to sign the theater contracts, Greb went to an Atlantic City resort for a well-deserved rest. The following day he acted as a second in a bout between his stablemate Cuddy DeMarco and fellow lightweight Sid Terris.

On September 4, with Greb still at the seashore, Mason arrived back in Pittsburgh. He announced that the proposed stage tour had been called off. Greb and Mason had decided it would be better to keep Greb in good form. The *Pittsburgh Post* would write, "Mason already has four matches lined up, which will keep Greb in shape."[17] This was one of the differences between Mason's management style and Engel's. Mason always kept feeding Greb a lot of fights that helped him stay in shape, as well as make more money. Another thing Mason was attempting to do was show everyone that Greb, unlike Wilson, would be a very active champion who took on all and any competition.

On September 10 the conquering hero arrived home. Greb arrived in Pittsburgh by train at 1:30 P.M. with a whole day's worth of festivities planned for him. For days leading up to his return the newspapers had been informing sports fans about the planned receptions that would take place.[18] When he stepped off the train Greb was greeted by Nirella's band and a vast group of mounted police. Greb's response was "smiling his smilingest and doffing his hat to the hearty welcome of the thousands."[19] The squadron of mounted police and the band then escorted Greb throughout the downtown streets of Pittsburgh to the City Council Building. At the foot of the building, dignitaries made speeches followed by Greb's speaking to the crowd.

The fleet of cars then made its way down Fifth Avenue while parade watchers waved signs and banners about Greb and his accomplishment. "Traffic stood still, cornermen saluted, youngsters along the line march shouted." The parade ended at the Elks Club located at Seventh Street and Duquesne Way, "where the new champion held an informal reception before attending a luncheon in his honor."[20]

The Elks Club was filled with a great many people paying homage to Greb, including jazz bands and vaudeville acts. The luncheon turned into a dinner and lasted until the evening. During the event Greb told a story of how he almost messed up the celebration schedule. Greb had started his train trip home the previous night and was scheduled to arrive in Pittsburgh at 10:30 A.M., three full hours before people were expecting him to arrive. The *Post* would write: "But Greb stayed on the train until it reached Greensburg and in the metropolis of Westmoreland county the middleweight champion of the world marooned himself until a convenient train came along and brought him in on time for the sendoff."[21]

With Greb having won the middleweight championship and previously the light heavyweight championship, there were thoughts of a third belt. The *New York Times* wrote after the fight that Greb "has expressed a desire to tackle Jack Dempsey in a ten-round bout."[22] Greb wasn't the only one who thought he had a chance against Dempsey now. On September 14, Dempsey fought Luis Angel Firpo at the Polo Grounds in New York, where Greb had just beaten Wilson. Jess Willard not only fought and lost to Dempsey, but was also at the Demspey-Firpo fight. A week later on September 20, Willard, former heavyweight champion, stated his opinion that Greb could beat Dempsey. When interviewed Willard said he thought Greb "is the only boxer who has a good chance to win a decision over Jack Dempsey today." The *Post* wrote that "he believed Greb's peculiar style of fighting would baffle Dempsey and that the Pittsburgher might be able to outpoint the champion."[23]

It seemed there were a lot of opportunities in front of Greb now. He was finally in control

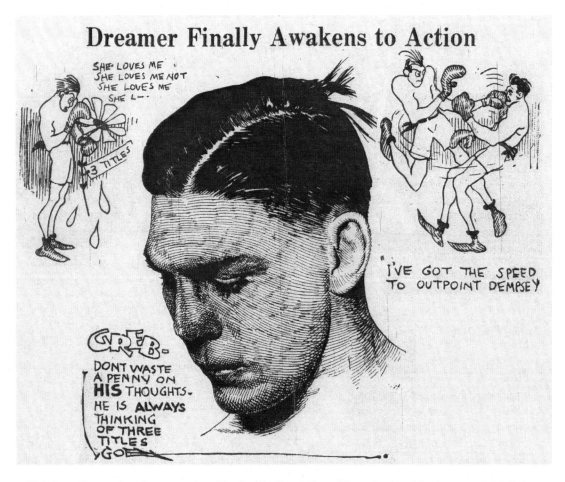

This is an illustration that was printed in the *Pittsburgh Post.* After winning titles in two weight divisions, it shows Greb dreaming of a third (*Pittsburgh Post-Gazette*).

and calling the shots. Greb would keep his promise to stay a very active champion and he defended the title against all comers. The middleweight championship reign of Harry Greb had finally begun, and after he finished, *Ring* magazine would rank him as the greatest middleweight there ever was.

11.

DEFENDING THE TITLE

Harry Greb's reign as middleweight champion lasted from 1923 to 1926. During these four years of dominance Greb acquired many nicknames such as "The Wildest Tiger," "The Iron City Express," "King of the Alley Fighters," "The Human Rubberball," "The Pittsburgh Wildcat" and "The Perpetual-Motion Machine," but the one he is best known as is "The Pittsburgh Windmill." All his nicknames were attempts to describe what he was like in the ring, and how he defended his title. During this golden age of boxing he was the undisputed pound-for-pound champion and would fight anyone who was willing to challenge him. While defending his title he continued to fight men from the top three weight divisions.

He had won the middleweight title at the end of August 1923. The third boxer he met as champion was middleweight Lou Bogash on October 22 at the First Regiment Armory in Newark, New Jersey. Bogash was born in Foggia, Italy, and had come to America in 1907. His birth name was Luigi Buccasio and he had started boxing at the age of fifteen. He began his career boxing out of Bridgeport, Connecticut, but would later have matches all over the country. During his career Bogash not only fought the best, he would also beat the best. Bogash defeated such great-caliber fighters as Mickey Walker, Tommy Loughran, Jock Malone, Mike McTigue, Mike O'Dowd, and Tiger Flowers.

The audience in the smoke-filled Armory enjoyed Greb's technique; there were yells of "admiration from ringside critics who marveled at his speed, endurance and ability to hit from any angle at any time." Regis M. Welsh wrote about Greb's "freak" style:

> Where Greb summons the unlimited energy he brought into play tonight will be as much a mystery as is his style which no one dares copyright. He led every minute of the way, seldom slowed down and at one stage of the game, in the sixth round, was measuring Louis for a right while propping his head into position for a left in a vain attempt to find out just how much Bogash could take and stand up.[1]

Bogash did enough to win three rounds and hold Greb even in two rounds, but the majority of the twelve-round fight was all Greb. The next day it was written: "The sustained virility of Greb's attack, his eagerness to go in and mix and the use of his clubbing right a la Firpo, along with a star right and left and a vicious left hook to the body, proved too much for Bogash." Greb was having such a great time in the ring that he was seen smiling during the fight. The New Jersey crowd had never seen Greb's unorthodox style before but soon learned to appreciate it and marvel at it. Welsh summed it up best when he wrote the next day, "Greb was Greb, that's all there was to it."[2]

Harry Wills sat at ringside for the fight to watch Greb's unique fighting technique. Wills sat in amazement, "and just smiled a broad smile as he watched every move." At the end of the fight Wills was asked what he thought. The great heavyweight was speechless and just "shook his head queerly when asked his opinion."[3]

After winning the bout Greb left New Jersey and traveled back to Pittsburgh to start training

Lou Bogash was inducted into the World Boxing Hall of Fame in 2000. After his boxing career he refereed for eight years, including some of Rocky Marciano's bouts (Antiquities of the Prize Ring).

for his next bout. His next fight was to be in a week against Canadian light heavyweight Soldier Jones, who outweighed Greb by almost twenty pounds. Greb weighed around 166 and Jones weighed about 185. Greb trained for most of the week leading up to the bout, and on November 3 the *Post* wrote: "Declaring himself fit for a hard battle, Harry Greb wound up his hard training yesterday and planned to do just a little light sparring work today as the final touch to his training plans for his ten-round bout with Soldier Jones in Motor Square Garden Monday night."[4]

These two boxers had met before, once in 1919 and once more in 1921. Greb had knocked out Jones in each of those fights, but Greb knew Jones had a big punch and had to be taken seriously.

Fight night finally arrived on November 5, 1923. The first round began with Greb forcing the fight while Jones "missed with lefts and rights." Greb hooked lefts and rights to the body and face while Jones continued to miss.

According to the *Pittsburgh Post*, "Both were swinging wild and Jones sent a left to the chin, which backed Greb up to the ropes. Jones hooked a left to the head and Greb went down." It was just one minute into the first round. Being blind in his right eye, he probably didn't even see the left punch coming. While he was being counted out, Greb "lolled and rolled about on the lower ropes." While the count continued Greb was able to "regain his feet after a count of eight and wobble about like a drunken man." Jones continued his attack "and another right caught Greb's chin." Greb went down again, this time holding on to Jones's legs. Referee Joe Keally had counted to four when Greb finally staggered to his feet. Greb went in for a clinch to try to clear his head. While Greb was still "groggy" Jones landed two more left hooks. Mason called for Greb from a corner since he was "staggering and did not know which corner to go to."[5]

In between rounds Greb sat "limp" on his chair while Mason tried to revive him. "Mason worked frantically but wisely over him, rubbed his tired legs back into life, massaged his ears and brought color back into his pale face."

Greb came out at the start of the second round still blinking, tired and groggy, but slowly recovering due to the help of his manager. After a minute of the round Greb had seemingly recovered, and it looked like he would survive. Then Jones landed two more left hooks to the head which rocked Greb again. Greb went in for a clinch then later landed a left and right of his own. These punches were able to delay Jones's attack until the bell rang to end the round.

When in his corner Greb was silent, but then halfway through the rest time he began to "straighten up in his chair and began talking to Mason." When the third round started the crowd was "standing on chairs, yelling and howling for Greb." This seemed to refresh Greb, who then "began moving, swinging, jabbing, hooking and throwing with both hands." With one of the best chins in boxing history, Greb had shaken off the cobwebs and finally recovered. Throughout the third round his energy continued to replenish itself with Greb throwing "right and left overhand punches to Jones' head and face."[6] Near the end of the third round Greb threw a punch that caused a "gaping cut" over Jones's right eye. The third round was awarded to Greb.

By round four Greb was not only fully recovered but was dominating Jones. He was even able to stagger Jones with a right to the chin. The *Post* wrote: "Greb was battering Jones to all sides of the ring at the bell. It was a terrific round and Greb had a big margin, sending Jones to his corner with his right eye closed."[7] Now, unbeknown to most people, both boxers were fighting with only one eye.

For the rest of the fight Greb proceeded to punish Jones so badly it was described as "a slaughter." Greb landed twenty unanswered punches in the fifth round, and by the sixth round "Jones was wobbling around. It was another round for Greb and Jones seemed more tired even than Greb was in the first two rounds." By the seventh Jones was "leg weary" and only managed to land two blows. Greb was back to his normal self and was completely dominating his opponent, who was staggering around groggily. At the end of the round the referee had to ask Jones if he wanted to continue. In round eight "Greb hooked a hard right to Jones' chin and Jones went down for the count of nine, Jones arose and seemed helpless as Greb pounded."[8]

Jones continued to stagger around at the start of round nine. During the round Greb punished Jones severely, "which made the soldier's face a mass of blood." Jones had one eye closed while blood flowed from his nose and mouth. The tenth round was much the same. When the fight ended Greb had lost the first two rounds but won the remaining eight in a very one-sided finish. It was said to be one of the biggest massacres Greb had dished out. A headline in the *Post* the next day read, "Pittsburgh's great boxer displays wonderful gameness and recuperative powers. Tears into Soldier Jones, earning verdict by taking last eight rounds."[9]

A few years later Greb would tell his friend Harry Keck, "The Soldier hits hard. He looks like a bum against somebody you never heard of and then turns around and looks like a champ for a few minutes against me."[10]

The next month Greb was to officially defend his title for the first time against Bryan Downey; the date for the fight was December 3. It was not only his first middleweight defense but also the first fight in Pennsylvania under the new McBride Law that legalized decisions in the state. Greb entered the ring weighing 161 pounds and Downey was a little over 158. Downey won the first round by a slight edge due to Greb's conservative fighting. It was thought Greb started his first title defense tentatively because he wasn't sure what techniques "constitute[d] fouls and fairs." This ended early when "Downey threw discretion to the winds, [and] Greb gave it a further toss."[11]

In the third round Greb "went back to his old methods of just swinging and landing no matter where the punches started." Greb landed a "hard right to the chin and a terrific left to the body"[12] which sent Downey through the ropes. One of the new McBride rules was that a three-foot platform had to be around the ring, as it is today, so Downey didn't fall to the floor. Downey got back into the ring and continued to be attacked.

From the third round on it was all Greb. By the later rounds, "Downey's face was a crimson red, he bore several cuts under the eyes and about the face, and Greb, taking a long chance of staging a knockout, began whaling away at the Columbus tough guy." Greb was often taking his right hand and throwing uppercuts as well as throwing it down from above, "always finding a landing place on Downey's battered face."[13]

During the fight Downey "became rough" and attempted to use some of the dirty tactics he had learned during his career. Because Downey was getting away with it Greb realized it was OK to use some himself. He then taught Downey a lesson he wouldn't forget. The *Post* the next day had the headline, "Downey Learns Tricks About Roughness." When the fight ended Greb had "outfought, outpunched, outgeneraled and outroughed Bryan Downey."[14] Greb had easily won his first official title defense.

Just ten days after the fight, Downey announced that he was retiring from the ring. A *Washington Post* article on December 13 described how the death of his infant daughter recently had been a great blow. Added to this was his devastating loss to Greb. "His recent setback at the hands of Harry Greb decided Downey to quit the ring."[15]

Greb's second official title defense was on January 18, 1924, and was a rematch against Johnny Wilson. The fight was scheduled for fifteen rounds and took place at Madison Square Garden. The champion weighed in for the fight at 158½ pounds while Wilson, now the challenger, weighed one pound more.

Greb fought a very clean fight, "conforming to every rule, fighting cleaner even than he did with Tunney." Greb stayed on the outside a lot early on in the fight while "wreaking havoc with his flinging right hook to the head and body and finally bringing blood from Wilson's mouth and opening a neat gash under his eye."[16] Wilson's best showing was early on, "when he flayed Greb with a vicious body attack."[16] Then Greb carried the fight but didn't show as much speed as in their previous battle. Wilson was said to have won the fourth round with the third, tenth and thirteenth being even. The rest of the fifteen rounds were all

Bryan Downey came from a family of boxers, including his two brothers, Joe and Anthony (Heavyweight collectibles.com).

Greb.[17] "The smiling champion looked, acted and boxed the part right down to his heels."[18]

In the last two rounds Greb stepped it up a notch and started showing his speed. He finished the fight strong and quick, completely dominating Wilson. When the fifteen rounds ended the 11,000 people in attendance heard the judges award the victory to Greb. Harry Newman wrote that Greb "dealt a thorough licking to Johnny Wilson." When the announcer, Joe Humphries, declared, "The winner — and still the champion, Greb, Greb the winner," Greb's manager, Red Mason, rushed into the ring. Mason was so excited he "attempted a running forward handspring that turned out to be a fearful bloomer." Mason fell down, but he quickly got up a very happy manager. The headline in the *Pittsburgh Post* the next day read, "Greb Retains Middleweight Title; Administers Lacing To Wilson."[19]

Also the following day Regis Welsh wrote in the *Pittsburgh Post*:

> The fight lacked any spectacular thrills, the only real fireworks in the ninth and eleventh, which Greb took by such a wide margin that it looked like a bad match. Harry had too much nerve, too much heart and too much ability for Wilson to come within reaching distance of him and the pasting the contender took tonight was just as complete as any ever administered a novice mixing with the titleholder.[20]

The following month Greb went on a seven-week summer vacation to California. He traveled with his manager Red Mason and his trainer/sparring partner Leo Caghill. The vacation began with Greb fighting Jack Reeves on February 22, 1924, in Oakland. It was a very "one-sided" bout and Greb had "the better of every round."[21]

Greb and Johnny Wilson (right) weighing in for their rematch. Red Mason is pictured between them (Antiquities of the Prize Ring).

Once that bout was taken care of the real vacation began and Greb enjoyed a much-deserved rest. After the vacation Greb would say, "Everything was lovely. Had a grand time and would have stayed longer." Greb continued, "California is a great place but I was getting sort of home-sick. If it hadn't been that we wanted to get back here where friends seem real, maybe we would have stayed longer." Greb arrived back in Pittsburgh on March 15. He talked about his future boxing plans: "I'm going to do plenty of fighting, starting next week with Fay Keiser in Baltimore."

Greb continued, "I hear that Lou Bogash and Ted Moore are to meet here next week. If Moore wins I'll fight him right here in Pittsburgh."[22]

A week after arriving back Greb fought his old nemesis Fay Keiser on March 24, 1924. The bout took place at the 104th Regiment Armory in Baltimore and was the ninth time these two boxers had fought each other. The bout was an official middleweight title defense with plenty of drama.

Greb had issues with the referee that was chosen. He didn't want referee Charley Short to officiate his title defense because of concerns over what would be allowed and what wouldn't be. It was said that Greb didn't want to be unjustly disqualified because of a questionable call from Referee Short.

It was written that Greb thought it would be a non-title bout. He didn't know it was going to be for the title until the day before. When he found out it was going to be an official title defense, Greb said, "I'm afraid Short will give Keiser my title on a foul. Fay fights dirty. He don't think nothing of fouling you but he squawks when you foul him back. He may go down yelling 'foul' and your referee might give him the title."[23]

The night of the fight Greb was in his dressing room with the situation still unresolved. The *Pittsburgh Post* explained, "State Chairman Latro Cogswell of the boxing commission and local Commissioner John Schuchman went to the champion's dressing room, while the crowd waited impatiently."[24] Greb was asking for a Pittsburgh referee named Al Foss to work the fight instead, but the commission wouldn't allow it.[25] The *Post* would go on to explain, "Greb would not accept Charley Short and finally compromised on Benny Franklin, the promoter of the show. Greb was fined for his stubbornness, but Franklin paid it rather than see the show fall flat."[26]

With Referee Franklin finally agreed upon, Greb and Keiser entered the ring to start the fight. The *Post* would write:

> To show the futility of Keiser's campaign tonight, Greb's hair, with its slick part, remained unruffled until about the fourth round when it became mussed up in a wrestling match on the ropes, while Keiser spouted blood from the nose and mouth and a trickle of crimson ran down his face from a nasty gash over the nose which Greb started in the fourth.[27]

Greb continued to batter Keiser around the ring in a very one-sided contest. Greb opened up in the eighth round when he "battered Keiser unmercifully without return." When the twelfth round finally arrived Greb put "everything into a right swing, flopped the groggy Keiser to the floor and saw him gamely get up and resume a hopeless task." The *Post* would go on to write that Keiser was "battered and bleeding, floored with a hefty right to the chin and then arising in a pitiful condition, [until] the referee humanely stepped in." Referee and promoter Franklin "acquiesced to the pleadings of the crowd and stopped the slaughter before any serious damage was done."[28] Greb had successfully defended his title with a twelfth-round TKO. It was the final time these two combatants would meet in the ring.

Greb's next bout, a rematch against Kid Norfolk, was supposed to take place during the first week of April, but it was postponed. On March 31, 1924, the *Beloit Daily News* ran an article titled "Greb Is Injured In Car Accident." The article stated how the bout had been "indefinitely postponed." The injury was described by Mason. "According to information received from Greb's manager, the champion received a bad cut over one eye in a motor accident Saturday. The injury, requiring four stitches, would make it impossible for Greb to box here Friday, the promoters were informed."[29]

The fight eventually took place a few weeks later, but Mason would eventually shed some light on what really caused the postponement. Later on Mason was interviewed by the *Chicago Tribune*. Here is an excerpt from the article:

Red Mason on the left, Harry Greb in the middle and Greb's trainer Leo Caghill on the right. This was taken in 1924 during their vacation in California (Heavyweightcollectibles.com).

About a year ago Greb's automobile was found on a country road with the windshield smashed and a couple of fenders banged up. Harry popped up in a hospital. Slightly injured, they said.

"That was bunk," Red Mason admitted afterward. "Greb was daffy over the dolls, and he thought he'd do better if he had his face fixed the way Dempsey did. He had a sort of horn over each eye from being cut and sewed up time after time; sort of a lump, like an awning over each eye, you know. Then he wanted his nose straightened. But he was afraid the mob would kid him for going to a beauty doctor, so he faked the smash-up and went in as a casualty.

"And the joke of it was," Mason laughed, "that when they got through operating on him them horns were worse than ever."[30]

The rematch with Kid Norfolk finally took place on April 19, 1924. It would be the first time these two fighters had seen each other since Norfolk had injured Greb's retina in their previous bout. This rematch took place at Mechanics Pavilion in Boston and the referee for the bout was Jack Sheehan. The contest was said to be "one of the toughest, roughest and ugliest battles ever staged here or elsewhere."[31]

The first two rounds were awarded to Greb. The two combatants traded vicious blows, with Norfolk focusing on a body attack for these first rounds. During this time Norfolk "shot at least two palpably low blows."

During the second round Norfolk was able to get Greb through the ropes:

Norfolk rushed clear across the ring, charged into Greb with head down, hit him with his shoulder and sent him careening through the ropes outside the ring into the press section. On recovering, Greb came back and cut loose with anything and everything and before another half minute had passed it was the grandest, roughest and most exciting go-as-you-please style of milling anyone has ever seen anywhere.

In the third round Greb "started hopping about and gave Norfolk a terrific lacing, but the Negro, weighing 172½ pounds, apparently in perfect shape, withstood it after being rocked about the ring twice." The round was said to be even.

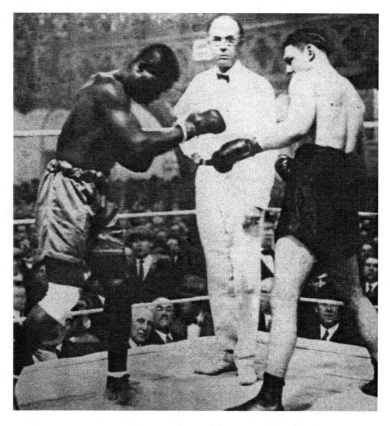

Greb and Kid Norfolk (left) before their rematch in 1924. Referee Jack Sheehan is in the center. The fight ended in the only disqualification of Greb's career (collection of Pugilistica.com).

Then in the fourth round things started to get ugly. "From the opening of the fourth round until the finish both did almost as they pleased, everything went, as Sheehan seemed helpless and powerless." Greb threw a great punch to Norfolk's mouth that "brought blood." After trading uppercuts, hooks, lefts and rights with Norfolk, Greb was awarded this round.

Referee Sheehan had a handful with these two fighters giving it their all and the crowd started chanting, "Let them fight the way they want!" This was what started the fifth round. Norfolk continued to go for what he was going for the whole fight: Greb's body. Norfolk kept punching Greb's left side "until it showed a mellow red." Greb kept fighting "full speed" on the outside and was apparently unaffected by Norfolk's body punches. When the bell finally ended the fifth round the crowd was going crazy, yelling in excitement because "they were getting more than they bargained for." Greb was awarded the fifth round.

The sixth round was three minutes of toe-to-toe slugging. Norfolk was holding Greb while punching with the other hand onto his body. This is a technique Greb would use himself in many fights. Greb was trying to get on the outside and fight from there. By the end of the sixth round they were standing in front of each other constantly trading blows. Then at the very end of the sixth round it got even crazier.

The newspapers would write:

> Just then the bell clanged a faint clang, and Norfolk sent a vicious right to Greb's head. The
> blow was a palpable foul, but Greb rushed after Norfolk, shot both hands to the head twice,

while the Negro kept pumping them into the body. For a full half minute they fought, until seconds, commissioners and police and what not jumped into the ring and led each fighter to his
corner.

Once the fighters were sent to their corners the referee made an announcement. Referee
Sheehan waved to Norfolk's corner and declared him the winner of the bout by a foul. Sheehan
then very quickly left the ring while the two fighters were still on their seats in their corners
wondering what had just happened.

> With Sheehan gone the crowd surged to the ringside to ascertain the verdict and it was then
> that Commissioner Gene Buckley made known the fact that, in his judgment, Norfolk was the
> first and real offender and that the body which governs the game here would likely take action
> to override the referee's verdict.

Norfolk then got his gloves removed and started to leave the ring. He left by way of the
side where Greb was sitting, "and rushed toward him." Greb rose from his chair and was waiting for Norfolk, not knowing what to expect. At this point Greb still had his gloves on and was
wondering what Norfolk was up to. Before something could happen between the two, "the police
and local officials interfered."

When Norfolk finally left the ring he was met with "menacing hoots" from the crowd, while
Greb left the ring with a great sendoff which "consisted of mingled hoots and cheers."

A day later a headline read, "Champ Not Blamed For Rough-Housing In Norfolk Fight."
Many critics were saying that Norfolk was to blame for starting the dirty tactics throughout the
fight, consisting of low blows and body-rushing Greb out of the ring and into the press area.
It was only after Norfolk had done these things that Greb started answering in kind.[32]

Norfolk was officially awarded the victory by a sixth-round DQ. Greb had won most of the
rounds, but it went down on his record as a disqualification loss. A week after the fight the Massachusetts Boxing Commission suspended both fighters from fighting in the state for six months.
That was the final time they fought.[33]

On June 13, 1924, Greb was nicknamed "The Pittsburgh Giant Killer" when he fought Martin Burke in Cleveland, Ohio. Burke was ten inches taller than Greb and outweighed him by
twenty pounds. Burke, a former sparring partner of Jack Dempsey's, had fought such great
heavyweights and light heavyweights as Bartley Madden, Carl Morris, Gene Tunney, Jim Coffey,
Billy Miske, Charley Weinert, Fred Fulton, Jack Renault, Tommy Loughran, and Homer Smith.
A day after the bout the *Pittsburgh Post* described the fight:

> Early in the fight a right uppercut by Greb opened a deep cut over Burke's nose and blood
> poured from the big fellow in streams. There were numerous cries to the referee to stop the
> bout. Burke, however, was not materially damaged and by reason of his persistent clinching
> and holding tactics he managed to weather the fight to the limit of ten rounds.[34]

Greb was said to have won every single round.

A few days later, on June 16, Greb fought Frank Moody in Waterbury, Connecticut. Moody
was touted as the best middleweight to ever come out of England. He had a powerful right-
hand punch and was considered a great threat to Greb. Moody had recently beaten Jock Malone and had become the first person to ever knock out Lou Bogash. The crowd of 20,000
spectators expected a terrific battle.

The following passage is Frank Moody describing the first round himself:

> He came tearing out of his corner at the first bell, leapt at me and started swinging both arms. I
> took most of his punches on my shoulders and arms. Then he came in close and hooked away with
> lefts and rights in an unceasing bombardment. Greb was never in one place for more than half of
> a second, and the swift lefts I shot at him hit only empty air as he bobbed and weaved, then

jumped in to clutch me with one hand and whale away with the other. He put me on the defensive right away and it was next to impossible to try to alter the state of affairs. Each rush was followed by a spell of infighting, with Harry pulling and pushing, punching under and over, here, there and everywhere. My arms were plastered with leather and although I jabbed, hooked and uppercut, it was like fighting a dozen men or an octopus with gloves on. Midway through the opening round Greb butted me under the chin and as my head went back he gave me the laces of his left glove and finished the stroke by jabbing his thumb into my right eye. The pain was deadly.[35]

The *Pittsburgh Post* wrote the next day: "Greb kept moving, weaving in and out with such speed that Moody never was able to find him." The newspaper would go on to write: "Greb dropped him in the fourth round from a right-hand punch. Moody was spread out flat on his back and it looked then as though he would not respond in time to continue."[36] Moody recovered and continued to be punished by Greb's constant assault. By the end of the fourth Moody went down again for the count of three, but he was able to make it back up onto his feet and survive the round. By the fifth round Greb closed Moody's right eye with a hard right punch. The round ended with Moody very hurt indeed.

When the sixth round began, Greb "continued his rushing attack" and "aimed at Moody's jaw." Moody was subjected to a "fusillade of punches" that was eventually too much for him. Moody was knocked down in the sixth round and couldn't get up in time. "Moody protested Referee Galvin's count, claiming that he was on his feet when the referee reached ten." What observers saw was Moody try to rise on the count of nine, and by the count of ten he was still attempting to rise. He was still so weak that by the count of ten, "he slipped back to the floor."[37] Greb had won the fight with a sixth-round knockout.

Greb's next bout was an official title defense on June 26, 1924. At Yankee Stadium in New York there was a charity show in aid of a Milk Fund and Greb was the headliner. Greb defended his title against Ted Moore in a fifteen-round bout. Yankee Stadium was packed with 50,000 fans whose total donation to the Milk Fund was $150,000. Other bouts on the card were Gene Tunney against Ermino Spalla, and Young Stribling against Tommy Loughran. The referee for the day was Eddie Purdy while Joe Humphries was the announcer.

Ted Moore weighed in at the 160-pound limit while Greb was 159½ pounds. In an article printed in *Boxing News* magazine, the tone of the fight is described: "From the start Greb produced a seemingly inexhaustible supply of energy and power that did not permit his opponent to open an offensive of his own. Moore had to defend himself against a ceaseless two-fisted attack to the face."[38]

Moore is credited with the sixth and seventh rounds, but the rest were all Greb. Only once did Moore land a good shot and that was in the ninth round. That punch woke Greb up and he started fighting harder. After the tenth round Moore had his right eye cut open and his nose was cut and bleeding. Greb was close to winning by a knockout twice, but instead chose to take the decision and give the crowd their money's worth. A headline the next day was "Briton Outclassed, Bewildered, Beaten By Garfield Boxer." Greb had successfully defended his title again although many observers were looking for a knockout.[39]

Greb's next bout was a newspaper decision on August 21, 1924, in Fremont, Ohio. His adversary for the ten-round bout was Tiger Flowers. Greb would eventually battle Flowers twice more a couple of years later for the title, but this was their first meeting.

The first round was said to be very fast. Both fighters threw a lot of left and right punches to the head and body, and the round was said to be even. The second round had a lot of power punches from both fighters, and Flowers was awarded this round. In the first half of round three both boxers focused on the body, but by the end of the round most of the punches were being aimed at the head. The third round went to Greb.[40]

Greb started quickening his pace in the fourth round. He started with a right to the head

The boxers of the Milk Fund getting their physicals. Greb is standing on the left looking upward, while Young Stribling is being examined by the doctors. Ted Moore is standing at the back of the doctor in white, with Gene Tunney behind him wearing a white shirt. Ermino Spalla is standing with his arms crossed. The other men shown are unidentified (Craig Hamilton collection, www.josportsinc.com).

that made Flowers go to the ropes. Then Greb sent a "hard right to the body which made Tiger back away." Both fighters missed some swings, but Greb was able to land a couple of good right hooks to the chin. The *Pittsburgh Post* wrote that "Tiger was slowing up" in this round. They exchanged blows until the end of the round, which Greb won.

The fifth round was awarded to Greb because by this time he was landing a lot of combinations. The next two rounds were said to be Flowers's best of the fight. Flowers landed a good right hand to the chin while Greb was stepping in, which made Greb back up to the ropes. The crowd started yelling, but Greb immediately started fighting back. Flowers threw a lot of effective punches but by the end of the seventh "seemed slowed up at the bell." Flowers seemed to have used up his energy reserves and the fight was all Greb's from here on out. In round eight, "the champion opened up at old speed. He shot rights and lefts to the head without return and made Tiger hold. Greb began weaving about, shooting rights and lefts and making Tiger miss." Round eight was awarded to Greb.

Greb "cut loose" in round nine. "He landed six rights and lefts without return and then sent two hard right uppercuts to the head." This round went to Greb also. Flowers "seemed tired at the bell" when the tenth and final round began. After both fighters gave their best, Greb was awarded the round.

Greb was given the victory after winning six of the ten rounds. Flowers won three rounds while the first round was judged even. The next day the headline in the *Pittsburgh Post* read, "Champion Harry Greb Beats Negro Boxer In 10 Slashing Rounds." Flowers was said to have been "easily outpointed."

Greb and Ted Moore (right) during their title bout, with referee Eddie Purdy looking on (Craig Hamilton collection, www.josportsinc.com).

The *Washington Post* also gave the verdict to Greb. The newspaper headline the next day read, "Greb Retains His Title In Fight With Negro."[41] The article would go on to say how Greb easily outpointed Flowers in eight of the ten rounds.

The *Oklahoman* had the headline, "Middleweight King Has Little Trouble In Beating Flowers." The article said how Greb used his "whirlwind attack to capture eight of ten rounds." Greb had been puzzled in the first round by "Flowers' southpaw boxing" but then "gauged this style correctly and was the leader in all but two rounds." It was even written that Greb "drew blood from his opponent early in the contest."[42]

The *New York Times* had the headline, "Greb Defeats Flowers." The short article told how Greb "easily outpoints Atlanta boxer in ten-round bout in Ohio."[43] The *Times* also awarded Greb eight of the ten rounds.

Greb would have seven more bouts in 1924, not losing any of them. Some of the fighters in those bouts included Jimmy Slattery, Gene Tunney, Tommy Loughran and Jimmy Delaney. *Ring* magazine would list Greb as their 1924 Fighter of the Year.

On January 1, 1925, Greb fought middleweight contender Augie Ratner at Madison Square Garden. Ratner was considered a major threat because he had recently beaten Ted "Kid" Lewis, fought Paul Berlenbach to a draw and knocked out Jack Delaney in the first round. Ratner fought many great boxers in his career including Mike McTigue, Johnny Wilson, Mike O'Dowd, Bryan Downey, Jock Malone, Lou Bogash, Dave Shade, and Jimmy Slattery.

Greb "bewildered, outfought and outroughed the highly touted Augie Ratner of New York."[44] When the ten-round fight was over Greb had won every single round. In the later rounds

Greb even started fighting flat-footed so as to try for a knockout. It wasn't to happen and Greb won the decision on points.

A few days later on January 6, 1925, Greb stopped off in Chicago and tried something he had never done before. He acted as official referee at the Arcade Gym, where some amateur bouts were being held. There were ten bouts total and Greb had a taste of what it was like to be the third man in the ring. Greb was known for not liking the fact that a referee had to be in the ring with him when he fought. He believed that referees should be outside the ring to allow the fighters more freedom. This made the image of Greb acting as a referee ironic and amusing.[45]

On April 17, 1925, Greb fought Johnny Wilson for a third time. The fight took place at the Mechanics Building in Boston and was a ten-round fight. It was a "sizzling battle" and better than the previous meetings. Both fighters won four rounds with two rounds even. "But Greb captured the decision because he was far more impressive in taking his four rounds than Wilson was in his four." Whenever Wilson started being effective, "the Pittsburgh lad put on a bit more steam and promptly checked the rally."[46]

Tiger Flowers received the nickname "The Fighting Deacon" because he was a deacon in his church. He was known to read the Bible daily and was very friendly. He eventually became the first African-American since Jack Johnson to hold a world title (Craig Hamilton collection, www.josportsinc.com).

On July 16, 1925, the promoter Floyd Fitzsimmons thought he would try another time to host a Greb-Dempsey fight. He had first tried back in 1920 after the two boxers sparred together. Fitzsimmons was hoping his "friendship with Dempsey" would enable him to get Dempsey to sign. The night of July 16 Fitzsimmons called Mason to start the ball rolling on a possible fight in Michigan City on Labor Day. Fitzsimmons was staying in New York at the time trying to persuade Dempsey to agree.[47]

Getting Dempsey to fight competitive fights was difficult because he wanted to retire undefeated. Jack Kearns, Dempsey's manager, said, "Dempsey's contention is that if he retires as an undefeated champion, he'd always in the future, be able to collect money as a showman in various capacities, whereas a defeated titleholder, the present and coming generations would relegate him into the pugilistic discard." Kearns would go on to say, "Jack is painting mental pictures of himself as a grand old man, being the hero of the ring as an undefeated champion."[48]

Dempsey had planned to fight Gene Tunney or Harry Wills at the end of the year under the promotion of Fitzsimmons, but needed a couple of "warm-up bouts" first. In a newspaper article on July 21 it was written:

> Dempsey said he wished to assure everybody that he hadn't retired and that he would box for promoter Floyd Fitzsimmons in the Sky Blue arena at Michigan City, Indiana late in September, provided Fitzsimmons could obtain a suitable opponent, and the terms were satisfactory. Dempsey said this would be one of the "warming up" bouts mentioned in his agreement with Rickard, which provided for one or two such contests before the match with Wills.[49]

Fitzsimmons was considering Harry Greb, Jack Renault, Tommy Gibbons, George Godfrey, Bartley Madden or Martin Burke for the warm-up bout.

A newspaper article titled "Greb Follows Dempsey Into Chicago" described how Greb traveled to meet Fitzsimmons to talk over the details of the fight. Regis Welsh, working for the *Pittsburgh Post*, wrote: "It has been the ambition of Greb's life to meet Dempsey." Before Greb left Pittsburgh to meet Fitzsimmons in Chicago he was interviewed. Greb said, "If Fitz makes the price right, there is nothing else to worry about. I'll take the match with Dempsey in a minute." Greb would go on to say,

> There was never a time that I did not think I could out-speed the champion and even though the chance is coming a few years later than it should, I'll take it. Dempsey has not been doing much for the last few years. I have been active and proved in the Walker fight that I still have something. Dempsey couldn't hit me at Benton Harbor a few years ago—maybe I can still make him look bad. Anyhow, if the money is right—but that fellow Fitzsimmons will have to put it in the bank first—I'll fight Dempsey in September or any time he wants. Gibbons fought him at Shelby for nothing, but my dough will have to be certain before I take the chance. The money is the only thing I'm worried about. If that is straightened out I'll be more than glad to take the chance.[50]

When Greb arrived in Chicago he met with Fitzsimmons and many Chicago sportswriters. In a newspaper article titled "Greb picked as Best Available Foe For Dempsey In Ten-Round Title Bout," it was reported that Greb "was chosen as the best available opponent for Dempsey in view of the fact that the heavyweight champion said that he could not be ready for an engagement with Gene Tunney or Harry Wills this year." The article would go on to say how Fitzsimmons was waiting on Dempsey to sign the contract before he would post $50,000 guaranteeing to stage the bout. Once Dempsey posted $25,000, then Fitzsimmons would post $50,000 and Greb would post $10,000. The article made it clear that "the middleweight titleholder boxed Dempsey two or three times in training camps with the result that Dempsey was unable to do very much with him."[51]

While the promoter was waiting on Dempsey to sign the contract, Greb and Mason agreed to the fight. In a *Chicago Tribune* article titled "Greb Willing To Battle Dempsey On Sept. 19 or 25," Mason was interviewed. He said, "Either date is satisfactory with us."[52] When Greb and Mason were in Tulsa, Oklahoma, for the Otis Bryant fight, they scheduled a meeting with Fitzsimmons "to sign articles for a ten-round title match with Jack Dempsey."[53]

On the eve of Greb's signing the contract, Dempsey refused to fight Greb. In an article titled "Won't Meet Greb," a spokesperson for Dempsey told the papers, "Dempsey has not signed to fight Greb at Michigan City." The spokesperson would go on to say, "Dempsey has decided that if he fights anyone at all in September, it will not be Greb. He will continue light training, however, in case some bout is arranged for him soon; but in case of delay in action, he will turn his attention toward other matters."[54]

Dempsey was said to have wanted to fight Bartley Madden instead of Greb. An article titled "Bartley Madden Likely To Take Greb's Place In Michigan Bout" stated, "Indications of Dempsey's disapproval of Harry Greb as an opponent in a fight this year increases Madden's chances of obtaining a title match."[55]

On August 3 Floyd Fitzsimmons, with contract in hand, was finally able to corner Dempsey in Los Angeles. The two met and "sat down hard" when Fitzsimmons wanted "immediate signing of papers for a bout between the champion and Harry Greb next September." The excuse Dempsey offered for his refusal to fight Greb this time was said to be that "the one fight he wanted was with Harry Wills."[56] Dempsey's manager Jack Kearns was interviewed about the Greb fight and referred back to the time when Greb had gotten the best of Dempsey years ago in the sparring matches. Kearns said, "The hell with that seven-year itch."[57]

Sports fans were denied the chance to see "two of the world's greatest fighters" fight for the title. "One a brute champion, the other, the fastest, trickiest and gamest of his pounds who ever pulled on a glove."[58] Grantland Rice would say that Greb was "a cross between a wildcat and a hornets' nest." Jack Dempsey said Greb was "the fastest fighter I ever saw."[59]

Greb went on to fight Ed "KO" Smith, Pat Walsh and Tommy Burns in August 1925. Greb knocked out Smith and Walsh in early rounds. Burns was a last-minute replacement for Jack Delaney, who had to cancel his fight with Greb; he was in the hospital for a throat operation.

Greb's next boxing match was on October 12, 1925, against Tony Marullo. It was a ten-round fight in Pittsburgh and Greb won every round. Greb beat Marullo again a month later and finished the year off by fighting Soldier Buck on December 14 in Nashville, Tennessee. Greb beat Buck in eight rounds and knocked Buck out of the ropes six times. It was clear that Greb was in great shape while defending his middleweight title.

12.

THE TUNNEY REMATCHES

When Greb soundly defeated Gene Tunney for the American Light Heavyweight Title in 1922, it was the first time they met in the ring. From 1922 to 1925 these two men fought each other five times. Greb reigned as middleweight champion starting in 1923 and Tunney reigned as heavyweight champion starting in 1927. When Greb thoroughly beat Tunney in a bloody battle on May 23, 1922, he became the first man to beat Tunney. When their careers were over Greb was the only man in history ever to have beaten Gene Tunney. While the first fight is legendary, their other four fights would be equally exciting and controversial.

After Greb beat Tunney in their first bout, he successfully defended his title against future Hall of Famer Tommy Loughran on January 30, 1923. The following month a Greb-Tunney rematch was scheduled for February 23. Both fighters trained for the fight, Tunney at his training quarters in Red Bank, New Jersey, and Greb at the Garden Gymnasium.

Tunney altered his technique to adapt to Greb's style. While Tunney was training for the bout he was helped out by lightweight champion Benny Leonard. Leonard had been ringside at the first fight and thought Tunney focused too much on Greb's head and not enough on his body.[1] Leonard taught him "to hit him in the heart" by throwing punches underneath Greb's elbows and landing them in the middle of his body. It was meant to take the wind out of Greb's sails.[2] Tunney added his own observations from fighting Greb the first time. Soon after their first fight Tunney said he saw something that made him think he could beat Greb. This was "the way Harry dropped his shoulder at times, the move he made when he threw a right hook."[3] Tunney went into this rematch hoping these little things, and his improvement as a boxer, would be enough to help him give a better showing than last time.

Greb was physically ready, finishing six fights in six weeks, but mentally he had other things on his mind. His wife Mildred had just come home from the spa where she had been fighting her tuberculosis. The doctors said she didn't have much time to live. Greb was staying at home with her and planned on continuing his care for her once this previously scheduled fight was completed.

A major difference in the rematch compared to the first time they fought was Billy Gibson. Billy Gibson was in Greb's corner during the first fight and acted as Greb's second. But Gibson had since left Greb's camp and had now become Tunney's new manager.[4] Just days before the fight was to take place, Gibson tried to put Greb on the defensive by petitioning the State Athletic Commission to "have a strict watch placed on Harry Greb."[5]

Gibson felt that Greb had committed fouls in the first fight and didn't want it to happen this time. Gibson pointed out to the commission that rule 6 of the New York boxing law stated, "Points should be deducted for a foul, even though it is unintentional and not of a serious enough nature to warrant disqualification."[6] In an interview in the *New York Times* on February 21, just two days before the fight, Gibson said, "I have decided to ask from the commission protection for Tunney against the violations of boxing rules by Greb. I am convinced that Greb disregards the boxing rules, which are part of the Walker law. I do not think Greb is deliberate in his violations, but at the same time I want to seek some assurances of protection for Tunney against Greb's holding and hitting and other unfair boxing tactics." Gibson's motives were very clear: he was asking the commission to talk with the judges of the fight and "instruct its officials for the title bout to pay particular attention to Greb's deportment in the ring and to penalize the Pittsburgh boxer for any infractions of the boxing rules."[7]

Gibson's actions created such unusual attention to the fight that many feared Greb would not receive a "square deal" in the bout. Many started to believe Greb would be a victim of an "injustice," that the fight was a "frame" and "a fix."[8] Greb's manager, Red Mason, accused Tunney's camp of "trying to 'intimidate' the New York officials into an anti–Greb bias."[9] It was such a threat that Greb's wife Mildred wrote a letter to the chairman of the State Athletic Commission, William Muldoon. In the letter Mildred pointed out that she had received "many anonymous communications by mail and wire predicting many things which Greb would encounter because of his alleged foul fighting tactics."[10] Mildred was looking for "relief and assurance" that it would be a fair fight.

Chairman Muldoon felt he had to come to Greb's defense and calm the tide of skepticism surrounding this bout. In the *New York Times* on the morning of the fight he announced, "So far as I know, there is nothing foul in Greb's boxing style. If there were he would have been disqualified long ago." Muldoon went on to say, "Yet I don't know of a single instance of Greb being disqualified because of a foul. I have assured him he will not be the victim of any injustice in the ring tomorrow night."[11] Muldoon's response was said to be "reassuring" to Mrs. Greb, but a shroud of uncertainty surrounded this fight before it even began.

The fight took place at Madison Square Garden in New York on February 23, 1923. The crowd viewed Tunney as the "hometown" boy from Greenwich Village, while Greb was said to have entered the fight a "marked man." This was demonstrated when the two fighters stepped into the ring. The packed house greeted Greb "with a warm reception" while Tunney was greeted "amid an ovation which lasted for more than a minute." The odds leading up to the fight had Greb the favorite, but after the controversy it had dropped down to even when the fighters entered the ring.[12] Greb weighed 165½ pounds while Tunney, at 174 pounds, outweighed him almost nine pounds when he entered the ring. The crowd was said to be "almost solidly behind Tunney" before the fight began.

Before the first round began, Referee Patsy Haley gave his instructions to the boxers. Greb asked Haley for advice on what was fair and what was questionable. Tunney stood there motionless while Greb demonstrated on Tunney's body different techniques he would use and asked Haley for his advice. The argument over style lasted "for several minutes." It was very clear that Greb was concerned that he would be disqualified for fighting the same way he always did. After the mid-ring consultation, both fighters went back to their corner to begin the bout.

During the first round Greb focused his punches on Tunney's head. Tunney seemed to have taken Benny Leonard's advice and focused on a body attack. In the second round Greb landed some punches to the head and body while Tunney continued countering to the midsection. After the bell Referee Haley went to Greb's corner and said to "be careful while throwing that right to the body." In the third round Tunney continued the body attack while Greb landed lefts and rights to the head. There were some hard punches exchanged in this round. After one wild exchange, "Tunney's left eye showed signs of blood." Greb seemed to be tentative to cut loose, not knowing what was acceptable or not. In between rounds, "Tunney looked worried as they attended to his eye."

In the fourth round the crowd "hooted" at Greb whenever they were in a clinch, thinking Greb was doing something rough. Tunney was seen using a "rabbit punch for the first time and was stopped." Tunney landed a right to the nose that "drew blood." Tunney also threw some effective uppercuts and seemed very strong in this round.

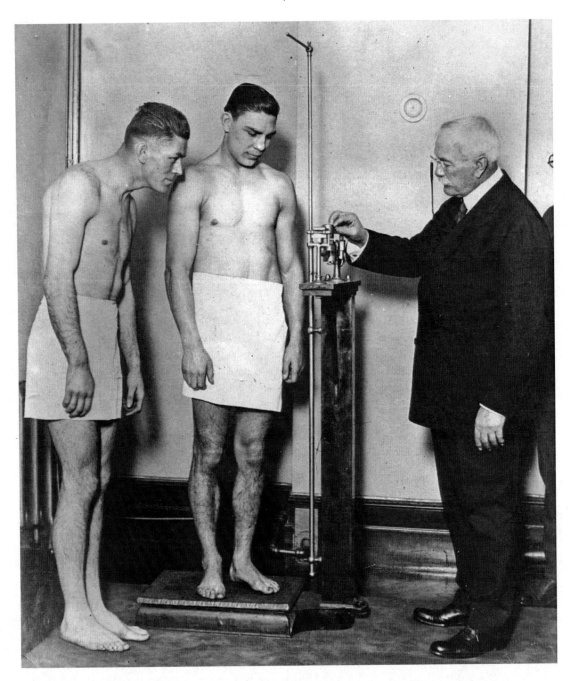

Tunney (left) strains to read Greb's weight on the scale as Commissioner William Muldoon balances the bar. This weighing-in was for their second bout, on February 23, 1923 (Craig Hamilton collection, www.josportsinc.com).

At the start of the fifth, Greb "started dancing around" for the first time in the fight. Tunney continued to pepper Greb's body with punches while having the better of the infighting. Before the bell Greb landed an overhand right to the ear and two more punches. Greb's left side was marked by Tunney's right-hand punches.

During the sixth round it was seen that Tunney was starting to tire. Greb landed a great right to Tunney's chin and followed it up with two lefts, while Tunney was still landing effective body punches. Greb landed a lot more in this round, but there wasn't much steam behind them.

In the seventh round Greb landed two rights to the body, "and then cut Tunney's eye with a left." Greb was able to repeatedly land rights to the jaw, "and Gene was visibly annoyed at his own inability to avoid them."[13] Before the bell Greb landed a left and a right.

With Tunney tiring, Greb was very busy in round eight. Greb began his two-handed attack while "Tunney seemed content to let Greb lead." Greb shot two hard rights to the head that backed Tunney up. Greb started feeling so comfortable he began holding Tunney with one arm while hitting him with the other. Greb was so in control that he measured Tunney with a left then scored a hard right to the chin that "sent Tunney back onto his heels." Greb forced Tunney to the ropes, where both fighters exchanged blows. It was written the next day that "it was a great round and Greb [was] having a great margin."

Before the ninth round, "Tunney and Gibson called Haley to their corner and [began] telling him about Greb's tactics." When the bell rang Greb walked out slowly, then landed "half a dozen blows to Tunney's chin" including "a fierce right-hand punch." In the clinches referee Haley started shouting "Let 'er go" to help separate the two boxers. They started fighting rough, and "science was abandoned by both fighters." Tunney drove Greb to the ropes and threw lefts and rights, while "Greb laughed." Greb threw "a left hand that opened a cut over Gene's right eye."[14] Tunney's body blows "were missing, while Greb was working up to his regular form. It was a tough round, but Greb seemed sure of himself as he walked to his corner at the bell." The two were compared to "longshoremen" in this round, which Greb won.

The tenth round started with a clinch. Greb landed a left hook, then threw lefts and rights to the body. A couple of Greb's punches were a little "wild" and "low" so the referee "cautioned him several times." Tunney continued to focus on Greb's body, but Greb retaliated with "four rights to Tunney's head." Immediately it was noticed that "Tunney's eye bore signs from a hard right." They went into a clinch and Greb threw lefts to the face. In the following clinch, "Tunney kept pounding Greb over the heart." Greb replied with a straight left punch that made Tunney's head fly back. They both threw body blows while Greb also added lefts and rights to the head. It was another round for Greb.

In the eleventh round, "Greb appeared to have his second wind, and pitched into Gene, swinging both hands for the head." Tunney went "head first" into a clinch while Greb "held out both arms" to show the referee that Tunney was clinching. Greb then "acted like a young lion" when he "chased Tunney around the ring, whaling away with both hands." He never stopped swinging while Tunney "seemed to have lost a lot of his steam." This was clearly Greb's round as he was "always the aggressor," but he continued to get hit in the stomach by Tunney's blows.

Near the start of round twelve the boxers traded punches and went into a clinch. "Greb let go with both hands." Referee Haley grabbed Greb and then "cautioned Greb for an alleged attempt at butting in the clinches and for a while it looked as if the referee was going to disqualify him." Haley kept on saying, "Don't do that, don't do that." Greb argued his case and was allowed to continue. They exchanged blows, but whenever Greb landed punches anywhere near the body, "the crowd began to say throw him out." It was noticed that "Greb was trying hard," but he was now cautious to "cut loose." Greb was able to land a right to Tunney's chin at one point, but the next time they clinched, "Haley again cautioned Greb and it was beginning to look bad for Greb as everything he did was found fault with." It was noticed that the referee was "making it hard for Greb." The round ended and Greb went to his corner. Referee Haley followed him to his corner and "cautioned him" again while the crowd cheered for Tunney, their hometown boy. Greb had been winning the rounds since the sixth, but was now forced to fight "desperately with the odds against him."

At the start of the thirteenth they clinched and "Greb was careful." Greb threw a hard right to the chin and then two uppercuts to the same target. Tunney was countering to the body. They traded punches in the center ring then Greb managed to force Tunney to a corner while the "crowd hooted." Greb landed a hard right to the chin "that rocked the Irishman." When Greb threw a left to Tunney's head, "Tunney complained to the referee." At the end of the round "Tunney wrestled his way out of a clinch and was warned for his roughness."

In the fourteenth they exchanged punches to the body. Then Tunney "leapt in with a right" that landed "flush on the jaw." It rocked Greb and the crowd got to their feet and "was in an uproar." Tunney continued his attack; "Greb, however, stood up under Tunney's heavy rights and lefts to the body." Greb was put on the defensive "for the first time in the bout but succeeded in blocking most of Tunney's punches." While Tunney focused his punches at the heart, Greb landed a left hook to the body at the bell.

Greb was middleweight champion. He often wore this kind of shirt while training (© Bettmann/CORBIS).

The crowd was still on their feet yelling as the two boxers shook hands in the ring before the start of the fifteenth and final round. Greb landed a left punch. It was noticed that "Tunney seemed afraid to lead." Greb continued to come out very strong as the round began, "and rocked Tunney with a succession of right uppercuts as they mixed at a speedy pace." Whenever Tunney landed to the body, "he was jolted by several smashes to the head in return." Greb was leading the round the whole time. As the round ended Greb hooked a left to Tunney's jaw.

The two judges for the bout were Charles E. Miles and Charles J. Meegan, with the referee, Patsy Haley, the deciding vote if needed. After Haley gathered the cards from both judges, the announcer, Joe Humphries, proclaimed Tunney the winner and new light heavyweight champion. It was a split decision with judge Charles E. Miles writing down Greb as the winner on his card. The other judge voted for Tunney, so Haley had to cast the deciding vote. Haley gave it to Tunney.[15] The verdict was greeted "with mingled acclaim and disapproval." Greb left the ring "amid a semi-hostile demonstration." The *New York Times* admitted that Greb was "fighting before a crowd which was openly hostile from the start."[16]

The controversy before the fight would be surpassed by the controversy about the split decision. The decision was a huge surprise to many who witnessed Greb leading and forcing the fight for most of the bout. Although it looked to many like Greb had won the fight, Haley later described why he cast the deciding vote for Tunney. The next day Haley declared "that Greb's foul tactics, including holding and butting, influenced the verdict which he and the judges gave to Tunney, despite the Pittsburgher's apparent margin on points." Haley's decision was so unpopular that he was assaulted on his way to the dressing room and there were numerous arrests. "One woman reached out of the railing and grabbed the gray-haired arbiter by the silvery locks, and the man [an assailant] missed a wild right intended for Haley's jaw. The second man the police took in, is said to have threatened Haley for his part in the 'deliberate steal' as he termed it."[17] There was also a threat on Haley later that night in an uptown billiard hall. All those arrested were native New Yorkers.

Many sportswriters witnessing the fight thought Greb had won, or at least that a draw should have been given. The *New York Herald* said the result "was probably the most outrageous decision ever rendered in New York State." Harry Newman for the *Chicago Tribune* wrote: "Most of the fans seemed to be of the opinion that a draw would have been more equitable." Westbrook Pegler, writing for the United News, wrote: "many on hand seemed to think that Greb was entitled to no worse decision than a draw."[18]

The decision was already controversial, but the aftermath was about to be made worse. Two days after the fight, in a *New York Times* article titled "Muldoon Says Greb Outpointed Tunney," the chairman of the New York State Boxing Commission declared that Greb should have received the decision. When interviewed after the bout Muldoon said, "The decision in Tunney's favor was unjustifiable, in my opinion." He went on to say, "I thought Greb should have received the decision after his determined fight."[19] In another interview Muldoon stated, "I heartily indorse every word regarding the bout, that appeared in the New York 'Herald' this morning." He went on to say, "While the fight was a rough one, Greb was no more blamable than Tunney." In an article titled "Haley's Decision Wrong in Opinion of Billy Muldoon," a bunch of ringside critics were asked for their results. Four gave the decision to Greb, five "insisted that a decision of a draw should have been registered,"[20] and four gave the fight to Tunney.

After the fight Greb and Mason were interviewed at the Pennsylvania Hotel in New York. Mason said, "I think Greb won and won handily. Greb himself thinks he won." Greb explained how both fighters were boxing rough. "According to the referee, Patsy Haley, I was fouling Tunney all through, when, as a matter of fact, Tunney was hitting me low in nearly every round."[21] Mason went on to say, "Greb is so sure he can beat Tunney anytime he boxes him that he is going to demand a return bout for the championship. I intend to go down to the offices of the State Athletic Commission on Monday and issue a challenge to Tunney on behalf of Greb. I will post a forfeit of $2,500 to bind the challenge."[22] Therefore, the stage was set for a second rematch to take place.

Greb returned home to take care of his ailing wife Mildred. He stayed by her bedside at their home until she passed away on March 18, 1923. Then, on August 31, Greb won the World Middleweight Title by beating Johnny Wilson. A third bout against Tunney was scheduled for December 10, 1923. It also took place at Madison Square Garden. Greb finished training for the fight the day before by running in Central Park and "doing some boxing, rope skipping and bag punching in the gymnasium."[23]

This bout was also a fifteen-round fight for the light heavyweight championship. However, the similarities ended there. There was no controversy leading up to the fight and the judges and referee were all changed, the referee for this bout being Lou Magnolia. Greb put on some extra weight for this bout and weighed in at 171½ pounds while Tunney was 175 pounds. Tunney again focused on Greb's body and did some more leading in this bout compared to the last one. At times during the fight "Greb's tactics bewildered the champion," but it didn't stop Tunney's "steady body fire." Greb's best round was the fifteenth when he "unleashed a furious attack that threatened for a moment to topple the champion. Setting a terrific pace in the closing round, Greb pummeled Tunney on the head and body, jarring the champion to his heels with several smashes."[24] However, it happened too late in the fight and Tunney was awarded a unanimous decision. Most of the critics awarded nine rounds to Tunney, four rounds to Greb and had two rounds even.

Greb fought a lot cleaner in this bout. Westbrook Pegler, writing for the United News staff, even wrote: "If there was foul work at the cross roads it must be scored against Tunney, who was guilty of butting on a few occasions."[25] There were still sportswriters and newspapers who thought Greb had won, but they were in a minority this time. Pegler was one of the people who thought Greb had won the fight, as was Regis M. Welsh for the *Pittsburgh Post*. Welsh wrote:

> Tunney, his eye cut, his mouth and nose bleeding, windblown and tired climbed out of the ring amidst loud hooting, while Greb, who won admiration by his clean, earnest and ever aggressive fighting, stood silently for a few seconds after greeting Tunney and listened to the jeering which boomed against the rafters as the prejudice of the local judges and referee became an established fact, instead of a myth or a dream or even a mistake.

After three battles between these boxers, most believed each fighter had won one bout with the other bout a draw. Because there were no knockdowns in any of the fights, people were still not convinced which fighter was the better light heavyweight. Tunney needed a more decisive victory against Greb to settle any unanswered questions. So a fourth bout was scheduled a year later.

The bout took place at the Olympic Arena in Cleveland, Ohio. Around 10,000 spectators in overcoats braved the cold air in the outdoor arena to see the fight. It was a ten-round bout with Matt Hinkel as the referee. The date was September 17, 1924. This time it was not to be a title defense, but a newspaper decision. The decision would not be in the hands of two judges and a referee, but would be decided by the sportswriters working for many newspapers. Whoever received the majority of the sportswriters' opinions in the newspapers the next day would be declared the winner of the bout.

Greb entered the ring first, close to eleven P.M.; with him was Mason and Tom Dolan as the second. Greb weighed 166 pounds this time, while Tunney outweighed him by nine pounds. Tunney arrived minutes later with Billy Gibson and Greb's old manager George Engel. Both boxers entered the ring without gloves but with their hands bandaged. The gloves were then put on and referee Hinkle argued with Greb about what was allowed in the bout and what wasn't. After the instructions were agreed upon the fight began.[26]

Greb started the first round fast and hard. Tunney focused on the body again, and Greb landed everywhere, mostly the head. There were a couple of clinches on the ropes, and it was said Greb had a slight advantage in the first round.

They were "dancing" early in the second round. Greb "kept ramming short rights to Tunney's head as Gene hammered the body in a clinch." Greb danced on the outside and picked his shots, then Tunney landed a bunch of shots to the body with both hands. They were both hitting the body when Greb forced Tunney to the ropes. It was said to be Tunney's round.

Greb picked it up in round three and "swarmed all over Gene with both hands to the head and body." Greb circled Tunney hooking lefts and rights to the body, while Tunney threw some short punches to the body. Greb "hopped in" with a left and right to his opponent's head and a hard left to the face. Greb then "followed this with another left and right to the head and again bounced into Tunney, who tried to stave him off." It began to look like "an alley fight" so it was no surprise that it was viewed as "Greb's round by a wide margin."

Tunney was able to slow Greb down a little in the fourth round using "a heavy body assault." The biggest punch of the round was when Tunney landed "a savage right under the heart." Greb responded quickly by tearing in "wildly," but it wasn't enough to win the round. Tunney won the fourth.

The *New York Times* wrote, "Greb was the aggressor in the fifth." The paper went on to say Greb "reached Tunney with sweeping rights and lefts to the head, while Tunney continued his body attack at close range." The *Pittsburgh Post* described how "Greb bounced off the ropes and hooked both hands hard to the head. Tunney's left eye was bleeding from a hard hook." It was Greb's round.

The sixth round was said to be "tame." Greb missed some swings while Tunney continued to hit his body. Most of the punches landed by both boxers were relatively light. The papers gave Tunney this round by "a shade." With four rounds left to go, the fight was even with each fighter winning three rounds each.

Greb started round seven fast while both fighters clinched and then "mauled one another on the ropes." Greb danced around Tunney while landing lefts and rights. The round was filled with "lively exchanges" as the fighters set "a furious pace." Tunney's punches were said to be more accurate while Greb's were going around Tunney's head and shoulders. When the round ended, "they were fighting so furiously that neither heard the bell." It was "a great round and even."

Greb started the eighth with a "wild fury." When he threw "a wild swing" he missed and almost fell over the top rope. Tunney then complained to the referee that Greb was butting him. Both fighters went into a clinch, then Tunney starting talking to Greb when they were close. Tunney won the round because of his "effective body punches."

In the ninth Greb landed two great rights to the body and a hard right to Tunney's head.

"Greb was hopping around and Tunney's only work came when they came in close." Greb landed two hard lefts to the face and was said to have been "forcing the fighting." Greb then "chased Tunney across the ring with a left and right to the head." Near the end of the round Greb threw "a straight left to the face and then staggered Gene with lefts and rights to the head." It was definitely Greb's round when the bell rang. With the tenth and final round up next, it was four rounds to Greb, four rounds to Tunney and one round even.

The fighters started the last round by walking to the center of the ring and shaking hands. Greb "flew" and "chased" Tunney at the start of the round while hooking three hard rights and a left to the head. Greb sent two rights to the head and a left to the stomach that made Tunney slip to the floor. Greb helped him up and then "smashed him with lefts and rights to the head." During the round they "exchanged punches in the center of the ring on even terms."

Greb in a posed publicity photograph (© Bettmann/CORBIS).

Later in the round Tunney drove Greb to the ropes where they traded punches. At the very end Greb missed a right to the head while Tunney also missed a right swing as the bell rang. The final round was judged to be a draw.

The *New York Times* wrote the next day that though they "fought at a furious pace, neither was damaged." They also wrote that Tunney left the ring with "a slight cut on his forehead." Another newspaper wrote that after the fight Tunney had a "cut above the right eye," and Greb was bleeding "from the mouth where several hard lefts had nailed him."

The result in most of the newspapers the next day was that the fight was an obvious draw. The *Washington Post* had a headline, "Greb And Tunney Go Ten Rounds To Draw." The article made it clear that the two boxers "fought ten rounds on fairly even terms here tonight, according to a majority of the newspaper experts at the ringside."[27]

The *New York Times* headline was "Tunney And Greb Draw In 10 Rounds." In the article they describe how Greb, outweighed by about ten pounds, was the aggressor and Tunney countered with a good body attack.

Referee Matt Hinkel later said he would have also ruled it a draw. Other newspapers that judged it a draw were the *Lima News* and the *Lincoln State Journal*. Some newspapers even listed Greb as the flat-out winner, but they were in the minority. With four fights completed, many believed the tally was one win for Greb, one win for Tunney and two fights drawn. These exciting fights left people wanting more, so six months later a fifth and final bout was scheduled. The fight was set for March 17, 1925.

On the last day of February, a couple of weeks before the fight, Greb was driving in Pittsburgh at night with two women in his car. At the entrance of Highland Park, five men held up Greb and his two female companions. The crooks stole a ring and $95. The incident was reported in the *Washington Post* with the headline "Harry Greb in Fight With Five Bandits." Normally when five men attack one man with two women, the five men would get away without a scratch, but not this time. The article described how Greb reported the robbery immediately and when the police went back to the scene of the crime the police "found the road spattered with blood as a result of the punishment inflicted upon the highwaymen."[28] Greb had beaten up the five robbers who attacked him.

The police later arrested George Seibert and E.A. Brendle, who were identified as a couple of the robbers. When Greb identified Mr. Brendle, age thirty-two, Brendle's wife and two children were crying and pleading his case to Greb. Greb was so touched that he offered to put up bond for his assailant to help get him released. The police rejected Greb's offer to help out his own robber.[29]

The Greb-Tunney fight had to be canceled immediately due to injuries Greb had received while beating up his attackers.[30] Jack Delaney and Young Stribling were asked to substitute for him in the Tunney fight, but they declined.[31] The fight was then rescheduled for March 27. On March 9 Greb arrived at Hot Springs, Arkansas, to begin a two-week training session for the rescheduled bout.[32] The intense training ended on March 23 when he left his camp at Hot Springs to travel by train to St. Paul, Minnesota, where the fight was to be held.[33] On his way Greb stopped off in Chicago on March 23, and worked out at the Arcade Gym. Whenever he was in Chicago he would train there. Later that evening Greb hopped on another train and arrived in St. Paul.[34]

When Greb and Tunney met in the ring for the final time, Tunney was just a year away from winning the heavyweight championship by beating Dempsey. Tunney was continuing to improve as a boxer and continuing to gain weight. This time he entered the ring weighing 181 pounds while Greb was only 167½. The ten-round bout took place on March 27th, 1925, at the St. Paul Auditorium and was witnessed by 8,000 fans. The betting odds for the fight went off at even money. Tunney said Greb entered the ring the way he always did, "with his hair brushed down with slickum and his face powdered."[35]

Greb strikes a menacing pose in the ring (© Bettmann/CORBIS).

The newspaper-decision bout was said to be the least exciting of all the fights. Greb started the first round by rushing Tunney to the ropes where he landed some light punches to the face. The round looked like light sparring with both boxers landing punches to the body. It was an uneventful "even" round.[36]

The highlight of the second round was when Greb "landed a left to Tunney's chin, which knocked Tunney back on his heels, and a right to the same place sent him spinning into the ropes." Tunney recovered but didn't do enough to win the round.

In the third round they fought aggressively in a neutral corner. While in the corner Greb was "whaling away with sweeping lefts and rights to the head, and Tunney, on the defensive, countered with long punches to the body." The *Chicago Daily Tribune* wrote that Greb "kept up his winning pace by getting a shade in the third."

In the fourth round Tunney focused on a body attack and was very effective. In the fifth round Tunney continued landing hits to the body. The punches were making Greb clinch to stop the attack. During the round referee George Barton warned Greb about using his elbows in the clinches.

Tunney was able to "slow up" Greb in the sixth round. It was filled with Tunney's applying a body attack that made Greb clinch to stop it. Greb attempted to move around Tunney on the outside, but whenever he landed a short punch, Tunney would reach his body with rights and lefts.

Round seven was even with both fighters landing punches to the face and body. Tunney won the eighth round by landing more hard body punches. Greb wrestled Tun-

Greb and Tunney (right) prior to their 1925 bout in St. Paul, Minnesota. Referee George Barton is in the middle (collection of Tony Triem).

ney to the ropes and the referee warned Greb again. Tunney "shook Greb with three short right uppercuts" that made Greb start fighting defensively in the round. The *New York Times* wrote: "Greb showed a flash of speed in the ninth, reaching Tunney with wild swings to the head, while Tunney continued his smashing body attack." This round and the next were extremely uneventful. The *Chicago Daily Tribune* described it as "little fighting, much clinching, and the crowd again showed their disapproval by booing. And some were so rude as to leave as early as the ninth round."

The tenth round began with both fighters swapping punches to the head. Later in the round Greb "scored half a dozen times with a left," while Tunney countered to the body. The fighters were clinched at the bell and the round was called even.

In the newspapers the next day this lackluster bout was declared won by Tunney. The *Chicago Daily Tribune* summed it up best with their headline that read, "Tunney Shades Greb In Sleepy Bout At St. Paul." The headline in the *New York Times* simply said, "Tunney Beats Greb In St. Paul Battle."

After the fight Greb visited Tunney in his dressing room. Years later Billy Gibson recounted their conversation. The two boxers hugged and Greb mentioned how Tunney was getting to be a bigger heavyweight now. Greb went on to tell Tunney,

Billy Gibson tells me you don't want to fight Tom Gibbons because you don't know what's going to happen. Listen, Gene, you're ready for anyone now. You'll lick Gibbons and you'll lick Dempsey. I know, I boxed with both of 'em. You got the style to lick 'em. You can't miss, kid, and when you're the big champ, remember it was Harry Greb who told you so.[37]

George Barton was in a corner of the dressing room and remembered that Greb's words "left a deep impression on young Tunney."

Tommy Gibbons was at ringside for the bout because the winner was to fight him next. When it was decided that Tunney had won, Gibbons said, "Tunney is a big, strong fellow and ought to give me a good hard fight." In the lobby after the fight Greb walked over to Gibbons and said to him, "Watch that guy down there; he's going to lick you." Greb was right. Tunney fought Gibbons a few months later in a fifteen-round fight at the Polo Grounds; Tunney knocked him out in the twelfth round.[38]

The next year, 1926, Tunney fought Dempsey for the heavyweight title in September. Before the fight Dempsey asked Greb to spar with him to help get ready to battle Tunney. Dempsey was heavily favored for the fight, but Greb told him, "I don't want to take your money. There's no way you can beat Gene Tunney."[39] Greb even put his money where his mouth was. Ed Van Every interviewed Greb when he said what he thought Tunney's chances were. "I am going out to place my first bet on Tunney. I have a chance to risk $1,000 against $2,500 on Gene's chances and I will have plenty more riding on Gene before I am through betting."[40] Greb knew what he was doing because he had boxed both fighters. Greb said, "I have boxed Dempsey and Tunney. You never know how good Tunney is until you do box him."[41] Tunney ended up beating Dempsey in the fight to win the heavyweight title.

Tunney said of his fights with Greb:

He had a real fighting background and an abundance of courage. To him I give credit for my rapid development from a novice to a world champion. I learned a lot from Harry, among other important fighting assets, the value of sharp shooting, for it was necessary to be a sharpshooter in order to catch Greb. He was always on the go—side-stepping, retreating, advancing—always moving, and watching him and studying him in our battles, I learned how to do as he did. It was he who taught me confidence, and I could see myself improve with each fight I had with him.[42]

Tunney wrote in his autobiography: "Few human beings have fought each other more savagely or more often than Harry Greb and I.... The first of the five is for me an enduring memory, a memory still terrifying.... All five of our fights were of that order of savagery."[43]

In another interview Tunney talked of Greb this way:

The moment we signed for a fight he was my enemy and he detested me. But after a fight it was a different matter and it remained that way until we were matched again. If ever an athlete deserved a monument to his greatness, to his endurance, to his sportsmanship, it was Harry Greb. Anything he did to you—and he did everything he could to dismember you—you could do back to him and he wouldn't complain.[44]

Long after their last fight, when Tunney was returning from Greb's funeral, Tunney described his feelings this way: "To me he was a great fighter." He then said, "...the greatest fighter I ever saw."[45]

13.

THE CHAMPION PLAYBOY

Much has been written about Greb's legendary exploits with women. Greb wasn't always as promiscuous as the famous tales suggest. He dated his future wife Mildred for years, and by all accounts they were always committed to one another. They got married on January 30, 1919, and during their five years of marriage Harry and Mildred were always faithful to one another and had a daughter named Dorothy. During Mildred's lengthy illness it was written: "For all the toughness in the ring, Greb found his young wife's imminent death unbearable."[1] Greb went to church every day to pray for her to get better. Her final passing so deeply affected him that the fighter who boxed every week had to take three months off before he was ready to step into the ring again. He went back to boxing in June, and then on his second fight back from his lay-off, he became the middleweight champion on August 31, 1923.

It is only after Mildred's death, and Greb's winning the middleweight title, that the tales begin. His sister, Ida Edwards, who eventually raised his daughter Dorothy, talked of his womanizing. "But he didn't run around with them during his marriage. I wouldn't want anything to reflect on Dorothy's children. It was only after the death of our Harry's wife that he really attained fame [chasing women]."[2]

Geoff Poundes once wrote of Greb's infamous playboy lifestyle this way: "That Harry had access to women is beyond doubt, although the multitude of anecdotes in this direction are surely exaggerated. Greb actually married his childhood sweetheart, Mildred Riley." Poundes would go on to write: "All reports are that Harry doted on both wife and daughter and was shattered by Mildred's death." He finally states: "It has also come to light that Greb carried a Bible with him everywhere he went. Can this be the insensitive deflowerer of women so often portrayed in everyday conversation?"[3]

Once Greb won the middleweight championship he was adorned with all the attention that came with it. The first credible account of Greb's taking advantage of being a famous eligible bachelor was when he fought Johnny Wilson in their title rematch on January 18, 1924. The fight took place at Madison Square Garden and Greb won. In a book titled *...a man from the past*, author Roy C. Higby recounts bumping into Greb at the Hotel Pennsylvania later that evening:

> I also remember the fellows took me to a prize fight in the old Madison Square Garden. The contestants were Harry Greb and Johnny Wilson. The fight went the full fifteen rounds and was won by Greb. Later I invited the boys to my room in the Hotel Pennsylvania where we had a bite to eat and a few drinks. Upon hearing some people in the hall, one of the fellows opened our door and invited them to join us. There were three ladies and two men, one of the latter being none other than Harry Greb, who didn't show many signs of having just completed a rough fifteen round prizefight. He was really a good fellow, and he had sandwiches and ginger ale with us, but no alcoholic beverage.[4]

That was what happened after the fight. What took place before the fight was described by Stanley Weston thirty years later. Weston wrote in 1954 about a conversation he had years earlier with Greb's manager Red Mason. Mason told Weston about the morning of the fight.

Greb ready for a night on the town (Antiquities of the Prize Ring).

We checked into the Hotel Pennsylvania the morning of the fight. Harry takes a doze and wakes about 2:30. We walk down to the lobby together and I can smell trouble. He's got that look in his good eye — the look that means fun for him and misery for me.

We sit and talk for about twenty minutes and then he says, "I think I'll go upstairs and get some more sleep." It sounds like a good idea so I say Okay.

About two hours later I go upstairs to the room and there's no Greb. I run outside looking for the bellboy. "Did you see Harry leave the room?" I ask him. "Leave?" says the punk. "He ain't been there all afternoon."

I rush over to the elevator and ask the boy where Greb is. "Sure, he got on the elevator about 3:00 o'clock," said the boy, "but he got off on the mezzanine. There were a couple of pretty dishes waiting for him and I ain't seen him since."

This was about seven o'clock, the fight was only three hours away and I can't find my fighter. So I start making the rounds of all his hangouts but I still can't find him. We're supposed to be in the Garden at 8:00 so there's nothing for me to do but wait in the dressing room.

Finally, at about half past nine, in walks Harry. He starts undressing and I say, "This is a fine time to show." He laughs and punches me playfully in the ribs. "What'cha worrying about, Red?" he wants to know, "We still got half an hour before we go on."[5]

Mason figured there was no use in arguing with him, so he let it go. Greb went into the ring and beat Wilson to win the fight. He then hooked up with the ladies again afterwards. This was a third-person account written thirty years after the event so some of the details may be in question. For example, Weston mentions Mason's saying it was after the Gibbons fight when detailed newspaper accounts of Greb's whereabouts discount that possibility.

There are other stories of Greb's seeing women before he entered the ring to fight. One such story took place a couple of months after the Wilson fight when Greb fought Fay Keiser on March 24, 1924. The fight was in Baltimore and Greb won by a knockout. Before the fight Greb was said to have unintentionally inconvenienced some hotel guests with his antics. Supposedly Greb and his entourage were traveling down the elevator in their hotel to the lobby on their way to the fight. They all stepped off the elevator but Greb stayed on. The elevator then traveled past all the floors and stopped between the top floor and the roof for "several minutes."

One of the entourage, interviewed years later, recounted the story this way:

> The girl operator had fixed him with an inescapable eye. So when we got out, she slammed the door before anyone else could get in and up she went with Greb, staying there until completion of a satisfactory merging of mutual interests. We was all happy, if guests waiting for the elevator wasn't, because it was the kind of roadwork that always sharpens the timing.[6]

Another alleged story of his playboy antics took place in the dressing room before a fight. Greb was taping his own hands before the bout when there was a knock at the door, and in came two women. James Fair wrote what he said happened next:

> Before anyone realized what was happening, he had herded his handlers and his opponent's observer into the opposition's dressing room and locked the door. While Mr. Albacker pounded frantically and emitted hysterical pleas for him to desist, he was enjoying life. When it was all over, he complimented the ladies on their finesse, paid them, told them that Hollywood scouts would sure as hell nab them, and sent them on their way. Then he unlocked the door to the joining dressing room and bandaged his hands for all to see.[7]

Greb looking dapper outside the ring. As champion he always made sure to look his best when he was out on the town (**Antiquities of the Prize Ring**).

Many of these stories are told in third-person accounts decades after they supposedly occurred. Their credibility is in question, but the fact that they are perpetuated adds to the myth surrounding the story of Greb's life. Even the great Nat Fleischer wrote that Greb loved illicit bars and the women who attended them.

However, one of Greb's closest friends, sportswriter Harry Keck, had a very different account of Greb's championship years. Keck worked as a sportswriter at the *Pittsburgh Post* and met Greb for the first time in 1914. Over the years they became close friends.[8] When Keck was interviewed in 1967 he remembered, "...at no time in his career could he have been regarded as a blonde-chasing dipsomaniac."[9] Keck knew the real Greb first-hand, not the myth, so his viewpoint should be taken more seriously.

While Greb was the bachelor champion he made sure to look good for the ladies. It has been said that before some fights he would bathe his face in Saint Anthony's Oil. He would also enter the ring with his hair neatly greased backed and combed. Some have also said he was seen with his face lightly powdered. Tunney once wrote: "Greb was curiously, oddly vain. He was concerned about his looks. Strange that anyone so careful of his face should have selected prize-fighting for a profession."[10] Indeed, Red Mason told the story (recounted earlier in this book) of how Greb faked a car accident so as to secretly fix his appearance for the ladies.

When stepping out on the town he would make sure he dressed nicely, often being seen in a suit. All of this physical vanity was a humorous contradiction because he was a rugged-looking prizefighter who was known as the most vicious fighter in the ring.

Around this time Greb met a nightclub dancer named Sally who was employed by the Shuberts in New York. Greb supposedly dated her and was said to have "introduced her to Tex Rickard as his future wife." Sally would say that Greb asked the Shuberts "to drape her figure in more clothes than the script called for."[11] Exactly when they dated each other is unknown, but it was very brief. Sally went on to marry a lawyer named Alfred Henry Bronis. Mr. Bronis would later try to sue Greb for the past "alienation of his wife's affection."[12]

After Greb's alleged antics he was ready for a more serious relationship. In late 1924 Greb met Louise Walton, who was a musical comedy actress.[13] They originally met while Miss Walton was "filling an engagement in Pittsburgh" at a local theater.[14] The two dated during this time, then she moved to Chicago to perform at a Chicago Loop theatre.[15] The show was titled *Plain Jane*, and performances started on November 23, 1924.[16] In the second act there was a prizefight routine.[17] The show originally started its run in New York City in May.[18] Louise Walton was originally from Cambridge, Massachusetts. She was a graduate of the Russell School of Larch Road, Cambridge, and the Sacred Heart Academy of Watertown.[19]

After Greb's fight against Frankie Ritz on November 25, 1924, in West Virginia, Greb took the rest of the year off. During this time his relationship with Miss Walton blossomed, and he traveled to Chicago to see her. He was very familiar with Chicago because for many years he would travel to Chicago by train on his way across country to and from different fights. He would often stay in Chicago for a few days and train at Kid Howard's Gym.

After they had dated for some time, Greb traveled to Chicago and proposed to Miss Walton. On December 18 the two went to City Hall to get a marriage license. The clerk was closing for the day but recognized the middleweight champion and stayed open to fill out the

Greb with his face powdered and his hair slicked back for the cameras (collection of Tony Triem).

In Palm Beach, Florida, Greb is playfully sparring for the cameras with Alaska Liederman. She was hoping to be one of the first female boxers in the country (© Bettmann/CORBIS).

paperwork. They had just been given the marriage license when Greb had a great idea. Although they had originally talked about getting married a couple of weeks later, spontaneous Greb thought that they might as well do it right then and there.[20]

Clutching the marriage license, they entered Judge Lawrence Jacob's night court. They needed a witness so Greb called his friend Kid Howard, the gym owner. While the three of them were in front of the judge a disagreement surfaced between the bride and groom.

The *Chicago Daily Tribune* explained, "When Louise promised Harry she would go through with the handcuffing act she had forgotten she had a contract with the *Plain Jane* company which required that she give two weeks notice before quitting the company. Now Harry wanted to wed on the spot but Louise insisted on waiting two weeks."[21]

During their conversation the judge informed them that the court was very busy, and he said they would have to clear the court if they couldn't agree. So the two lovebirds "agreed to disagree, at least for the time being." They then went out to dinner at a "chop house," where Kid Howard ran into them later on. They came to the conclusion that they would try again two weeks later.[22] Greb left for Pittsburgh the next day to train at the Lyceum Gym for his New Year's Day fight against Augie Ratner.[23]

Greb fought Ratner in Pittsburgh and gave him "an unmerciful whipping, winning every round."[24] Greb then left Pittsburgh to try to marry Miss Walton one more time.[25] Greb arrived in Chicago on January 4. The next day, January 5, the marriage ceremony was attempted again. This time the ceremony was at St. Thomas of Canterbury Church and was officiated by Father Malloy. Miss Walton's parents traveled from Boston to be there.

Unfortunately, another surprise was to unfold. The *Chicago Daily Tribune* again explained:

> At the last minute it was discovered that neither the prospective bride nor groom had received permission for the marriage from their diocesan authorities. Father Malloy declared he could not go through with the wedding and advised them to wait until they had received the necessary permission and then have the ceremony performed either in Boston or Pittsburgh among their friends.[26]

Later that night the press interviewed Miss Walton at the theater where she was performing. She informed the press that she wasn't sure about the marriage. "She declared that Greb wanted her to leave the stage, while she wants to continue her career."[27]

Greb focused on training for his bout against Bob Sage, which was taking place on January 9 in Detroit. Greb won "every one of the ten rounds from Bob Sage."[28]

A couple of months later in Pittsburgh was when Greb had his previously mentioned run-in with the five bandits outside of the Highland Park entrance. He was in a car with two unnamed women when they were held up. The bandits only got away after Greb had beaten them up first. When the police came back to investigate they saw the blood on the street from Greb's defensive pummeling. Two of the men were eventually found and arrested. It is unknown who the two women in the car were.

Then, in the first week of June 1925,

Greb poses in warm-up gear (collection of Tony Triem).

Greb went back to Chicago. It is believed that Greb's relationship with Miss Walton probably ended around this time. The *Chicago Daily Tribune* described an incident with Greb that took place on June 3 in Chicago. Greb was arrested on a "disorderly conduct charge after an automobile chase over several blocks on a north side street." The article described the situation. "As a policeman approached an automobile on a street corner to investigate a woman's scream," he said "Greb stepped into a taxicab and drove away, halting after the officer fired several shots. Five other occupants of the automobile, including two women, were also arrested." Everyone who was arrested posted a thirty-dollar forfeit but later failed to appear at their hearing.[29] After this event there are no other accounts of Greb with Miss Walton.

In June of 1925 Greb started training for his upcoming middleweight title defense against Mickey Walker. The bout was scheduled to take place at the Polo Grounds in New York on July 2, 1925. Around this time Greb started dating a woman he would stay with until the day he died. Her name was Naomi Braden.

Naomi Braden came from a large family that had been raised on a Pennsylvania dairy farm. Her first two siblings died at birth. Then there were five sisters, one brother, then Naomi,

Naomi Braden. The photograph is believed to have been taken sometime in the 1930s. Her resemblance to Greb's late wife, Mildred, is evident (courtesy of Sally Braden, Naomi Braden's great-niece).

and two more siblings after her. It is unknown how Harry and Naomi first met. Unlike Greb's last girlfriend, Naomi Braden wasn't in entertainment.[30]

Greb traveled to New York to train for the Walker fight and Naomi Braden went with him. Miss Braden is seen in the only film footage that exists of Greb, shot on July 2, 1925. There was a newsreel film crew documenting Greb's training at "Philadelphia" Jack O'Brien's gym in New York. The gym was located at 52nd Street and Broadway. Greb was having his final workout there, as well as being officially weighed in[31] before the big fight to defend the middleweight championship against Mickey Walker, the welterweight champion.

In the film footage featuring Miss Braden, Greb is jumping rope, and when he is finished she walks to Greb and wipes off his sweaty face with a towel. Then she clowns around by putting up her fist as if to throw a punch. Greb playfully smiles and leans his head back, as if not wanting to get punched. Greb promised to propose to Miss Braden after he beat Walker.

Greb did propose to Miss Braden soon after the boxing match. When she became his fiancée Greb finally told Miss Braden that he had lost his sight in his right eye. She promised him that she wouldn't say anything to anyone. She never told a soul until after his death, when she finally told her brother.

Their relationship continued through 1925 and was still going strong into 1926. When May 1926 arrived Greb was surprised when he found out he was being sued by a former girlfriend. The nightclub dancer, Sally Bronis, was suing him for $100,000 on a "breach of promise charge."

In a New York newspaper Greb's only response was printed. One of Greb's friend's stated, "Harry says he hardly knows the girl."[32] Greb had briefly dated Sally a while earlier and had supposedly promised to marry her, "in letters and telegrams."

When August 1926 arrived Greb again went to New York, now for his rematch with Tiger Flowers. This time Greb was handed a summons for a second time. Attorney Harry H. Oshrin informed Greb that he was being sued by the "outraged husband" of Sally Bronis. Alfred Henry Bronis was now asking for $250,000 for the "alleged alienation of his wife's affection."[33] Mr. Bronis had become an attorney and was said to have pressured his wife into suing Greb because he thought they could make some money. When she backed out in May, he sued on her behalf in August.

This lawsuit eventually went nowhere and Greb never had to pay anything. Greb's relationship with Naomi Braden was not affected by this and they stayed engaged. Greb and Miss Braden agreed to marry, and set the date for around the end of November or the first part of December of 1926. Because of Greb's untimely death the ceremony never happened, but she was always by his side. In the *New York Times* dated October 23, 1926, it is stated, "His fiancée, Miss Naomi Braden of Pittsburgh, was at his side when the end came."[34] A *New York Times* article titled "Greb's Fiancée Keeps Vigil Beside His Body" reiterates that Miss Braden "was at his bedside when he died." Even during his funeral she "kept a sorrowful vigil over the body."[35]

A few years later Miss Braden eventually married a man by the name of Jake Goldstein. They lived in Florida for many years, where they owned a hotel/resort off the beach. Naomi passed away around 1970. According to Sally Braden, Naomi Braden's great-niece, Naomi never talked that much about Greb after his death. She would always start to cry when talking about him, so no one ever asked her any questions.[36]

Many tales of Greb's exploits with women are greatly exaggerated. He was married faithfully to a woman he loved for five years after dating her for years before that. After her death he sowed some wild oats but eventually settled down a little. Greb then had two lengthy relationships with women he was engaged to. Many of the myths surrounding Greb's alleged womanizing throughout his career are perpetuated by people's opinion of how they would like a boxer to act.

James Fair's biography about Greb, *Give Him to the Angels,* focuses a great deal on Greb's alleged playboy ways and was written with little research. According to Greb's friend, sportswriter Harry Keck, Mr. Fair was Keck's ringside telegrapher and covered many of Greb's New York fights with him. Fair became "enamored of Greb" and wrote his book in just ninety days. It has been written about Fair's biography that it was just "a chronicle of Greb's alleged sexual exploits, not a biography of a great fighter. When Greb's family threatened to sue, the book was withdrawn from the market."[37] Throughout the years many magazine and newspaper articles have used quotes from Fair's book that simply perpetuate the same stories. In a 1964 interview with Harry Cleaveline, Keck said, "With each passing year, the Greb legend gets sillier and sillier." Keck goes on to say how Greb's "alleged skirt chasing" gets perpetuated in the press with the stories just "rehashes of the same old balderdash." Keck went on to say, "The stealing goes on and on — and there's no end in sight. Next thing you know, some idiot will insist Greb had three arms."[38]

14.

THE BULLDOG MEETS THE WINDMILL

In 1925 Harry "The Pittsburgh Windmill" Greb battled Mickey "The Toy Bulldog" Walker. The fight became one of Greb's most famous encounters. Walker had become a great welterweight by fighting Jack Britton, Dave Shade, Soldier Bartfield, Pal Reed, Lou Bogash, Jock Malone and Owen Phelps. Many of these men weighed much more than Walker. On November 1, 1922, Walker won the World Welterweight Title by defeating Jack Britton in a fifteen-round bout. As champion, Walker started defeating many of his challengers by knockout. By 1925 Walker had knocked out ten opponents as well as defeating Pete Latzo, Jock Malone, Lew Tendler, Mike McTigue, and Bert Colima by decision. With this impressive string of wins and a knockout punch, some expected Walker to beat Greb.

The World Welterweight Champion was scheduled to battle the World Middleweight Champion on July 2, 1925. Matchmaker Jimmy DeForest and promoter Humbert Fugazy put it together. Leading up to the fight on June 29 the *Pittsburgh Press* wrote an article titled "Gamblers Pick Greb To Lose." The article explained why the New York gamblers favored Walker. Greb's "whirlwind tactics" where expected to give Walker some trouble early on but betters envisioned Walker winning the decision or winning by a knockout. Many believed Greb was "going too low in weight"[1] and it would deplete his energy. Others believed Greb, now in his twelfth year in boxing, was just too old for a young champion in his prime like Walker.

Although these concerns were valid, the main reason why Walker was now favored was that the New York betters were "paying considerable attention to the stories that have been floating around about Greb's habits, and figure that the life he has been leading has finally sapped enough of his vitality to make him a mark for a man of Walker's caliber." This concern was reiterated in an article titled "Walker Favored To Defeat Greb." This article stated that "reports were that Harry was not in the best of condition, but these could not be substantiated."[2]

The title bout was originally scheduled for June 19, but was rescheduled when Walker announced he had a foot ailment. Walker had gotten an ingrown toenail on one of his big toes and had some work done to it, then canceled the fight on June 10.[3] The fight was then rescheduled for July 2.

The fight was the headline of the Italian Hospital Fund at the Polo Grounds in New York. The baseball park was located at 155th Street and Eighth Avenue, and was the same location where Greb had won the World Middleweight Championship from Johnny Wilson in 1923. Other boxing matches on the card were Harry Wills against Charley Weinert, Jimmy Slattery against Dave Shade and Jack Sharkey against Joe Lynch. An impressive card, it included five future Hall of Famers.

Greb trained for the fight at his Atlantic City camp for ten days. His chief sparring partner was middleweight George Courtney of the Paddy Mullins stable. Courtney stated that Greb was "in almost perfect condition, mentally and physically."[4]

Greb then left the camp and arrived in New York City on June 29. He continued his training

Mickey Walker (left) and Harry Greb sign the contract to battle each other. Matchmaker Jimmy DeForest is pictured in the middle chewing his cigar (Craig Hamilton collection, www.josportsinc.com).

at "Philadelphia" Jack O'Brien's gym with his workouts consisting mostly of "hand ball and shadow boxing." Just a few days before the fight, Greb stepped on the scales weighing 163¼ pounds. Walker was still training at Johnny Collin's camp at Summit, New Jersey, where he would box twelve rounds with four different sparring partners.[5]

On July 1 Greb had a public weighing at O'Brien's gym in front of hundreds of fans. When he stepped on the scales he weighed 158½ pounds, well beneath the middleweight limit. Regis Welsh wrote: "Greb proved that this is one fight he has taken seriously and one in which he will probably be more like the old Greb than he has been in the last three years."[6] Harry Keck told of who was at the weigh-in with Greb. "With Greb at the gymnasium, besides O'Brien, who took almost a fatherly interest in him, were James Mason, Greb's manager; Tom Dolan and a number of Pittsburgh friends. Greb said that Eddie Deasy, one of his particular pals, planned to come by airplane, and that he did not expect him until tomorrow."[7] When Greb left the gym he returned to the Claridge Hotel, where he had made his headquarters.

On July 2, the *Gazette Times* wrote what Greb's diet was designed to help him to make the middleweight limit:

> He drank a pint of malted milk with an egg in it and later had dinner, consisting of two chops and salad with mayonnaise dressing as ordered by O'Brien, who has been watching his diet as well as his training since he came here from Atlantic City last Sunday. Before going to bed, Greb had a glass of ale; last night he had two glasses, and he said he awoke feeling great this morning. He weighed an even 160 pounds at the end of yesterday's workout.[8]

Greb was interviewed the day before the fight and had this to say:

> They tell me Walker is a great fighter, a good puncher and a pretty good ring general. I had that
> in mind when I first started to train and maybe that is the reason that I feel so fit today. I will
> make Walker use these things from the first bell on. I am certain that even though he is a good
> fighter I will show him a few things he doesn't know and make certain that I am his master.[9]

Greb was expecting his speed and experience to make the difference. In another interview
Greb said, "I'll win in a walk." He continued,

> I look for it to be a one-sided fight after the early rounds. I don't think Mickey can keep up
> with me in speed. I am sure he cannot knock me out and I am not going to try and knock him
> out. I will be satisfied to win by an undisputable margin on points.[10]

Greb was once an 8–5 favorite to win the fight. Now that people saw how fit he was, the
odds of Greb's winning were increasing to 2–1 just a day before the fight. Greb wanted to bet
on himself to win so he did something the night before the fight to change the odds. Stanley
Weston would write:

> It seems a group of gamblers, including Arnold Rothstein, Sam Boston and Mike Best were
> shooting the breeze in front of Lindy's Restaurant. It was about two in the morning. Suddenly a
> yellow cab rolled up to the curb and out fell Harry Greb, in a drunken stupor. Rothstein, who
> had bet a bundle on Harry, looked down at the guy who was going to carry his marbles and
> broke into a cold sweat. Two heavily painted showgirls hopped out of the cab and helped Greb
> back inside. Then the cab shot away. The gamblers looked at each other and then, as if a tor-
> nado had struck, they disappeared in different directions, heading for the nearest telephones.
> They called all over the country and hedged their bets off Greb and onto the well conditioned
> Walker.[11]

Greb was said to have continued this fake act all over town at different establishments
where he knew gamblers would be. Walker wrote of this charade in his biography and said, "It
was Harry's intention to have the gambling mob think he had been drinking heavily. The ruse
worked."[12] The odds soon changed to make Walker the favorite. The news of Walker's being
favored to win "brought a grin from Greb."[13] He was said to have then bet thousands of dollars on himself to win the fight. When Greb was at the weigh-in on fight day a reporter, "who
had been tipped off that Greb had been drinking heavily the night before, asked him how he
felt." "I feel fine," Greb grinned. "How do you feel?"[14] This story of Greb's trying to change the
odds the night before the fight was first reported many decades later and may not be true.

The fight finally took place the next day with Greb weighing 159 pounds and Walker weighing 152. Over 60,000 fans were there to see this fifteen-round title fight, and the referee was Ed
Purdy. There was a thirty-minute delay between the title fight and the semifinal because Walker
was late getting to the baseball park. When he finally arrived he entered the ring first. Teddy
Hayes was Walker's second for the fight instead of Jack Kearns.

Kearns, who also managed Dempsey, had recently become Walker's manager and hadn't
agreed to allow Dempsey to fight Harry Wills, so the New York Boxing Commission put Kearns
and Dempsey on the "unfavorable" list.[15] Kearns didn't even have a license to manage in the
state so he was suspended. Kearns was now banned from entering the Polo Grounds to be
Walker's second. Hayes had been with Walker throughout all the training sessions and was ready
to step in and be in Walker's corner for the fight. After Walker and Hayes entered the ring, Greb
and Mason soon followed. Walker would write in his biography: "As we stood waiting in our
corners for the bell, I bent down to bless myself as I did in all my fights. Greb, watching me,
grinned and did the same."[16]

When the first round began both fighters started fast. Walker used some hard left hooks

The Polo Grounds, where the Greb-Walker title fight took place. The Polo Grounds was home to the New York Giants and the New York Yankees baseball teams. The previous time Greb fought there was when he won the World Middleweight Championship against Johnny Wilson in 1923.

and focused mostly on the body. The *Gazette Times* wrote that in this round, "Greb worked his trick of getting behind his opponent, confusing but not hurting him."[17] Walker landed a hook to the body as well as a left hook to the jaw that "stung" Greb on both occasions. Greb landed many rights to the head throughout the session, but Walker was said to have won the first round.

At the start of the second round Walker landed "a hard left to Greb's stomach." Walker was then low with a left and was warned by the referee. After that Greb started picking up the speed. "Greb drove a right to the face, which drew blood from Walker's nose." With Walker trying to land lefts and rights to the body, "Greb forced him to a corner and literally rained punches on him." Greb landed a big right to Walker's eye, and Walker retaliated with lefts and rights to the body. "Greb was standing flat-footed, but finally Walker went to the floor, but was up in an instant and they stood toe to toe in what seemed the greatest slugging match ever staged." The punch that took Walker to the floor was a left to the jaw. The *New York Times* stated that Walker was sent to "his glove tips," while the *Chicago Daily Tribune* wrote Walker went "to his knees." Just before the bell rang Walker "staggered" Greb with a right which some say was to the jaw while another source said it was to the ear. Greb was said to have won that round.

Early in the third there was some clinching while they both focused on body punches. Greb started using his right, sometimes missing and sometimes landing on his opponent's head or face. Walker hooked to the body, then Greb grazed him with another right to the face. They both landed left hooks to the head and rights to the kidneys. It was another round for Greb by "a close but slight shade."

At the start of the fourth Greb "hopped" out of his corner and landed a hard left hook to the head and another to the body. Walker returned with a left hook to the body. Greb then threw a left to the jaw and a right to Walker's head. It was noticed in this round that "Walker's early speed was gone and Greb was fighting him flatfooted." Greb started wrestling Walker, then threw a left and right to his face. It was written that "Greb sent a wild right which landed on Walker's back, then Harry wrestled Mickey around, again getting behind him. Harry sent another left to the body and knocked down a left to the head by Mickey. Greb, who was taking matters fairly easy at this stage, laughed as Mickey tried to free his arms in a clinch." Walker landed more punches to the body. Then Greb blocked a right punch, "and brought a smear of blood from Walker's mouth." It was a clear round for Greb.

The fifth round consisted of both boxers' focusing on both the head and body. Greb started using uppercuts more often in this round. He landed a left to the face which "sent Walker's head back and they clinched on the ropes." It was noticed that Walker's nose was bleeding. It was another round for Greb.

It was much of the same in the sixth round. "Greb pinned Walker on the ropes and pounded him on the body with rights and lefts." Later in the round Greb landed "four uppercuts to Mickey's chin." Then Greb took control when he "held Walker with his left and pounded his kidneys with the right. He repeated the operation. Greb again went completely around Walker but did no damage." Greb was getting the better of the exchanges including when they clinched and this round was Greb's also.

The seventh round was full of surprises. The fighters came out of their corners slowly. They went "head to head" and when Walker threw a right to the body, Greb countered with two lefts to the head. Walker was throwing wild and trying to hold his rival. It was said they were "fighting like a couple of heavyweights." "Time after time" Greb forced Walker to the ropes until he accidentally "pushed Mickey outside the ropes, but they shook hands and resumed fighting." Near the end of the round the two fighters were in a clinch. Referee Purdy "slipped to the floor in the excitement." Purdy had twisted his leg and one of the boxers had to step over him. "The crowd got a great kick out of it and started to count." Then Purdy "nearly upset Walker in his clumsy effort to get away from nothing. Greb assisted the referee to his feet." It was later discovered that Purdy had dislocated his right knee. Purdy handled the rest of the bout on one leg and was seen grasping the ropes often for assistance. The bell rang and it was Greb's round because he was "the aggressor almost throughout."

Greb didn't waste any time in the eighth when he went after his opponent and "chopped a half dozen rights to the head." Then both fighters landed hard right hooks to the stomach, and Walker started landing some hard left hooks to the body. In a clinch, "Greb clubbed his right to the head." Walker returned with a few more effective body punches, and Greb landed a left to the face. "Greb sent four short rights in close and Walker kept pumping to the body." Greb was said to have "uppercut repeatedly with his right to the face." The round ended after Greb landed "a left and three lefts to the body and Walker by mistake went to the wrong corner as the bell hit." The *Pittsburgh Post* reported, "Mickey was entitled to a draw in this round with his hard punches to the body."

Early in the ninth round Greb landed "three hard uppercuts to Walker's chin." Greb followed this up by landing "a half dozen light lefts to the body." Walker then landed a "light" left to Greb's mouth. It was observed that "Greb pinned Walker on the ropes and smothered Walker with lefts and rights to the body." Greb was starting to effectively block Walker's left hook. "In a clinch Greb continued to pound the body while he held Walker locked as if in a vise." Greb was trying to use his weight advantage to ride his opponent and tire him out. According to the *Pittsburgh Press* there were some Walker fans who yelled, "Push him away from you and you can beat him."[18] Then Greb landed a left jab to the mouth "which bore Walker to the floor." Walker then threw "a hard left to the body and again Greb rushed him wildly to the ropes. The referee spoke warningly to Greb." Right before the bell sounded Greb "sent Walker's head back with a right uppercut and drove a left and right to the body at the bell." Greb won the round.

At the start of round ten Greb came out dancing and landed two left jabs, and made Walker miss a left to the body. Greb was able to "dance away without a return." "Greb sent Walker to the ropes twice with lefts and rights to the face." Walker started dancing and landed a left and right to Greb's head, but Greb followed with an uppercut. Greb "leaped in with a volley of rights and lefts to the head." "Greb dropped over a hard right to the head which set Walker back on his heels. Greb spun Mick around again with two lefts to the face." Walker then landed a right to the jaw but missed a left as Greb tied him up on the ropes. They were sparring when the bell finally sounded to end the round, which was awarded to Greb.

In the beginning of round eleven, "Greb toyed with Walker and then shot two rights and a half dozen lefts to the head." Soon after this exchange it was noticed that "Greb drew more blood from Mickey's mouth." They both exchanged punches, focusing mainly on the head. "They fought like wild men and once more Greb sent Walker to the floor as they milled around." The *New York Times* stated, "Greb came in all the time and as Referee Purdy tried to separate the men, he fell for a second time." At the end of the round they were in another clinch while Greb landed lefts and rights to Walker's body. Greb won the round "by a wide margin."

Walker opened round twelve with rights and lefts to his opponent's head. "Walker crossed a right to the head and as Greb came in swinging rights and lefts to the body and head, Walker hooked a left to the face and body." Walker seemed to have gotten some of his energy back and was seen "forcing the fight." "Greb staggered Mickey with a right hand to the ear and then nailed him with a left as Mike fell against the ropes." When Greb landed punches, Walker "nailed him with a left and right to the face. It was an unexpected sport by Walker and gave him the round."

Greb started the thirteenth landing a straight left to the mouth. He then threw a left and right to the head, following up with a left to the body. Walker landed a couple of punches to the head, and Greb started moving around a little more in this round. "At close quarters Greb clubbed his right to the body and head." Near the end of the round, "Greb forced Mickey to the ropes and showered him with lefts and rights to the jaw." Greb finished with a right to the jaw that "rocked" Walker and forced him back onto the ropes. With his back on the ropes Walker received "a shower of rights and lefts to the jaw." The round was Greb's.

Greb opened the fourteenth by landing a straight left to Walker's face. Greb then also shot a left and right to the head. At this time, "The referee fell to the ropes." "Greb sent four lefts and rights to the mouth. Greb manhandled Walker, doing as he pleased with him." Greb was rushing his opponent around the ring throwing rights. Then Greb "staggered Walker with a terrific right to the jaw. Walker was groggy and helpless on the ropes but Greb was too tired to follow his advantage." It was reported that Walker was "out on his feet, but gamely stayed on his feet as Greb hooked lefts and rights to the body."

Walker remembered the punch this way when he wrote:

> I saw his right hand coming. I can still see it. It looked as big as a balloon shooting toward me. I raised my left shoulder to protect my chin, confident I could block the blow. But somehow, it slipped past and landed high on my jaw. I was knocked ragtime, not off my feet, but I was silly. You know, like a man walking in a dream. It nearly tore off my roof.[19]

Walker would go on to write: "The clip on the chin he fed me had me on queer street for a half hour after the fight."[20]

Greb continued to punish him with shots to the head and body, "as Mickey covered his jaw from a shower of lefts and rights." While Walker was "groggy" Greb "leaped in" with two-fisted body punching. "Greb pounded Walker unmercifully, but couldn't locate a vital spot. Walker was out on his feet at the bell and Greb showed him to his corner."

Walker described what happened in his corner in between these rounds. "Hayes dragged me back to my corner. He doused cold water over me. The smelling salts under my nose cleared my head. But my left eye was completely closed and the right eye wasn't much better."[21]

Both fighters shook hands at the start of the fifteenth and final round. Greb continued exactly where he had left off in the previous round when he "rushed Walker to the ropes, pumping rights and lefts to the face at close quarters." Walker seemed to have recovered slightly in between rounds and was able to land several lefts and rights to his rival's head. Walker managed to land a left and right to Greb's jaw. "Greb pressed Walker on the ropes, where he pounded Mickey with rights and lefts to the face, which brought the blood under Walker's right eye." The right eye was "badly cut." Walker gamely threw some punches to the head and forced Greb to his corner. Both men looked a little tired. "Greb hooked two lefts and a right to Walker's head." At the end of the round Greb "drove a right to the jaw and uppercut a right to the chin at close quarters." Walker was just punching wild at this time, "trying to land a haymaker." They were still sparring when the bell rang to end the fight. The final round was Greb's.

The *Pittsburgh Post* awarded Greb twelve of the fifteen rounds, with Walker winning the first and twelfth. Round eight was said to be even. The championship rounds were said to be Greb's best. "Walker, puffed, bleeding and bewildered in the thirteenth round, left himself open for a flash in the fourteenth and like a streak of lightning Greb sent out an overhead right and caught Mickey flush on the chin." It was also written that, "Greb hooked vicious right uppercuts, shot slashing hooks and jabs at Walker's head and face until the little Irishman looked as though he had put his face into an electric fan." The near knockout was said to be the highlight of the night. As the fight wore on, "it was only a question of how badly Walker would be beaten."[22]

Greb not only won, but also looked great doing it:

> Greb tonight was a master boxer who turned fighter in an instant. He bewildered Walker at nearly every stage, took the hardest raps the heavier puncher landed and still had stamina left to finish in a blaze of speed and glory. It has been a long time since Greb won a decision so far away.[23]

In an article the next day titled "Middleweight King Has Easy Time With Welter Champion," Regis Welsh wrote:

> But it was not the margin of victory, but the manner in which it was accomplished which made the champion look better tonight than he has any night since his memorable fight at the Garden with Tommy Gibbons. Walker never had a real chance to win and it was only his indomitable spirit which carried him across to the final bell.[24]

The newspaper headlines the next day told the story. The *Pittsburgh Press* wrote: "Walker Is Beaten In Hot Clash." The *New York Times* wrote: "Greb Keeps Title." The *Washington Post's* headline was, "65,000 Fans Watch Greb Retain Title In Walker Battle."

Walker himself commented on Greb's victory:

> He could hit from impossible angles. Once, after Harry missed a right to my face, he spun all the way around so that his back faced me. I relaxed my guard and waited for him to turn around. But before I knew what was happening, his left was stuck in my mouth. I still don't know how he did it, but he hit me while his hands faced in the opposite direction.

The impressive victory was appreciated by even the hardest of boxing fans. Regis Welsh would write the next day that he interviewed a "previously prejudiced" boxing man who had this to say about Greb now: "Greb is a marvel fighter whose real worth will not be appreciated until he has passed on. Some day he will go the way of all the others, down and out, but who dares guess how long it will be in coming."[25]

Greb decided to stay in New York over the July 4 holiday and go to his Atlantic City training quarters a few days later. Later on the night of the fight some say Greb and Walker ran into each other by chance outside a club. The stories say how they "fought all over again, free of charge, in the street, with no holds barred." John Lardner and James Fair were under the belief that the fight never happened. Lardner said of the story:

> I heard it when I first came here, and I have heard it at least once a year ever since, sometimes two or three times a month. Everyone who tells it tells it differently—different place, different words, different outcome. Fair is of the opinion that it is untrue, or apocryphal, and I agree with him. True or not, it shows you that Greb was a great man and a natural born hitching-post for legends.

Lardner would go on to say:

> The gist of it is that Greb and Mickey Walker, after fighting a tremendous fifteen-round fight for the World Middleweight Championship, which Greb won, met later the same night by chance and fought all over again, free of charge, in the street, with no holds barred. I estimate that I have listened to 120 versions of this story, all given as gospel. I have heard that the street fight occurred in front of the Silver Slipper, Billy LaHiff's Tavern, Texas Guinan's, Barney Gallant's and Joe Madden's. I have heard that the fight occurred on the street, on the sidewalk, in a nightclub lobby, and in the open door of a taxicab. Of the 120 versions, 116 say that Greb almost killed Walker and four say that Walker almost killed Greb. Walker, the only living potential eyewitness, sometimes says it's true and sometimes denies it, sometimes says he beat Greb in the street and sometimes says he would have if they'd fought in the street. I suspect Mickey is so attached to Greb as a legend that he would remember something even if nothing ever happened. That is the kind of effect Greb had.[26]

Stanley Weston described how the second fight occurred outside Billy LaHiff's Tavern, located on West 48th Street in Manhattan.[27] Weston wrote that when the title bout ended around 11:30 P.M., Walker cleaned himself up and went to the club to meet his manager, Doc Kearns, who had been listening to the fight there because he wasn't allowed to be at the fight. When Walker entered the club,

> He walked inside and who should he see at the front table but Harry Greb. Mickey had to pass Harry's table in order to get to Kearns and his girl. Billy LaHiff stood there and he was plenty nervous. He knew what would happen to his joint if these two guys got into an argument. The two fighters looked at each other and then Greb stood up. A smile crossed over his face. "Sit down Mick and have a drink." Walker, who was clenching his fists suddenly relaxed. He was stunned but pleased. Walker grinned and sat down. "I can use one," he said—"I had a tough night."[28]

Weston wrote how the two boxers sat at the table and shot the breeze for a while. Then Greb said, "Say, Mickey, I hear Bill Duffy has quite a joint in the Silver Slipper Café. What say we jump over and see what goes?" Weston would go on to write:

> So they walked outside, into the warm summer night and Harry hailed a cab. He opened the door and in his best manners bowed low and said, "After you, Mickey." Walker returned the bow and started to get into the taxi. Suddenly he stopped short and turned to Greb. "I just want you to know—you Dutch rat—that you never would have won tonight if you hadn't stuck your thumb in my eye." Walker had one foot in the cab but before he could get all the way inside, Harry grabbed him by the back of his neck and ripped him out onto the sidewalk. The smile Greb wore all evening disappeared, he scowled and his battered face twitched in anger. "Why you Irish lug," he yelled, "I could lick you the best night you ever saw. Even right now I could do it."[29]

Walker described what happened next in his biography, *The Toy Bulldog and His Times*. Walker wrote that Greb started taking his coat off before fighting Walker. Walker seized this opportunity. "When the coat was halfway off, I bounced one off his chin. The punch would have kayoed any other man — but not Greb." Walker continued, "We slugged away and people came running over to see what it was all about." Walker described that when the fight started the only spectators were a newspaper boy, the cab driver and the doorman. When the street fight was over, "there may have been a few dozen people watching."[30]

Walker finally wrote: "We'd probably be fighting yet if a giant Irish cop on the beat named Pat Casey had not pulled us apart and heaved us into separate taxicabs."[31]

Greb's good friend Harry Keck said of those stories that night, "I was with Greb, from the time we left the Polo Grounds after Harry's brilliant victory, until we checked into a mid-town hotel. We didn't even see Walker."[32] Keck would also say, "The Walker 'second fight' continues to be one of the legends of boxing. Walker says it happened; I say it didn't. If he's happy with it, let him have it. There is such a thing as a man telling a story so often he believes it."[33]

Just days after the fight, on July 4, Red Mason suffered an accident outside his home. Mason was rushed to the West Penn hospital, "facing the possibility of losing sight of his left eye in consequence of a fourth of July accident." The *New York Times* wrote: "A fireworks display piece exploded prematurely as Mason was bending over it, filling the left eye with gunpowder and slightly injuring the right eye."[34]

The next day Mason went to Mercy Hospital and was treated by his own surgeon. The explosion was mostly on his left side and it took several days to determine the extent of the injuries to the eye. The right eye, "although injured, is likely to be saved."[35]

On July 7 Mason was still in the hospital with both eyes heavily bandaged. X-rays were taken to determine "how badly the left eyeball has been injured by the concussion and gunpowder."[36] This eye injury added to the similarities between the lives of Mason and Greb. Both men were in the sport of boxing, both were married on January 30, both had wives that died prematurely, both were left to raise their only offspring, which happened to be daughters, both daughters' names were Dorothy and now both men had eye injuries. Luckily for Mason, his eye injury healed after a couple of weeks and he was back to his normal routine. Greb's eyesight, on the other hand, was slowly getting worse. Greb could see nothing out of his right eye. There was concern that it would start spreading to his other eye soon, but he continued fighting and living in the fast lane.

Greb would have some bad luck of his own a month and a half later on the night of August 19, 1925. The *Oklahoman* recounts what happened. "Greb and two other men had set out in the fighter's automobile for Erie, Pa., where Greb was to meet Jimmy Darragh in an American Legion boxing match Friday night. Twelve miles from here on descending a hill, the fighter's car met two others. Slamming on the brakes, the wheels locked and the Greb car slid and overturned. Passing autoists rushed Greb to this city. His companions were not seriously hurt."[37] The accident was said to have occurred "near Bakerstown."[38]

The *Chicago Daily Tribune* described what happened next:

> He was brought to the West Penn hospital, where physicians said he sustained two fractured ribs and cuts and bruises on his back and chest. The extent of internal injuries he may have suffered will not be known until x-ray photographs have been made, it was said. The champion's condition was declared to be serious, but not necessarily dangerous.[39]

The concern was due to the fact that the fractured ribs were near to his left lung, which made breathing difficult.[40] When Mason was interviewed about the crash he said Greb would have to stay in the hospital for two to three weeks. This meant Greb would have to cancel some upcoming fights, including one against Jimmy Slattery that was set for September 13.[41]

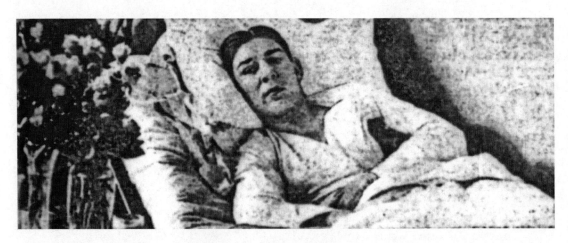

Greb in a hospital bed after a car accident. He broke two ribs and injured his back and chest. Greb later said he never felt the same after this accident. In the picture his left arm is being propped up to protect his ribs (© Bettmann/CORBIS).

When Greb was interviewed in the hospital days after the accident he said,

> I guess I won't see any action for a couple of months, maybe longer and that means the loss of a big bout in New York that had been tentatively arranged for next month. This hospital vacation is going to keep me out of shape and even when I do get on my feet again it'll take some time before I can reach fighting shape.[42]

Greb eventually recovered, but six months later he said, "You know, I have never been right since that auto accident last summer. I showed that in my fight with Tony Marullo at Motor Square and again at New Orleans."[43]

15.

THE BEST OF HIS TIME

Many boxing fans and historians judge a boxer's place in history on who he fought during his time in the ring, and how well he did in those fights. It is from this perspective that many view Harry Greb as the greatest middleweight boxer who ever lived, as well as the greatest boxer of his era. During a time when there were only eight divisions in the sport, Greb battled the past, present and future champions in the top three weight divisions, beating every single one of them that had the courage to test himself against Greb.

The men Greb defeated who were middleweight champions at one time in their career were George Chip, Al McCoy, Johnny Wilson, Tiger Flowers, and Mickey Walker. The middleweight title claimants he defeated were Jeff Smith, Bryan Downey, Eddie McGoorty, and Frank Mantell. The champion light heavyweights he beat were Tommy Loughran, Mike McTigue, Jack Dillon, Battling Levinsky, Jimmy Slattery, and Maxie Rosenbloom. He scored a victory over heavyweight champion Gene Tunney, as well as Jack Dempsey in sparring exhibitions. These are just the champion titleholders he defeated. Greb also fought and beat most of the top contenders in all of these weight classes.

The champions of his time admired Greb's speed, ferocity, endurance and will to win. Heavyweight champion Jack Dempsey said of Greb, "The fastest fighter I ever saw."[1] Previous heavyweight champion Jack Johnson is said to have sparred with Greb in a four-round exhibition at Kid Howard's gym in Chicago. Johnson is quoted as saying to Greb, "You're the fastest man your size I've ever seen."[2] Middleweight champion Mickey Walker remembered Greb this way: "Harry Greb I think was the greatest fighter I ever fought." Walker would go on to say, "He was one of the greatest that ever stepped in the ring." Hall of Fame welterweight champion Jimmy McLarnin once told an admirer, "If you thought I was great, you should have seen Harry Greb."

The accolades from his fellow champions are almost endless. Heavyweight champion Gene Tunney put it this way: "Greb is the gamest man I ever met and the most remarkable product I have ever seen in the ring."[3] Tunney also said, "Greb was one of the greatest fighters of all time."[4] Light heavyweight champion Tommy Loughran said,

> Boxing fans now have no conception of what it was like thirty to forty years ago. They can't understand what the competition was, how good Greb had to be to do the things he did. In my weight alone we had Jack Delaney, Paul Berlenbach, Young Stribling, Mike McTigue, Georges Carpentier, Battling Levinsky, Jim Slattery, Battling Siki, Gene Tunney — and several rough middleweights and heavyweights we fought. On top of the heap was Harry Greb, weighing a hundred and sixty pounds, and able to lick them all.[5]

It wasn't just his fellow champions that thought Greb was the best of his time. *Ring* magazine in 2001 listed Greb as "the greatest middleweight of all time."[6] Boxing Hall of Fame cut man and trainer Whitey Bimstein said, "I don't put nobody over Greb."[7] Boxing Hall of Fame writer Damon Runyon simply wrote: "Greb was one in a million."[8] Analyst Max Kellerman once said, "Greb ... the more ya find out about him, the more you realize it was HE and not Benny Leonard, who was the greatest fighter of the twenties."[9] Dempsey also compared the two when he stated, "Hell. Greb is faster than Benny Leonard."[10] Lightweight champion Benny Leonard tended to agree when he said, "Harry was more than just a fighter, he had that inborn spark and sixth sense which made him great. I was always thankful that I weighed twenty pounds less than he did."[11]

Greb would battle eleven International Boxing Hall of Fame champions in official bouts and beat every single one of them. Greb also met three more Hall of Fame boxers in sparring or exhibition matches, which included Jack Dempsey, Frank Klaus and allegedly Jack Johnson. Of the eleven International Hall of Fame boxers he officially fought, many have already been discussed, including Mike Gibbons, Tommy Gibbons, Kid Norfolk, "Philadelphia" Jack O'Brien, Tiger Flowers, Gene Tunney and Mickey Walker. The remaining legendary boxers will be discussed in this chapter, and they include Jack Dillon, Battling Levinsky, Tommy Loughran, Jimmy Slattery and Maxie Rosenbloom. Also covered will be his battles against World Light Heavyweight Champion Mike McTigue and World Middleweight Champion Frank Klaus.

Early in Greb's career he had a chance to step into the ring against former middleweight champion Frank Klaus. Klaus had been born and raised in Pittsburgh, just like Greb. Klaus was managed by George Engel during his career, just like Greb had been at one point. Klaus had won the middleweight championship in 1912 by beating Georges Carpentier in France, and while champion he fought Jack Dillon, Billy Papke, Jimmy Gardner and Eddie McGoorty. Klaus finally lost the title on October 11, 1913, when he was beaten by George Chip. After fighting Chip one last time a couple of months later, Klaus retired from the ring. Nat Fleischer ranked Klaus the Number-Six Middleweight of all time. He was inducted into the Ring Hall of Fame in 1974.

Five years after his retirement Frank "Bearcat" Klaus had an exhibition bout with Greb. This would be the only exhibition that Klaus ever appeared in and it was on February 7, 1918. It took place at the Penn Avenue Power House in Pittsburgh at 34th Street and Penn Avenue. The big event was to raise money for the Camp Lee Draftees' Tobacco Fund. The benefit boxing show consisted of nine bouts with Greb and Klaus as the main event. Each bout was three two-minute rounds.[12]

During the exhibition both fighters "decided to make it as hot as they could."[13] Klaus still showed some ring instinct and was willing to mix it up a little. Then, between the second and third rounds people dragged Tommy Gibbons from the crowd and brought him into the ring. The crowd wanted Gibbons to be one of Greb's opponents in the exhibition, but that wasn't to happen. Gibbons then left the ring and the final round of the exhibition bout commenced. When the bout ended it was seen as a passing of the torch between the two Pittsburgh middleweights, Klaus "the old" and Greb "the new."

The newspapers weighed in on the results the next day. Since both fighters were from the hometown of Pittsburgh, the *Pittsburgh Post* wouldn't give a decision. Iowa's *Waterloo Evening Courier* and Wisconsin's *Daily Northwestern* both wrote, "Greb won from Frank Klaus."[14]

Early in Greb's career he met legend Jack Dillon. Nat Fleischer ranked Dillon as the Number Three All-Time Light Heavyweight, and he was inducted into the International Boxing Hall of Fame in 1995. He started his career in 1908 and fought out of his home state of Indiana. Dillon's birth name was Ernest Cutler Price and during his career he was known as "The Hoosier Bearcat" and "Jack the Giant Killer." He got the latter nickname for beating bigger men and doing it in a style similar to Dempsey's. By the time he fought Greb in 1917 he had already fought Jim Corbett, George Chip, Mike Glover, Jimmy Gardner, Mike "Twin" Sullivan, Battling Levinsky, Frank Klaus, Hugo Kelly, Joe Thomas, Buck Crouse, "Fireman" Jim Flynn, Jack Lester, Al Norton, Dan "Porky" Flynn, Ed "Gunboat" Smith, Tom "Bearcat" McMahon, Billy Miske, Tom Cowler, Frank Moran, Mike Gibbons and Al McCoy.

In 1912 he claimed the middleweight championship of the world when he beat Leo Houck by a six-round TKO when Houck refused to come out of his corner for the seventh round. This title, however, wasn't officially recognized. In 1914 he claimed the vacant light heavyweight title when he beat Battling Levinsky on April 14. He defended the title claim against Bob Moha, Frank Mantell and Charley Weinert, whom he knocked out. Dillon defended the title three times against Levinsky until Levinsky beat him on October 24, 1916. A year later Dillon fought Greb in the first of two bouts.

The fight took place at Forbes Field on July 30, 1917, and it was the very first time a boxing show had taken place at the baseball stadium. While Greb was training for the fight he injured himself when a sparring partner elbowed him in the forehead. There was swelling, but it was high up on the forehead and wasn't expected to have any bearing on the fight. Dillon was in excellent shape and was training at his Broadripple training quarters in his home state of Indiana. Dillon had a couple of sparring partners to help his speed and two heavyweight sparring partners to develop his strength and power.[15]

Jack Dillon in 1919, a year after his second fight with Greb. Dillon has been inducted into both the Ring and International Boxing Halls of Fame (collection of Pugilistica.com).

The day before the fight they had an unofficial weigh-in at the Lyceum Gym, where both were currently training. Dillon "stripped down to 158½," while Greb "in his street clothes weighed 165."[16] When fight night arrived Forbes Field had an estimated 10,000 boxing fans filling the seats.

Greb had only been boxing for around five years while Dillon was closing in on a decade, but Greb was still viewed as the "master" schooling Dillon. Greb had "complete mastery of the fight" and was said to have won every round except for the fourth, which was even. Greb used his constant punching style that "out-gunned, out-maneuvered and out-guessed" his opponent. Greb threw constant punches from the outside and often circled Dillon. Greb hit him so often that Dillon was too busy dodging punches and only "occasionally" did he attempt a counterattack. The next day it was written that, "Greb keeps so busy fighting that he doesn't allow anyone else to fight."[17]

As early as the second round Greb's onslaught could be seen on Dillon's face. "Dillon bled at the mouth from the second round on." Dillon usually had an expressionless face, but against Greb he "registered rage, disappointment and blind, helpless fury as the fight progressed."

Dillon's only good round was the fourth, when he resorted to throwing haymakers to try to catch Greb. At the very beginning of the round he rushed Greb into a neutral corner and landed a big right "flush against Harry's jaw." This punch had knocked out many heavyweights and light heavyweights Dillon had fought in the past, but Greb had a great chin. "This mighty blow had no disastrous consequence for Greb." Greb then made his way across the ring and got Dillon in a clinch, and after a few seconds he soon recovered. It was written: "So quickly did Harry rally from the effects of this blow that ten seconds later he was pumping them into Dillon with an added ferocity."[18] Greb was the aggressor for the rest of the round with Dillon landing only four more effective punches. Greb rallied so effectively that the round was said to be even. It was the only round of the fight that was even close.

By the seventh round Greb's constant and unending onslaught was paying off. In this round, "Dillon was within a narrow margin of going down and out under a pitiless drumfire." Greb's attack had him "dazed, sick, staggering and weary," but he kept going. Not only did Greb shower his opponent with punches from the outside, he bettered Dillon on the infighting also. It was written: "Even at straight, old-fashioned, toe-to-toe slugging Greb proved himself more than Dillon's equal. He could hit with greater rapidity and score twice while Dillon was letting his ponderous punches underway." Even in the clinches Greb "showed uncanny ability to guess from whence Dillon's punches were coming and to twist, squirm or writhe away from those he could not block."[19]

When the fight was over Greb was declared the overwhelming victor. The *Post* would write: "No words can adequately describe Greb's complete mastery of the fight." After the bout Greb was seen "unmarked from the fight." The *Chicago Tribune* headline the next day was "Greb Hands Out Real Trimming To Jack Dillon."[20]

The two combatants met once again in a scheduled twelve-round fight on March 4, 1918, at the Coliseum in Toledo, Ohio. As early as the opening round it was clear that Greb was Dillon's superior. Greb had Dillon's nose "almost reduced to a pulp in this round from continual jabbing." When the third round arrived Dillon was groggy and had to hold on to Greb "to save himself." In the fifth round, "Greb staggered Dillon against the ropes with terrific right swings to the head and the face."[21] Greb continued to rush him and maintained a savage attack for the rest of the fight.

It was estimated that Greb landed fifty blows to Dillon's jaw and chin. Greb's attacks and dancing made Dillon "appear to be standing still." As the bout continued it was clear Dillon didn't have a chance of winning. It was written that "Greb's attack on Dillon was so persistent and so full of punishment that the vast crowd became disturbed and many left the Coliseum before the bout was over."[22]

Another future Hall of Famer Greb battled around this time was Light Heavyweight Champion Battling Levinsky. Levinsky had claimed the World Light Heavyweight Title when he beat Jack Dillon on October 24, 1916 in Boston. Levinsky then defended his title for the next year while fighting the likes of Billy Miske, Carl Morris, Ed "Gunboat" Smith, Bob Moha, Tommy Gibbons and Bartley Madden.

On September 6, 1917, Greb and Levinsky fought at Forbes Field in Pittsburgh. It would be the first of six fights they had against each other. Each fight would be while Levinsky was claiming the World Light Heavyweight Title. It was a newspaper decision, so for Greb to gain the title he not only had to win, he had to knock the champion out. Levinsky entered the ring three inches taller than Greb and an estimated twenty to twenty-five pounds heavier.

Before the fight Greb trained at the Lyceum Gym. He was training so hard that he damaged a ligament in his leg so the fight was postponed for four days. The leg healed and Greb gave an open training exhibition at the Lyceum Gym a couple of days before the fight. The *Pittsburgh Post* stated, "Most of the work consisted of hard bouts with his numerous sparring partners." One of the sparring partners was George Hook, the big policeman. People were interested in seeing how Greb would handle this big man because Levinsky outweighed Greb by a similar ratio. After the exhibition the *Post* wrote: "Levinsky's weight, reach and height advantage is not going to save him from defeat unless he can show a great deal in addition to that. Greb's speed and aggressiveness discount that advantage."[23]

Levinsky weighed a little over 180 pounds to Greb's 160 pounds. Levinsky was also three inches taller, with Greb 5'8" and Levinsky 5'11" tall. With all this against him, Greb was extremely confident of a win; he even urged friends to place bets on him. Since Greb first saw Levinsky fight he had asserted that he could whip him.

The fight was very tough with Levinsky using his size advantage "laying on Greb and bearing down on him at every opportunity." Levinsky was planning on wearing Greb down and

Battling Levinsky in 1915, two years before he first fought Greb (collection of Pugilistica.com).

catching him in the later rounds, but the opposite was to happen. Greb was the aggressor throughout the fight. Levinsky was puzzled by Greb because he had never encountered his "sort of perpetual-motion fighting machine."[24]

For the first five rounds Greb fought "his usual hurricane fashion, jabbing, hooking, hauling and clubbing." His blows were landing "often and clean, and the cumulative effect was deadly." When Levinsky wanted to box close, Greb stayed on the outside. When Levinsky wanted to box outside, Greb went in close and didn't give him room to swing, or just moved away very fast. All this kept Levinsky off his game and "puzzled" him throughout the fight. He just couldn't understand Greb's unique style, which continued to adapt and counter whatever his next move was.

In the sixth round Greb landed a combination that consisted of a left to the body, a right to the head, and finally a big left to the jaw "that shook Levinsky to his toes." Greb followed all this with another left to the jaw that caused Levinsky's footing to be "uncertain." After Levinsky went into a clinch to survive, Greb landed another left and right to his face. Levinsky survived the round, but it was clearer than ever that Greb was winning this bout and hurting Levinsky quite a bit.

Levinsky was getting frustrated and began the eighth round by head-butting Greb in the chest, which was followed by a warning from the referee. Then Levinsky showed he had something to offer when he landed a hard right to the stomach, which made Greb laugh. It was effective, though, and slowed Greb down for the rest of the round.

Greb resumed his dominant attack when early in the ninth he landed "a terrific hook to the mouth that made Levinsky stand stock still." By the tenth and final round Levinsky was just trying to survive the fight by "fighting for the sound of the gong." Greb, on the other hand, was trying to knock out his exhausted foe. Late in the round Greb landed a powerful right to the jaw, "and Levinsky dropped into Greb's corner." When he finally got up Greb rushed him again, but, unfortunately for Greb, there were only seconds left. With Greb on a verge of a knockout the bell rang to end the round and the fight. Levinsky had barely survived.

Greb was awarded the victory by completely dominating Levinsky and winning eight of the ten rounds. The remaining two rounds were said to be even. In his dressing room after the fight Levinsky said, "Wasn't I rotten. Gee, wasn't I rotten." After his response it was written: "A lot of fighters have felt the same way about it after a session with Greb, whose speed and tactics discount their traditionally correct fighting."

Greb was interviewed after the fight and responded,

> Had he been my size I surely would have knocked him out. It took me a few rounds to get him down to my size and then he wasn't in the fight. He never gave me any trouble except for one body blow in the eighth round. I am sure I would have stopped him had the tenth round gone a minute longer for he was tired and hanging on even before I knocked him down just before the bell. I would now be the Light Heavyweight Champion if our bout had been a twelve or fifteen-round affair instead of a ten-rounder.[25]

The two would fight five more times in the next two years with Greb winning every single time. However, the title never changed hands because Greb didn't win any of the fights by a knockout. Their final bout took place on September 3, 1919, and Greb was said to have won every round. Levinsky finally lost his title the next year when he was knocked out by Georges Carpentier on October 12, 1920. Levinsky was inducted into the International Boxing Hall of Fame in 2000.

Mike McTigue was a World Light Heavyweight Champion who fought Greb twice. Born in Ireland, he began boxing in 1909 around the age of seventeen. After turning pro he fought out of New York and captured the World Light Heavyweight Title in 1923 after beating Battling Siki. The twenty-round bout took place in Dublin, Ireland. While champion, McTigue fought Tommy Loughran, Young Stribling and Mickey Walker, but he lost the title in 1925 when Paul Berlenbach beat him in a fifteen-round bout in New York.

Before McTigue became champion he fought Greb once in 1918 and in a rematch in 1919. The first bout took place at the Moose Club in Cleveland on March 11. McTigue weighed 158 pounds for this ten-round newspaper-decision bout. The battle was said to be very one-sided with Greb winning almost every round. Greb hit McTigue "several hundred times" in the bout while McTigue only landed "four or five times." Greb didn't inflict too much damage but was able to open a cut over McTigue's left eye. McTigue seemed close to being knocked out a few times while he "lay over on the ropes with but little defense." McTigue was also described as "helpless and so unwilling to strike back, but so willing to embrace with both arms."[26] Greb won while McTigue just clinched most of the time. According to the local Ohio newspaper, the *Newark Advocate*, Greb was "an easy winner in nine rounds, one round being even, according to newspaper critics."[27]

They had their rematch the following year with similar results. The fight took place on December 12, 1919, in Endicott, New York, and was just two days after Greb beat Clay Turner in a ten-round bout.

In an outcome similar to that of the first fight, Greb won every round but one as he was just "too shifty and aggressive." Greb almost had a knockout in the fifth round but McTigue "stuck to his guns" and survived. Greb's attack was so overwhelming that McTigue "had trouble defending himself." Greb was beating his foe "badly," especially near the end of the bout. By the time the final round came, "the fans were calling to Greb to put his man out."[28] McTigue was able to stay on his feet and Greb won by newspaper decision. The local New York paper, the *Olean Times*, simply wrote that "Greb outfought Mike McTigue."[29]

Between the years 1922 and 1924 Greb would battle another future Hall of Famer a total of six times, this one by the name of Tommy Loughran. Loughran was known as the "Phantom of Philly" because he hailed from that fair city. Nat Fleischer ranked him as the Number Four All-Time Light Heavyweight. He would eventually win the title in 1927 against Mike McTigue, but only after fighting Greb many times.

The first time they battled was on July 10, 1922, after Greb had won the American Light Heavyweight Title from Gene Tunney just a couple of months earlier. The fight was a newspaper-decision bout that took place in Philadelphia, with Greb weighing 167 pounds and Loughran weighing a little over 163.

The day before the bout Greb said, "He's the one fighter whom I have never met, whom outsiders seem to think has a chance. Maybe he has and, if he beat the fellows they say he did, maybe he will have. But I am out to prove tomorrow that the middleweight title belongs to me."[30]

World light heavyweight champion Mike McTigue (**Antiquities of the Prize Ring**).

Loughran fought well for the first five rounds, proving himself "a capable foeman." It was not until after the fifth round that "Greb really had an advantage worth bragging about."[31]

Early in the sixth round Greb got a cut over his left eye, "but toward the middle of the round Greb, seeming to sense that Loughran was fighting well, cut loose a jumping attack and from then on, except a hard flurry in the eighth, had Loughran well in hand." It was written that "there was little doubt that the longer it went the better Greb got." Greb was awarded the victory in a tough battle. Loughran was "cuffed and clouted, battered and buffeted, by a style of attack he knew little about." Greb's experience was said to have made the difference.

The next time they fought was another newspaper-decision bout which took place on January 15, 1923, at Motor Square Garden in Pittsburgh. Greb made sure to train well for the fight; he worked out at the Lyceum Gym and sparred up to the day before the fight.[32]

Greb weighed in at 168¼ pounds while Loughran was 3¾ pounds lighter for this fifteen-round fight. Loughran started off fine by landing some effective body blows in the first few rounds. However, after that it was all Greb's fight. Greb started blocking blows with his forearms and then punching Loughran in return. Loughran looked like "a novice" while "the lacing he took was at times pitiful." In the eighth and tenth rounds Loughran was weak in the legs and "wobbly." When the final bell rang, Loughran had "a gaping cut over his left eye and the blood streaming from his mouth and nose."[33]

Loughran was most effective when Greb stayed on the outside, so Greb didn't do that very often, instead staying on the inside and throwing effective right uppercuts. The next day it was written that "never has Greb won so decisively and never did he show the eagerness to go and do things as he did last night." Greb won by a very wide margin.

A couple of weeks later they fought for a third time. This bout had an official decision, and was the first official defense of Greb's American Light Heavyweight Title. The fifteen-round judged bout took place at Madison Square Garden in New York on January 30, 1923.

Both men weighed 166 pounds before the bout. Loughran was effective in the first three rounds using a straight left jab with a kick that kept Greb at bay. Then, however, Greb stepped it up a notch and overwhelmed his opponent. Greb was very effective on the infighting and kept Loughran on the defensive for the rest of the fight. Loughran would sometimes hold on to Greb to weather the storm, but Greb would just punch away using both hands. On the inside Greb sometimes used his head to butt Loughran's chin, and in the tenth Loughran tried to claim foul and stop the punishment he was receiving, but referee McPartland would have none of it and just "waved him back to work."[34]

In the last three rounds Loughran tried to make a comeback, but it was too little too late. Greb's overwhelming lead in the fight was too much to overcome. When the fight ended Greb was awarded the victory and was said to have given Loughran a "masterful lacing." Loughran's early rounds were not enough when Greb used his "windmill tactics" for the remainder of the fifteen-round fight. Greb had successfully defended his title against a future Hall of Famer.

Tommy Loughran. He was a light heavyweight from Philadelphia and has been inducted into the International Boxing Hall of Fame (Craig Hamilton collection, www.josportsinc.com).

They fought three more times with Loughran squeaking out a controversial win in the first of them, but Greb responded with a clear-cut win in their next ten-round decision bout. Their final match-up took place on October 13, 1924, in Philadelphia and was judged a draw.[35] Loughran was inducted into the International Boxing Hall of Fame in 1991.

Also in 1924 Greb was to meet another future legend, Jimmy Slattery. They met only once and it was a six-round decision bout on September 3, 1924. Slattery was a light heavyweight who fought out of Buffalo, New York, and he was inducted into the International Boxing Hall of Fame in 2006. He was 5'11" tall and weighed 163 pounds when he met Greb in the ring. Greb trained for the fight at Conneaut Lake in the Mercer County Spa. It was expected to be a battle of speed.[36]

A total of 15,000 boxing fans filled Bison Stadium to watch the young light heavyweight contender take on the current middleweight champion. During the first two rounds Slattery used his quickness

Light heavyweight James Slattery. Both his father and brother died of tuberculosis. After his 1925 knockout loss to Paul Berlenbach, Slattery was said to have started drinking heavily (collection of Pugilistica.com).

and two-handed attack while "fighting fiercely and gave as good as he got in the exchanges."[37] During these six minutes, Slattery "cut loose with everything he had."

According to the *New York Times*, "The fight was all Greb's after the second round."[38] During the third it was clear that Slattery had used up his energy trying to keep up a terrific pace. At the end of the third round Greb landed a hard right hook over Slattery's right eye, which started bleeding. With Greb just warming up, the third round was judged even.[39]

In the fourth, Greb "got after him with both hands, fighting like a demon and scoring to the head and body. Blood steaming down Slattery's face." It was thought that "the sensation of his own blood trickling down his face and body took some of the heart out of him." In the fifth round Greb picked up the pace and fought even more aggressively. It was written that Greb "continued his terrific onslaught and poor Slattery, burned out, and his inexperience leaving nothing in reserve, was buffeted about, even forgetting to protect himself."[40] Greb won the fifth round by a very large margin with a possible knockout in reach.

In the sixth and final round Greb started a great rally. He threw a right and two uppercuts to Slattery's chin. Then Greb landed a big uppercut to the chin. With an additional left and right to the head, Slattery was "staggered" while Greb backed him around the ring. After another onslaught by Greb, Slattery could do nothing but save himself by holding on. Then while very weak Slattery "slipped and fell" on the canvas. Greb helped him back up and the fighting continued. By the end of the final round, "Slattery was always there to be hit, the dazzling speed had gone from his legs and arms and he was nothing but a willing, game, inexperienced kid, glad to stay the limit."[41]

After the final bell rang Greb was announced the winner. According to the *New York Times*, Greb was "undamaged at the finish."[42] Slattery left the ring "with his face covered with blood from the first cut he had suffered in the profession, and his body puffing under the concentrated attack which Greb cut loose once Slattery had shown signs of tiring."[43] Despite Slattery's being from the same state as where the fight took place, "the decision was a popular one and Greb was given an ovation."[44]

A few years later Slattery won the vacant NBA World Light Heavyweight Title by beating Maxie Rosenbloom on August 30, 1927. Four months later Slattery lost the title against Tommy Loughran. Slattery then won the NYSAC Light Heavyweight Title in 1930 by squeaking out a win against Lou Scozza. But he lost that title four months later when he was beaten by old rival Maxie Rosenbloom in a fifteen-round bout on June 25, 1930.

In 1925 Greb had been fighting at full speed for twelve years and people were wondering when time was going to catch up with him. In early July Greb had successfully defended his middleweight title against Mickey Walker. The next fight Greb had was against tough New York middleweight Maxie Rosenbloom. It was written that "Slapsie" Maxie Rosenbloom "felt that he was to be the one who would catch Greb slipping."[45] The ten-round bout took place in Cleveland, Ohio, on July 16th, 1925.

The first three rounds were said to be Rosenbloom's best, while Greb was trying to figure out how to combat him. During these rounds Rosenbloom was focusing mainly on the body but with little effect. At the start of the fourth round Greb's famous slicked-back hair "still wore its original part."[46] Greb started being more effective and continued his work on Maxie in the fourth and fifth.

In the sixth round Greb really "opened up, danced and pranced, hooked and slugged" with Rosenbloom receiving some severe punishment. Greb's "unexpected outburst" surprised Rosenbloom, who didn't know how to defend himself against it. All of a sudden Rosenbloom "seemed to weaken." By the end of the sixth round Rosenbloom was "breathing hard, the blood streaming from his battered mouth and nose and his cauliflower ear."[47]

Maxie Rosenbloom in 1928. Rosenbloom would end his sixteen-year career with 299 official bouts. It only took Greb thirteen years to reach that number. Rosenbloom averaged around eighteen and a half fights a year while Greb averaged twenty-three bouts a year (collection of Pugilistica.com).

In the seventh Greb continued the attack on his "wobbly" victim, throwing a short right to the chin that "dropped Maxie full length on the floor. As the referee tolled off the seconds it began to look as though Maxie was to be counted out."[48] According to the *New York Times* he found the strength to rise to his feet on the "count of seven."[49]

Greb just coasted to a win for the rest of the fight. The *Pittsburgh Post* wrote: "So long as Maxie wanted to fight Greb tore in and fought; when Maxie got tired Greb eased up. At no time was the champion exerted to the limit of his capabilities." When the bell rang it was clear that the "unmarked" champion had won the fight. The papers the next day made it clear that Greb had easily won this newspaper-decision bout. In an Ohio article titled "Greb Wins Fight," the *Zanesville Signal* wrote that "Greb led all the way, carrying the fight to Rosenbloom, shooting both hands to the head and body at will."[50]

Five years later Rosenbloom would go on to win the World Light Heavyweight Title when he beat Jimmy Slattery on June 25, 1930. He would successfully defend that title for more than four years until he lost it against Bob Olin on November 16, 1934. Rosenbloom was inducted into the International Boxing Hall of Fame in 1993.

Years after his fight with Greb, Rosenbloom talked with the NEA news service. During the interview he reminisced about his bout with Greb. "What an education I got in the ring," Maxie said. "I ran away from my manager when I was nineteen. When I came back, he punished me by getting me a fight with Harry Greb."[51] He wasn't the only champion who felt that way after a fight with Greb.

16.

THE TRAGIC HERO

The coming of 1926 marked the 13th year Greb had been boxing as a professional. Most fans were amazed that Greb had maintained his massive fight schedule and was still at the top of his game. What they didn't know was that he had been boxing completely blind in one eye for the past four years. Greb was always known to fight the best competition out there, even if he had to cross the color line. This is why he allowed African-American Tiger Flowers a shot at his world title in 1926.

Greb had previously beaten Flowers on August 21, 1924, in a ten-round bout. Since then Flowers had had a string of impressive victories including wins against Johnny Wilson, Ted Moore, Lou Bogash, Pal Reed, Jock Malone, "Allentown" Joe Gans and Frank Moody. He had also fought Jack Delaney, Chuck Wiggins and Mike McTigue. Flowers had moved up in the middleweight ranks since he last fought Greb, so Greb decided to give him a controversial title shot.

Jack Johnson had won the heavyweight title in 1908, but since then the white boxing establishment had vowed not to give another African-American boxer a shot at any title. The only way for them to make sure there was never another African-American champion was to make sure they never even fought for a title. This "color line" continued after Johnson lost his title in 1915. Greb never cared about any color line and first fought African-Americans Jack Blackburn and Willie Langford while Johnson was still heavyweight champion. When Greb became World Middleweight Champion he still continued to fight African-Americans. He fought Detroit middleweight Kid Lewis in Pittsburgh on January 22, 1925. Now in 1926, Greb was going to do something that no one had done for almost twenty years: allow an African-American to fight for a world boxing title. This legendary fight would help slowly usher in a slightly fairer playing field for boxers of any race. After this fight it would be eleven years until the color line was truly broken when Joe Louis won the World Heavyweight Championship. Greb had become part of the solution instead of part of the problem.

The Greb-Flowers title fight was held at Madison Square Garden on February 26, 1926. Greb trained for the fight at "Philadelphia" Jack O'Brien's gym in New York. He arrived there around a week before the fight and weighed around 165½ pounds. As of February 23 Greb was sparring eight rounds a day against southpaws to simulate Flowers's style. He would also play some handball with Red Mason. His good friend Eddie Deasy, along with other Pittsburghers, had arrived that day from Pittsburgh. With three days to go before the fight Greb weighed around 164 pounds.[1]

The next day was February 24 and Greb continued his training with an early-morning run. Photographers had arrived at the gym as well as Mike McTigue, Clay Turner and hundreds of fans. Greb and Mason played handball with a bet on the line; the stakes were that the loser had to pay for the entourage's dinner that night. When that was completed Greb sparred with 135-pound lightweight Johnny Mack for speed, and then with 210-pound heavyweight Young Sully for power. After the workout Greb weighed in at 162¼ pounds. Everyone was very excited on how easily Greb was making weight with two days before the fight. The odds for the fight at this time favored Greb 3 to 1.[2]

On February 25, just one day before the fight, Regis Welsh would write:

> Confident that he can once more defy the laws of nature and the fond hokum of tradition, Harry Greb, still a champion at the age of thirty-two, still a windmill after thirteen years of campaigning, today wrote finis to the short training campaign which has prepared him for his title defense tomorrow night with Tiger Flowers, the first Negro title challenger since the famous days of the "White Hopes."

Greb finished the day weighing 162 pounds. He was expected to be under 160 pounds by the next day, "with the drying out process which is due to begin tonight."[3] According to the *New York Times* on the morning of the fight, the odds for Greb to win had gone down to 8 to 5.[4] This was due to Flowers's impressive speed and how well he looked in training camp.

On fight night Greb weighed 158½ pounds while Flowers weighed 159½. Frank Getty, a United News staff correspondent, wrote how they entered the ring. "A roar of applause greeted the appearance of Greb, while Flowers came in almost unnoticed." Ed "Gunboat" Smith, a boxer once knocked out by Greb, was the referee for the fifteen-round fight. The two judges were Tom Flynn and Charles Mathison. The bell for the first round rang at 9:51 P.M.

The first round began with a clinch when Greb went into Flowers's corner. Flowers returned with a two-fisted attack. During the round Greb missed with a left and a right. Greb was fighting defensively until he "lashed out with a right to the jaw, which sent Flowers staggering back, but in the rally that followed Flowers had the better of it. Greb opened a cut over Flowers's left eye with a right as the gong sounded."[5] The bell quieted the roaring crowd. Regis Welsh, at the fight for the *Pittsburgh Post*, said it was Flowers's round.

In the beginning of round two Flowers was able to land often and "backed Greb around the ring." The crowd was starting to be concerned about Greb's showing to this point. Then Greb picked up the pace and "tore into Flowers." After a clinch, "Greb landed his right to the Tiger's left eye and drew blood." This was followed by Greb's sending "a vicious left hook to head and right to body, taking some steam out of the Tiger." Flowers was able to land effectively to the body. Greb started using his footwork by moving around Flowers and trying to measure him, but Flowers moved out of the way every time. It was Greb's round "by a shade" according to Welsh.

In round three, "Flowers was slapping with his open glove." After Flowers's mugging he landed "two vicious rights, opening a deep gash over Greb's eye. As the blood came down over his face he tried to put everything into a right hand, but the Negro stepped outside and drove both hands to body. Greb's face was a crimson smear as Flowers landed to the head." This was the first time either of Greb's eyes had been cut in three full years. The last cut occurring in a fight against Bob Roper. The crowd cheered when Greb "hooked two to the chin," but then Flowers took his elbow and "tore into Greb's eye," which made the crowd yell. Flowers was using some rough tactics. The boxers continued fighting after the bell until the "referee had to part them." Welsh wrote that it was another round for Flowers.

Round four began with cautious sparring. Greb landed rights and lefts to the body while Flowers focused on the head. Greb landed "a hard right to the ribs," while the challenger landed "a right to the neck." Greb landed a right to the heart that made Flowers clinch. The excitement started when Greb "backed Flowers to the ropes and uppercut him in again close. The crowd went wild as they stood toe to toe tearing away at each other." According to the *Washington Post*, "Greb punched Flowers all over the ring with such a versatile and speedy attack that the Tiger could do nothing but attempt to cover up. Flowers was groggy at the bell." Greb won the round on Welsh's scorecard.

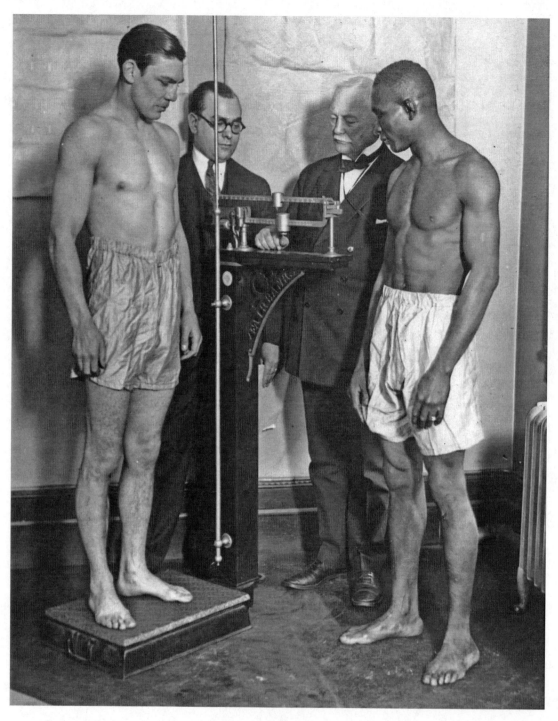

Boxing Secretary Bert Stand (second from left) helps Commissioner William Muldoon weigh in Greb while Tiger Flowers looks on (Craig Hamilton collection, www.josportsinc.com).

At the start of round five, "Flowers became more cautious waiting for Greb to lead, but finally hooked right to body." Greb started leading but was swinging "wildly and without effect as he backed Flowers to the ropes." It was noticed that both fighters seemed a little tired and slow after the pace of the previous round. Flowers was effectively landing long-range rights and lefts as he "pecked at the champion's face and body." Welsh gave Flowers a "slight shade" for the round.

In round six both fighters were fighting wildly, missing a lot of their punches early on. "Greb battered Flowers to the ropes with his crushing right. Greb attempted to measure the challenger but the Tiger ran away." According to the *Pittsburgh Post*, "There was little damage by the rally and not much fighting in the round which was even."

Round seven had the two boxers in a clinch while Flowers landed some effective blows. "Greb suddenly swung a right to the jaw and Flowers went back to the ropes but the challenger blocked most of Greb's blows in a furious mix-up." Greb's "long left" jab was doing a good job at "keeping Flowers outside." Both fighters were landing some good punches. Greb was described as being slightly more aggressive and effective than the challenger and won the round by a shade, but it could have gone either way.

In round eight, "Flowers's southpaw style appeared to bother Greb." They both landed good body punches, and later in the round Greb "mugged" his opponent with a left to the head. It was noticed that Greb was walking "flatfooted," but he then picked up the pace. "Greb let fly with right hook to chin following with right uppercut to body. Greb began swinging with right driving Flowers to ropes." This right was so powerful it "sent Flowers half-way across the ring." Then Greb "finally opened up in true style and let loose with both hands in the center of the ring." They were fighting so fast when the bell rang that they didn't even hear it, "and the referee again had to part them." Welsh saw it as Greb's round.

Greb started round nine aggressively, making Flowers hold. "Greb's boxing became evident when the punches that had caught him in early rounds went unnoticed. They went head to head with Flowers willing to stand his ground." Greb twice threw a punch, then "turned Flowers around." This didn't have any noticeable effect because Flowers just covered up and "blocked Greb's efforts." Later in the round Flowers landed a left to the mouth that made Greb "wince." At the end of the round, "Greb tore in and landed left and right to head at the bell." According to the *Washington Post*, "Greb caught Flowers off balance and almost toppled him with a crashing right, but the bell prevented a follow up." Welsh said it was "a good round and even, Greb getting the break on account of his aggressiveness."

In round ten Flowers was beating Greb to the punch and landing his left often. Greb landed some effective uppercuts, "which sent Tiger's head back." Greb was focusing on the head while Flowers landed on the body. At the bell, "Greb struck a terrific right to the chin." Welsh gave Greb the round by "a slight shade."

The eleventh round was very close with both fighters landing good punches to the head and face. Then in the twelfth, "Harry opened up in true form in this round, driving Flowers with half a dozen rights and lefts to head. He shot another right to head and two uppercuts to chin, then sent Flowers head back with left hooks." One of the rights to Flowers's jaw "spun him around." During every exchange Greb was "rushing" his opponent and landing "his famous left hook." During a "wild mix-up" Greb "punished him severely with half a dozen uppercuts." Then Greb started wrestling Flowers around the ring until he "finally pushed him through the ropes, while the crowd roared disapproval. Flowers came back tearing into the body." Right before the bell sounded Greb was "nailing Flowers in close." The crowd "hooted Greb for holding and hitting." There were some rough tactics, but it was clearly Greb's round according to Welsh.

In round thirteen the two boxers stood toe-to-toe exchanging lefts and rights as the crowd screamed in enjoyment. "The Tiger was still in good form and backing Greb around the ring doing most of his work in the clinches." Throughout the active round both fighters landed often with rights and lefts. At the very end, Greb "pushed Flowers through the ropes" while the crowd "hooted" in disapproval. They were clinching when the bell rang. Welsh gave the round to Greb.

At the start of round fourteen, "Flowers slapped to the head and ribs with open gloves. Both appeared somewhat tired and the pace slackened. They clinched more often." According to the *Washington Post*, "Flowers appeared thoroughly on the defensive, with Greb doing all the leading." While Greb was tearing in he "wrestled Flowers to the ropes bringing more jeers from the crowd as Flowers countered with a right to the chin." Then Flowers "wrestled Greb to the ropes landing a right." The *Pittsburgh Post* gave the round to Greb.

In the beginning of the fifteenth and final round both fighters shook hands in the center of the ring. "Greb opened up in the style they looked for in the opening rounds but Flowers came back and traded punches with him." They both exchanged lefts to the body, then went into a clinch. They followed that up with rights, again to the body. "Greb was wrestling and holding." According to the *Pittsburgh Post*, "Greb missed Flowers by a foot and they both looked like a couple of clowns. Neither one landed. Greb was again off balance and again wrestled Flowers to the ropes. He hooked two long lefts to the chin at the bell." The *Washington Post* wrote that the round ended when "Flowers landed a downward stab to the face." The *New York Times* wrote: "They exchanged rights to the face at the final bell." Welsh decided that Flowers had won the last round.

Welsh wrote what happened next. "At the close of the fifteenth round the crowd began to roar. In what seemed like hours, but was only a few seconds, Joe Humphries came to the center of the ring. For an instant he spread both hands, intimating a draw, and the gladdened Flowers rose from his chair to go over to Greb." It seemed that Flowers would have been happy with the verdict of a draw. Then, however, came the final announcement. "The winner and new middleweight champion of the world, Tiger Flowers."[6] The passionate Greb was shocked by the verdict and was seen teary eyed in his corner. The man who was blind in his right eye had finally lost the title that he seemed "to love more than his life."[7] The *Post* would describe it as "the taking away of the title from a champion who had never been on the floor, a champion who had never failed to keep trying, but of a champion who was so far off his accustomed form that it seemed as though his name was not Greb."[8]

The two judges, Tom Flynn and Charles Mathison, ruled for Flowers, but the referee saw it differently. "Gunboat" Smith, the third man in the ring, said Greb was the winner. If the judges had disagreed then Smith's vote would have been the deciding factor. However, with the judges unanimous, Smith's verdict didn't change anything. What may have been going through the referee's mind was written about the next day. "It might have been that Smith could not as many others see that Flowers without a knockout, without punishing the champion to any visible or serious effect, had sufficient margin to carry off the golden derby."[9] Flowers had now successfully become the first African-American boxing champion since Jack Johnson.

Frank Getty wrote: "Many experts figured that the worst the former champion should have had was a draw, for Greb was the stronger puncher, and at times had Flowers in real trouble."[10]

The reason for the judges' verdict was said to be "Harry's inability to put usual speed and accuracy behind his windmill attack." Some thought Greb had over-trained for the bought, while others said Greb just didn't look like his normal self. Many believed that Flowers won the fight not because of how well he fought, but on the less-than-normal showing from Greb. According to the Associated Press, "Boxing critics argued that the margin obtained by the Negro was too small for a title to change hands, although it was generally admitted that he had won under the rules of the New York State Athletic Commission, which provide that all bouts must be decided by rounds gained."[11]

Hype Igoe, writer for the *New York World News*, scored the fight as Greb the winner by rounds. As Igoe saw it, Greb had won seven rounds, Flowers five, and three rounds were even. Welsh, for the *Pittsburgh Post*, had a similar scorecard with Greb winning by rounds. He had Greb winning eight rounds, Flowers five and two rounds even. Getty, for the United News, wrote: "The worst the former champion should have had was a draw."[12]

Greb's response the next day was, "I would like to have another chance because I think that if I get myself right I can beat that fellow and once more get back to the top of the heap." Greb would go on to say,

> You know, I have never been right since that auto accident last summer. I showed that in my fight with Tony Marullo at Motor Square and again at New Orleans. The story was broadcast last night that in my dressing room I made the remark that I would quit the game. This is all wrong. I intend fighting, not so much as before, but enough to get ready again for Flowers.[13]

The auto accident Greb was referring to was the one on August 19, 1925, after he fought Mickey Walker.

Greb said,

> I'm going home tomorrow night and within a few days will leave Pittsburgh for Hot Springs, Arkansas. A month there, working hard and taking care of myself should bring me back to the form I always had — and then I'll tackle Flowers. Too much training for this fight made me stale, the weight may have hurt me, but I feel that I am a better fighter than I was last night and a better fighter than Flowers was. I'm not squawking, I'm not even thinking of it, but along about the twelfth round last night I figured I had enough lead to gamble with. The verdict was a shock to me but then you must figure that Flowers is a great fighter. I knew that and said it when we met at Fremont two years ago, as his awkward style with his abundance of speed, makes him one of the toughest fellows in the business. But there are no good middleweights except us, and we will meet again, sure as you're alive. Then will come my chance, and instead of quitting the ring when Flowers beat me, I will retire as the middleweight champion who came back and proved that he had the stuff in him.[14]

Greb completed his interview by saying,

> I couldn't get going early last night, and when I did it was only in flashes. But even at that I thought I did enough to protect my title. I was surprised by the decision, but hope that when the time comes those who are now feeling sorry for me will learn that I can fight back.[15]

Tiger "The Fighting Deacon" Flowers graciously said he would fight anyone the New York State Athletic Commission wanted him to. Flowers, who was a steward in the Butler Colored Methodist Church of Atlanta, said, "Every round of the fight last night, I repeated to myself a part of the 144th Psalm, 'Blessed be the Lord, my strength, which teacheth my hands to war and my fingers to fight.'"[16]

On March 1, a few days after the fight, Regis Welsh interviewed Heavyweight Champion Jack Dempsey in New York. Dempsey first asked Welsh how Greb was doing. Dempsey said, "Bet he doesn't feel any too good and I think I'll stop over and see him for a minute because now is the time he needs friends." Then Dempsey "incidentally let out a secret that lies deep in his heart." Dempsey stated, "He was, and I believe, still is a great fighter — but for the life of me, I can't understand why he gave a Negro a chance to take that title away from him." Welsh described this prejudice as "Dempsey's innermost secret."[17]

On March 2 Greb and Mason went to the New York Boxing Commission. They presented a certified check for $2,500 to bind a challenge to fight Flowers again. The commission said that it wasn't binding until six months so Greb and Mason walked over to Madison Square Garden to talk with matchmaker Jess McMahon. While there, Flowers and his manager Walk Miller happened to arrive. "After a preliminary discussion and then a private one with the matchmaker, Miller and Flowers agreed to give Greb another chance, and articles were drawn and signed before even the contestants seemed to realize what was going on."[18] The date of the rematch was May 21, 1926.

Flowers then graciously said, "You gave me a chance to be a champion — now I'm going to return the favor and let you have a chance. All I want is enough time in between to let the doctor work on me for a few minor operations and engage in a few little bouts. Then you and I will be at it again."[19]

Greb was interviewed again on March 8th and had this to say: "I'm never going to let it be said that I stuck in the game after I should have quit. Why should I? I have all the money I'll ever need. When I get through with this next Flowers fight I'll have something like $200,000 left out of my earnings." He went on to say, "The young fellows are never going to slap me around. But I do want a chance to get back on top again, and then I'll step out. I want my friends to remember me as a winning fighter." Greb then mentioned to the interviewer that if he should retire, "he would likely open a gymnasium in Pittsburgh and perhaps promote a few boxing shows on the side."[20]

Greb traveled to Hot Springs and stayed there with Mason for about a month. Then Greb traveled to New York in the first week of April with some rather surprising news. He announced that he had broken up with his longtime manager and would never work with him again. In an interview with Welsh, Greb explained the circumstances. "Yes, the story that I have asked for a severance of contract with Mason is true. He has tried to pull something on me that I won't stand for and I have asked the boxing commission to take up my case and see that once and for all I'm through with a fellow who cheated me, even when I was looking."[21]

Greb then went into the details of the break.

> The day I went to the office of the boxing commission to weigh in for Flowers, Mason said to me that I would have to have my New York license renewed as it had expired and I could not fight without having one. So, after I weighed in we went into the outer office of the commission and there Mason showed me three sheets of paper, each of which he asked me to sign. The top one was the application for the license renewal and I signed it without reading because I knew what it was as the printed form was familiar to me. The other two sheets I just turned up at the bottom and signed, believing that they were duplicate copies of the license application. Now, it turns out that Mason had inserted under the top form, two copies of the contract, dating for two years from February 26, in which he increased his percentage from 25 per cent, which he has been getting since we have been together, to 33 and a third per cent.[22]

Greb went on to explain:

> I had no idea this was what he had done and it never bothered me. When we went to Hot Springs the old arguments, which we have been having for years, broke out again and Mason told one of the boys there: "I got that Dutchman hooked and he don't know it. He signed a two-year contract with me in New York not so long ago and I'm going to hold him to it." This made me investigate the thing and for that reason I left Hot Springs and came East, giving out the story that I was coming over to spend Easter at Atlantic City. Today I told my story to the commission and they told me they would call Mason here and hear his side of it before taking action. But regardless of what the commission may do, I have fought my last fight under Mason. He cheated me, or tried to, and that ends it.[23]

The next day Greb said,

> This thing has been brewing for a long while and it came to a head when I learned that Mason had short changed me more than $1,000 when he paid me my share of the bout with Flowers. It was not until four days after Mason handed me what he said was my share of the purse that I discovered he was holding out more than $1,000. I accused him openly of trying to gyp me and that started the whole affair — although other and similar things entered into it.[24]

A month later, on May 8, 1926, the New York State Boxing Commission stated, "The contract, signed and sworn to, was not genuine, and as far as they are concerned Greb from now on is his own manager."[25] The date of the Flowers rematch was now moved from May 21 to sometime in August. With Greb handling his own affairs his next boxing match was on June 1, 1926, against Art Weigand. It was a ten-round bout in New York. Greb was an "easy winner" when he won eight of the ten rounds. Now that Greb had finished his first boxing match since their argument, Mason hired an attorney. Mason was now suing Greb, claiming their contract was legal and he should get his share of future purses.

It was said to be "well known in New York fight circles" that Greb had approached other people to manage his affairs, but they were "laying off until they learned Mason's attitude." People were expecting Mason to do something after Greb fought again. One of the managers Greb was looking at to work with was Jimmy Johnston, who managed Mike McTigue. Johnston was currently denying this, but many believed he would be managing Greb's affairs when Greb fought for the title again against Flowers.[26]

Mason's appeal eventually made it to New York's Supreme Court. On June 14, Justice Charles L. Guy ruled that the contract that Greb signed was valid and legal. Greb had to fight under Mason's management and Mason was to receive 33 percent of any purse.[27] This announcement came just one day before Greb was to box again in Pennsylvania.

Greb was scheduled to fight "Allentown" Joe Gans on June 15, 1926, in Wilkes-Barre, Pennsylvania. Gans was an African-American fighter who was to be tough competition to help Greb get into shape for Flowers. Gans had previously knocked out Roland Todd and had a "furious" battle with Flowers. When he fought Flowers he "opened up a cut on the champion's left eye that has kept Tiger idle since and knocked him out of several battles, including one with Greb at the Garden." Greb was ready for Gans and said, "I just wish I had been in as good shape as I am now the night I took on Flowers and the title never would have changed hands."[28]

Greb easily won the ten-round fight against Gans. "Newspaper men credited Greb with at least six of the rounds, called two or three even, and could give Gans the benefit of the doubt in only one." Greb was seen to have regained his old speed and never allowed his opponent to settle in one position long enough to throw an effective punch. Greb "smothered him in a shower of gloves" and he was "fresh and strong at the finish."[29]

The title rematch against Flowers was rescheduled for August 19, 1926. Leading up to the fight, Greb started training with and being handled by Jimmy Johnston. Johnston was expected to be in Greb's corner on fight night, but due to Mason's contract's being upheld, a third of Greb's winnings would still go to Mason. Mason was expected to keep a close eye on the proceedings from a front row seat.

Johnston was an experienced and influential New York manager. His influence supposedly helped his boxer, Mike McTigue, win a controversial decision against Flowers a year earlier. Flowers supposedly dominated McTigue in the bout, but Johnston's influence was rumored to have swayed the judges to give the bout to McTigue. No one was raising a bigger fuss about this than Flowers's manager, Walk Miller. Miller was now saying that Johnston was trying to fix this bout also, this time for Greb to win. Miller was so afraid that this fight with Greb was "in the bag" for Greb that he went to the New York Boxing Commission and stated his concern. Miller asked that his boxer get a "square deal" on fight night.[30]

Just a couple of days before the fight it seemed Johnston would not even be able to be in Greb's corner on fight night. On August 16 Johnston's wife died so he was expected not to be able to make it to the bout.[31] When fight night finally arrived Flowers was the 8 to 5 favorite, but on light betting.[32] Both fighters made weight by coming in around one pound under the middleweight limit. Flowers entered the ring first at around 9:37, "and was given a fairly good reception." Greb entered the ring with his new handler Jimmy Johnston and with Charlie Johnston. Greb was given "a wild ovation as he rushed up the ring steps and galloped through the ropes. Greb seemed full of pep and anxious to start and rushing over greeted Flowers like an old friend."[33]

The two judges for this fifteen-round title fight were Charles F. Mathison and Harold Barnes, while Jim Crowley was the referee. When the bell rang to start the fight, "Greb lashed out with both hands, started like the Greb of old and before the thing was a minute old, had the Negro champion staggering backward." Flowers was focusing mainly on a body attack. Greb was seen "moving about like the cat he was years ago and in a manner which brought cheers from the crowd, Greb bounced in and out, weaved around Flowers with consummate skill and ease, sometimes bewildering the Negro."[34]

Other than Greb's starting a little sooner and looking a little fresher, the fight was similar to the previous one, but much more aggressive. After a clinch in the second round, an old cut over Greb's left eye started bleeding. Then in the sixth round Greb returned the favor by opening a cut over Flowers's left eye. The only knockdown of the fight occurred in round eight. Welsh wrote: "Greb shot a hard short right to the champion's chin. Down like a log went Flowers, rolled over and scampered to his feet like a scared rabbit."[35]

In the eleventh round Greb "once more rocked Flowers with a smashing right hand to the mouth, which brought blood from the champion's lips. Then came the wildest excitement, both mauling, tugging, wrestling, fouling and doing everything but the stand up sort of fighting which local judges are accustomed to scoring." The remainder of the bout was a very rough affair. Flowers accused Greb of thumbing, while Flowers landed repeated low blows, "and frequently backhanded."[36]

The fourteenth round was said to be Greb's best, "which by all appearances put the fight in the bag for Greb." Throughout the round Greb "battered the Tiger about." Then in the fifteenth it continued to be "a wild exchange" which included more "mauling and tugging and wrestling." During this round Greb "draped Flowers over the ropes and shoved him almost to the floor." This was viewed as counting heavily against Greb as "the judges were seen to make copious notes on the offense." If there was any question about Greb's stamina it was definitely put to rest in the fifteenth round when Greb was seen "bounding, swinging, tearing around like a fighter who had just started to show his real stuff."

The round ended and the verdict was announced. It was another split decision. The two judges scored the bout for Flowers, while referee Jim Crowley had Greb as the winner. The *New York Times* let it be known how close the voting was when they told of the scorecards. On both judges' scorecards they had Flowers winning seven rounds, Greb winning six rounds, and two rounds even. Flowers was given

Greb's new manager, Jimmy Johnston. He was born in England and his family came to New York when he was twelve. In the 1930s, while still a successful boxing manager, he became a matchmaker for Madison Square Garden. He is now in the International Boxing Hall of Fame as a manager/promoter.

rounds 2, 5, 8, 9, 10, 12, 13. Greb was given rounds 1, 4, 6, 11, 14 and 15. The third and seventh were said to be even.[37]

The *Pittsburgh Post's* front-page headline the next day read, "Greb

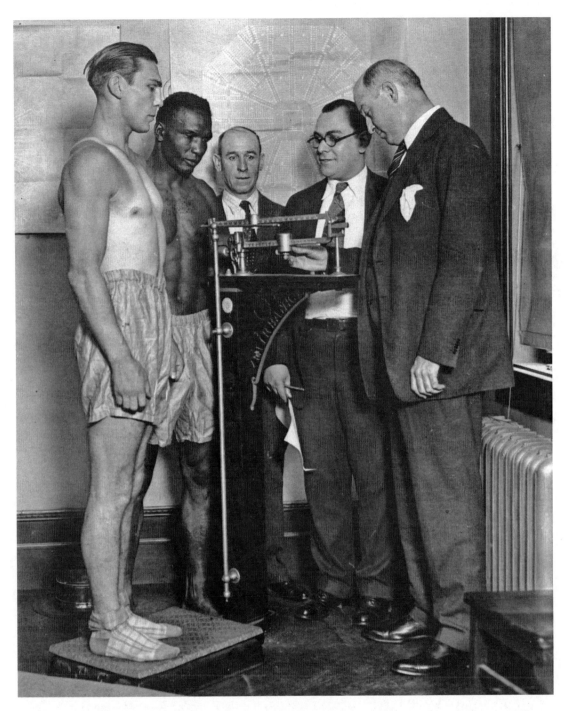

Jim Farley (right), the New York State Boxing Commissioner in 1926, weighs in Greb and Tiger Flowers for their last meeting. Boxing Secretary Bert Stand is next to Farley. The man in the center is unidentified (Craig Hamilton collection, www.josportsinc.com).

Wins Most Rounds But Flowers Retains Crown."[38] The *Post* wrote: "Greb honestly won that fight tonight," while Flowers "didn't show enough tonight to honestly merit the verdict in his favor." Regis Welsh had Greb winning nine rounds, Flowers four, and the third and ninth rounds even. Welsh would write: "In view of this tabulation there must have been something radically wrong." It was believed there were two factors that led to the discrepancy in the judges' scorecards.

The first issue was the rumors that the fight was in the bag for Greb before it started. This ended up working against Greb when it was believed that the judges overcompensated due to this rumor's being in the public eye. Every local paper ran the story of the conspiracy against Flowers, stating that "New York had said that its future fight game was in jeopardy." This was all due to Greb's making Johnston his handler. Welsh wrote:

> Greb, making one of the gamest comebacks in the history of the ring, fighting with courage and velocity which made it look as though he was in the full bloom of youth instead of a veteran campaigner and an ex-champion, paid the penalty of what a few weeks ago looked to him to be a smart move, by having in his corner a man whose influence was flung into the teeth of men who are engaged to count them up as they see them and render the verdict according to their honest judgment.[39]

The second factor that influenced the judges' scorecards was Greb's roughhouse tactics. Welsh wrote:

> It was unofficially whispered about the ring after the crowd had thinned out that Greb's ring tactics, some of which were unwarranted pushing and mauling which once sent Flowers through the ropes, militated heavily against clean scoring and swinging the thing universally in Flowers' favor.[40] ... The champion had been floored and this usually is enough to win by, but in the final counting this seemed to have been overlooked, discounted by Greb's foul tactics in the eyes of the judges.

Round eight ended up being the deciding round. Greb had knocked the champion down onto the canvas and had dominated during the round, but both judges scored the round for Flowers. The *Post* would write: "Winding up Greb caught Flowers with a terrific right to the stomach and the champion hit the floor." This would normally be a 10–8 round in Greb's favor. The *New York Times* describes the knockdown differently: "Flowers simply got his feet tangled up as he dug a left to the body and he squatted in Greb's corner."[41] It was said that the judges took into account Greb's foul tactics and scored the round against him. Greb continued fighting after the bell and this is believed to have been a factor. The *Washington Post* wrote of the incident: "Greb connected with a right to the chin just before the bell. The challenger plunged after the Tiger to continue the attack and had to be chased to his corner by the referee."[42] Flowers wasn't without his own roughhouse tactics during the round. He wrestled Greb to the canvas to the point of Greb's almost falling out of the ring. The *Chicago Daily Tribune* put it best when they wrote: "It was a hard fight to score, for they were both so bad that it became a case of assigning the blame at the end of each round instead of awarding credit."[43]

The *New York Times* described what happened after the verdict was announced. "The verdict, however, was not a popular one. The crowd thought that Greb should have received the decision, judged by the shower of straw hats and torn papers which flooded the arena when the verdict was announced."[44]

After the verdict two of Greb's "women friends" started some trouble. The two "went around the ring after the decision had been rendered attacking those they believed responsible for the verdict. One of the girls slapped Dick Murphy, the veteran Western Union chief in the mistaken belief that he was one of the judges."[45] The identity of the ladies is unknown.

Greb was interviewed a day after the fight and had this to say: "Well, that was one fight I won if I ever won any." Many newspapers agreed with Greb: "Many unofficial thousands were of the opinion that he had won." The *Post* would write: "One official, the referee, Jimmy Crowley, voiced his opinion that way on the ballot, while several of the unofficial newspaper judges, here and out of town recorded decisions in his favor. So, although it was likely the thing which marked the end of his fighting career, Greb had the solace of having some friends left."[46] No matter how close the fight was, it was clear Greb's best years were behind him.

The next month Greb entered the hospital to have some work done on his right eye. On September 16 the *New York Times* and other newspapers were given the story that Greb "submitted to an operation for the removal of a traumatic cataract from his right eye in the Atlantic City Hospital."[47] He was expected to stay in the hospital for a week with his eye covered.

This was a cover story to hide the real reason Greb was being operated on. Greb was having his right eye completely removed, then replaced with a glass eye. His personal physician, Dr. Carl S. McGivern, would explain the circumstances months later. "Harry Greb was made blind by a blow on his right eye during a fight with Kid Norfolk, Negro heavyweight, in New York City in 1921. He told no one about it." McGivern would go on to say, "I felt, and so did other physicians, that eventually the condition of the right eye would spread to the left eye and the gallant fighter would be totally blind. So last August he came here in the greatest of secrecy to have the operation performed." It should be noted that McGivern incorrectly remembered the procedure taking place in August, when it is documented to have taken place in September.

Dr. McGivern continued by saying:

> He entered a private hospital in Atlantic City under the name of Harry Brown and the difficult operation was performed by Dr. Gustav Guist, an eminent eye specialist of Vienna, Austria, who was visiting me here at the time. Dr. Guist's method, which involved the use of a special stone eye, was so successful that it was difficult for even a close observer to detect the difference between the real eye and the false one.

Dr. McGivern finished by stating,

> The secrecy was maintained and it was given out that a cataract had been removed from the eye. I am glad to be able to tell the truth now, as it reflects credit upon Greb's bravery and clears me of any charge of having assisted in the removal of a cataract from a blind eye.[48]

With people still believing Greb simply had a cataract removed, Greb continued his normal routine outside boxing. When he was released from the hospital a week after his operation, Greb was seen at the Dempsey-Tunney fight. The bout took place on September 23 in Philadelphia. Greb had seen both of them in training and was on record as saying he thought Tunney would win the fight if Dempsey didn't knock him out in the first few rounds. Greb was seen a day before the Dempsey-Tunney fight when "he showed up in Philadelphia wearing a black patch over the eye."[49] Greb's prediction came true when Tunney won the heavyweight championship.

During this time Greb had a conversation with his friend Happy Albacker about his intentions for the future. He told Albacker that he planned on opening a gymnasium in downtown Pittsburgh.[50] Albacker said, "He told me that he would not fight again and was contemplating taking over a floor in the then new building which houses the 5 & 10-cent store at Sixth Ave. and Smithfield St." Greb went on to say, "I'm going to go on talking about fighting Flowers again. I want to keep before the public until I get the business started. The fans soon forget you when you're through fighting."[51] He was also heard to say how he planned to promote the occasional boxing match.

Around the first week of October, Greb was in another auto accident. It was rumored that he was driving his car and tried to avoid hitting two farmers whose wagons were obstructing the road. The Associated Press would write: "In the automobile accident, in which his car plunged over an embankment, the wound from the operation was opened and several bones in the nose were fractured, causing him to breathe improperly."[52] The *Washington Post* would write: "Greb had complained of suffering from severe headaches and also dizziness since the accident."[53]

On October 21 Greb returned to Atlantic City, "primarily to have his eye treated." He traveled there with his fiancée, Naomi Braden. It was written: "He was in Atlantic City for final treatment of the optic, and for what he considered minor injuries received in the Pittsburgh accident."[54] While he was at the hospital, an "examination proved that his nasal passages had been entirely blocked." After consultation, "he decided on the operation for the removal of the fractured bones."[55]

Dr. McGivern explained the details of the operation. "The operation was started under local anesthesia and later during its course this was supplemented by nitrous oxide and oxygen gas. He left the operating table apparently in good condition at 8:30 last night."[56] Miss Braden was with him in the hospital the entire time.

Greb survived through the night but Dr. McGivern describes what happened the next morning on October 22. "At 10 o'clock this morning his heart began to fail and rapidly grew weaker despite the administration of stimulants until he died at 2:30 o'clock this afternoon."[57] Miss Braden, "who was at his bedside when he died, kept a sorrowful vigil over the body."[58]

The New York Times explained, "Following the operation Greb fell into a state of coma from which he failed to rally, and death was attributed to heart failure super induced by the shock of the operation combined with the injuries received in the accident."[59]

Dr. Weinberg was another physician that was present during the operation. On October 23 he was interviewed and declared that death was due to a blood clot on the brain related to Greb's auto accident. Dr. Weinberg stated, "Evidently a piece of bone extending from the bridge of the nose to the floor of the skull had been fractured in such a manner that a blood clot was formed in the brain." He went on to say,

> The fracture formed an obstruction in the nasal passages, making it impossible for him to breathe through his nose. He wished to reenter the ring, and it was necessary that this obstruction be removed. During the course of the operation, when the bone was removed, it permitted the blood to rush into the brain, thus bringing about the hemorrhage which resulted in his death.[60]

On October 23 Harry Greb's coffin was brought to an undertaking establishment in Atlantic City for a quick funeral. "His coffin was banked with flowers sent by friends and boxing enthusiasts."

After the immediate local funeral his body was taken to Pittsburgh for the official funeral and burial. His sister, Ida May Edwards, was immediately put in charge of the funeral arrangements.[61] His body arrived by train at East Liberty Station in Pittsburgh at 8:20 in the morning on October 24. Four people had traveled with the casket from Atlantic City: Greb's father Pius Greb, Greb's sister Ida with her husband J. Elmer Edwards, and Miss Naomi Braden. The body was immediately taken to the local undertaking establishment to be prepared for the funeral.

The funeral was to be held at the home of Ida and Elmer Edwards, where Greb's daughter Dorothy was staying. The address was 1130 Jancey Street, in the East End of Pittsburgh. Another sister, Kathryn Greb Brink, was in town, while the third sister, Clara Greb, was arriving from Spokane, Washington. Clara was now married and known as Mrs. Roy Briggs.[62] While the official funeral would be held a few days later, people were allowed to pay their respects to Greb during visitation at his sister's house.

On October 25 there were many tributes for Greb. The Rev. James R. Cox of Old St. Patrick's Church spoke on the radio describing "the spiritual side of Greb's life." During local boxing matches, various boxing clubs draped portraits of Greb in their rings. The crowd bowed their heads and taps was played after the timekeeper tolled the count of ten. "Floral tributes almost beyond count have arrived at the Edwards home since the body was taken there, and scores of telegrams of condolence have also been received."[63]

During the day "thousands" passed in and out of the home of Greb's sister, "to view the remains of the former middleweight champion." Many condolences also arrived, including

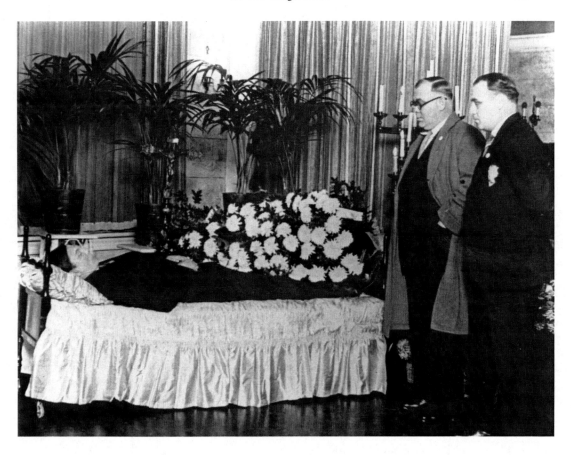

Greb lying in state in Atlantic City, where two unidentified mourners pay their respects (Antiquities of the Prize Ring).

telegrams from Pete Latzo, Johnny Wilson, Joe Dundee, Jimmy Delaney and Jack Dempsey. Dempsey wrote to the family, "I have lost one of my best friends and the world one of its great champions. In your hour of bereavement allow me to express my heartfelt sympathy."[64]

Gene Tunney wrote in the local newspaper: "To realize that the great windmill, the untiring, game, courageous boxer has passed away, can hardly be believed. To me Greb became a pal, and he gave me all sorts of encouragement for my fight which eventually made me champion." Tunney would go on to say,

> Greb taught me to fight, because I centered my mind on how to beat him, the man whom other heavies had trouble conquering with his speed and courage. Never did a better fighter of his pounds live and never did any fighter try so hard to win, do so much to keep the boxing game alive and never, in all fight history, has any fighter ignored physical obstacles like Greb did.[65]

Mason had this to say:

> Greb was the greatest fighter of his weight that ever lived. He was afraid of nothing and could fight like a wildcat. He and I differed on matters of policy several times, and, although feelings became strained more than once, I never lost track of the fact that Greb was a marvelous fighter. A week before Greb went down to be operated upon, he and I patched up all our differences, and Harry expressed the opinion that he would easily beat Flowers at catchweights, if they were matched again. I have a deep respect for Greb and his ability and I am deeply shocked at the news of his sudden death. Greb, as I said before, is one of the greatest fighting men of all time.[66]

No one knew yet that Greb had been fighting the last years of his career blind in one eye, but On October 26 the news of his having a glass eye for the last month finally leaked. Ida Edwards commented,

> Harry didn't want to let anybody know about it. It was to have been a secret just among members of the family and a few intimate friends and the surgeons who operated on him. Harry was sensitive about the affliction that made it necessary for him to have this done, and even in death I am sure he would not have wanted the world to know about it.[67]

On October 27 the official funeral began. At 9:30 in the morning the day's events began at Ida's house. So many flowers arrived they had to be turned over "to various hospitals and asylums throughout the city." They included an additional two "truckloads" of floral arrangements that arrived that day. The funeral procession then made its way to St. Philomena's Catholic Church, where Greb used to attend. Many thousands of fans accompanied the pallbearers carrying Greb in the middle of the closed off streets.

The ten official pallbearers included his manager Red Mason. Also included were Greb's long-time friends who often traveled with him, Eddie Deasy, Tom Dolan and Happy Albacker. Greb's secretary Jack White, his former sparring partners Jack Barry and Leo Caghill. The remaining pallbearers included Gene Tunney, who came in from Cleveland, Councilman Daniel Winters, and Sam Pender.[68]

The *Pittsburgh Press* wrote: "In the next hour and 10 minutes the procession wound slowly along Negley Ave., Fifth Ave. and Beachwood Blvd. to the church." The funeral left the church a little before noon. A "cortege" of thirty-one cars and 5,000 mourners then accompanied the carried casket to Calvary Cemetery. The casket was lowered while a war veteran sounded taps from his bugle.[69] The specific interment location is Section W, Lot 40, Grave 5.

Greb's brother-in-law, Elmer Edwards, was interviewed a day before the funeral. He talked of how Greb acted in his last month.

> For the last month or so, Harry has been rather despondent. He spoke often of death and seemed spiritless in many ways. When he discussed matters pertaining to the future, he would preface his remark with "If I live, I may do it" and he spoke several times of what arrangements should be made for the care of little Dorothy Mildred, his seven-year-old daughter, in the event of his death. He requested that he be buried from our home when he died and also stipulated that he wished to be buried beside his wife, who died four years ago.[70]

Elmer continued,

> A week ago last Saturday, Harry gave a birthday party for his daughter at our home, and he spent considerable time playing with the children. Ordinarily he preferred the company of grownups, but on this occasion he seemed to sense that he would not have another such opportunity for fraternizing with the youngsters. Judging from his conduct for the several weeks immediately preceding his death, now that I look back on them, I am firmly convinced that he had a premonition of his fate.[71]

On October 27 the *New York Times* ran an article that finally divulged the fact that Greb had been fighting blind for half a decade. Greb's personal physician, Dr. Carl S. McGivern, was interviewed and stated, "Harry Greb was made blind by a blow on his right eye during a fight with Kid Norfolk, Negro heavyweight, in New York City in 1921."[72]

Ida Edwards became executrix of the Greb will on October 29. Greb had left behind $75,000 in savings, a very large sum of money in 1926. Ida and her husband, Elmer, were made guardians of Greb's daughter, Dorothy. They eventually moved into Greb's house at 6444 Jackson Street, in the East End, where they lived for decades. Naomi Braden eventually married Jake Goldstein and moved to Florida, where they owned a hotel/resort off the beach. Red Mason continued to live in Pittsburgh for nine more years. He died of a heart attack on August 15, 1935. Greb's daughter, Dorothy, married Harry Wohlfarth when she was twenty-one. They remained married and had three children, a son and two daughters. They named their son Harry Greb Wohlfarth, while their daughters were named Suzanne and Mary Kay. They eventually moved to Conneaut Lake, Pennsylvania, where they lived until Dorothy passed away in 2001 at the age of eighty-one.

17.

THE MYTHS GROW WHILE
THE LEGEND FADES

John Lardner once wrote: "You can call a man well-known when many things are said about him by many people, but when many things both true and untrue are said about him — in other words, when a mythology begins to grow up around him — the man is truly famous." Lardner was referring to the myths that surrounded Greb during his life and continued to grow and spread like wildfire after his passing. He would go on to write: "More stories are told about Greb than about any man in his field, living or dead; including John L. Sullivan. More lies are told about him, and more honest fictions— all in his honor, all as a tribute. He's bigger than Stanley Ketchel, better than Paul Bunyan."[1]

To know who Harry Greb really was you must try to separate the fact from the fiction. Many of the tall tales surrounding him came about during his lifetime and were difficult to distinguish from the truth because he encouraged some of them. Others he just didn't care enough about to correct. He wasn't bothered if a newspaperman he never met made up stories about him to sell some papers. As long as it didn't hurt anybody, he didn't care. Greb was "a great man and a natural hitching-post for legends."[2] Some of the fantastic stories started after he passed away and it was discovered he had been secretly blind in his right eye for many years of his career. This was true, but seemed so unbelievable that people kept adding to it.

There are usually five myths that still follow Greb to this day.

The first myth is that he never trained for his bouts. Some of the yarns that were spread described "a thirteen-year campaign in defiance of all laws and rules of training and conditioning such as the average mortal must follow." It was also written that he was "breaking most of the rules of training laid down by the experts in the way of food, drink, sleep and modes of living."[3] With great amazement and admiration it was said the only training he did before a fight was with "babes and booze."[4]

This couldn't be further from the truth. Newspaper quotes throughout this book have detailed Greb's training habits. Even though he fought every week or two he was still in the gym training or outside running. Early in his career he trained at Pittsburgh's Garfield Athletic Club. Greb's usual training regimen during this time included going six rounds with relays of different boxing partners, men from many different weight classes. He would also run ten miles, have extensive exercises in the gym and finish with a rubdown.[5] From early in his career, and continuing into 1920, he would predominantly train out of the Lyceum Gym located at 110 Washington Place in Pittsburgh.[6] It was located across the street from the Epiphany Catholic Church, where he got married. He trained vigorously and often against smaller men for speed and heavyweights for power. His sparring increased from six rounds with relay partners up to nine rounds before his big fights. Greb even suffered bruises and cuts before a fight because he trained so hard.[7]

During 1921 and 1922, while managed by George Engel, Greb started training out of the Motor Square Boxing Club in Pittsburgh. It was located at 5900 Baum Boulevard in East Liberty. Even then he would still be seen at the Lyceum Gym on occasion. Under Engel's management he started having many fights in New York because Engel was based there. When in New York Greb would train at "Philadelphia" Jack O'Brien's Gym located at 1658 Broadway.[8] A typical workout there would consist of many hours of sparring, handball, pulleys and long runs in Central Park.[9] He would also make his training quarters in Manhasset, Long Island.[10] Greb even stopped at Billy Grupp's Gymnasium, also in New York.

When Greb went back to Red Mason in 1923 they built their own training camp at Conneaut Lake, Pennsylvania. He and Mason had it built before he fought Wilson for the middleweight championship. Once he won the title Greb was in the spotlight so this camp, located forty minutes outside of Pittsburgh and far away from the press, helped Greb focus on staying in shape. Between 1923–1926 he would still work out in Pittsburgh at the Lyceum Gym and the Motor Square Garden.[11] He would also spend some weeks at a training camp in Atlantic City and at the camp in Manhasset, Long island.[12]

When Greb traveled to out-of-state fights he would work out in local gyms. When going across country by locomotive he would often stop over in Chicago and go to Kid Howard's Arcade Gymnasium.[13] It was run by Howard Carr, also known as Kid Howard, and was located at 62 West Madison Street.[14] Greb would also spend time at Hot Springs, Arkansas, to condition himself before some big fights.[15] When in Michigan, Greb would work out at the Detroit A.C., located at 241 Madison Avenue.[16]

Before many fights Greb would stage public workouts to help drum up awareness and hopefully increase attendance. These would be for a few hours each over two days and be open to the press and consist of sparring, rope skipping and calisthenics.[17]

The fact that Greb trained before his bouts is even caught on film. The only film footage of Greb that exists is of him working out for his bout with Mickey Walker. The newsreel footage shows Greb at "Philadelphia" Jack O'Brien's Gym. On the film Greb is shadow boxing, jumping rope, hitting the punching bag, doing sit-ups and calisthenics, stretching, sparring and playing handball.

Not only is his professional work ethic documented in newspapers and video, it is also stated by people who were close associates of his. Harry Keck was a sportswriter for the *Pittsburgh Post* and had covered Greb's career since 1914, his second year as a professional boxer. They started out as acquaintances and then became close friends over the years. Keck was at ringside for every local fight and traveled to the out of state fights also. It has been written that "Keck was with Greb throughout his career and conversed with him in Pittsburgh the night before the great middleweight died on an operating table in Atlantic City."[18] Keck stated frequently that Greb trained very hard "and very diligently. He did road work and a lot of gym work and swimming. The canard that he was a physical freak who didn't need to train is just another of the many Greb fables. Fact is, Harry, like so many of the old timers, used one fight as preparation for the next."[19] Keck would also explain, "Don't forget — he fought so often that this training didn't have to be the elaborate month-long ritual modern fighters make of it."[20]

Cuddy DeMarco was a stablemate of Greb and was interviewed after Greb passed away. DeMarco had this to say about Greb's training: "Harry always was in shape for a fight and he never cared who his opponent was. And he never failed to train religiously for a fight, either. He was in the gym every day."[21] The story that Greb never trained is simply untrue.

The second myth surrounding Greb is that he was a heavy drinker. This was started when Greb was still alive and he actually helped to create it. Greb wanted to fight Johnny Wilson in 1923 for the middleweight title. Wilson had been ducking Greb for years, so Greb supposedly traveled to New York just to trick Wilson into thinking he was out of shape. Stanley Weston

Greb training for a fight later in his career (Antiquities of the Prize Ring).

tells the story this way: "Enlisting the aid of some New York bartenders, all of whom liked him, Harry spent hours drinking colored water and acting like a drunk. The news got around that he was 'training' as usual, and finally reached the ears of Wilson." Johnny said to his manager, "Now's the time for me to fight that bum. The only time."[22]

From then on the rumor of Greb's heavy drinking habits continued. It worked so well Greb was said to have used it again to change the odds before the Mickey Walker fight in 1925. Greb wanted to bet on himself before the fight, but he was a 2–1 favorite. It is said Greb pulled up in a cab very late the night before the fight outside Lindy's Restaurant in New York, as well as many other establishments. Many heavy gamblers where hanging out there so Greb fooled them into thinking he was drunk. He "stumbled" out of the cab and waved "a drunken greeting" to the gamblers. George Engel, Greb's old manager, said, "Consequently, various drinking establishments all over town were treated to the sight of Harry Greb falling drunkenly out of a cab accompanied by a couple of wide-eyed blondes."[23] The girls would then help him back into the cab and they would drive to another establishment. Looking so drunk the night before the fight was said to have changed the odds so Greb could bet on himself.[24]

According to his sister, Ida Edwards, Greb often fooled people into thinking he was a heavy drinker. When Greb knew in advance that reporters would be interviewing him, Ida explains what he would do.

> He would watch for them and when he saw them he would yell to Elmer or to me to bring him a drink and a cigarette. He would be smoking and drinking when they arrived and their stock question was usually, "How on earth can you dissipate this way and beat great fighters like Tunney?" Greb would shrug his shoulders, empty the glass and order another slug. The reporters didn't know it was just plain unadulterated ginger ale and that he didn't inhale the cigarette smoke."[25] Ida would go on to say, "And quite often they produced the desired result. They put him on the short end of the betting and he would wager thousands of dollars on himself to win, sometimes at huge odds.[26]

Many people closest to Greb would say the same thing his sister did. Bernard "Happy" Albacker was one of Greb's closest friends. Albacker once said,

> I was probably as close to Greb as any person. I saw him in practically all of his fights and rarely left him at any time." He would go on to say, "Greb never drank a drop of liquor. He would drink an occasional bottle of ale to build up his strength after trying to make weight or sometimes a glass of champagne, but never the hard stuff. You might have heard stories of Greb sitting in a nightclub roaring drunk. But not Harry. He would either dump his drinks under the table, spill them or pass them to others at the table. He liked to give off the impression that he was "tight."[27]

Greb's preference for ginger ale was even noticed by others. Roy Higby wrote in his book *...a man from the past* how he spent some time with Greb in the Hotel Pennsylvania after the Johnny Wilson rematch in 1924. Greb and a buddy were with three girls and partied with Higby and his friend in their hotel room because Greb was also staying on the same floor. They had alcohol in the room that people were drinking, but not Greb. Higby wrote: "He was really a good fellow, and he had sandwiches and ginger ale with us, but no alcoholic beverage."[28]

When interviewed about this subject Harry Keck had said, "He drank sparingly"[29] as well as saying Greb "would take an occasional drink."[30] *Ring* magazine editor Nat Fleischer was also aware that Greb was a fastidious trainer, but that he preferred to cultivate a reputation for excess. The story that Greb was a heavy drinker is simply untrue.

The third myth that is synonymous with Greb is that he was the dirtiest fighter that ever lived. Later on in his career when he started losing his sight he did fight rougher, but no more than some other experienced fighters of his day. Often his opponent would inflict these tactics upon him first before he would unleash the fouling in return. Tunney, who fought Greb five times in some of the roughest fights of Greb's career, is on record as saying, "I categorically state that as far as I know, Harry Greb was NOT a foul fighter. He gave no quarter, nor did he ask quarter." Tunney went on to say,

In my first fight with him, at the old Madison Square Garden, my nose was broken in the first 10 seconds. My seconds said that Greb butted me with his head. This I do not accept as factual; and if his head was the weapon, rather than his fists, my head should not have been where it was. Personally, I think he hit me with an overhand right. When Greb got into the ring with someone who tried to foul him, then he would throw the whole encyclopedia at his opponent. Probably this is the reason why he got the reputation of being a foul fighter.[31]

Augie Ratner fought Greb twice and said, "Greb was a clean fighter with me. He was so fast and tireless that you had to be in top shape to fight him. I think those who saw our twenty-rounder in New Orleans would agree that it was a good one — and a clean one."[32] Ratner was interviewed again and stated,

Sure, I've read those stories about Greb being the dirtiest fighter who ever lived. I didn't see him in all his fights, but those I did see were wild and woolly affairs — mostly because of Greb's hurricane style. I saw men much bigger than Harry deliberately foul him, and then all hell did break loose, because Harry always gave as good as he took. Outside the ring, he was a personable guy with nice manners.[33]

During the time Greb fought, boxing was less regulated and strict rules in the ring were not always enforced, as they are today. The sport was only a couple of decades removed from bare-knuckle fighting. The first World Heavyweight Champion under the Queensberry rules was Jim Corbett, who defeated John L. Sullivan in 1892. Greb started fighting as a pro just twenty-one years later, in 1913. There were many "foul" maneuvers done in the ring back then that were commonplace in a rough bout.

Shown here is a newspaper illustration that demonstrates the six fouls most commonly used by many fighters during Greb's era. The Harry Wills vs. Charley Weinert fight is mentioned, as well as the Wills vs. Firpo fight and the Greb vs. Walker fight. The first example of commonly used foul tactics is "Pulling an opponent in with the left and smashing at his body with the right, as Wills did all through his fight with Firpo."[34] In a few fight descriptions in this book this technique is described and was effectively used by Greb.

Another panel of the cartoon states, "How Wills slipped his left around Weinert's neck while socking him with the right. Many fighters use this trick. An apology follows and of course that gives the referee an excuse for overlooking the foul." It is documented that Greb also used this technique on occasion.

The illustration also mentions, "Clever work. Missing with a right hook and sinking the bony wrist into the other boxer's side just below the ribs." Also demonstrated is "Pushing an opponent between the ropes and holding him there for a pasting, as Greb did many times to Mickey Walker."

The next maneuver looks like a punch but is actually a thumbing. "This is considered an artistic stunt when 'pulled' so neatly that the referee can't see it. A light jab is delivered with half extended fingers and the thumb deftly poked into the opponent's eye." This was more easily accomplished back then because boxing gloves had less padded thumbs that were more flexible.

The last technique is described as "mugging." "Often crudely done by modern boxers but said in scientific circles to be very effective, especially if used with a little pressure of the thumb." "Captain" Bob Roper often inflicted this upon Greb during their rough bouts.

Harry Keck was asked if Greb was dirtier than other fighters of his time and he responded, "Each rehash of the Greb legend is more sickening than the one before it. A foul fighter? Take a look at the record; there's your answer. Harry was disqualified only once in a career that spanned almost fourteen years and more than 300 fights."[35] The fight Keck was referring to was the Kid Norfolk fight on April 19, 1924. It was an example of an opponent inflicting the foul

FOULS--BY SOMEONE WHO THINKS HE KNOWS

-BY EDGREN

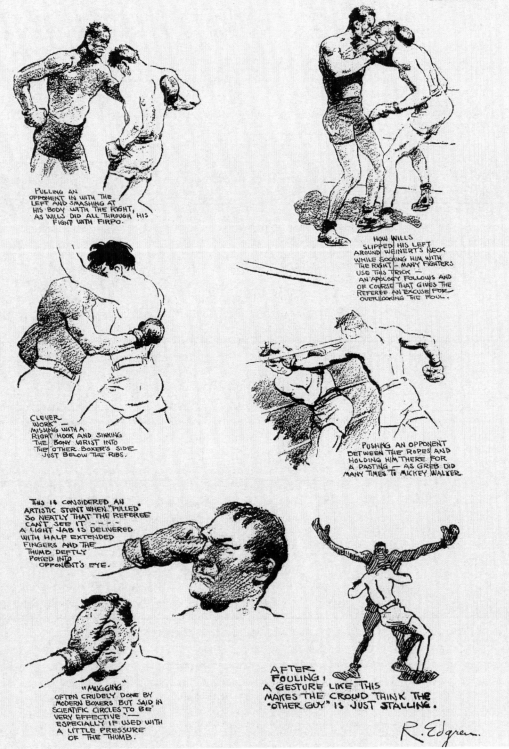

An illustration from the *Pittsburgh Post* during the 1920s. It shows the boxing fouls many fighters used in the ring during that era. Greb was not the only boxer to use these techniques (*Pittsburgh Post-Gazette*).

tactics on Greb first, then Greb returning the actions. Norfolk was said to have charged Greb head down and butted him through the ropes in round two. The referee didn't disqualify Norfolk so he continued fouling Greb, including many punches into Greb's groin. Only after all this did Greb then retaliate with similar tactics which resulted in disqualification when both fighters continued to fight after the bell had rung.

Bob Roper is another fighter who inflicted rough tactics on Greb first, which caused Greb to retaliate. Descriptions of Roper fights during his career clearly show Roper as a much dirtier fighter than Greb ever was. Roper was disqualified in at least six fights with some ending in riots.

Chuck Wiggins was another boxer who was far dirtier than Greb ever was. Wiggins fought approximately half the number of fights in his career that Greb did, but even with fewer bouts Wiggins was still disqualified for dirty tactics in eight of them. When Greb was asked about the nine incredible fights they had together he simply said Chuck Wiggins was "the best butter I ever butted with."[36]

Although Greb wasn't the dirtiest fighter who ever lived, he surely wasn't the cleanest either. Stanley Weston once wrote:

> And the funny part is that he wasn't ashamed of the things he did. "I fight to win" he used to say. "I'll bang 'em with my head, give 'em the thumb and the rabbit, and if it'll help, I'll kick 'em. This is a tough business and the only way to survive is to be tougher than the other guy." When caught in a foul act by the referee, Harry would never apologize.[37]

Even Gene Tunney, who stated Greb didn't foul, would contradict himself later on when he stated, "...He thumbed me. He butted me. He tried to kill me.... Anything he did to you — and he did everything he could to dismember you — you could do back and he wouldn't complain...."[38] Greb supposedly said this on the subject: "Boxing ain't the noblest of arts, and I ain't its noblest artist."[39] Many rough tactics were used by experienced boxers back then and Greb was no exception. Greb started using them late in his career to help compensate for his blindness, and it coincides with the exposure he was receiving as the middleweight champion. However, by no means was Greb the dirtiest fighter ever; that is just another exaggeration.

The fourth myth that follows Greb is that his name wasn't even Greb. A year after his death a sportswriter made up a story that the real name on his birth certificate was in fact "Berg." The story goes that Greb thought the name sounded too Jewish and might have cost him some fans and boxing engagements so he reversed the letters in his name so they read G-R-E-B instead of B-E-R-G.

Keck commented, "Someday I might get around to writing the real Greb story. Trouble is, I don't know what I'd do with it after I wrote it. I queried a few editors on it some years ago and found they preferred the myth, which they held was a better story, even down to the Berg-spelled-backwards angle."[40] Keck has said most of the Greb stories were just rehashed from one newspaper or magazine article to another. "The stealing goes on and on — and there's no end in sight. Next thing you know, some idiot will insist Greb had three arms."[41]

In a 1954 magazine article titled "Harry Greb or Harry Berg," the facts were finally revealed. Printed in the article was a copy of Greb's birth certificate which clearly showed that his last name had always been "Greb." In the article Greb's old manager George Engel stated, "Now getting back to this business of Greb's name which is supposed to be Berg. That's a lot of nonsense. And printed on this page is a certified true copy of his birth certificate to prove it."[42]

Harry got his name from his father, who was Pius Greb. Pius Greb came from Germany, where some Greb relatives still reside today. I have spoken with a few Greb relatives in Germany and it is very clear that the name was always Greb. His family's U.S. Census results, as well as his birth certificate, all confirm that his name was always Greb.

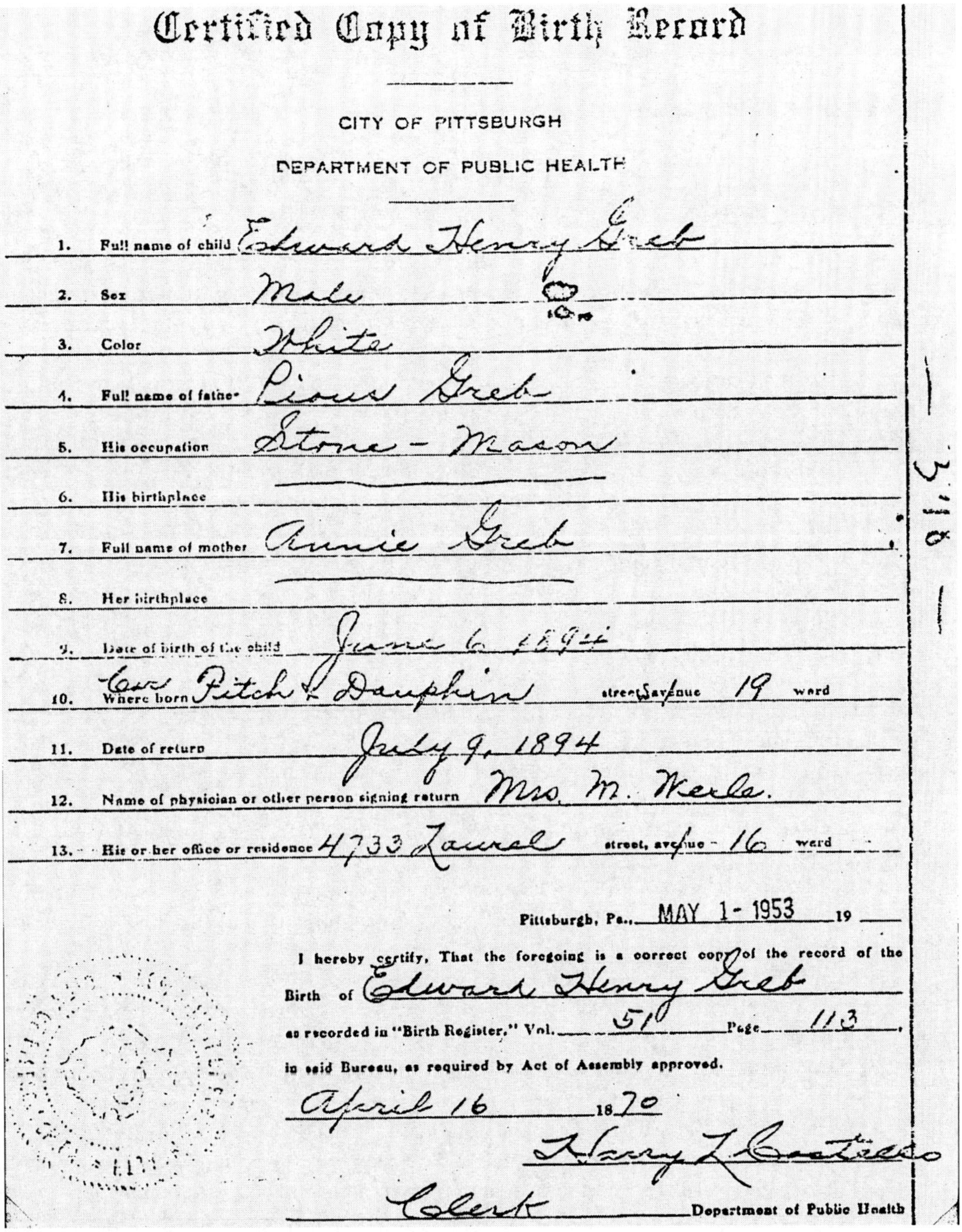

Certified Copy of Birth Record

CITY OF PITTSBURGH

DEPARTMENT OF PUBLIC HEALTH

1. Full name of child *Edward Henry Greb*
2. Sex *Male*
3. Color *White*
4. Full name of father *Pious Greb*
5. His occupation *Stone - Mason*
6. His birthplace
7. Full name of mother *Annie Greb*
8. Her birthplace
9. Date of birth of the child *June 6, 1894*
10. Where born *Cor Fitch & Dauphin* street, avenue *19* ward
11. Date of return *July 9, 1894*
12. Name of physician or other person signing return *Mrs. M. Merle.*
13. His or her office or residence *4733 Laurel* street, avenue *16* ward

Pittsburgh, Pa., **MAY 1 - 1953** 19___

I hereby certify, That the foregoing is a correct copy of the record of the

Birth of *Edward Henry Greb*

as recorded in "Birth Register," Vol. *51* Page *113*,

in said Bureau, as required by Act of Assembly approved.

April 16 18*70*

Harry L Costello

Clerk ___Department of Public Health

A copy of Harry Greb's birth certificate. He was born Edward Henry Greb and went by the name Harry Greb. Note that he was born in his father's car at the corner of Dauphin and Fitch Street. Fitch Street was also known as Millvale Ave. The Greb family home was at 138 N. Millvale Avenue (collection of Tony Triem).

The fifth and final myth is that Greb fought for years with a glass eye. This is more of a half-truth. After he retired following the final bout with Tiger Flowers, Greb did get a glass eye surgically implanted. However, he only had it for the last two months of his life, and Greb never fought while he had the glass eye.

A week after Greb's death his personal eye physician, Dr. Carl S. McGivern, was interviewed.

In an article in the *New York Times* on October 27, 1926, Dr. McGivern explains why the glass eye had not been put in sooner:

> Several years ago [Greb] was advised by physicians and friends to have the eye removed, but refused to do so in the fear that it would be discovered that he was half blind and he would be barred by the boxing commissions and promoters from the ring.[43]

People combined the facts that he was blind for many years with the fact that he eventually received a glass eye. Therefore, it was assumed he had the glass eye the whole time he fought blind. That is not true: Greb never fought while he had the glass eye; it was implanted after he retired.

The fact that stories, even false ones, continue about Greb is a tribute. As John Lardner once wrote: "They do not tell lies or believe myths about just anyone, which speaks well for Greb's enduring and mythological quality."[44]

As the decades passed after Greb's death, when people talked of him the stories would become larger than life. However, while the people who saw him fight started fading away, so did the memories of Greb. Unfortunately, no fight films exist of any of his bouts. This just adds to the mystery surrounding him and the lack of exposure to his history. When there are boxing highlight films from the Greb era on TV or video, all the greats can be seen and remembered, but never Greb. Because each generation of fight fans doesn't have the ability to watch his fights or his unique fighting style, he continues to be a mystery.

Almost every great opponent of Greb's has fight footage captured on film. It is extremely unusual for a middleweight boxing champion of his time to have had no fights recorded. Listed here are just some of his opponents who you can see on film today: Bill Brennan, Tommy Gibbons, Mike Gibbons, Gene Tunney, Mike O'Dowd, Tommy Loughran, Mickey Walker, Ace Hudkins, Ted Jamieson, George Chip, Jimmy Delaney, Roland Todd, Kid Norfolk, Soldier Jones, Bartley Madden, Mike McTigue, Battling Levinsky, Joe Chip, Eddie McGoorty, and Al McCoy. Many were not even champions, but all were beaten by Greb.

Greb contemporaries whom he didn't fight but have bouts captured on film include Jack Delaney, Georges Carpentier, Paul Berlenbach, Les Darcy, Jimmy Clabby, Battling Siki, Benny Leonard, and Ted "Kid" Lewis.

Boxing fights have been filmed since 1897 when Bob Fitzsimmons fought Jim Corbett for the heavyweight title. Although most of the bouts first filmed were heavyweight bouts, filming eventually spread to the other weight classes. Even middleweight champions before Greb exist on film today, including Billy Papke, Stanley Ketchel, George Chip, Al McCoy, Les Darcy, and Mike O'Dowd. All of these champions were recorded well before Greb ever won a title.

Although no fight films exist of Greb today, it doesn't mean they weren't filmed at one time. There are four Greb fights that were confirmed to have been filmed: the first Greb-Tunney fight in 1922, Greb-Walker in 1925; and the two Greb-Flowers fights in 1926. There may have been others, but these four have been confirmed. There were newspaper ads for the Greb-Walker fight telling how the film was to be shown in theaters. It has also been told how "Greb always spoke of the hot overhead lights made especially for filming the fight."[45] The first Greb-Tunney bout was even catalogued by the American Film Institute. They have it titled as *The Tunney-Greb Boxing Match (1922)* by J.C. Clark Productions. It was released in June of 1922 and consisted of four reels. Some of the Greb-Flowers matches were included in the film *The Fighting Deacon* (1926) also known as *The Life Of Tiger Flowers*. This film was also held by the AFI and consisted of five reels.

Unfortunately, these films were made on nitrate stock and deteriorated over the years. Even before they deteriorated, many were shown in theaters and then recycled to save money. Many were recycled during the world wars because of the silver content in the film. There were also laws at the turn of the century that prohibited owning or showing fight films, so many were sold overseas or kept hidden by collectors.

The most sought-after fight films in history are of Greb. *Ring* magazine in October 2000 listed the top ten most sought-after films of fights that were known to have been filmed. On the top of the list was Greb-Tunney 1, with the second highest in demand being the Greb-Walker fight.[46] The hope is that somewhere in the world some person or establishment finds one of these films in a collection. Nitrate film lasts thirty to eighty years in perfect condition, then it disintegrates. Unless it was copied onto safety film, the content is lost forever.

The famous fight collector Jim Jacobs searched for a Greb fight his whole life. He and his partner, Bill Clayton, once owned the largest collection of fight films in the world. After Jacobs died in 1988, Clayton sold the collection to ESPN, where they are shown on the network. Jim Jacobs once said, "If somebody — somebody astute about fight films, not just a guy who knows nothing about collecting—found, say, Greb footage in his cellar or attic, and he called me for a deal, I would trade him anything I have in my collection for whatever he has of Harry Greb."

The hope that one surfaces is fueled by a surprising discovery that happened in 1991. The University of South Carolina was doing renovation and discovered some newsreel films in boxes. On one of the newsreels was what is now known as *The Greb Training Film*. It consists of just a few minutes of Greb training before his bout with Mickey Walker. It shows Greb signing the contract as well as training at "Philadelphia" Jack O'Brien's Gym. He is sparring, jumping rope, playing handball, hitting the speed bag, doing calisthenics and smiling for the camera. After being lost for sixty-six years it was an amazing find. Boxing Hall of Fame inductee and *Ring* magazine owner and publisher Stanley Weston wrote an article for *Ring* magazine in 1991 describing the discovery. In the article Weston says, "To have an opportunity to see Harry Greb alive and in the prime of life was beyond my wildest dreams, comparable for a fight film collector to seeing Abraham Lincoln delivering the Gettysburg Address or Napoleon bidding farewell to his troops at Waterloo."[47] Fight film collectors, boxing historians and Greb fans still search to this day for any elusive film of Greb actually boxing in one of his fights.

Even with the men Greb beat available for viewing on film, since no known footage exists of Greb fighting them, Greb's fighting style and technique still remain a mystery. This adds to his mystique, as well as his not being remembered. As the old saying goes, "Out of sight, out of mind." Therefore, memorabilia about Greb have become some of the most expensive and rare collectors' items for boxing enthusiasts, while Greb's story and fights are mostly unknown to the casual fight fan. We are only left with stories and record books telling of a man who was the best of his generation and possibly the best of all time.

In 1960 Stanley Weston eloquently said it best when he wrote:

> But there has not been another Harry Greb, nor is there likely to be. With all the others there is something to prevent them from being called "The Fighter," the way Greb was called "The Fighter." Even Robinson, probably the best fighting machine since the Golden Age that Greb himself dominated, has his imperfections. If not in the ring, outside it. For once a man becomes a champion, he is the property of all the people. He must walk in the image they create for him. And although Ray Robinson came close to being the perfect fist fighter, he was only half a champion in the eyes of even his noisiest fans. He was money-hungry and conniving, a king who scorned the bows and cheers of his subjects. This earns only respect — it does not earn love. And they loved Harry Greb. They loved him because it was as though each fight fan had taken a ball of clay and formed it to his own idea of what a prizefighter should be, and it came out Harry Greb. There was a sense of possession there. They owned him. And so they loved him.[48]

Appendix A:
Greb's Complete Fight Record

This fight record includes amateur bouts and exhibitions.
"ND" stands for Newspaper Decision.

1913 Amateur

Mar 10	W.J. Miller	Waldemeir Hall, Pittsburgh, PA.	W3	
Mar 11	Al Storey	Waldemeir Hall, Pittsburgh, PA.	W3	
Mar 12	Red Cumpsten	Waldemeir Hall, Pittsburgh, PA.	W4	
Apr 4	George Koch	Cleveland, A.C., Cleveland, OH.	W4	
May 8	Red Cumpsten	East Liberty A.C., Pittsburgh, PA.	KO 3	

1913 Professional

May 29	Frank Kirkwood	Exposition Hall, Pittsburgh, PA.	ND 6	Win
Jul 19	Battling Murphy	Old City Hall, Pittsburgh, PA.	ND 6	TKO 2
Aug 13	Lloyd Crutcher	Jefferson Theatre, Punxsutawney, PA.	ND 6	KO 1
Oct 11	Hooks Evans	Old City Hall, Pittsburgh, PA.	ND 6	Loss
Oct 22	Mike Milko	Tariff Club, Pittsburgh, PA.	ND 6	Draw
Nov 17	Mike Milko	Southside Market House, Pittsburgh, PA.	ND 6	Win
Nov 29	Joe Chip	Old City Hall, Pittsburgh, PA.	ND 6	KO by 2
Dec 6	Harvey Sherbine	Old City Hall, Pittsburgh, PA.	ND 6	Win
Dec 12	Terry Nelson	Mishler Theatre, Altoona, PA.	ND 6	KO 3

1914

Jan 1	Whitey Wenzel	Old City Hall, Pittsburgh, PA.	ND 6	Win
Jan 10	Whitey Wenzel	Old City Hall, Pittsburgh, PA.	ND 6	Win
Mar 2	Mickey Rodgers	Central Rink, Steubenville, PA.	ND 10	W DQ 5
Apr 14	Fay Keiser	Duquesne Gardens, Pittsburgh, PA.	ND 6	Win
May 13	Fay Keiser	Southside Market House, Pittsburgh, PA.	ND 6	Draw
May 25	George Lewis	Southside Market House, Pittsburgh, PA.	ND 6	Win
May 29	Whitey Wenzel	Academy Theater, Pittsburgh, PA.	ND 6	Draw
Jun 15	Walter Monoghan	Waldemeir Hall, Pittsburgh, PA.	ND 6	Win
Jun 29	Irish Gorgas	Waldemeir Hall, Pittsburgh, PA.	ND 6	Win
Jul 20	John Foley	Waldemeir Hall, Pittsburgh, PA.	ND 6	Win
Jul 27	George Lewis	Central Rink, Stuebenville, OH.	ND 10	Win
Aug 10	Irish Gorgas	Waldemeir Hall, Pittsburgh, PA.	ND 6	Win
Aug 24	Whitey Wenzel	Waldemeir Hall, Pittsburgh, PA.	ND 6	Draw
Aug 31	John Foley	Waldemeir Hall, Pittsburgh, PA.	ND 6	Win

Sep 26	Jack Fink	National A.C., Philadelphia, PA.	ND 6	Win
Nov 14	Terry Martin	National A.C., Philadelphia, PA.	ND 6	Win
Dec 7	Joe Borrell	Olympia A.C., Philadelphia, PA.	ND 6	Loss

1915

Jan 1	Billy Donovan	Nonpareil A.C., Philadelphia, PA.	ND 6	Draw
Jan 8	Howard Truesdale	Nonpareil A.C., Philadelphia, PA.	ND 6	Win
Jan 12	Billy Miske	Fairmount A.C., Philadelphia, PA.	ND 6	Draw
Jan 25	Jack Blackburn	Duquesne Gardens, Pittsburgh, PA.	ND 6	Win
Feb 10	Harry "KO" Baker	Duquesne Gardens, Pittsburgh, PA.	ND 6	Win
Mar 4	Whitey Wenzel	Highland Club, Pittsburgh, PA.	ND 6	Win
Mar 6	Tommy Mack	W. Beau St. Rink, Washington, PA.	ND 6	Win
Mar 13	Jack Lavin	McKeesport, PA.	ND 6	Win
Mar 25	Harry "KO" Baker	Duquesne Gardens, Pittsburgh, PA.	ND 6	Win
Apr 15	Whitey Wenzel	Highland Club, Pittsburgh, PA.	ND 6	Loss
Apr 22	Joe Borrell	Duquesne Gardens, Pittsburgh, PA.	ND 6	Draw
May 24	Whitey Wenzel	Duquesne Gardens, Pittsburgh, PA.	ND 6	Win
May 31	Fay Keiser	West Side A.C., Connellsville, PA.	ND 6	Win
Jun 25	Fay Keiser	Old Moose Hall, Cumberland, MD.	ND 10	Draw
Jul 8	Red Robinson	Keystone Park, Kerenton, PA.	EXH 6	
Jul 12	Tommy Gavigan	Duquesne Gardens, Pittsburgh, PA.	ND 6	Win
Jul 21	George Hauser	Elwyn Grove, Elwyn, PA.	ND 6	KO 6
Jul 22	Fay Keiser	Old Moose Hall, Cumberland, MD.	ND 10	Win
Aug 23	Al Rogers	Duquesne Gardens, Pittsburgh, PA.	ND 6	Win
Sep 13	Al Rogers	Duquesne Gardens, Pittsburgh, PA.	ND 6	Win
Oct 18	George Chip	Duquesne Gardens, Pittsburgh, PA.	ND 6	Draw
Nov 16	Tommy Gibbons	Auditorium, St. Paul, MN.	ND 10	Loss
Dec 16	Perry "Kid" Graves	Power Auditorium, Pittsburgh, PA.	ND 6	TKO by 2

1916

Feb 26	Walter Monoghan	Power Auditorium, Pittsburgh, PA.	ND 6	Draw
Apr 1	Kid Manuel	Power Auditorium, Pittsburgh, PA.	ND 6	Win
Apr 27	Grant "Kid" Clark	Casino, Johnstown, PA.	ND 6	NC 5
May 6	Whitey Wenzel	Charleroi Rink, Charleroi, PA.	ND 6	Win
Jun 3	Kid Manuel	Power Auditorium, Pittsburgh, PA.	ND 6	KO 1
Jun 17	Whitey Wenzel	Baseball Park, New Kensington, PA.	ND 10	Win
Jun 26	George Chip	Coliseum, New castle, PA.	ND 10	Loss
Aug 7	Al Grayber	Power Auditorium, Pittsburgh, PA.	ND 6	Win
Aug 28	Jerry Cole	Power Auditorium, Pittsburgh, PA.	ND 6	Win
Sep 4	Fay Keiser	Amphitheatre, Cumberland, MD.	W 10	
Oct 16	Jackie Clark	Armory, Lonaconing, MD.	W 10	
Oct 21	Harry "KO" Baker	Power Auditorium, Pittsburgh, PA.	ND 6	Win
Nov 4	Bob "KO" Sweeney	Power Auditorium, Pittsburgh, PA.	ND 6	Win
Nov 8	Willie Brennan	Park Opera House, Erie, PA.	ND 10	Win
Nov 14	Jackie Clark	Armory, Lonaconing, MD.	KO 3	
Nov 17	Willie Brennan	Broadway Auditorium, Buffalo, NY.	ND 10	Win
Nov 24	Tommy Burke	Broadway Auditorium, Buffalo, NY.	ND 10	Win
Nov 27	George "KO" Brown	Power Auditorium, Pittsburgh, PA.	ND 6	Win
Dec 26	Bob Moha	Broadway Auditorium, Buffalo, NY.	ND 10	Win

1917

(37 bouts this year)

Jan 1	Joe Borrell	Power Auditorium, Pittsburgh, PA.	ND 6	Win
Jan 13	Eddie Coleman	Charleroi Rink, Charleroi, PA.	ND 10	KO 2
Jan 20	Jules Ritchie	National A.C., Philadelphia, PA.	ND 6	TKO 4
Jan 29	Fay Keiser	Maryland Theatre, Lonaconing, MD.	W 20	
Feb 10	Mike Gibbons	National A.C., Philadelphia, PA.	ND 6	Loss
Feb 12	Willie Brennan	Broadway Auditorium, Buffalo, NY.	ND 10	Win
Mar 5	Frankie Brennan	Power Auditorium, Pittsburgh, PA.	ND 6	Win
Mar 20	Tommy Gavigan	Orpheum Theatre, McKeesport, PA.	ND 10	TKO 5
Mar 23	Young Herman Miller	Casino, Johnstown, PA.	ND 10	TKO 5
Apr 2	Young Ahearn	Power Auditorium, Pittsburgh, PA.	ND 6	KO 1
Apr 14	Al Rogers	Charleroi Rink, Charleroi, PA.	ND 10	Win
Apr 16	Zulu Kid	Power Auditorium, Pittsburgh, PA.	ND 6	Win
Apr 30	Al McCoy	Exposition Hall, Pittsburgh, PA.	ND 10	Win

(For world middleweight title — unofficial "ND" bout. Must win by knockout)

May 3	Jackie Clarke	Narrows Park Rink, Cumberland, MD.	Draw 20	
May 9	Harry "KO" Baker	West End Theatre, Uniontown, PA.	ND 10	KO 5
May 19	Jeff Smith	Broadway Auditorium, Buffalo, NY.	ND 10	Win
May 22	George Chip	Exposition Hall, Pittsburgh, PA.	ND 10	Win
Jun 14	Frank Mantell	West End Theatre, Uniontown, PA.	ND 10	KO 1
Jul 2	Albert "Buck" Crouse	Exposition Hall, Pittsburgh, PA.	ND 10	TKO 6
Jul 30	Jack Dillon	Forbes Field, Pittsburgh, PA.	ND 10	Win
Sep 6	Battling Levinsky	Forbes Field, Pittsburgh, PA.	ND 10	Win
Sep 11	Jeff Smith	Auditorium, Milwaukee, WI.	ND 10	Win
Sep 14	Jack London	St. Nicholas Arena, New York, NY.	TKO 9	
Sep 17	George "KO" Brown	Highland Park, Dayton, OH.	TKO 9	
Sep 22	Battling Kopin	Charleroi Rink, Charleroi, PA.	ND 10	TKO 3
Sep 25	Johnny Howard	Broadway Sporting Club, Brooklyn, NY.	TKO 9	
Oct 6	Billy Kramer	National A.C., Philadelphia, PA.	ND 6	Win
Oct 11	Gus Christie	Broadway Auditorium, Buffalo, NY.	ND 10	Win
Oct 19	Len Rowlands	Auditorium, Milwaukee, WI.	ND 10	Win
Oct 23	Gus Christie	Armory, Chattanooga, TN.	W 8	
Nov 2	Soldier Bartfield	Broadway Auditorium, Buffalo, NY.	ND 10	Loss
Nov 19	George Chip	Heucks Opera House, Cincinnati, OH.	ND 10	Win
Dec 3	Willie Meehan	Olympia A.A., Philadelphia, PA.	ND 6	Win
Dec 5	George "Kid" Ashe	Cambria Theatre, Johnstown, PA.	ND 10	Win
Dec 8	Terry Martin	Charleroi Rink, Charleroi, PA.	ND 10	KO 3
Dec 17	Gus Christie	Heucks Opera House, Cincinnati, OH.	ND 12	Win
Dec 25	Whitey Wenzel	Turner Hall, Pittsburgh, PA.	ND 10	Win

1918

Jan 4	Terry Kellar	Orpheum Theatre, McKeesport, PA.	ND 10	Win
Jan 14	Battling Kopin	Charleroi Rink, Charleroi, PA.	ND 10	KO 1
Jan 21	Augie Ratner	Dauphine Theatre, New Orleans, LA.	W 20	
Jan 29	Zulu Kid	Casino Hall, Bridgeport, CT.	W 14	
Feb 4	Jack Hubbard	Armory, Lonaconing, MD.	KO 3	
Feb 7	Frank Klaus	Power Auditorium, Pittsburgh, PA.	EXH 3	
Feb 18	Bob Moha	Peoples Theatre, Cincinnati, OH.	ND 10	Win
Feb 25	Mike O'Dowd	Auditorium, St. Paul, MN.	ND 10	Loss

(For world middleweight title — unofficial "ND" bout. Must win by knockout)

Mar 4	Jack Dillon	Coliseum, Toledo, OH.	ND 12	Win

Mar 11	Mike McTigue	Moose Hall, Cleveland, OH.	ND 10	Win
Mar 18	Willie Langford	Broadway Auditorium, Buffalo, NY.	ND 6	Win
May 4	Jim Coffey	U.S.S. Recruit, Union Square, NY.	EXH 3	
May 4	Joe Bonds	U.S.S. Recruit, Union Square, NY.	EXH 3	
May 13	Al McCoy	Peoples Theatre, Cincinnati, OH.	ND 10	Win
May 15	Clay Turner	Casino Hall, Bridgeport, CT.	W 15	
May 20	Soldier Bartfield	Forbes Field, Pittsburgh, PA.	ND 10	Win
May 24	Ed "Gunboat" Smith	Madison Square Garden, New York, NY.	ND 6	Win
May 29	Soldier Bartfield	Swayne Field, Toledo, OH.	ND 15	Win
Jun 20	Zulu Kid	Madison Square Garden, New York, NY.	ND 6	Win
Jun 24	Frank Carbone	Casino Hall, Bridgeport, CT.	W 15	
Jul 4	Bob Moha	Three-I League Park, Rock Island, IL.	ND 10	Win
Jul 6	Harry Anderson	Cleveland Park, Cleveland, OH.	EXH 4	
Jul 16	Soldier Bartfield	Shibe Park, Philadelphia, PA.	ND 6	Draw
Jul 27	Eddie McGoorty	Drill Hall, Fort Sheridan, IL.	ND 10	Win
Aug 6	Battling Levinsky	Shibe Park, Philadelphia, PA.	ND 6	Win
Aug 9	Clay Turner	Baseball Park, Jersey City, NJ.	ND 8	Win
Sep 21	Billy Miske	Forbes Field, Pittsburgh, PA.	ND 10	Win
Dec 11	Corp./Sgt. Baker	Royal Albert Hall, London, England	KO 1	
Dec 12	Pvt. Ring	Royal Albert Hall, London, England	L 4	

(The previous two Navy bouts are not added to his official record)

1919

(A record 45 bouts this year)

Jan 14	Leo Houck	Armory A.A., Boston, MA.	W 12	
Jan 20	Young Fisher	Grand Opera House, Syracuse, NY.	ND 10	Win
Jan 23	Paul Samson-Koerner	Southside Market House, Pittsburgh, PA.	ND 10	Win
Jan 27	Soldier Bartfield	Memorial Hall, Columbus, OH.	ND 12	Win
Jan 31	Tommy Robson	Cleveland A.A., Cleveland, OH.	ND 10	Win
Feb 3	Len Rowlands	Southside Market House, Pittsburgh, PA.	ND 10	TKO 4
Feb 10	Bill Brennan	Olympian Arena, Syracuse, NY.	ND 10	Win
Feb 17	Battling Levinsky	Broadway Auditorium, Buffalo, NY.	ND 10	Win
Feb 28	Chuck Wiggins	Coliseum, Toledo, OH.	ND 12	Win
Mar 3	Chuck Wiggins	Elks Club, Detroit, MI.	ND 8	Win
Mar 6	Leo Houck	Fulton Opera House, Lancaster, PA.	ND 6	Win
Mar 17	Bill Brennan	Duquesne Garden, Pittsburgh, PA.	ND 10	Win
Mar 25	Harry "Happy" Howard	Cambria Theatre, Johnstown, PA.	ND 10	Win
Mar 31	Billy Miske	Duquesne Gardens, Pittsburgh, PA.	ND 10	Win
Apr 2	Tommy Madden	Majestic Theatre, Butler, PA.	ND 10	KO 2
Apr 7	Young "Caveman" Fisher	Olympian Arena, Syracuse, NY.	ND 10	Win
Apr 8	George "One-Round" Davis	Broadway Auditorium, Buffalo, NY.	ND 10	Win
Apr 25	Leo Houck	Mercantile Building, Erie, PA.	ND 10	Win
Apr 28	Battling Levinsky	Auditorium, Canton, OH.	ND 12	Win
May 6	Clay "Chief" Turner	Armory A.A., Boston, MA.	W 12	
May 8	Willie Meehan	Duquesne Gardens, Pittsburgh, PA.	ND 10	Win
May 13	Bartley Madden	Broadway Auditorium, Buffalo, NY.	ND 10	Win
May 26	Tommy Robson	Olympian Arena, Syracuse, NY.	ND 10	Win
Jun 16	Joe Borrell	Shibe Park, Philadelphia, PA.	ND 6	TKO 5
Jun 18	Harry "Happy" Howard	Mercantile Building, Erie, PA.	ND 10	Win
Jun 20	Yankee Gilbert	Park Casino, Wheeling, WV.	ND 10	TKO 4
Jun 23	Mike Gibbons	Forbes Field, Pittsburgh, PA.	ND 10	Win
Jul 4	Bill Brennan	Convention Hall, Tulsa, OK.	W 15	
Jul 14	Battling Levinsky	Shibe Park, Philadelphia, PA.	ND 6	Win

Jul 16	George "KO" Brown	Park Casino, Wheeling, WV.	ND 10	Win
Jul 24	Joe Chip	Idora Park, Youngstown, OH.	ND 12	Win
Aug 11	Terry Kellar	Highland Park, Dayton, OH.	W 15	
Aug 23	Bill Brennan	Forbes Field, Pittsburgh, PA.	ND 10	Win
Sep 1	Jeff Smith	Idora Park, Youngstown, OH.	ND 12	Win
Sep 3	Battling Levinsky	State Fair Grounds, Wheeling, WV.	ND 10	Win
Sep 18	Silent Martin	Coliseum, St. Louis, MO.	ND 8	Win
Oct 13	Sailor Ed Petroskey	Olympia A.C., Philadelphia, PA.	ND 6	Win
Nov 17	George "KO" Brown	Auditorium, Canton, OH.	ND 12	Win
Nov 24	Larry Williams	Southside Market House, Pittsburgh, PA.	ND 10	Win
Nov 27	Zulu Kid	Nonpareil Club, Beaver Falls, PA.	ND 10	Win
Nov 28	Soldier Jones	Broadway Auditorium, Buffalo, NY.	ND 10	KO 5
Dec 10	Clay "Chief" Turner	Broadway Auditorium, Buffalo, NY.	ND 10	Win
Dec 12	Mike McTigue	Ideal Pavilion, Endicott, NY.	ND 10	Win
Dec 15	Billy Kramer	Southside Market House, Pittsburgh, PA.	ND 10	Win
Dec 22	Clay "Chief" Turner	National A.C., Philadelphia, PA.	ND 6	Win

1920

Feb 6	Zulu Kid	New State Armory, Kalamazoo, MI.	ND 10	Draw
Feb 21	"Captain" Bob Roper	Exposition Hall, Pittsburgh, PA.	ND 10	Win
Mar 9	Clay "Chief" Turner	Armory, Akron, OH.	ND 12	Win
Mar 17	Tommy Robson	Industrial Building, Dayton, OH.	ND 12	Win
Mar 22	Larry Williams	Exposition Hall, Pittsburgh, PA.	ND 10	Win
Mar 25	George "KO" Brown	Denver Stadium, Denver, CO.	W 12	
Apr 5	"Captain" Bob Roper	Denver Stadium, Denver, CO.	W 12	
May 15	Tommy Gibbons	Forbes Field, Pittsburgh, PA.	ND 10	Loss
Jun 2	Clay "Chief" Turner	Ice Palace, Philadelphia, PA.	ND 8	Win
Jun 28	Frank Carbone	Convention Hall, Rochester, NY.	ND 10	Win
Jul 5	Bob Moha	Auditorium, Canton, OH.	ND 12	Win
Jul 8	Larry Williams	Bison Stadium, Buffalo, NY.	ND 10	Win
Jul 27	Jack Dempsey	Dempsey Training Camp, New York, NY.	EXH 4	
Jul 28	Jack Dempsey	Dempsey Training Camp, New York, NY.	EXH 4	
Jul 29	Jack Dempsey	Dempsey Training Camp, New York, NY.	EXH 2	
Jul 31	Tommy Gibbons	Forbes Field, Pittsburgh, PA.	ND 10	Win
Aug 14	Bob Moha	Cedar Point Arena, Cedar Point, OH.	ND 10	Win
Aug 20	Chuck Wiggins	New State Armory, Kalamazoo, MI.	ND 10	Win
Aug 28	Ted Jamieson	Ramona Park, Grand Rapids, MI.	ND 10	Draw
Sep 1	Jack Dempsey	Benton Harbor, MI.	EXH 3	
Sep 2	Jack Dempsey	Benton Harbor, MI.	EXH 3	
Sep 3	Jack Dempsey	Benton Harbor, MI.	EXH 2	
Sep 6	Chuck Wiggins	Stadium, Benton Harbor, MI.	ND 6	Win
Sep 22	Ted Jamieson	Auditorium, Milwaukee, WI.	ND 10	TKO 6
Oct 21	Ed "Gunboat" Smith	Springbrook Park, South Bend, IN.	ND 10	KO 1
Oct 28	Mickey Shannon	Exposition Hall, Pittsburgh, PA.	ND 10	Win
Nov 10	Bartley Madden	New State Armory, Kalamazoo, MI.	ND 10	Win
Nov 22	Bob Moha	Auditorium, Milwaukee, WI.	ND 10	Win
Dec 11	Jack Duffy	Motor Square Garden, Pittsburgh, PA.	ND 10	TKO 6
Dec 21	"Captain" Bob Roper	Mechanics Hall, Boston, MA.	W 10	
Dec 25	Jeff Smith	Motor Square Garden, Pittsburgh, PA.	ND 10	Win

1921

Jan 20	Johnny Celmars	Coliseum, Dallas, TX.	W 10	
Jan 29	Pal Reed	Mechanics Hall, Boston, MA.	W 10	
Feb 25	Jeff Smith	Mechanics Hall, Boston, MA.	W 10	
Mar 16	Jack Renault	Exposition Hall, Pittsburgh, PA.	ND 10	Win
Apr 1	Happy Littleton	Louisiana Auditorium, New Orleans, LA.	ND 15	Win
Apr 6	Jack Renault	Mount Royale Arena, Montreal, Quebec	ND 10	Win
Apr 11	Soldier Jones	Armories, Toronto, Ontario	ND 10	KO 4
May 4	Bartley Madden	Motor Square Garden, Pittsburgh, PA.	ND 10	Win
May 13	Jimmy Darcy	The Arena, Boston, MA.	W 10	
May 20	Jeff Smith	Louisiana Auditorium, New Orleans, LA.	Draw 15	
May 28	Chuck Wiggins	Springbrook Park, South Bend, IN.	ND 10	Draw
Jun 24	Chuck Wiggins	Three-I League Park, Terre Haute, IN.	ND 10	Draw
Aug 29	Kid Norfolk	Forbes Field, Pittsburgh, PA.	ND 10	Win
Sep 5	Chuck Wiggins	Cliffside Park Arena, Cliffside, KY.	ND 10	Win
Sep 20	Joe Cox	Palace Of Joy S.C., Coney Island, NY.	W 12	
Oct 24	Jimmy Darcy	Broadway Auditorium, Buffalo, NY.	W 10	
Nov 4	Charley Weinert	Madison Square Garden, New York, NY.	W 15	
Nov 11	Billy Shade	Motor Square Garden, Pittsburgh, PA.	ND 10	Win
Nov 25	Homer Smith	Laurel Gardens, Newark, NJ.	TKO 5	
Dec 6	Fay Keiser	Ice Palace, Philadelphia, PA.	ND 8	Win
Dec 23	Whitey Allen	Olympian Arena, Syracuse, NY.	TKO 6	

1922

Jan 2	Chuck Wiggins	Heucks Opera House, Cincinnati, OH.	ND 10	Win
Feb 1	Hugh Walker	Armory, Grand Rapids, MI.	ND 12	Win
Feb 20	Jeff Smith	Freeman Ave. Armory, Cincinnati, OH.	ND 10	Win
Mar 13	Tommy Gibbons	Madison Square Garden, New York, NY.	W 15	
May 12	Al Roberts	Armory A.A., Boston, MA.	KO 6	
May 23	Gene Tunney	Madison Square Garden, New York, NY.	W 15	
	(Won American light heavyweight title)			
Jun 26	Hugh Walker	Forbes Field, Pittsburgh, PA.	ND 10	Win
Jul 10	Tommy Loughran	Baker Bowl, Philadelphia, PA.	ND 8	Win
Sep 26	Al Benedict	Coliseum, Toronto, Ontario	ND 10	KO 2
Sep 29	"Captain" Bob Roper	Armory, Grand Rapids, MI.	ND 10	Win
Oct 27	Larry Williams	National A.C., Marieville, RI.	TKO 4	
Nov 10	"Captain" Bob Roper	Broadway Auditorium, Buffalo, NY.	W 12	

1923

Jan 1	"Captain" Bob Roper	Motor Square Garden, Pittsburgh, PA.	ND 12	Win
Jan 14	Jack Munro	Pittsburgh Lyceum, Pittsburgh, PA.	EXH 3	
Jan 15	Tommy Loughran	Motor Square Garden, Pittsburgh, PA.	ND 10	Win
Jan 22	Billy Shade	4th Regiment Armory, Jersey City, NJ.	ND 12	Win
Jan 30	Tommy Loughran	Madison Square Garden, New York, NY.	W 15	
	(Retained American light heavyweight title)			
Feb 5	Pal Reed	Laurel Gardens, Newark, NJ.	ND 12	Win
Feb 16	Young "Caveman" Fisher	Olympian Arena, Syracuse, NY.	W 12	
Feb 23	Gene Tunney	Madison Square Garden, New York, NY.	L 15 (split)	
	(Lost American light heavyweight title)			
Jun 16	Len Rowlands	Craft's Five Acres, Uniontown, PA.	ND 10	KO 3
Aug 31	Johnny Wilson	Polo Grounds, New York, NY.	W 15	
	(Won world middleweight title)			

Oct 4	Jimmy Darcy	Forbes Field, Pittsburgh, PA.	ND 10	Win
Oct 11	Tommy Loughran	Mechanics Hall, Boston, MA.	L 10	
Oct 22	Lou Bogash	First Regiment Armory, Newark, NJ.	ND 12	Win
Nov 5	Soldier Jones	Motor Square Garden, Pittsburgh, PA.	ND 10	Win
Nov 15	Chuck Wiggins	Armory, Grand Rapids, MI.	ND 10	Win
Dec 3	Bryan Downey	Motor Square Garden, Pittsburgh, PA.	W 10	

(Retained world middleweight title)

Dec 10	Gene Tunney	Madison Square Garden, New York, NY.	L 15	

(For American light heavyweight title)

Dec 25	Tommy Loughran	Motor Square Garden, Pittsburgh, PA.	W 10	

1924

Jan 18	Johnny Wilson	Madison Square Garden, New York, NY.	W 15	

(Retained world middleweight title)

Feb 22	Jack Reeves	Auditorium, Oakland, CA.	W 4	
Mar 24	Fay Keiser	4th Regiment Armory, Baltimore, MD.	TKO 12	

(Retained world middleweight title)

Apr 19	Kid Norfolk	Mechanics Hall, Boston, MA.	LF 6	
May 5	Jackie Clark	Franklin Stadium, Kenilworth, MD.	TKO 2	
May 12	Pal Reed	Motor Square Garden, Pittsburgh, PA.	W 10	
Jun 6	George Kenneally	St. Bonaventure College, Allegany, NY.	EXH 2	
Jun 6	Frank Zenke	St. Bonaventure College, Allegany, NY.	EXH 4	
Jun 12	Martin Burke	New Olympic Arena, Cleveland, OH.	ND 10	Win
Jun 16	Frank Moody	Brassco Park, Waterbury, CT.	KO 6	
Jun 26	Ted Moore	Yankee Stadium, Bronx, NY.	W 15	

(Retained world middleweight title)

Aug 21	Tiger Flowers	Amphitheatre, Freemont, OH.	ND 10	Win
Sep 3	Jimmy Slattery	Bison Stadium, Buffalo, NY.	W 6	
Sep 15	Billy Hirsch	Wabash Field, Mingo Junction, OH.	ND 10	TKO 8
Sep 17	Gene Tunney	Olympic Arena, Cleveland, OH.	ND 10	Draw
Oct 13	Tommy Loughran	The Arena, Philadelphia, PA.	D 10 (split)	
Nov 11	Ray Nelson	Midway Auditorium, Phillipsburg, PA.	KO 3	
Nov 17	Jimmy Delaney	Motor Square Garden, Pittsburgh, PA.	W 10	
Nov 25	Frankie Ritz	State Fair Park, Wheeling, WV.	TKO 3	

1925

Jan 1	Augie Ratner	Motor Square Garden, Pittsburgh, PA.	W 10	
Jan 9	Bob Sage	Arena Gardens, Detroit, MI.	ND 10	Win
Jan 19	Johnny Papke	Weller Theatre, Zanesville, OH.	ND 12	TKO 7
Jan 22	Kid Lewis	B.P.O. Elks #11, Pittsburgh, PA.	EXH 3	KO 1
Jan 30	Jimmy Delaney	Auditorium, St. Paul, MN.	ND 10	Win
Feb 17	Billy Britton	Measley's Auditorium, Allentown, PA.	W 10	
Mar 27	Gene Tunney	Auditorium, St. Paul, MN.	ND 10	Loss
Apr 17	Johnny Wilson	Mechanics Hall, Boston, MA.	W 10	
Apr 24	Jack Reddick	Coliseum, Toronto, Ontario	W 10	
May 1	Quintin Romero Rojas	Arena Gardens, Detroit, MI.	ND 10	Win
May 6	Billy Britton	Fairmont Avenue, Columbus, OH.	W 12	
May 29	Tommy Burns	Tomlinson Hall, Indianapolis, IN.	ND 10	Win
Jun 1	Soldier Buck	Jefferson County Armory, Louisville, KY.	ND 10	Win
Jun 5	Jimmy Nuss	Palestra, Marquette, MI.	ND 10	KO 5
Jul 2	Mickey Walker	Polo Grounds, New York, NY.	W 15	

(Retained world middleweight title)

Jul 16	Maxie Rosenbloom	Taylor Arena, Cleveland, OH.	ND 10	Win
Jul 23	Billy Britton	Fairgrounds, Columbus, KS.	W 10	
Jul 27	Ralph Brooks	The Forum, Wichita, KS.	ND 10	Win
Jul 31	Otis Bryant	Floto Bowl, Tulsa, OK.	KO 3	
Aug 4	Ed "KO" Smith	Memorial Hall, Kansas City, KS.	KO 4	
Aug 12	Pat Walsh	Airport, Atlantic City, NJ.	ND 10	TKO 2
Aug 17	Tommy Burns	Fairgrounds Coliseum, Detroit, MI.	ND 10	Win
Oct 13	Tony "Young" Marullo	Motor Square Garden, Pittsburgh, PA.	W 10	
Nov 13	Tony "Young" Marullo	Coliseum Arena, New Orleans, LA.	W 15	

(Retained world middleweight title)

Dec 14	Soldier Buck	Page Arena, Nashville, TN.	W 8	

1926

Jan 11	Roland Todd	Coliseum, Toronto, Ontario	W 12
Jan 19	Joe Lohman	Auditorium, Omaha, NE.	W 10
Jan 26	Ted Moore	Vernon Arena, Vernon, CA.	W 10
Jan 29	Buck Holley	Legion Stadium, Hollywood, CA.	TKO 5
Feb 3	Jimmy Delaney	Auditorium, Oakland, CA.	W 10
Feb 12	Owen Phelps	Capital City A.C., Phoenix, AZ.	W 10
Feb 26	Tiger Flowers	Madison Square Garden, New York, NY.	L 15 (split)

(Lost world middleweight title)

Jun 1	Art Weigand	Broadway Auditorium, Buffalo, NY.	W 10
Jun 15	"Allentown" Joe Gans	Barons Park, Wilkes-Barre, PA.	W 10
Aug 19	Tiger Flowers	Madison Square Garden, New York, NY.	L 15 (split)

(For world middleweight title)

APPENDIX B:
1923 MIDDLEWEIGHT CHAMPIONSHIP
BODY MEASUREMENTS

The following measurements of Harry Greb were taken before his 1923 Middleweight Championship bout against Johnny Wilson:

Age: 29
Height: 5' 8½"
Weight: 158 lbs.
Chest Expanded: 41"
Chest Normal: 36"
Neck: 15"
Waist: 32"
Reach: 71½"
Biceps: 14½"
Forearm: 11½"
Wrist: 7½"
Thigh: 21½"
Calf: 13½"
Ankle: 8½"

CHAPTER NOTES

Chapter 1

1. "Harry Greb or Harry Berg," *Boxing and Wrestling Magazine* (February 1954).

2. Ancestry.com. 1900 United States Federal Census [database online]. Provo, UT: The Generations Network, Inc., 2004. Original data: United States of America, Bureau of the Census. Twelfth Census of the United States, 1900. Washington, D.C.: National Archives and Records Administration, 1900. T623, 1854 rolls. http://content.ancestry.com/iexec/?htx=View&r=an&dbid=7602&iid=PAT623_1361-0785&fn=Prus&ln=Greb&st=r&ssrc=&pid=51322123 (accessed April 30, 2007)

3. Ancestry.com. 1910 United States Federal Census [database online]. Provo, UT: The Generations Network, Inc., 2006. For details on the contents of the film numbers, visit the following NARA web page: NARA Original data: United States of America, Bureau of the Census. Thirteenth Census of the United States, 1910. Washington, D.C.: National Archives and Records Administration, 1910. T624, 1,178 rolls. http://content.ancestry.com/iexec/?htx=View&r=an&dbid=7884&iid=PAT624_1302-0929&fn=Lius&ln=Gribb&st=r&ssrc=&pid=23770678 (accessed April 30, 2007).

4. James Fair, *Give Him to the Angels* (New York: Smith and Durrell, 1946), p. 145.

5. *Ibid.*, p. 24.

6. *Ibid.*, p. 146.

7. *Ibid.*

8. Fair, p. 25.

9. Ancestry.com. 1910 Census. http://content.ancestry.com/iexec/?htx=View&r=an&dbid=7884&iid=PAT624_1302-0935&fn=Walter&ln=Gimmel&st=r&ssrc=&pid=122772766 (accessed January 13, 2008).

10. Ancestry.com. 1910 Census. http://content.ancestry.com/iexec/?htx=View&r=an&dbid=7884&iid=PAT624_1302-0929&fn=Lius&ln=Gribb&st=r&ssrc=&pid=23770678 (accessed April 30, 2007).

11. *Ibid.*

12. "Harry Greb or Harry Berg."

13. Jim Jab, "Fine Bouts Staged by Amateurs," *Pittsburgh Press*, March 11, 1913.

14. "Amateur Tourney at Lawrenceville Closes Tonight," *Pittsburgh Press*, March 12, 1913.

15. "Amateur Tourney Brought to Close," *Pittsburgh Press*, March 13, 1913.

16. "Three Pittsburgh Amateur Boxers Win at Cleveland," *Pittsburgh Press*, April 5, 1913.

17. "Gibbons Here for Big Bout," *Pittsburgh Press*, May 29, 1913.

18. Thomas M. Croak, "The Professionalization of Prizefighting: Pittsburgh at the Turn of the Century," *Western Pennsylvania Historical Magazine* 62 (October 1979): pp. 336–337.

19. *Ibid.*

20. Croak, p. 338.

21. Nat Fleischer, *The Ring* (September 1936).

22. "Gibbons Here for Big Bout," *Pittsburgh Press*, May 29, 1913.

23. *Pittsburgh Post*, May 30, 1913.

24. *Pittsburgh Press*, July 20, 1913, p. 4.

25. *Pittsburgh Post*, October 12, 1913.

26. *Pittsburgh Post*, November 18, 1913.

27. Harry Cleaveline, "The Harry Greb Story," *Boxing Illustrated* (May 1967).

28. *Pittsburgh Press*, November 29, 1913.

29. *Pittsburgh Press*, November 30, 1913.

30. *Ibid.*

31. *Pittsburgh Post*, December 1, 1913.

Chapter 2

1. Jim Jab, "Christie Landed a Sleep Producer," *Pittsburgh Press*, January 11, 1914.

2. Harry Keck, "Greb Is Winner Over Wenzel in Hard-Fought Encounter," *Pittsburgh Post*, March 5, 1915.

3. *Pittsburgh Post*, May 7, 1916.

4. "Harry Greb Wins Over Fay Keiser," *Pittsburgh Post*, July 23, 1915, p. 11.

5. *Pittsburgh Post*, December 7, 1921.

6. Jim Jab, "Foley Is Mark for His Foe," *Pittsburgh Press*, July 21, 1914, p. 20.

7. Jim Jab, "Foley Victim of Worst Ever Ring Beating," *Pittsburgh Press*, September 1, 1914, p. 20.

8. Kevin R. Smith, *The Sundowners: The History of the Black Prizefighter 1870–1930*, vol. 2, part 1 (Lulu, 2006), p. 81.

9. "With the Boxers," *Pittsburgh Post*, January 22, 1915, p. 11.

10. Florent Gibson, "Glove-Dodging His Specialty," *Pittsburgh Post*, January 26, 1915, p. 11.

11. Description of Greb-Baker fight taken from Harry Keck, "Harry Greb Scores Victory Over Baker in Vicious Bout," *Pittsburgh Post*, February 11, 1915.

12. Harry Keck, "Boxing Public Proves Loyalty by Patronizing Shows of Merit," *Pittsburgh Post*, March 7, 1915, sports, p. 2.

13. Harry Keck, "Greb Duplicates Victory Over KO Karry Baker," *Pittsburgh Post*, March 26, 1915, p. 11.

14. Harry Keck, "Greb Pulls a New One," *Pittsburgh Post*, April 20, 1915, p. 14.

15. Harry Keck, "Harry Greb Held to Draw in Bout with Joe Borrell," *Pittsburgh Post*, April 23, 1915, sports, pp. 1–3.

16. "Graves and Greb Finish Training," *Pittsburgh Press*, December 14, 1915.

17. "Greb and Graves Fit for Battle," *Pittsburgh Press*, December 15, 1915.

18. Description of Greb-Graves bout taken from Jim Jab, "Greb Called Quitter in Graves Bout," *Pittsburgh Press*, December 17, 1915; Pitts-

burgh Post, December 17, 1915; and *Milwaukee Free Press*, December 17, 1915.

19. "Says Greb Now Is Two-Handed Boxer," *Pittsburgh Press*, February 22, 1916.

20. "Monoghan Says He Will Make Greb Run," *Pittsburgh Press*, February 24, 1916.

21. Jim Jab, "Greb Shaded by Monoghan in Good Bout," *Pittsburgh Press*, February 27, 1916.

22. "Grayber to Meet Millet Tonight in Greb's Place," *Pittsburgh Press*, March 18, 1916.

23. "Greb Claims His Left Arm Is Strong," *Pittsburgh Press*, March 29, 1916.

24. *Pittsburgh Post*, June 4, 1916.

25. "Harry Greb Wants to Fight Grayber," *Pittsburgh Press*, March 30, 1916.

26. "Greb Hopeful of Landing KO Blow," *Pittsburgh Press*, August 3, 1916.

27. "Greb and Grayber Both Want Mason to Second Them," *Pittsburgh Press*, August 6, 1916.

28. "Greb and Grayber Will Box," *Pittsburgh Press*, August 7, 1916.

29. Description of Greb-Grayber bout taken from Jim Jab, "Grayber and Greb in Draw," *Pittsburgh Press*, August 8, 1916.

Chapter 3

1. "Harry Greb Was Busiest Boxer in Country Last Year," *Pittsburgh Post*, January 3, 1918.

2. Florent Gibson, "Borrell Beaten by Harry Greb," *Pittsburgh Post*, January 2, 1917.

3. "Greb, Ahearn, McAndrews and Gradwell on Edge," *Pittsburgh Post*, April 2, 1917.

4. Florent Gibson, "Greb Stops Ahearn in Opening Minute," *Pittsburgh Post*, April 3, 1917.

5. Harry Keck, "K.O. Greb Tackles Zulu Kid Here April 19," *Pittsburgh Post*, April 4, 1917.

6. Florent Gibson, "Greb Won't Be Affected by Fright in Big Bout," *Pittsburgh Post*, April 27, 1917.

7. *Ibid.*

8. *Ibid.*

9. Description of the Greb-Al McCoy fight taken from Harry Keck, "Fight by Rounds," *Pittsburgh Post*, May 1, 1917; and Harry Keck, "Local Middleweight Beats Champion in Every Round," *Pittsburgh Post*, May 1, 1917.

10. Harry Keck, "Sporting Chit-Chat," *Pittsburgh Post*, May 2, 1917.

11. Florent Gibson, "Madison Miner Working Like a Beaver for His Fight," *Pittsburgh Post*, May 20, 1917.

12. Harry Keck, "Sporting Chit-Chat," *Pittsburgh Post*, May 8, 1917.

13. "Darcy Near Death; Fight Days Over," *Pittsburgh Post*, May 20, 1917.

14. Harry Keck, "Greb Fights Jeff Smith in Buffalo Tuesday; Goes 50-Rounds in 10 Days," *Pittsburgh Post*, May 5, 1917.

15. Description of the Greb-George Chip fight taken from Harry Keck, "Fight by Rounds," *Pittsburgh Post*, May 23, 1917; and Florent Gibson, "Youngster Beats Ex-Champ, but Has Mitts Always Full," *Pittsburgh Post*, May 23, 1917.

16. "Infected Teeth Result in Death of Antipodean," *Pittsburgh Post*, May 25, 1917.

17. "Harry Greb to Meet Mantell at Uniontown," *Pittsburgh Post*, May 27, 1917.

18. Florent Gibson, "Greb's Head Cut Open; Uniontown Fight Off," *Pittsburgh Post*, May 28, 1917.

19. "Greb Stops Mantell in 70 Seconds," *Pittsburgh Post*, June 15, 1917.

20. Description of the Greb-Buck Crouse fight taken from Harry Keck, "Fight by Rounds," *Pittsburgh Post*, July 3, 1917; and Florent Gibson, "Buck Has Seconds Toss Sponge into Ring After Barely Surviving Sixth," *Pittsburgh Post*, July 3, 1917.

21. Gibson, "Buck Has Seconds Toss Sponge."

22. "Greb's Title Claim Popular with fans," *Pittsburgh Post*, July 16, 1917.

23. Florent Gibson, "Greb, Also, Would Box 'Poilu' for Red Cross," *Pittsburgh Post*, August 27, 1917.

24. *Ibid.*

25. Florent Gibson, "Greb and Levinsky Resume Training for Thursday Night's Bout," *Pittsburgh Post*, September 5, 1917.

26. Florent Gibson, "Greb Worries Bat Levinsky Almost Down to His Size," *Pittsburgh Post*, September 7, 1917.

27. Harry Keck, "Interesting View of Greb Is Taken by Western Critic," *Pittsburgh Post*, September 14, 1917.

28. "Greb Kayos Terry Martin in Third Round," *Pittsburgh Post*, December 9, 1917.

29. "Harry Greb Was Busiest Boxer in Country Last Year; Earned $28,753," *Pittsburgh Post*, January 3, 1918.

Chapter 4

1. "Among the Boxers," *Pittsburgh Post*, January 7, 1918.

2. George A. Barton, "Greb Outpoints O'Dowd in Ten-Round Struggle," *Pittsburgh Post*, March 3, 1918.

3. *Ibid.*

4. Fred R. Coburn, "Harry Greb Has Shade Over O'Dowd," *Pittsburgh Post*, March 3, 1918.

5. Harry Keck, "Greb Really Defeated O'Dowd, Minneapolis Scribes' Stories Show," *Pittsburgh Post*, March 3, 1918.

6. *Ibid.*

7. "O'Dowd Handed Shade in Bout Against Greb," *Chicago Daily Tribune*, February 26, 1918, p. 18; "O'Dowd Has Edge on Greb in Ten Rounds," *Washington Post*, February 26, 1918, p. 10; "O'Dowd Wins by Shade," *New York Times*, February 26, 1918.

8. George A. Barton, "Greb Outpoints O'Dowd in Ten-Round Struggle," *Pittsburgh Post*, March 3, 1918.

9. Keck, "Greb Really Defeated O'Dowd."

10. "Greb Beats Langford," *Pittsburgh Post*, March 19, 1918.

11. "Harry Greb Seriously Ill," *Milwaukee Free Press*, April 14, 1918.

12. "Greb to Return for Fight Here After Display," *Pittsburgh Post*, May 4, 1918.

13. "Bouts Boost Recruiting," *New York Times*, May 5, 1918, p. 20.

14. *Ibid.*

15. "Greb and Ray Box in Gotham," *Pittsburgh Post*, May 5, 1918.

16. "Harry Greb Enlists, Then Trains for Bout," *Milwaukee Free Press*, May 9, 1918.

17. "Harry Greb Beats McCoy," *Pittsburgh Post*, May 14, 1918.

18. Florent Gibson, "Greb Battles Turner in Bridgeport Tonight," *Pittsburgh Post*, May 15, 1918.

19. "Greb Beats Turner," *Pittsburgh Post*, May 16, 1918.

20. Florent Gibson, "Greb and Bartfield Set for Go Tonight," *Pittsburgh Post*, May 20, 1918.

21. *Ibid.*

22. Description of the Greb-Bartfield fight Taken from Harry Keck, "Detailed Story of Greb's Triumph Over Bartfield," *Pittsburgh Post*, May 21, 1918.

23. *Ibid.*

24. Florent Gibson, "Greb Boosts Bartfield; Will Meet Him Again," *Pittsburgh Post*, May 22, 1918.

25. "Greb Beats Bartfield Badly in Toledo Ring," *Pittsburgh Post*, May 30, 1918.

26. Harry Keck, "Sporting Chit-Chat," *Pittsburgh Post*, May 31, 1918.

27. "Greb Plays with Zulu Kid in Red Cross Tournament," *Pittsburgh Post*, June 21, 1918.

28. *Pittsburgh Post*, January 30, 1918.

29. "Harry Greb Writes," *Pittsburgh Post*, July 28, 1918.

30. "Fulton and Dempsey, Also McGoorty and Greb, Battle Today," *Pittsburgh Post*, July 27, 1918.

31. Ray Pearson, "Greb Wins Service Title by Handing M'Goorty

Licking," *Pittsburgh Post*, July 28, 1918.
32. *Ibid.*
33. *Ibid.*
34. "Greb to Go to Sea Soon," *Pittsburgh Post*, October 6, 1918.
35. Harry Keck, "Greb Drives New Car Like He Fights; Help!" *Pittsburgh Post*, October 12, 1918.
36. *Ibid.*
37. *Ibid.*
38. Harry Keck, "Greb to Fight Carpentier in London," *Pittsburgh Post*, November 11, 1918.
39. *Ibid.*
40. *Ibid.*
41. Harry Keck, "Ten Bouts, 48 Rounds of Boxing in Big Show," *Pittsburgh Post*, November 17, 1918.
42. "Harry Greb Wins Bout. Ritchie Mitchell Loses," *Daily Northwestern*, December 11, 1918; "American Boxer Wins First Mill," *Sandusky Star Journal*, December 11, 1918; *Evening State Journal* and *Lincoln Daily News*, December 11, 1918; "Greb Scores One-Round Kayo in London Ring," *Pittsburgh Post*, December 12, 1918.
43. "Yankee Boxers Sweep British Off Their Feet Greb Is Eliminated," *Pittsburgh Post*, December 13, 1918; "It's Up to Eddie and Mike," *Kansas City Star*, December 12, 1918; *Daily Northwestern*, December 13, 1918.
44. "Yankee Boxers Sweep British Off Their Feet Greb Is Eliminated," *Pittsburgh Post*, December 13, 1918.
45. Harry Keck, "Among the Boxers," *Pittsburgh Post*, December 31, 1918.

Chapter 5

1. Harry Keck, "Harry Greb to Wed Late This Month," *Pittsburgh Post*, January 7, 1919.
2. *Ibid.*
3. Harry Greb Wohlfarth, phone interview by author, July 5, 1998.
4. Harry Keck, "Harry Greb to Wed."
5. *Ibid.*
6. *Ibid.*
7. Harry Keck, "Among the Boxers," *Pittsburgh Post*, January 12, 1919.
8. Harry Keck, "Greb Flays Sampson, but Can't Stop Him," *Pittsburgh Post*, January 24, 1919.
9. Harry Keck, "Among the Boxers," *Pittsburgh Post*, January 30, 1919.
10. "Greb Beats Bartfield; Floors Him," *Pittsburgh Post*, January 28, 1919.
11. Harry Keck, "Big Boxing Week; Three Shows and Greb's Wedding On," *Pittsburgh Post*, January 26, 1919.
12. *Ibid.*
13. Harry Keck, "1,000 See Greb Wed; 100 Attend Breakfast," *Pittsburgh Post*, January 31, 1919.
14. *Ibid.*
15. *Ibid.*
16. Ancestry.com. 1910 Census. http://content.ancestry.com/iexec/?htx=View&r=an&dbid=7884&iid=PAT624_1302-0888&fn=Emanuel+L&ln=Kelly&st=r&ssrc=&pid=122770700 (accessed April 30, 2007).
17. Harry Keck, "1,000 See Greb Wed; 100 Attend Breakfast," *Pittsburgh Post*, January 31, 1919.
18. *Ibid.*
19. "Greb Finds Robson Easy," *Pittsburgh Post*, February 1, 1919.
20. Harry Keck, "Greb May Receive Second Knockout of Career Tomorrow Night Brennan Promises It," *Pittsburgh Post*, March 16, 1919.
21. Harry Keck, "Bill Brennan Beaten in Every Round of Bout," *Pittsburgh Post*, March 18, 1919.
22. "Greb's Manager's Wife Critically Ill," *Pittsburgh Post*, March 20, 1919.
23. Keck, "Bill Brennan Beaten in Every Round."
24. "Greb's Manager's Wife Critically Ill," *Pittsburgh Post*, March 20, 1919.
25. Harry Keck, "Greb-Miske Battle Tomorrow Night to Set Crowd Record," *Pittsburgh Post*, March 30, 1919.
26. "Miske New Papa," *Pittsburgh Post*, April 1, 1919.
27. Description of the Greb-Miske fight taken from Harry Keck, "Eight of Ten Rounds Won by Local Battler," *Pittsburgh Post*, April 1, 1919.
28. Description of the Greb-Borrell fight taken from "Last-Round Rally Wins for Leonard; Greb KO's Borrell," *Pittsburgh Post*, June 17, 1919.
29. "H. Greb Becomes Angry," *Pittsburgh Press*, June 21, 1919.
30. *Ibid.*
31. Description of the Greb-Mike Gibbons fight taken from Gibby, "Barrage of Gloves Launched by Harry Confuses Phantom; Takes early Lead," *Pittsburgh Post*, June 24, 1919.
32. "Greb Will Set New Boxing Mark for Year," *Pittsburgh Post*, September 7, 1919.
33. "Greb-Smith Battle Off; Why? Boils!" *Pittsburgh Post*, September 21, 1919.
34. *Ibid.*
35. "Boxing Club Closes Until Winter Season," *Cumberland Evening Times*, September 22, 1919, p. 8.
36. "Greb Beats Petrosky All Over Arena," *Pittsburgh Post*, October 14, 1919.
37. "Greb Will Go After Jack Dempsey After Moran Bout," *Hamilton Daily News*, October 27, 1919, p. 8.
38. *Lima Times-Democrat*, October 21, 1919, p. 13.

39. Gibby, "Greb Gives Brown Hard Beating, but Greek Stays Limit," *Pittsburgh Post*, November 18, 1919.
40. "Greb Cancels Bout," *Trenton Evening Times*, December 29, 1919.
41. Harry Keck, "Harry Greb to Wed Late This Month," *Pittsburgh Post*, January 7, 1919.

Chapter 6

1. Grantland Rice, "King of All the Marvels," *Collier's* (February 20, 1926).
2. *Pittsburgh Post*, August 7, 1918.
3. "Greb-Dempsey Fight Probable; Two Promoters Offer Purses," *Pittsburgh Post*, July 21, 1919.
4. *Ibid.*
5. *Ibid.*
6. *Ibid.*
7. Paul Francis Kennedy, "Pittsburgh's Iron City Express," *Tribune Review*, August 30, 1988.
8. Bill Stern, "The Man Dempsey Wouldn't Fight," *Male Magazine* (October 1953).
9. "Harry Greb Laces Kellar and Floors the Referee," *Pittsburgh Post*, Jan 5, 1918.
10. "Greb Bids Farewell by Trouncing Larry Williams at Expo," *Pittsburgh Post*, March 23, 1920.
11. "Greb Pleases Buffalo Fans in Fast Bout," July 9, 1920.
12. "Dempsey May Box Greb," *Washington Post*, March 15, 1920.
13. "Dempsey Spars with Greb at Gotham Camp," *Pittsburgh Post*, July 28, 1920.
14. *Ibid.*
15. "Greb Puts Eye on Jack; Doug Plays Referee," *Pittsburgh Post*, July 30, 1920.
16. *Ibid.*
17. *Ibid.*
18. Description of the Greb-Tommy Gibbons fight taken from Florent Gibson, "Pittsburgher Wins Seven of 10 Rounds; Fight Ends in Rain," *Pittsburgh Post*, August 1, 1920.
19. "Greb Proves Easy Victor Over Meehan," *Pittsburgh Post*, December 4, 1917.
20. *Ibid.*
21. *Pittsburgh Post*, May 9, 1919.
22. "Greb Defeats Gunboat Smith in Red-X Bout," *Pittsburgh Post*, May 25, 1918.
23. *Tacoma News Tribune*, October 22, 1920.
24. "Smith Quits in Fifth Round of Greb Bout," *Pittsburgh Post*, November 26, 1921.
25. *Pittsburgh Post*, March 17, 1921.
26. "Greb Defeats Jack Renault at Montreal," *Pittsburgh Post*, April 7, 1921.
27. *Pittsburgh Post*, May 14, 1919.
28. *Pittsburgh Post*, November 11, 1920.

29. "Greb Stops Benedict in Second; Ready for Siki Anytime or Place," *Pittsburgh Post*, September 27, 1922.

30. "Greb Awarded Decision Over Cox in Gotham," *Pittsburgh Post*, September 21, 1921.

31. "Dempsey Given Stiff Workout by Harry Greb," *Pittsburgh Post*, September 2, 1920.

32. "Dempsey Satisfied with His Condition," *New York Times*, September 2, 1920, p. 10.

33. *Ibid.*

34. *Ibid.*

35. "Greb Splits Dempsey's Tongue in Final Workout for Billy Miske," *Washington Post*, September 3, 1920.

36. "Big Battlers Work Out at Top Speed," *New York Times*, September 3, 1920, p. 16.

37. *Ibid.*

38. "Greb Splits Dempsey's Tongue."

39. "Big Battlers Work Out at Top Speed," p. 16.

40. "Choice of Referee for Fight Delayed," *New York Times*, September 4, 1920, p. 13.

41. "Choice of Referee for Fight Delayed," p. 13.

42. "Greb May Meet Dempsey," *New York Times*, November 30, 1920, p. 19.

43. *Ibid.*

44. "Greb Defeats Roper; Gives Fans Surprise—Touted as Logical Contender for Dempsey," *Pittsburgh Post*, December 22, 1920.

Chapter 7

1. "Greb Breaks with Manager; Goes with Engel," *Chicago Daily Tribune*, December 31, 1920.

2. *Ibid.*

3. Jack Conway, "6,000 See Greb Win Over Reed," *Boston*.

4. "Harry Greb Wins Decision Over Pal Reed in Faneuil A.C. Bout," *Boston Post*, January 30, 1921.

5. Interview with Adam M. Reed, relative of Pal Reed.

6. *Ibid.*

7. "Greb Winner Over Wiggens in Tough Bout," *Pittsburgh Post*, September 6, 1921.

8. "The Human Windmill—#5 All-Time Great," *Boxing News*, August 14, 1998.

9. *Portland Oregonian*, May 14, 1921.

10. "Greb Defeats Jim Darcy in Buffalo Bout," *Pittsburgh Post*, October 26, 1921.

11. Regis M. Welsh, "Crowd Braves Cold to Witness Darcy Get Great Lacing," *Pittsburgh Post*, October 5, 1923.

12. "Greb Carries Shade Along,

Winning in Motor Square Bout," *Pittsburgh Post*, November 12, 1921.

13. *Ibid.*

14. *Ibid.*

15. Westbrook Pegler, "Weinert Takes Great Lacing from Icky," *Pittsburgh Post*, November 5, 1921.

16. *Ibid.*

17. "Greb Winner Over Wiggins in Tough Bout," *Pittsburgh Post*, September 6, 1921.

18. Regis M. Welsh, "Greb and Norfolk Meet Tomorrow in Forbes Field Ring," *Pittsburgh Post*, August 28, 1921.

19. Description of the Greb-Norfolk fight taken from Regis M. Welsh, "Garfield Battler Wins Six Rounds; Negro Takes Four," *Pittsburgh Post*, August 30, 1921.

20. "Greb Had a Glass Eye for Past Two Months," *New York Times*, October 27, 1926.

21. Dr. Albert Ackerman, telephone interview by author, June 11, 2007.

22. Dr. Scot A. Brower, telephone interview by author, June 26, 2007.

23. Ingrid Kreissig, *Primary Retinal Detachment: Options for Repair* (New York: Springer, Berlin, Heidelberg, 2005), p. 5.

24. Harry Cleaveline, "The Harry Greb Story—Part Two," *Boxing Illustrated* (June 1967); Harry Cleaveline, newspaper article, May 7, 1978.

25. Dr. Anthony Andrews, telephone interview by author, September 21, 2007.

26. *Sun Telegraph*, December 8, 1920.

27. "Mickey Shannon Dies After Knockout in Bout with Roberts," *Chicago Daily Tribune*, December 9, 1920.

Chapter 8

1. "Wilson Calls Off Bout," *New York Times*, January 3, 1922, p. 22.

2. "Wilson Is Barred by N.Y. Commission," *New York Times*, January 4, 1922, p. 21.

3. "Wilson Suspended in Sixteen States," *New York Times*, January 17, 1922, p. 21.

4. Harry Greb, "Can't Stop Me," *Pittsburgh Post*, March 13, 1922.

5. Tommy Gibbons, "I'll Win," *Pittsburgh Post*, March 13, 1922.

6. Regis M. Welsh, "Garfield Boxer Carries Battle," *Pittsburgh Post*, March 14, 1922, p. 10.

7. "Shamrock in Greb's Glove Factor in Win Over St. Paul Harp," *Pittsburgh Post*, March 15, 1922, p. 10.

8. Description of the Greb-Tommy Gibbons fight taken from "The Fight by Rounds," *Pittsburgh Post*, March 14, 1922, p. 10.

9. "Bout Is Stirring from End to End," *New York Times*, March 14, 1922, p. 21.

10. *Ibid.*

11. *Pittsburgh Post*, March 14, 1922, front page.

12. Igoe, "One-Punch Fighter Cannot Beat Greb, Belief of Expert," *Pittsburgh Post*, March 16, 1922.

13. Harry Greb, "Size Not Only Asset for Champion," *Pittsburgh Press*, March 22, 1922.

14. Harry Newman, "Seized for Walsh Perjury," *Chicago Daily Tribune*, March 14, 1922, p. 1.

15. Harry Greb, "Gibbons Struck Only Three Hard Blows," *Pittsburgh Press*, March 20, 1922.

16. *Ibid.*

17. Regis M. Welsh, "Garfield Battler Offered Theatrical Contract; Will Return to Pittsburgh Soon," *Pittsburgh Post*, March 15, 1922, p. 10.

18. "Greb Will Appear at Gayety Theater Here All Next Week," *Pittsburgh Post*, March 17, 1922.

19. Harry Keck, "Welcome Home Keeps Greb Hopping; Forced to Show Best Footwork," *Gazette Times*, March 21, 1922.

20. *Ibid.*

21. Regis M. Welsh, "Parade, Speeches and Great Turnout Feature Welcoming," *Pittsburgh Post*, March 21, 1922, p. 10.

22. Harry Keck, "Greb May Fight Dempsey; Won't Box Mike Gibbons," *Gazette Times*, March 24, 1922.

23. "Dempsey Will Give Greb Chance to Win Heavyweight Crown," *Oklahoman*, March 21, 1922, p. 10.

24. "Dempsey Will Box Greb After Tour," *New York Times*, April 12, 1922, p. 29.

25. Igoe, "One-Punch Fighter Cannot Beat Greb."

26. Harry Greb, "Size Not Only Asset for Champion."

Chapter 9

1. "Mrs. Greb Hears Fight," *Pittsburgh Post*, May 24, 1922.

2. New York World, April 25, 1922.

3. The round-by-round description of the first Greb-Tunney bout was collated from reports in the May 24, 1922, *New York Times, Nashville Tennessean, Pittsburgh Post,* and *Pittsburgh Press,* and Nat Fleischer, *Gene Tunney: Enigma of the Ring* (New York: F. Hubner, 1931).

4. Jack Cavanaugh, *Tunney: Boxing's Brainiest Champ and His Upset of the Great Jack Dempsey* (New York: Random House, 2006), p. 138.

5. Gene Tunney, *A Man Must Fight* (Boston/NY: Houghton Mifflin, 1931), p. 69.

6. Fleischer, *Gene Tunney: Enigma of the Ring.*
7. *Ibid.*
8. John Lardner, "King of the Alley Fighters," *Boxing Yearbook* (1959).
9. Fleischer, *Gene Tunney: Enigma of the Ring.*
10. *Ibid.*
11. Mel Heimer, *The Long Count* (New York: Atheneum, 1969).
12. Tunney, p. 69.
13. Grantland Rice, *The Tumult and the Shouting* (New York: A.S. Barnes, 1954), p. 140.
14. Heimer, *The Long Count.*
15. Tunney, *A Man Must Fight.*
16. Rice, p. 140.
17. Stanley Weston, "Harry Greb—The Pittsburgh Windmill," *Boxing and Wrestling Magazine* (October 1954).
18. Fair, *Give Him to the Angels*; Lardner, "King of the Alley Fighters."
19. Wikipedia, "Tuberculosis: Study and Treatment," http://en.wikipedia.org/wiki/Tuberculosis (accessed August 1, 2007).
20. "Harry Greb Hands Beating to Roper in Buffalo Fight," *Pittsburgh Post*, November 11, 1922.
21. *Ibid.*
22. *Ibid.*
23. *Ibid.*
24. "Greb Seeking Title Battle," *Washington Post*, November 25, 1922, p. 16.
25. Excerpts from interviews with Dr. Albert Ackerman on June 11, 2007, Dr. Scot A. Brower on June 26, 2007, and Dr. Anthony Andrews on September 21, 2007.
26. "Harry Greb's Eyes Under Treatment," *Washington Post*, December 3, 1922, p. 59.
27. "Greb Enters West Penn Hospital for Treatment; Plans Big Winter Program," *Pittsburgh Post*, December 2, 1922.
28. "Greb Leaves Hospital Today; May Fight at Local Club New Years," *Pittsburgh Post*, December 7, 1922.
29. "Decision Depends on Doctor's examination of His Eye," *Oklahoman*, December 19, 1922, p. 16.
30. "Greb-Engel Split, Rumor in Gotham," *Pittsburgh Post*, November 15, 1922.
31. "George Engel Denies Rumor of Break with Greb; Going to Coast," *Pittsburgh Post*, November 16, 1922.
32. "Greb Leaves Hospital Today."
33. William A. White, "Near-Riot Follows Exchanges Between Rivals After Bell," *Pittsburgh Post*, January 2, 1923.
34. *Ibid.*
35. *Ibid.*
36. "Lid Clamped Down Upon Raw Tactics in Local Fistiana," *Pittsburgh Post*, January 3, 1923.

37. William A. White, "Boxing Commission Reinstates Greb; Champion Absent," *Pittsburgh Post*, January 9, 1923.
38. Regis M. Welsh, "Move May Pave Way to Reunion; Champ Still Undecided," *Pittsburgh Post*, January 15, 1923.
39. "Drops Californian in Seventh; Makes Impressive Showing," *Pittsburgh Post*, January 23, 1923.
40. "Greb-Gibbons Bout Off," *Chicago Daily Tribune*, Match 8, 1923, p. 15.
41. Cavanaugh, *Tunney: Boxing's Brainiest Champ*, p. 177.
42. "Harry Greb's Wife Is Dead," *Chicago Tribune*, March 19, 1923, p. 27.
43. Cleaveline, "The Harry Greb Story—Part Two."

Chapter 10

1. Regis M. Welsh, "Greb, Threatened with Poisoning, Undergoes Knife," *Pittsburgh Post*, May 8, 1923.
2. *Ibid.*
3. "Harry Greb Recovering; Surgeons Say Operation on Boxer's Arm Is a Success," *New York Times*, May 9, 1923, p. 17.
4. Regis M. Welsh, "Greb Fight Halted Because of Rain," *Pittsburgh Post*, June 16, 1923.
5. Stanley Weston, "Harry Greb—Portrait of an Immortal," *Boxing Illustrated/Wrestling News* (November 1960).
6. *Ibid.*
7. Regis M. Welsh, "Bout Means Test for Two Battlers Long Out of Action," *Pittsburgh Post*, August 19, 1923.
8. "Greb Worsted by Connellsville Cops," *Washington Post*, July 7, 1923, p. 11.
9. Ed Fritz, "The Middleweight Feud Between Harry Greb, Al McCoy and the Chip Brothers, George and Joe," *The Veteran Boxer Magazine-Three Star Issue* (1949).
10. Description of the first Greb-Wilson fight taken from "Boston Italian Loses Crown in Bout of Fifteen Rounds Before Small New York Crowd," *Pittsburgh Post*, September 1, 1923; "Johnny Wilson Relieved of Crown by Harry Greb," *Everlast Boxing Record*, 1924, pp. 51–53.
11. Weston, "Harry Greb—Portrait of an Immortal."
12. "Comments on Current Events in Sports," *New York Times*, September 3, 1923.
13. *Chicago Daily Tribune*, September 16, 1923, p. H5.
14. "Greb Now Yearns for Other Titles" *New York Times*, September 2, 1923.

15. "Greb Openly Denies Jumping Mason to Go Back to Engel," *Pittsburgh Post*, September 2, 1923.
16. *Ibid.*
17. Regis M. Welsh, "Reception Planned for Greb Monday on Arrival Home," *Pittsburgh Post*, September 5, 1923.
18. "Local Fans to Welcome Greb Today," *Gazette Times*, September 10, 1923.
19. "Greb Arrives Home, Parade and Dinner Part of Welcome," *Pittsburgh Post*, September 11, 1923.
20. *Ibid.*
21. *Ibid.*
22. "Greb Now Yearns for Other Titles."
23. "Greb Only Boxer Who Has Chance to Beat Jack," *Pittsburgh Post*, September 21, 1923.

Chapter 11

1. Regis M. Welsh, "Though Extended to Limit, Local Battler Outpoints Louie Bogash Decisively," *Pittsburgh Post*, October 23, 1923.
2. *Ibid.*
3. *Ibid.*
4. "Greb Puts Finishing Touches on for Jones Bout at Motor Square," *Pittsburgh Post*, November 3, 1923.
5. Regis M. Welsh, "Champion Dropped Twice in Opening Round, Comes back," *Pittsburgh Post*, November 6, 1923.
6. *Ibid.*
7. *Ibid.*
8. *Ibid.*
9. *Ibid.*
10. Cleaveline, "The Harry Greb Story—Part Two."
11. Regis M. Welsh, "Clevelander Gets Terrific Lacing in Decision Inaugural," *Pittsburgh Post*, December 4, 1923.
12. *Ibid.*
13. *Ibid.*
14. *Ibid.*
15. "Downey to Retire from Fight Game," *Washington Post*, December 13, 1923, p. 17.
16. Hype Igoe, "Trying to Outbox Bounding Harry, Wilson's Mistake," *Pittsburgh Post*, January 19, 1924.
17. Regis Welsh, "Champion Shows Remarkable Form After Tipping Scales One Pound Below Contender," *Pittsburgh Post*, January 19, 1924.
18. Hype Igoe, "Trying to Outbox Bounding Harry, Wilson's Mistake," *Pittsburgh Post*, January 19, 1924.
19. Harry Newman, "Ex-Champion Has No Kick Coming, Says Harry Newman," *Pittsburgh Post*, January 19, 1924.
20. Westbrook Pegler, "With K.O. Wallop Greb Could Easily Put Wop

to Sleep," *Pittsburgh Post*, January 19, 1924.

21. "Harry Greb Wins," *Pittsburgh Post*, February 23, 1924.

22. Regis M. Welsh, "Greb Gets Home; Deplores Blowup of Berlenbach Bout," *Pittsburgh Post*, March 16, 1924.

23. "Harry Greb and His 297 Enemies," *World Boxing* (April 1924).

24. Regis M. Welsh, "Fight Is Stopped in Twelfth Round to Halt Slaughter," *Pittsburgh Post*, March 25, 1924.

25. James R. Fair, "The Wildest Tiger," *Esquire* (March 1942).

26. Regis M. Welsh, "Fight Is Stopped in Twelfth Round."

27. *Ibid.*

28. *Ibid.*

29. "Greb Is Injured in Auto Accident," *Beloit Daily News*, March 31, 1924.

30. "Greb Gets Bad Break," *Chicago Tribune*, November 21, 1926, p. A5.

31. Round-by-round description of Greb-Norfolk fight taken from Regis M. Welsh, "Wild Excitement Prevails as Referee Charges Champ with Slugging After Bell," *Pittsburgh Post*, April 20, 1924.

32. Regis M. Welsh, "Champ Not Blamed for Rough-housing in Norfolk Battle," *Pittsburgh Post*, April 21, 1924.

33. "Norfolk Defies Suspension; Greb Victim of Clique," *Pittsburgh Post*, May 13, 1924.

34. "Pittsburgh's Champ Wins Every Round Against Burly Foe," *Pittsburgh Post*, June 13, 1924.

35. Weston, "Harry Greb — Portrait of an Immortal."

36. "Touted Englishman Suffers Terrific Lacing from Champ," *Pittsburgh Post*, June 17, 1924.

37. *Ibid.*

38. Gilbert Odd, "Tough-guy Ted took on Greb the Great," *Boxing News*, July 28, 1989.

39. Regis M. Welsh, "Briton Outclassed, Bewildered, Beaten by Garfield Boxer," *Pittsburgh Post*, June 27, 1924.

40. Round-by-round description of the first Greb-Flowers fight taken from "Blow-by-Blow of Greb-Flowers Clash in Ohio Ring," *Pittsburgh Post*, August 22, 1924.

41. "Greb Retains His Title in Fight with Negro," *Washington Post*, August 22, 1924.

42. "Middleweight King Has Little Trouble in Beating Flowers," *Oklahoman*, August 22, 1924, p. 12.

43. "Greb Defeats Flowers," *New York Times*, August 22, 1924.

44. Regis M. Welsh, "Touted Gotham Star Outclassed; Prelim Flashes Make Hit," *Pittsburgh Post*, January 2, 1925.

45. "Harry Greb Toils as Ref. at Arcade Amateur Bouts," *Chicago Daily Tribune*, January 7, 1925.

46. "Greb Shows Fine Form in Winning Over Johnny Wilson," *Pittsburgh Post*, April 18, 1925.

47. "Greb-Shade Match Practically closed; $65,000 for Harry," *Pittsburgh Post*, July 17, 1925.

48. Frank Smith, "Rumors of Dempsey's Retirement Verified as Champ Sends Letter to Friend," *Pittsburgh Post*, April 14, 1925.

49. Regis M. Welsh, "Greb Follows Dempsey into Chicago; May Take Michigan City Offer," *Pittsburgh Post*, July 21, 1925.

50. *Ibid.*

51. "Greb Picked as Best Available Foe for Dempsey in Ten-Round Title Bout," *Pittsburgh Post*, July 24, 1925.

52. "Greb Willing to Battle Dempsey on Sept. 19 or 25," *Chicago Daily Tribune*, July 25, 1925, p. 6.

53. "What's This Mean?" *Pittsburgh Post*, July 31, 1925.

54. "Won't Meet Greb," *Pittsburgh Post*, July 31, 1925.

55. "Bartley Madden Likely to Take Place in Michigan Bout," *Pittsburgh Post*, July 31, 1925.

56. "Greb-Dempsey Off," *Pittsburgh Post*, August 4, 1925.

57. John Lardner, "King of the Alley Fighters," *Boxing Yearbook*, 1959.

58. "How Game Is Greb?" *Pittsburgh Post*, July 26, 1925.

59. Lardner, "King of the Alley Fighters."

Chapter 12

1. Cavanaugh, *Tunney: Boxing's Brainiest Champ*, p. 173.

2. Bert Randolph Sugar and the editors of *The Ring* magazine, *The Great Fights* (New York: Gallery Books, 1984), p. 55.

3. Mel Heimer, *The Long Count* (New York: Atheneum, 1969), p. 47.

4. "Billy Gibson, Greb's Second in Tunney Bout Last Year, Yells for Harry to Obey Rules," *Pittsburgh Post*, February 22, 1923.

5. "Gibson Takes Step to Protect Tunney," *New York Times*, February 21, 1923.

6. "Billy Gibson, Greb's Second in Tunney Bout."

7. "Gibson Takes Step to Protect Tunney."

8. "Muldoon Reassures Title Holder's Wife," *Pittsburgh Post*, February 23, 1923.

9. Sugar et al., *The Great Fights*, p. 55.

10. "Greb to Receive Fair Treatment," *New York Times*, February 23, 1923.

11. *Ibid.*

12. Description of the second Greb-Tunney bout is taken from "Tunney Regains His Ring Honors," *New York Times*, February 24, 1923; "Fight by Rounds," *Washington Post*, February 24, 1923; and "The Story of a Victory Earned — But Denied," *Pittsburgh Post*, February 24, 1923.

13. Sugar et al., *The Great Fights*, p. 55.

14. *Ibid.*

15. Charles F. Mathison, "Haley's Decision Wrong in Opinion of Billy Muldoon," *Pittsburgh Post*, February 25, 1923.

16. "Tunney Regains His Ring Honors," *New York Times*, February 24, 1923.

17. Regis M. Welsh, "Greb Is Heralded as Actual Winner in Many Quarters," *Pittsburgh Post*, February 25, 1923.

18. "What Others Thought," *Pittsburgh Post*, February 24, 1923.

19. "Muldoon Says Greb Outpointed Tunney," *New York Times*, February 25, 1923.

20. Mathison, "Haley's Decision Wrong."

21. "Greb Issues Challenge to Tunney," *Pittsburgh Post*, February 27, 1923.

22. "Muldoon Says Greb Outpointed Tunney."

23. Jack Lawrence, "Greb Will Battle Wilson in Garden; Tunney Expects K.O.," *Pittsburgh Post*, December 9, 1923.

24. "Gene Tunney's Body Attack Enables Him to Win Over Greb," *Pittsburgh Post*, December 11, 1923.

25. Westbrook Pegler, "Pegler Declares Greb Won by Big City Block," *Pittsburgh Post*, December 11, 1923.

26. Description of the fourth Greb-Tunney bout on September 17, 1924, taken from "Tunney and Greb Draw in 10 Rounds," *New York Times*, September 18, 1924, p. 26; and "Blow by Blow, Round by Round, of Greb-Tunney Fight in Cleveland," *Pittsburgh Post*, September 18, 1924.

27. "Greb and Tunney Go Ten Rounds to Draw," *Washington Post*, September 18, 1924.

28. "Harry Greb in Fight with Five Bandits," *Washington Post*, March 2, 1925.

29. "Greb Offers to Bail His Assailant," *New York Times*, March 5, 1925.

30. "Greb-Tunney Bout Cancelled," *New York Times*, March 4, 1925.

31. "Delaney, Stribling Avoid Tunney Bout," *Washington Post*, March 5, 1925.

32. "Harry Greb in Training," *Washington Post*, March 5, 1925.

33. "Greb Goes to St. Paul," *New York Times*, March 24, 1925.

34. "Greb Leaves for Tunney Bout Friday," *Chicago Daily Tribune*, March 24, 1925.

35. Tunney, *A Man Must Fight*.

36. Description of the March 27, 1925, Greb-Tunney bout taken from "Tunney Beats Greb in St. Paul Battle," *New York Times*, March 28, 1925; "Tunney Shades Greb in Sleepy Bout at St. Paul," *Chicago Daily Tribune*, March 28, 1925, p. 16; and "Gibbons Watches Two Great Rivals in Poor Exhibition," *Pittsburgh Post*, March 28, 1925.

37. Weston, "Harry Greb, The Pittsburgh Windmill."

38. "A Good Fighter, Says Gibbons, After Seeing Tunney Beat Greb," *New York Times*, March 29, 1925.

39. Paul Francis Kennedy, "Pittsburgh's Iron City Express," *Tribune Review*, August 30, 1998.

40. Ed Van Every, "Harry Greb's Career," *The Everlast Boxing Record*, 1927.

41. Tunney, *A Man Must Fight*.

42. Fleischer, *Gene Tunney: Enigma of the Ring*.

43. Kennedy, "Pittsburgh's Iron City Express."

44. Fair, *Give Him to the Angels*.

45. Fleischer, *Gene Tunney: Enigma of the Ring*.

Chapter 13

1. Cavanaugh, *Tunney: Boxing's Brainiest Champ*, p. 174.

2. Fair, *Give Him to the Angels*, p. 144.

3. Geoff Poundes, "The Legendary Harry Greb," *Boxing Monthly* (February 1991).

4. Roy C. Higby, *...A man from the past* (New York: Big Moose, 1974), p. 123.

5. Weston, "Harry Greb — The Pittsburgh Windmill."

6. Fair, *Give Him to the Angels*.

7. *Ibid.*, pp. 82–83.

8. Harry Cleaveline, "A Tale of Two Harrys," *Boxing Illustrated* (August 1980).

9. Cleaveline, "The Harry Greb Story — Part One."

10. Kennedy, "Pittsburgh's Iron City Express."

11. "Sues Harry Greb Breach Promise," *Olean Evening Times*, May 5, 1926.

12. "Hubby of Girl Sues H. Greb," *Times* (Hammond, Indiana), August 21, 1926.

13. "Harry Greb Coming Here to Be Married," *Chicago Daily Tribune*, January 1, 1925.

14. "Harry Greb to Wed Miss Walton After Big Bloomer Here," *Chicago Daily Tribune*, December 23, 1924.

15. *Ibid.*

16. "Theaters," *Chicago Daily Tribune*, October 29, 1924, p. 21.

17. "Plain Jane Opens," *New York Times*, May 13, 1924.

18. *Ibid.*

19. "Harry Greb to Wed Miss Walton."

20. Frank Smith, "Champion Harry Greb Flits from a Matrimonial Web," *Chicago Daily Tribune*, December 19, 1924, p. 29.

21. *Ibid.*

22. Smith, "Champion Harry Greb Flits."

23. Regis M. Welsh, "Greb May Lose Championship in Battle with Ratner Here Today," *Pittsburgh Post*, January 1, 1925.

24. Regis M. Welsh, "Greb Gives Ratner Beautiful Lacing," *Pittsburgh Post*, January 2, 1925.

25. "Harry Greb Coming Here to Be Married."

26. "Greb Has Close Call in Alter Bout," *Chicago Daily Tribune*, January 5, 1925, p. 18.

27. *Ibid.*

28. "Detroit Collegian in Plucky Battle Against Champion," *Pittsburgh Post*, January 10, 1925.

29. "Pinched!" *Chicago Daily Tribune*, June 4, 1925, p. 22.

30. Sally Braden, interviewed by author through email, 2005.

31. "Harry Scales 158? Pounds; Is Confident," *Gazette Times*, July 2, 1925.

32. "Sues Harry Greb Breach Promise."

33. "Hubby of Girl Sues H. Greb."

34. "Harry Greb Dies After Operation," *New York Times*, October 23, 1926.

35. "Greb's Fiancée Keeps Vigil Beside His Body," *New York Times*, October 24, 1926.

36. Sally Braden, interviewed by author through email, 2005.

37. Cleaveline, "A Tale of Two Harrys."

38. *Ibid.*

Chapter 14

1. Ralph Davis, "Gamblers Pick Greb to Lose," *Pittsburgh Press*, June 29, 1925, p. 20.

2. "Walker Favored to Defeat Greb," *Pittsburgh Press*, June 29, 1925, p. 21.

3. "Walker Hurts Toe, Greb Bout Halted," *New York Times*, June 10, 1925, p. 21.

4. "Greb Lands in New York to Finish Work for Walker," *Pittsburgh Post*, June 30, 1925.

5. *Ibid.*

6. Regis M. Welsh, "Champion Primed, in Best of Shape; I'll Win-Harry," *Pittsburgh Post*, July 2, 1925, p. 10.

7. Keck, "Harry Scales 158? Pounds."

8. *Ibid.*

9. Welsh, "Champion Primed."

10. Keck, "Harry Scales 158? Pounds."

11. Weston, "Harry Greb — The Pittsburgh Windmill."

12. Mickey Walker and Joe Reichler, *The Toy Bulldog and His Times* (New York: Random House, 1961), p. 96.

13. "Greb Lands in New York to Finish Work for Walker," *Pittsburgh Post*, June 30, 1925.

14. Walker and Reichler, *The Toy Bulldog and His Times*, p. 96.

15. "Walker Will Meet Greb Without Aid of Famous Pilot," *Pittsburgh Post*, July 1, 1925.

16. Walker and Reichler, *The Toy Bulldog and His Times*, p. 96.

17. Description of the Greb-Walker fight was taken from "Greb-Walker Detail Told Round by Round," *New York Times*, July 3, 1925, p. 8; "Round by Round in Big Fights," *Chicago Daily Tribune*, July 3, 1925, p. 13; "Harry Greb-Mickey Walker," *Pittsburgh Post*, July 3, 1925, p. 11; and *Gazette Times*, July 3, 1925.

18. Jim Jab, "Walker Is Beaten in Hot Clash," *Pittsburgh Press*, July 3, 1925, p. 12.

19. Walker and Reichler, *The Toy Bulldog and His Times*, p. 97.

20. *Ibid.*, p. 98.

21. *Ibid.*, p. 97.

22. Regis M. Welsh, "Middleweight King Has Easy Time with Welter Champion," *Pittsburgh Post*, July 3, 1925, p. 9.

23. *Ibid.*

24. *Ibid.*, p. 11.

25. "Pittsburgh Boxer Finally Credited by Gotham Rooters," *Pittsburgh Post*, July 4, 1925, p. 11.

26. John Lardner, "How to Be Legendary," unknown newspaper, July 15, 1946.

27. Kiley Rogers, "You Can't Train on Babes and Booze!" *The Police Gazette* (August 1961).

28. Weston, "Harry Greb — The Pittsburgh Windmill."

29. *Ibid.*

30. Walker and Reichler, *The Toy Bulldog and His Times*, pp. 100–101.

31. *Ibid.*, p. 101.

32. Cleaveline, "A Tale of Two Harrys."

33. Cleaveline, "The Harry Greb Story — Part One."

34. "Greb's Manager Is Hurt," *New York Times*, July 7, 1925, page 17.

35. "Red Mason Fighting for His Sight," *Pittsburgh Post*, July 6, 1925.

36. "Greb Signed for Cleveland Bout July 14," *Pittsburgh Post*, July 7, 1925.

37. "Harry Greb Is Hurt in Smash," *Oklahoman*, August 21, 1925, p. 15.

38. "Harry Greb Injured," *Beloit Daily News*, August 21, 1925.

39. "Down for the Count," *Chicago Daily Tribune*, August 21, 1925.

40. "Two Months Rest Needed by Champion After Upset," *Pittsburgh Post*, August 22, 1925.

41. "Greb Must Stay in Hospital for at Least Two Weeks," *Chicago Tribune*, August 22, 1925.

42. "Two Months Rest Needed by Champion."

43. Regis M. Welsh, "Will Start Home Today; Plans for Early Comeback," *Pittsburgh Post*, February 28, 1926.

Chapter 15

1. Lardner, "King of the Alley Fighters."

2. Ken Merritt, "The Immortal Harry Greb," *The Ring* (August 1992).

3. Rice, "King of All the Marvels."

4. Rolfe Garrett, "Harry Greb — Windmill of the Ring," *The Arena*, July 10, 1929.

5. Weston, "Harry Greb, Portrait of an Immortal."

6. William Dettloff, "20 Greatest Middleweights of All Time," *The Ring* (January 2001).

7. Merritt, "The Immortal Harry Greb."

8. Weston, "Harry Greb — The Pittsburgh Windmill."

9. *ESPN Friday Night Fights*, November 27, 1998, Max Kellerman.

10. Lardner, "King of the Alley Fighters."

11. Weston, "Harry Greb — The Pittsburgh Windmill."

12. "Greb and Klaus in Final Bout of All-Star Program," *Pittsburgh Post*, February 7, 1918.

13. "Greb and the Bearcat," *Pittsburgh Post*, February 8, 1918.

14. *Waterloo (Iowa) Evening Courier*, February 8, 1918; *Daily Northwestern* (Oshkosh, Wisconsin), February 8, 1918.

15. "Dillon and Greb Ready for Battle Tonight," *Pittsburgh Post*, July 30, 1917.

16. Florent Gibson, "Icky Takes Nine Rounds of Fight; Other One Is Even," *Pittsburgh Post*, July 31, 1917.

17. *Ibid.*

18. *Ibid.*

19. *Ibid.*

20. "Greb Hands Out Real Trimming to Jack Dillon," *Chicago Tribune*, July 31, 1917.

21. "Greb Hands Dillon Another Bad Lacing," *Pittsburgh Post*. March 5, 1918.

22. *Ibid.*

23. Florent Gibson, "Greb and Levinsky Resume Training for Thursday Night's Bout," *Pittsburgh Post*, September 5, 1917.

24. The Greb-Levinsky fight description taken from Harry Keck, "Fight by Rounds," *Pittsburgh Post*, September 7, 1917; and Florent Gibson, "Greb Worries Levinsky Almost Down to His Size," *Pittsburgh Post*, September 7, 1917.

25. Harry Keck, "Bring Gibbons for Next Bout Here, Says Greb," *Pittsburgh Post*, September 7, 1917.

26. "Soft for Greb; Ward Also Wins," *Pittsburgh Post*, March 12, 1918.

27. "Greb Was Easy Winner," *Newark Advocate*, March 12, 1918.

28. "Greb Licks McTighe at Binghamton," *Pittsburgh Post*, December 13, 1919.

29. "Last Night's Fights," *Olean Times*, December 13, 1919.

30. Regis M. Welsh, "Greb and Loughran Battle in Philly Ball Park Tonight," *Pittsburgh Post*, July 10, 1922.

31. Fight description taken from Regis M. Welsh, "Light Heavy Champ Wins on Experience Over Younger Foe," *Pittsburgh Post*, July 11, 1922.

32. Regis M. Welsh, "Move May Pave Way to Reunion; Champ Still Undecided," *Pittsburgh Post*, January 15, 1923.

33. Regis M. Welsh, "Philadelphian Gets Terrific Lacing in One-sided Battle," *Pittsburgh Post*, January 16, 1923.

34. Westbrook Pegler, "Gets Late Start, but Finishes in Whirlwind Style," *Pittsburgh Post*, January 31, 1923.

35. "Loughran Gets Draw with Greb After Judges Disagree," *Pittsburgh Post*, October 14, 1924.

36. Regis M. Welsh, "Greb and Slattery Meet in Buffalo in Six-Round Bout," *Pittsburgh Post*, September 3, 1924.

37. "Greb Gets Decision," *New York Times*, September 4, 1924.

38. *Ibid.*

39. Regis M. Welsh, "Pittsburgh's Champ Has Buffalo Idol Tottering at Bell," *Pittsburgh Post*, September 4, 1924.

40. *Ibid.*

41. *Ibid.*

42. "Greb Gets Decision."

43. Welsh, "Pittsburgh's Champ Has Buffalo Idol Tottering."

44. "Greb Gets Decision."

45. Regis M. Welsh, "Rosenbloom Proves Easy Victim for Harry Greb," *Pittsburgh Post*, July 17, 1925.

46. *Ibid.*

47. *Ibid.*

48. *Ibid.*

49. "Greb Beats Rosenbloom," *New York Times*, July 17, 1925.

50. "Greb Wins Fight," *Zanesville Signal*, July 17, 1925.

51. Cleaveline, "The Harry Greb Story — Part Two."

Chapter 16

1. Regis M. Welsh, "Harry Impresses Gym Crowd with Speedy Workout," *Pittsburgh Post*, February 24, 1926.

2. "Capacity Audience to See Harry and Tiger Sway Punches," *Pittsburgh Post*, February 25, 1926.

3. Regis M. Welsh, "Harry and Tiger Both Confident as Battle Nears," *Pittsburgh Post*, February 26, 1926.

4. "Greb Is Favored in Flowers Bout," *New York Times*, February 26, 1926, p. 19.

5. Description of the February 26, 1926, Greb-Flowers fight was taken from the *Pittsburgh Post*, February 27, 1926; the *New York Times*, February 27, 1926; and the *Washington Post*, February 27, 1926.

6. Regis M. Welsh, "Pittsburgh Fighter Far Off Form," *Pittsburgh Post*, February 27, 1926, pp. 1, 17.

7. "Gunner Smith, Once Defeated by Greb, Furnishes Vote as Referee to Harry," *Pittsburgh Post*, February 27, 1926.

8. Regis M. Welsh, "Pittsburgh Fighter Far Off Form," pp. 1 and 17.

9. "Gunner Smith, Once Defeated by Greb."

10. Frank Getty, "Ex-Champ Trained Too Fine, Experts at Ringside Agree," *Pittsburgh Post*, February 27, 1926.

11. "Ex-Champ Trained Too Fine."

12. *Ibid.*

13. Regis M. Welsh, "Will Start Home Today; Plans for Early Comeback," *Pittsburgh Post*, February 28, 1926.

14. *Ibid.*

15. *Ibid.*

16. "Willing to Fight Anyone Selected Within 3 Months," *Pittsburgh Post*, February 28, 1926.

17. Regis M. Welsh, "Fallen Champion Follows Zivic in Unexpected Defeat," *Pittsburgh Post*, March 2, 1926.

18. "Negro Champ Eager to Show Former Win Not Fluke," *Pittsburgh Post*, March 3, 1926.

19. *Ibid.*

20. "Greb Hopes to Retain Title, Lick Berlenbach and Retire from Ring," *Washington Post*, March 9, 1926, p. 15.

21. Regis M. Welsh, "Fighter Alleges Pilot Tricked Him Signing Contract," *Pittsburgh Post*, April 7, 1926.

22. *Ibid.*

23. *Ibid.*

24. "Greb Says Mason Gypped Him," *Pittsburgh Post*, April 8, 1926.

25. "Board Upholds Fighter's Plea of Trickery in Signature," *Pittsburgh Post*, May 8, 1926.

26. "Ex-Champion Must Appear in Gotham Courts for Answer," *Pittsburgh Post*, June 2, 1926.

27. "Reverses Opinion of Boxing Board in Contract Fuss," *Pittsburgh Post*, June 15, 1926, p. 13.

28. *Ibid.*, p. 14.

29. "Greb Easily Defeats Gans in Ten Rounds," *Pittsburgh Post*, June 16, 1926, p. 15.

30. "Johnston, Reputed Influential, Likely Away from Corner," *Pittsburgh Post*, August 17, 1926, p. 12.

31. *Ibid.*

32. "Flowers Favorite!" *Pittsburgh Post*, August 19, 1926, p. 12.

33. Regis M. Welsh, "Greb Wins by Rounds, Flowers Retains Crown," *Pittsburgh Post*, August 20, 1926, p. 15.

34. *Ibid.*

35. *Ibid.*

36. *Ibid.*

37. James P. Dawson, "Flowers Retains Title, Beats Greb," *New York Times*, August 20, 1926.

38. Welsh, "Greb Wins by Rounds," p. 15.

39. *Ibid.*

40. *Ibid.*

41. Dawson, "Flowers Retains Title."

42. "Round by Round," *Washington Post*, August 20, 1926, p. 15.

43. Westbrook Pegler, "Deacon Tiger Outhugs Greb in Slow Bout," *Chicago Daily Tribune*, August 20, 1926.

44. Dawson, "Flowers Retains Title."

45. Frank Getty, "Fair Ones Storm Ringside at Close, Attack Wire Chief," *Pittsburgh Post*, August 20, 1926.

46. Regis M. Welsh, "Passed Up Chances to Win Back Title, Not Claiming Foul," *Pittsburgh Post*, August 21, 1926.

47. "Greb Operated On," *New York Times*, September 17, 1926, p. 16.

48. "Greb Had a Glass Eye for Past Two Months," *New York Times*, October 27, 1926, p. 31.

49. "Here's That Greb Story Again," unknown New York newspaper.

50. Fair, *Give Him to the Angels*, p. 183.

51. "Here's That Greb Story Again."

52. Associated Press, "Bone Broken in Nose in Auto Crash Here Is

Primary Cause of Death," *Pittsburgh Post*, October 23, 1926, p. 1.

53. "Brain Clot Was Fatal to Greb," *Washington Post*, October 24, 1926, p. M24.

54. "Harry Greb Dies After Operation," *New York Times*, October 23, 1926, p. 21.

55. Associated Press, "Bone Broken in Nose in Auto Crash," p. 1.

56. "Harry Greb Dies After Operation," p. 21.

57. *Ibid.*

58. "Greb's Fiancée Keeps Vigil Beside His Body," *New York Times*, October 24, 1926, p. S10.

59. "Harry Greb Dies After Operation," p. 21.

60. "Brain Clot Was Fatal to Greb," p. M24.

61. *Ibid.*

62. "Fighter's Body to Arrive Here Early This Morning," *Pittsburgh Press*, October 24, 1926.

63. "Tribute to Be Paid to Greb," *Pittsburgh Press*, October 25, 1926.

64. "Tunney Will Be Pallbearer at Greb Funeral Tomorrow," *Gazette Times*, October 26, 1926.

65. Regis M. Welsh, "Passing of Ex-Champion Throws Heavy Pall Over Gotham," *Pittsburgh Post*, October 23, 1926, pp. 9, 12.

66. "Greb, Dead, Is Praised by Pugilistic Experts," *Pittsburgh Post*, October 23, 1926.

67. "Greb Relatives Regret Secret of Glass Eye Became Known," *Gazette Times*, October 27, 1926.

68. "Final Honors Will Be Paid Dead Boxer at Funeral Today," *Pittsburgh Post*, October 27, 1926.

69. "Harry Greb Is Laid to Rest," *Pittsburgh Press*, October 27, 1926.

70. "Harry Spoke Constantly of End—Despondent for Last Month," *Gazette Times*, October 27, 1926.

71. *Ibid.*

72. "Greb Had a Glass Eye for Past Two Months," p. 31.

Chapter 17

1. Lardner, "How to Be Legendary."

2. *Ibid.*

3. Rice, "King of All the Marvels."

4. "You Can't Train on Babes and Booze!"

5. "With the Boxers," *Pittsburgh Post*, January 22, 1915.

6. "Greb Heads Lyceum Show on Thursday," *Pittsburgh Post*, April 19, 1925.

7. "Greb's Head Cut Open; Uniontown Fight Off?" *Pittsburgh Post*, May 28, 1917.

8. "Gentle Arts Claim Philadelphia Jack," *New York Times*, December 24, 1931.

9. Regis M. Welsh, "Champion Favored to Defeat Briton in Milk Fund Show," *Pittsburgh Post*, June 26, 1924.

10. "Harry Greb Preparing for Championship Tilt with Johnny Wilson Next Friday," *Pittsburgh Press*, August 26, 1923.

11. Regis M. Welsh, "Greb May Lose Championship in Battle with Ratner Here Today," *Pittsburgh Post*, January 1, 1925.

12. "Greb Signs for Three Bouts," *Pittsburgh Post*, July 10, 1925.

13. "Greb Leaves for Tunney Bout Friday," *Chicago Daily Tribune*, March 24, 1925, p. 22; "Fulton and Dempsey, Also McGoorty and Greb, Battle Today," *Pittsburgh Post*, July 27, 1918.

14. "Howard's Gym Team Out to Win Golden Gloves," *Chicago Daily Tribune*, June 25, 1932, p. 17; "Eckersall's Gossip of the Boxers," *Chicago Daily Tribune*, July 30, 1926, p. 20.

15. "Tunney Eases Up," *Pittsburgh Post*, February 22, 1925.

16. "Greb to Meet Rojas Tonight at Detroit," *Pittsburgh Post*, May 1, 1925.

17. "Greb and Delaney Stage Workout in Public at Garden," *Pittsburgh Post*, November 15, 1924.

18. Cleaveline, "A Tale of Two Harrys."

19. Cleaveline, "The Harry Greb Story — Part One."

20. Cleaveline, "A Tale of Two Harrys."

21. Les Biederman, "Harry Greb, Greatest Fighter, Died in East 20 Years Ago Today," newspaper article, October 22, 1946.

22. Weston, "Harry Greb — Portrait of an Immortal."

23. Poundes, "The Legendary Harry Greb."

24. Fair, *Give Him to the Angels*.

25. Poundes, "The Legendary Harry Greb."

26. Fair, *Give Him to the Angels*.

27. Biederman, "Harry Greb, Greatest Fighter, Died in East 20 Years Ago Today."

28. Higby, *…a man from the past*, p. 123.

29. Cleaveline, "The Harry Greb Story — Part One."

30. Cleaveline, "A Tale of Two Harrys."

31. Cleaveline, "The Harry Greb Story — Part One."

32. *Ibid.*

33. Cleaveline, "A Tale of Two Harrys."

34. R. Edgren, "Fouls — By Someone Who Thinks He Knows," *Pittsburgh Post*, July 26, 1922.

35. Harry Cleaveline, "Was Harry Greb World's Greatest Fighter?," newspaper article, May 7, 1978.

36. Bob Mee, "The Human Wind-

mill—#5 All-Time Great," *Boxing News,* August 14, 1998.

37. Weston, "Harry Greb—The Pittsburgh Windmill."

38. Cleaveline, "The Harry Greb Story—Part One."

39. Fair, *Give Him to the Angels.*

40. Cleaveline, "The Harry Greb Story—Part One."

41. Cleaveline, "A Tale of Two Harrys."

42. "Harry Greb or Harry Berg."

43. "Greb Had a Glass Eye for Two Months."

44. Lardner, "How to Be Legendary."

45. Eric Bottjer, "The Reel Deal!" *The Ring* (October 2000).

46. *Ibid.*

47. Stanley Weston, "Harry Greb Is Alive," *The Ring* (August 1991).

48. Weston, "Harry Greb—Portrait of an Immortal."

BIBLIOGRAPHY

Books

Cavanaugh, Jack. *Tunney: Boxing's Brainiest Champ and His Upset of the Great Jack Dempsey.* New York: Random House, 2006.

Everlast Boxing Record 1924. New York: Everlast Sports Publishing, 1924.

Everlast Boxing Record 1927. New York: Everlast Sports Publishing, 1927.

Fair, James. *Give Him to the Angels.* New York: Smith and Durrell, 1946.

Fleischer, Nat. *Gene Tunney: Enigma of the Ring.* New York: F. Hubner, 1931.

Heimer, Mel. *The Long Count.* New York: Atheneum, 1969.

Higby, Roy C. *...A man from the past.* New York: Big Moose, 1974.

Kreissig, Ingrid. *Primary Retinal Detachment: Options for Repair.* New York: Springer, Berlin, Heidelberg, 2005.

Rice, Grantland. *The Tumult and the Shouting.* New York: A.S. Barnes, 1954.

Sugar, Bert Randolph, and the editors of *The Ring* magazine. *The Great Fights.* New York: Gallery Books, 1984.

Tunney, Gene. *A Man Must Fight.* Boston/NY: Houghton Mifflin, 1931.

Walker, Mickey, and Joe Reichler. *The Toy Bulldog and His Times.* New York: Random House, 1961.

Kennedy, Paul Francis. "Pittsburgh's Iron City Express." *Tribune Review* (August 30, 1988).

Lardner, John. "King of the Alley Fighters." *Boxing Yearbook* (1959.

Mee, Bob. "The Human Windmill—#5 All-Time Great." *Boxing News* (August 14, 1998).

Merritt, Ken. "The Immortal Harry Greb." *The Ring* (August 1992).

Odd, Gilbert. "Tough-guy Ted took on Greb the Great." *Boxing News* (July 28, 1989).

Poundes, Geoff. "The Legendary Harry Greb." *Boxing Monthly* (February 1991).

Rice, Grantland. "King of All the Marvels." *Collier's* (February 20, 1926).

Rogers, Kiley. "You Can't Train on Babes and Booze!" *The Police Gazette* (August 1961).

Smith, Kevin R. *The Sundowners: The History of the Black Prizefighter 1870–1930.* Vol. 2, Part 1. Lulu, 2006.

Stern, Bill. "The Man Dempsey Wouldn't Fight." *Male Magazine* (October 1953).

Weston, Stanley. "Harry Greb Is Alive." *The Ring* (August 1991).

_____. "Harry Greb—Portrait of an Immortal." *Boxing Illustrated/Wrestling News* (November 1960).

_____. "Harry Greb—The Pittsburgh Windmill," *Boxing and Wrestling Magazine* (October 1954).

Magazine Articles

Bottjer, Eric. "The Reel Deal!" *The Ring* (October 2000).

Cleaveline, Harry. "The Harry Greb Story—Part One." *Boxing Illustrated* (May 1967).

_____. "The Harry Greb Story—Part Two." *Boxing Illustrated* (June 1967).

_____. "A Tale of Two Harrys." *Boxing Illustrated* (August 1980).

Croak, Thomas M. "The Professionalization of Prizefighting: Pittsburgh at the Turn of the Century." *Western Pennsylvania Historical Magazine* 62 (October 1979).

Dettloff, William. "20 Greatest Middleweights of All Time." *The Ring* (January 2001).

Fair, James. "The Wildest Tiger." *Esquire* (March 1942).

Fritz, Ed. "The Middleweight Feud Between Harry Greb, Al McCoy and the Chip Brothers, George and Joe." *The Veteran Boxer Magazine—Three Star Issue* (1949).

Garret, Rolfe. "Harry Greb—Windmill of the Ring." *The Arena Magazine* (July 10, 1929).

"Harry Greb and His 297 Enemies." *World Boxing* (April 1969).

"Harry Greb or Harry Berg." *Boxing and Wrestling Magazine* (February 1954).

Newspapers

Selected newspaper articles, 1913 to 1926, from:
Beloit Daily News
Boston Post
Chicago Daily Tribune
Chicago Tribune
Cumberland Evening Times
Daily Northwestern (Oshkosh, WI)
Gazette Times (Pittsburgh, PA)
Hamilton Daily News
Milwaukee Free Press
Nashville Tennessean
New York Times
New York World
Oklahoman
Olean Evening Times
Pittsburgh Post
Pittsburgh Press
Portland Oregonian
Sun Telegraph
Tacoma News Tribune
The Times (Hammond, IN)
Trenton Evening Times

The Tribune Review
Washington Post
Waterloo Evening Courier (IA)
Zanesville Signal

Libraries

The Carnegie Library of Pittsburgh (Oakland)
Library & Archives of the Historical Society of Western
    Pennsylvania

Interviews and Personal Communications

Ackerman, Dr. Albert
Andrews, Dr. Anthony
Braden, Sally
Brower, Dr. Scot A.
Garvey, the Rev. James W., of the Epiphany Church
Greb, Christopher
Reed, Adam M.
Weston, Stanley
Wohlfarth, Harry Greb
Web Sites
Ancestry.com
Chicagotribune.com
Harrygreb.com
history.navy.mil
navyhistory.org
Newspaperarchive.com
nytimes.com
old-picture.com
washingtonpost.com
Wikipedia.com

Visual Sources

ESPN Friday Night Fights, November 27, 1998, Max Keller-
    man.
Harry Greb — Preview (aka *The 1925 Greb Training Film*),
    VHS (The University of South Carolina, Newsfilm Li-
    brary).

Public Documents

United States of America, Bureau of the Census. Twelfth
    Census of the United States, 1900. Washington, D.C.:
    National Archives and Records Administration, 1900.
United States of America, Bureau of the Census. Thirteenth
    Census of the United States, 1910. Washington, D.C.:
    National Archives and Records Administration, 1910.
United States of America, Bureau of the Census. Fourteenth
    Census of the United States, 1920. Washington, D.C.:
    National Archives and Records Administration, 1920.

Additional Sources for Research (not cited in book)

Books

Durant, John, and Edward Rice. *Come Out Fighting.* New
    York: Duell, Sloan and Pearce, 1946.
Fleischer, Nat, and Sam Andre. *Pictorial History of Boxing.*
    New York: Citadel Press, 1959.
Oates, Joyce Carol. *On Boxing.* New York: Dolphin/Dou-
    bleday, 1987.

Magazine Articles

Daniel, Daniel M. "Boxing Hall of Fame — Tunney, Greb,
    Walker and Leonard." *The Ring* (November 1955).
Dorgan, Ike. "Greb May Duplicate Feat of Bob Fitzsim-
    mons." *The Ring* (April 1922).
Harvey, John. "The Sugar Ray of His Day." *Sports Illus-
    trated* (March 30, 1987).
Kofoed, Jack. "Harry Greb — The Human Windmill." *Fight
    Stories* (April 1943).
Lardner, John. "The Golden Rule." *Newsweek* (February 4,
    1957).
Mann, Arthur. "Ring Terror — The Story of Harry Greb
    (Part One)." *Sport Story Magazine* (First February, 1937).
_____. "Ring Terror — The Story of Harry Greb (Part
    Two)." *Sport Story Magazine* (Second February, 1937).
_____. "Ring Terror — The Story of Harry Greb (Part
    Three)." *Sport Story Magazine* (First March, 1937).
Merrill, Edward. "The Human Windmill." *The Ring* (No-
    vember 1932).
"The Only Fight Gene Tunney Ever Lost." *Boxing Pictorial*
    (March 1977).
Roberts, George. "Fights Never To Be Forgotten." *National
    Police Gazette* (November 1958).
"Ten Dirtiest Fights of All Time." *The Ring* (December
    1997).
"The Toughest Alley Fighter Who Ever Lived!" *Boxing Leg-
    ends* (Spring 1981).

Newspapers

Lardner, John. "How to Be Legendary." Unknown newspa-
    per (July 15, 1946).
Other Pittsburgh newspapers:
Pittsburgh Daily Dispatch
Hilltop Record
Pittsburgh Leader
Oaklander
Pittsburgh Sun

Web Sites

Boxrec.com
Cyberboxingzone.com

INDEX